10    $3.00
      Policy

D0500326

This item is no longer property
of Pima County Public Library
Sale of this item benefited the Library

THE COMMUNIST

FRANK MARSHALL DAVIS: THE UNTOLD STORY OF BARACK OBAMA'S MENTOR

PAUL KENGOR, PH.D.

THRESHOLD
EDITIONS

MERCURY
INK

NEW YORK   LONDON   TORONTO   SYDNEY   NEW DELHI

THRESHOLD
EDITIONS

MERCURY
INK

Threshold Editions/Mercury Ink
A Division of Simon & Schuster
1230 Avenue of the Americas
New York, NY 10020

First Threshold Editions / Mercury Ink hardcover edition October 2012

THRESHOLD EDITIONS and colophon are trademarks of Simon & Schuster.com.
MERCURY INK is a trademark of Mercury Radio Arts, Inc.

Certain material in this book originally appeared in different form in Paul Kengor, *Dupes:
How America's Adversaries Have Manipulated Progressives for a Century* (ISI Books, 2010).
Permission for use granted by publisher.

For information about special discounts for bulk purchases,
please contact Simon & Schuster Special Sales at 1-866-506-1949
or business@simonandschuster.com.

The Simon & Schuster Speakers Bureau can bring authors to your live event. For more
information or to book an event, contact the Simon & Schuster Speakers Bureau
at 1-866-248-3049 or visit our website at www.simonspeakers.com.

Designed by Ruth Lee-Mui

Manufactured in the United States of America

10 9 8 7 6 5 4 3 2

Library of Congress Cataloging-in-Publication Data

Kengor, Paul, 1966–
  The communist : Frank Marshall Davis : the untold story of Barack Obama's mentor /
by Paul Kengor. —Hardcover ed.
    p. cm.
  Includes bibliographical references.
    1. Davis, Frank Marshall, 1905–1987. 2. Davis, Frank Marshall, 1905–1987—Political
and social views. 3. Davis, Frank Marshall, 1905–1987—Influence. 4. African American
political activists—Biography. 5. Political activists—United States—Biography.
6. Communist Party of the United States of America—History 20th century. 7. Labor
movement—United States—History—20th century. 8. African American journalists—
Biography. 9. African American poets—Biography. 10. Obama, Barack—Friends and
associates. I. Title.
    E185.97.D28K36 2012
    070.92—dc23
    [B]
                                                    2012019601
  ISBN 978-1-4516-9809-1
  ISBN 978-1-4516-9815-2 (ebook)

In memory of

HARRY TRUMAN,

*who was viciously smeared by American communists
for fighting the good fight against Stalin and the Soviets*

and dedicated to

SPYRIDON MITSOTAKIS,

whose remarkable research compelled this book

They'll train you so good, you'll start believing what they tell you about equal opportunity and the American way and all that sh-t.

—Frank Marshall Davis to Barack Obama,
Dreams from My Father

I'm tired of being beaned with those double meaning words like "sacred institutions" and "the American way of life" which our flag-waving fascists and lukewarm liberals hurl at us day and night.

—Frank Marshall Davis, *Chicago Star,*
communist newspaper, November 9, 1946

Contents

Introduction: Past Is Prologue   1

1. Growing Up Frank   21

2. Atlanta, 1931–32: The Communists Swarm to Scottsboro   30

3. Frank's Work for the *Atlanta Daily World* (1931–34)   53

4. Paul Robeson and Progressive Dupes   62

5. Back to Chicago: "Peace" Mobilization and Duping the "Social Justice" Religious Left   73

6. War Time and Party Time (1943–45): Frank with CPUSA and the Associated Negro Press   88

7. The Latter 1940s: Frank and the Chicago Crew   105

8. The *Chicago Star*: Comrades, "Progressives," and Soviet Agents   118

9. Frank's Writings in the *Chicago Star* (1946–48)   124

10. Frank Heads to Hawaii   142

11. Frank in the *Honolulu Record* (1949–50): Target, Harry Truman   154

12. Frank in the *Honolulu Record* (1949–50): Other Targets, from "HUAC" to "Profits" to GM   165

13. Frank and the Founders   181

14. 1951–57: Frank on Red China, Korea, Vietnam, and More   193

15. Mr. Davis Goes to Washington   204

16. Frank versus "the Gestapo"   214

17. American Committee for Protection of Foreign Born   220

18. When Frank Met Obama   229

19. When Obama Leaves Frank: Occidental College   246

20. Frank Re-Emerges—and the Media Ignore Him   268

21. Conclusion: Echoes of Frank   285

    Motivation and Acknowledgments   299

    Appendix: Frank Marshall Davis Documents   305

    Notes   317

    Index   369

Introduction: Past Is Prologue

I pledge myself to rally the masses to defend the Soviet Union, the land of victorious socialism. I pledge myself to remain at all times a vigilant and firm defender of the Leninist line of the Party, the only line that insures the triumph of Soviet Power in the United States.[1]

—American Communist Party's Oath of Allegiance, 1935[2]

THE PEOPLE WHO influence our presidents matter.

Any worthy biographer of a president starts with those who influenced the president. To ignore such figures would be scholarly or journalistic negligence.

I know this well. I have personally written biographies of figures as diverse as Hillary Clinton, George W. Bush, and Ronald Reagan, among others. In every case I started by taking a hard look at the people who influenced these leaders. Consider, for example, the influences on two of my subjects:

Ronald Reagan's mentor was Ben Cleaver. A pastor at the First Christian Church in Dixon, Illinois, Cleaver was a father figure to Reagan during his teen years, right up to college. The University of Chicago theology graduate was intellectual and patriotic, given to invoking Washington and Lincoln, whether from the pulpit or to the local American Legion.[2]

The kind of instruction Ronald Reagan got from Reverend Cleaver was in the tradition of an exceptional America, a Shining City on a Hill, a "light unto the nations" that "cannot be hidden," which ought to "shine before men." This divinely inspired, blessed nation stood in contrast to "the heart of darkness" that was the Soviet Union.[3] America was to be a model, a guiding light proclaiming liberty to the captives. The American way was a good way.

Many years removed from Cleaver, those messages were embedded in Reagan's soul. "I've spoken of the shining city all my political life," President Reagan said in his January 1989 Farewell Address. "In my mind it was a tall, proud city built on rocks stronger than oceans, windswept, God-blessed."

It was like Ben Cleaver speaking from the grave.

Hillary Clinton is not only a prominent modern liberal but she was also the chief rival for the 2008 Democratic presidential nomination that went to Barack Obama. Today she serves as President Obama's secretary of state. Clinton's mentor was Don Jones, youth minister at First Methodist Church in Park Ridge, Illinois. Just like Cleaver to Reagan, Jones entered Hillary's life at adolescence and influenced her right up to her departure for college. Fresh out of divinity school at Drew University, Reverend Jones constantly interacted with Hillary and other teens, especially through his Thursday evening "University of Life" program.[4]

Jones saw in Hillary a precocious youngster, and advised her on the wider world. Hillary stopped by Jones's office after school or on summer afternoons, eager to talk. Jones had her read Tillich, Niebuhr, Søren Kierkegaard, Dietrich Bonhoeffer; they had lengthy discussions.[5]

To be sure, some conservative writers have decried Jones's influence, a man of the Religious Left who converted Hillary from the conservative "Goldwater girl" of her father to the liberal she became. But whether Don Jones from the liberal side or Ben Cleaver from the conservative side—or various other mentors to our presidents—these men loved America. No one questioned their dedication to the American way of life. They wholeheartedly professed, enthusiastically proclaimed, and even preached it.

Virtually all prominent leaders throughout American history have had well-publicized mentors. For example, among Democrats: President Franklin Delano Roosevelt often remembered the impact of his former headmaster, Endicott Peabody, an Episcopalian minister. President Jimmy Carter declared the "profound effect" of Admiral Hyman Rickover.[6] President Bill Clinton cited J. William Fulbright of Arkansas, the longest-running chair of the Senate Foreign Relations Committee.[7] Vice President Al Gore pointed to Roger Revelle, a Harvard environmental scientist.[8] Vice President Joe Biden speaks fondly of the late New York senator Daniel Patrick Moynihan.[9]

The list of such people and their mentors is long, but to detail it would simply belabor an obvious point: *The people who influence our leaders matter.*

THE FRANK MARSHALL DAVIS FACTOR

Among biographical subjects I have covered, none wrote about their mentors in their memoirs like Obama did with Frank Marshall Davis. In Reagan's memoirs, *An American Life*, Reagan never once mentioned Ben Cleaver.[10] Hillary Clinton, in her memoirs, *Living History*, mentioned Don Jones very little. While noting Jones's influence on matters like "social justice," Hillary does not speak of Jones affecting her "life" in the way Obama did of Frank Marshall Davis in his memoirs, *Dreams from My Father*.[11] Compared to Reagan and Hillary, not to mention other mentors, Obama speaks far more of Frank Marshall Davis in his memoirs, and certainly more substantively. And yet, no journalist or scholar hesitates to acknowledge Ben Cleaver as a mentor to Reagan or Don Jones as a mentor to Hillary. So, why do biographers—actually, *liberal* biographers—hesitate to do so for Obama's *Frank*? In this book, readers will quickly learn the obvious answer: Because neither Ben Cleaver nor Don Jones was a pro-Soviet member of Communist Party USA.

I have no doubt that this is why Obama was careful to never once give Frank Marshall Davis's full name in *Dreams from My Father*.

Liberal biographers have responded in kind, exhibiting a very unjournalistic, unscholarly bias to their subject, dutifully doing backflips to protect Barack Obama. Such is the sort of scandalous neglect we have witnessed from our media in its shielding of Barack Obama—a bias that Mrs. Clinton herself noticed most acutely, understanding that the bias probably cost her not merely the Democratic Party's nomination to the presidency but the White House itself.

It is scandalous that so little attention has been paid to Frank Marshall Davis and his influence on our president. The general public knows little to nothing about this man. Liberal journalists, historians, scholars, and pundits would never tolerate such self-imposed ignorance if facing a conservative president influenced by a figure this extreme to the right.

Nonetheless, Barack Obama's left-leaning biographers have either willfully ignored Frank Marshall Davis or seriously downplayed his influence and communist leanings. Of everything written on Obama over the years, no book has focused specifically on Frank. And now, after considerable time researching and writing on the subject, I understand why: No president has been influenced by a figure as politically troubling as this one.

Here are the facts, and they are indisputable: Frank Marshall Davis was a pro-Soviet, pro–Red China, card-carrying member of Communist Party USA (CPUSA). His Communist Party card number was 47544.[12] He did endless Soviet propaganda work in his newspaper columns, at every juncture agitating and opposing U.S. attempts to slow Stalin and Mao in the late 1940s and early 1950s. He favored Red Army takeovers of Poland, Czechoslovakia, Yugoslavia, and Central and Eastern Europe as a whole. In China, he urged America to dump the "fascist" Chiang in support of Mao's Red forces. He wanted communist takeovers in Korea and Vietnam. He was adamantly, angrily anti-NATO, anti–Marshall Plan, anti–Truman Doctrine. He argued that U.S. officials under President Harry Truman—whom he portrayed as a fascist, racist, and imperialist—and under secretaries of state George Marshall and Dean Acheson were handing West Germany back to the Nazis, while Stalin was pursuing "democracy" in East Germany and throughout the Communist Bloc. He portrayed America's leaders as "aching for an excuse to launch a nuclear nightmare of mass murder and extermination" against the Chinese and the Soviets—and eager to end all civilization. His writings were breathtakingly irresponsible and shamelessly outrageous. A Reverend Jeremiah Wright sermon or Professor Bill Ayers lecture is tame by comparison.

Frank Marshall Davis toed the Soviet/Stalinist line unflinchingly, unerringly, unabashedly. He was the prototype of the dedicated CPUSA foot soldier and loyal Soviet patriot who dutifully served the Motherland. He wrote for and edited communist newspapers in Chicago and Honolulu. For the *Chicago Star*, he was founder and executive editor. Known among locals as the "*Red Star*," it was an unapologetically pro-Soviet/communist weekly run by closet CPUSA members. Some of its contributors, as I will show, were actual Soviet agents. Certain contributors and even some board members—dear friends and mentors of Frank—had not only been trained in Moscow but took up full-time residence there.

In the *Chicago Star*, Frank and his comrades mocked the claims of Winston Churchill (whom Frank detested) that an Iron Curtain was being erected by Stalin in Europe; to the contrary, they maintained that the only "Iron Curtains" were those being erected by Frank's worst demons: anticommunists in the American press and General Motors. The problem was not Stalin's *Iron Curtain*, scoffed Frank Marshall Davis, but "G.M.'s iron curtain," being raised by "General Motors' Hitlers."

Frank Marshall Davis's political antics were so radical that the FBI placed him on the federal government's Security Index, which meant that he could be immediately detained or arrested in the event of a national emergency, such as a war breaking out between the United States and the USSR.

TARGET: DEMOCRATS

Here is a wake-up call for President Obama's Democratic base: Frank's targets were chiefly Democrats, especially Harry Truman. In fact, before Frank joined the Communist Party, he had supported Republicans, not Democrats. In 1936 and 1940, he actually worked for the presidential campaigns of Alf Landon and Wendell Willkie, whom the GOP ran against FDR.

Why target Truman? Frank's peak period of procommunist, pro-Soviet writings was 1946–51, when Stalin's Red Army was rampaging through Eastern Europe and erecting an Iron Curtain in front of a path of conquest, blood, and destruction. Standing in Stalin's way was a former Missouri farmer/haberdasher-turned-politician named Harry S. Truman, president from 1945 to 1953. This means that Frank's most bitter foes, whom he tarred and feathered and eviscerated in his writings, were not Republicans but Democrats, including leading members of Truman's administration, from Secretary of State George Marshall to Attorney General Tom Clark.

George Marshall, of course, is an American icon. His name and integrity require no elaboration. As for Tom Clark's credentials, Truman appointed Clark to the Supreme Court, and his descendants include the left's longtime antiwar luminary Ramsey Clark. Tom Clark eventually stepped down from the high court when Ramsey, his son, was himself appointed attorney general—by President Lyndon Johnson. In stepping down, Tom Clark opened the historic vacant seat that was filled by Thurgood Marshall, America's first African-American Supreme Court justice.

Clark's Justice Department—not to mention various Democrat-run Senate and House congressional committees—painstakingly compiled exhaustive lists of subversive communist fronts, which correctly listed numerous groups that were close to Frank or of which Frank had been an active member. Frank labeled Clark a red-baiting, witch-hunting, violence-inspiring racist and "assassin" of civil rights: "White Supremacist Tom Clark."[13]

As for Harry Truman, Frank's *Chicago Star* trashed him with headlines like "WHITE HOUSE TO WHITE HOODS: KKK HAILS TRUMAN'S POLICY AS ITS OWN" and "TRUMAN KNIFES HOPE FOR PEACE."

These Democrats were not like the Nancy Pelosi Democrats of today. They were old-time, anticommunist, Cold War Democrats. And Frank Marshall Davis despised them.

To say that Frank Marshall Davis was brutal to his critics is an understatement. His rhetoric was incredibly inflammatory. He was unrelenting in describing his opponents as "fascists," "racists," "Klansmen," "Nazis," "storm troopers," "mini-Hitlers," and on and on. His unflagging, over-the-top language, over the course of decades, was downright obscene. Joe McCarthy's most demagogic statements about

Harry Truman and George Marshall are kind compared to Frank's fusillade.

Speaking of Joe McCarthy, liberals today try to portray Frank as a victim of McCarthyism. To the contrary, Frank did not deal with McCarthy, a Republican; it was Democrats who pursued Frank and his comrades, especially Democrats on the Senate Judiciary Committee. When Frank was called to Washington to testify on his pro-Soviet activities, it was by Democrats. And the Republican committee member who questioned Frank happened to be the very senator who led the fight to censure Joe McCarthy.[14] It was a Democratic Senate that, in an official 1957 report titled "Scope of Soviet Activity in the United States," publicly listed Frank as "an identified member of the Communist Party." In fact, throughout the vast majority of its existence, the House Committee on Un-American Activities, which Frank and his leftist friends denounced as the House "*Un-American* Committee," was run by Democrats, stretching from Rep. Martin Dies (D-TX), to Rep. Francis Walter (D-PA), to Rep. Richard Ichord (D-MO), among others. In other words, critics of this book looking for an anti-Democrat bias are in for a shock: It was Frank Marshall Davis himself who displayed the worst bias toward Democrats. If anything, this book is a sustained *defense* of the Democrats whom Frank did battle with.

But it is not a defense of *all* Democrats. After all, when Frank honed his pen to slash and gash racist segregationists in his columns, they were almost always Democrats—Southern Democrat New Dealers like Congressman John Rankin and Senator Theodore Bilbo (both from Mississippi). Those Democrats I certainly do not defend.

Finally, one last sobering warning for Democrats: After all of those blistering attacks on their party, Frank hopped in bed with the Democrats—but only to use them, just as he and fellow communists had long exploited the "progressive" label. Once the Hawaiian Communist Party went underground, with Henry Wallace's Progressive Party having collapsed, Hawaii's Reds changed their tactics, concentrating instead on infiltrating the Democratic Party, even running their members in local elections to seize delegate positions. One of those who not only urged this tactic but was himself elected to a Democratic precinct was Frank

Marshall Davis.[15] For America's Reds, it was the start of a long march to operate within the Democratic Party, transforming it from the party of Harry Truman and John F. Kennedy to the party of Nancy Pelosi and Barack Obama.

FRANK'S INFLUENCE ON OBAMA

Amid this political theater, Frank Marshall Davis came into Barack Obama's life in the 1970s. Importantly, his deep roots in the far left had not dried up by the time he was sharing his life's wisdom with a young Obama. Among the material housed in communist archives is a February 15, 1979, document from the New York–based American Committee for Protection of Foreign Born (ACPFB), which, at that point, was one of the oldest remaining communist fronts operating in the United States. The Seventy-eighth Congress had identified ACPFB as such way back in 1944 in its seminal two-thousand-one-hundred-page investigative report of front groups. The report noted that the ACPFB "was founded by the Communist Party in order to exploit racial divisions in the United States for its own revolutionary purposes."[16] The standard party line by ACPFB and by CPUSA was that America was rife with a racism that had been completely abolished by Stalin's USSR—an absurd thesis that Frank himself advanced in his columns.

That Frank Marshall Davis would choose to remain with this particular front so late in life is very revealing. And yet, there was Frank's name on the letterhead, in February 1979, right alongside old Communist Party hacks like Abe Feinglass and "social justice" pastors like William Howard Melish.[17] This was just before Barack Obama headed off to college at Occidental, and, as we shall see, not without Frank's input.

Frank Marshall Davis had a distinct influence on Obama during their years together in the 1970s. The exact extent of that influence will be one of the subjects analyzed in detail throughout this book. But for now, as a snapshot, consider some remarkable similarities between the ideas in Frank's columns and the political actions and thinking of Obama.[18] Frank Marshall Davis:

- Rejected and blasted Winston Churchill;
- Vilified and targeted General Motors, a company that he would have been thrilled to nationalize;
- Advocated wealth redistribution from (in his words) greedy "corporations" to "health insurance" and "public works projects";
- Favored taxpayer funding of universal health care;
- Supported government stimulus and trumpeted the public sector over the private sector;
- Constantly bashed Wall Street;
- Marched in May Day parades;
- Dismissed traditional notions of American exceptionalism and framed America not as selflessly serving the post–World War II world but instead as selfishly flaunting its so-called "mountainous ego" and "racist-imperialist-colonialist" ambitions;
- Warned God-and-gun-clinging Americans about huckster preachers and instead sought the political support of the "social justice" Religious Left for various causes and campaigns;
- Perceived the Catholic Church as an obstacle to his vision for the state;[19]
- Confidently declared certain government actions "constitutional" or "unconstitutional";[20]
- Excoriated the "tentacles of big business," bankers, big oil, the "Big Boys," "excess profits," corporate fat cats and their "fat contracts," "millionaires" and "rich men," and the wealthy;
- Attacked "GOP" tax cuts that "spare the rich" and that only "benefit millionaires";
- Singled out the "corporation executive" for not paying his "fair" share;
- Used slogans such as "change" and "forward."[21]

The list goes on and on, this is merely a sample, and it frequently bears an uncanny resemblance to Obama's own words and actions.

Among those, Frank likewise preached a mantra of "change," which he pushed in his very first column for the inaugural edition of his *Chi-*

cago Star. Among the forms of change pushed by the *Star's* contributors was the socialized medicine championed by Sen. Claude "Red" Pepper (D-FL). Pepper's landmark (albeit failed) health-care legislation was overseen by his chief of staff, Charles Kramer, who we now know was a Soviet agent—one of several who contributed to the *Star.*[22] With Frank, Pepper was one of the leading contributors to the *Star's* op-ed page, along with Howard Fast, winner of the 1953 Stalin Prize.

One can even discern a lasting impression in Frank's comments disparaging "the American way," which were recalled by Obama in *Dreams from My Father.*[23] Frank's long-held condescending, snide view of the American way—dating back to *Chicago Star* columns in the 1940s—constituted his parting words of wisdom to Obama before the young man left for college.

Frank Marshall Davis almost surely helps explain how America's current president developed into a man of the left early on in life, ultimately ranked by *National Journal* as the most left-leaning member of the U.S. Senate—to the left of Ted Kennedy, Barbara Boxer, Hillary Clinton, and everyone else—in the final year before he ran for president. At the very least, he surely sheds light on how Obama was on the farthest reaches of the left when arriving at Occidental College in 1980. That, too, is a subject I detail in this book, relying in particular on the testimony of Dr. John Drew, who knew Obama at Occidental, and knew him (at the time) as a fellow Marxist.[24] If Barack Obama was indeed once a Marxist, and specifically at Occidental, just after leaving Hawaii, then Frank Marshall Davis would likely have been a primary, explanatory influence.

Frank Marshall Davis's eye-opening, disturbing background seems a certain missing link in the political life and narrative of Barack Obama. The man now in charge of the mightiest economic engine in the history of humanity was influenced, to some notable degree, by a pro-Soviet CPUSA member.

Given the fact that we look into the most personal details of candidates' lives, from their bedroom to their taxes, it is absurd to think that looking into someone who was clearly influential in our president's life could somehow be seen as off-limits or not important. But that, of course, is exactly how critics will attempt to portray this work. They will say that Obama never took Frank seriously, that they were not very close at all, or that Obama simply ignored Frank's radical political views. While Frank's precise political influence on Obama is not completely clear, Frank was much more to Obama than anyone working with the president would care to admit.The people who influence our presidents matter—and are certainly worthy of our scrutiny.

WHAT SORT OF "MENTOR"?

Radical influences on Barack Obama, from Jeremiah Wright to Bill Ayers, have gotten plenty of attention over the years. Questions about those influences have been so prominent that they were raised during presidential debates, with Obama forced to explain the relationship. In one debate during the Democratic primary, Hillary Clinton raised the Ayers issue, and even the *New York Times* gave the Obama-Ayers relationship front-page treatment.[25] But neither Wright nor Ayers, by Obama's own accounting, had an influence approximating that of Frank Marshall Davis.

But what, exactly, was the nature of that influence? Is it accurate to describe Frank as a "mentor" to Obama, as others have done?[26] And, even if it seems clear that Frank was at least *a* mentor to some meaningful degree, was he *the* mentor to Obama?

On the basis of all of my research, I believe that no other individual can claim the title.

Frank Marshall Davis is the closest thing that the adolescent Obama had to a mentor. The only competitor was Obama's maternal grandfather, Stanley Dunham. Actually, "competitor" is not a good word, given that Dunham introduced Frank to Obama for the purpose of mentoring. It is fascinating that Frank and the Obama family shared an unlikely geographical path, with Frank moving from Kansas to Chicago to Honolulu, and with Barack Obama's family living in Kansas before moving to Honolulu—where Dunham introduced Frank to Barack—and then (for Barack) on to Chicago. Obama's mother, Ann, was born in Kansas (1942) and died in Honolulu (1995); Frank was born in Kansas (1905) and died in Honolulu (1987). Stanley Dunham was the interconnector linking these remarkably coincidental parts together. Both Stanley and Frank grew up in Kansas in the 1920s.[27]

Witnesses attest to an unmistakable, meaningful impact by Frank on Obama. In light of the appraisals of these witnesses, as well as biographical profiles by liberals and conservatives alike,[28] the word "mentor" might *understate* the relationship.[29] Consider these testimonies, none of which come from conservative anti-Obama sources:

1. A major August 2008 profile by the Associated Press called Frank Marshall Davis an "important influence" on Obama, one whom Obama "looked to" not merely for "advice on living" but as a "father" figure. Frank was there when Obama "struggled to find mentors." According to the AP, Frank was "an intriguing figure" whom Obama sought in lieu of "a father he hardly knew," handpicked by Obama's maternal grandfather for that purpose.[30]

2. The *London Telegraph* called Frank an "early influence" and form of "counsel," to whom Obama "gravitated . . . at moments of doubt."[31]

3. The *New York Times*, carefully avoiding any incriminating details about "Frank," including his full name, acknowledged that Obama "took refuge" in him.[32]

4. Columbia-educated professor Dr. Gerald Horne, a man of the far left who has studied both Frank and Obama, and who has written extensively on this period in Hawaii, wrote that Frank was "a decisive influence" in helping Obama "find his present identity."[33]

5. Maya Soetoro-Ng called Frank "a point of connection, a bridge if you will," to Obama. Maya would know; she is Obama's half sister.[34]

6. David Remnick, Pulitzer Prize–winning reporter for the *Washington Post* and *New Yorker*, and author of *The Bridge*, the definitive biography of Barack Obama, quotes Dawna Weatherly-Williams, Frank Marshall Davis's next-door neighbor and dear friend. (Weatherly-Williams was so close to Davis that she called him "Daddy," and was actually present the first time Obama and Frank met in the early 1970s.) She described the Davis-Obama relationship as very influential, with Frank affecting Obama on "social justice," on "life," on "what's important," and on no less than "how to use" his "heart" and "mind."[35]

7. Dr. Kathryn Takara, a University of Hawaii professor of ethnic and black studies, is a Frank Marshall Davis biographer who knew Davis for fifteen years. Davis spoke to her classes, and she often visited with him, discussing his life and currents news and events. They were so close that Frank spoke to her the day he died. Takara's colleagues described her biography of Frank as "brilliant," "wonderful," "masterful," "compelling," "painstaking," "poignant," "astute," "insightful," and "important." Takara raved about Frank, commending his "dedication to social justice" and his work as a "catalyst for change."[36] Takara said that Frank and Obama's grandfather were "closest friends,"[37] and that Frank "nurtured a sense of possibility" in Obama. This, Takara said, is evident "in the way that Barack Obama carries himself, walks and talks."[38] She states that Frank handed on to Obama "a sense of believing that change can happen."[39]

Given that "change" became the one-word mantra of Barack Obama and the entire Obama political movement, this is no small statement. The very title of the Obama team's 2008 campaign book was *Change We Can Believe In*—words that precisely echo Takara's description of Frank's influence on Obama.[40] This suggests a consequential influence not only on Obama and his election, but on America itself. That belief in change, and making change happen, has, for better or worse, changed a nation forever.

Speaking of which, the innumerable deferential books that were rushed out to help elect Obama president in 2008 contained frequent, warm references about Frank's mentorship. These highly sympathetic liberals seemed unaware of the (literal) red flags posed by mentioning Frank. To cite just one example, Garen Thomas's book, *Yes We Can: A Biography of Barack Obama*, stated: "Barack looked to Frank for some hint of whom he should become as an adult."[41] It is ironic, and I am sure that Thomas, given his support of Obama, did not intend this, but that statement alone provides plenty of support for the idea that the public deserves to know much more about Frank Marshall Davis.

That is likewise true for a tribute book by Ron Jacobs, titled *Obamaland: Who Is Barack Obama?* A loving, large, glossy, photo-filled book, it includes more than thirty Hawaiian natives as contributors. He provides a well-detailed look at Obama from an on-the-ground Hawaiian perspective, replete with arguably more facts on Obama's Hawaii years than any other work. Jacobs calls Obama "the most heralded person in world history," who "leads America and the world into brighter and more peaceful times." As for Obama's influences, Jacobs pictures (literally) Frank Marshall Davis first. "There is little doubt that young Barack Obama's notions of black manhood were nurtured by Frank Marshall Davis," writes Jacobs. More than that, Jacobs lists "writers of whom he [Frank] told Barry Obama—Booker T. Washington, W.E.B. DuBois, Langston Hughes, James Baldwin and others." Of Frank, Jacobs adds: "Obama visited and drank with the old black man. . . . How much transfusion of their brotherly blood took place between the two?" Jacobs concludes: "God bless Frank Marshall Davis. Amen, *aloha* and *mahalo* for being The Man when Barack Obama needed him most."[42]

Other pro-Obama books have echoed Frank's influence.

Richard Wolffe, a man of impeccable liberal credentials who covered Obama's 2008 campaign for *Newsweek* and as an MSNBC analyst, wrote the best-selling, highly acclaimed *Renegade: The Making of a President.* In it, he sets up an interview with Obama by noting how the young Obama had been "distanced from more positive influences, from community and mentors." In the next paragraph, Wolffe brought in Frank, whom he described as "eccentric" but "engaging" and whom "Obama sought out . . . for advice."[43]

Another scholar from the left who points to Frank is James Kloppenberg. In his Princeton University Press work, *Reading Obama: Dreams, Hope, and the American Political Tradition,* which is flattering in its praise of Obama and was adoringly reviewed by a grateful *New York Times,*[44] Dr. Kloppenberg makes multiple references to Frank, at times with soaring eloquence.[45] In one of the most ironic passages, Professor Kloppenberg asks, "Have the economic advisers Obama has brought into his administration fulfilled the prophecy of Frank Davis?"[46]

That, of course, is precisely what many of us fear.

Obama himself has spoken about Frank's influence. As David Remnick notes, "Davis, by Obama's own accounting, made the young man feel something deep and disorienting."[47]

Indeed, in his memoirs, Obama notes that Frank offered him advice at several life-changing levels: on race, on college, on women, on his mind, on his attitudes, on life. "I was intrigued by old Frank," Obama wrote, "with his books and whiskey breath and the hint of hard-earned knowledge behind the hooded eyes."

Obama's memoirs feature twenty-two direct references to "Frank" by name, and far more via pronouns and other forms of reference. Frank is a consistent theme throughout the book, appearing repeatedly and meaningfully in all three parts, which are titled "Origins," "Chicago," and "Kenya." He is part of Obama's life and mind, by Obama's own extended recounting, from Hawaii—the site of visits and late evenings together—to Los Angeles to Chicago to Germany to Africa, from adolescence to college to community organizing. Frank is always one of the few (and first) names mentioned by Obama in each mile marker upon his historic path from Hawaii to Washington.[48]

As we will see, when Frank is not physically with Obama each step of the way, Obama literally imagines him there—pictures him there, visualizes him. He felt a connection to Frank that he painfully concedes he was unable to find in his mother, father, stepfather, grandfather, grandmother, siblings, or anyone else who comprised his origins and life journey. Frank is a lasting, permanent influence, an integral part of Obama's sojourn. And, as we will also see, Obama's parting thoughts from Frank—on achievements and accomplishment—redound to the Oval Office today.

Even then, Obama was smart enough to never once dare use Frank's full name anywhere in the entire book, no doubt understanding the political danger of conceding such a close, abiding association with a man of Frank's political past and proclivity. He was especially wise to avoid Frank's political/ideological thinking. *Dreams from My Father* was written in the 1990s when Obama likely had no thought about even running for president. Had he been writing memoirs as a presidential candidate in say 2006 or 2007, and aware that some enterprising researcher might scare up Frank's old CPUSA propaganda work, he might have banished Frank from his memoirs altogether—unfair as that would have been.

To that end, Obama's cheerleaders and court composers among liberal journalists and academics might wish to censor Frank from

Obama's narrative, to retroactively expunge him from Obama's own autobiography. Yet that was something Obama himself found impossible to do. Liberals would like to blacklist the communist Frank, but they cannot, because Obama himself could not. They cannot make Frank go away, because Obama could not.

THE SEEDY SIDE OF FRANK

This book is not intended to be a comprehensive biography of Frank Marshall Davis. There are many facets of Frank's life that I have skipped that otherwise would be included in a standard biographical treatment, particularly the seedy side of his life, meaning the perverse sexual material that has been widely disseminated on the internet or appears in Frank's own writings. The internet is rife with scandalous accusations about various sexual preferences by Frank, and (most bizarre) about how those choices might have affected his literal relations with Obama and Obama's family. This material is usually the first thing that pops up in web searches on Frank and Obama.

Those offended by speculation on Frank's sordid sexual adventures need to understand that it began with Frank himself. Frank wrote a quasi-pornographic biography—described by some as a "memoir"—a novel called *Sex Rebel*, under an alias, "Bob Greene."[49] Bob's sexual exploits, from bisexuality to seducing barely teenage girls (a thirteen-year-old named "Anne"), are graphically revealed. They are shared without shame. Frank's own memoirs, *Livin' the Blues*, conceded his authorship of *Sex Rebel*.[50] He happily admitted it, stating that he "could not truthfully deny that this book, which came out in 1968 as a Greenleaf Classic, was mine."[51] The only question is to what extent the exploits are fictional or nonfictional, biographical or autobiographical, desired experiences or actual experiences.[52]

Discussing this material would not be completely inappropriate for this book, given that Frank's sexual life and practices are not unrelated to his communist philosophy. As anyone who has studied or been involved in the communist movement knows, communists were proudly loose in their morality, including their sexual morality. This is traceable not only to the moral relativism of the likes of Lenin, Trotsky, and Stalin, but to Marx himself, who wrote openly in *The Communist Manifesto* of the "abolition of the family" and of communism abolishing "eternal truths," "all religion, and all morality." "The communist revolution is the most radical rupture with traditional relations," conceded Marx. "Its development involves the most radical rupture with traditional ideas."[53]

In religiously keeping with the philosophy they adhered to, American communists engaged in radical forms of extramarital relations, unacceptable even by today's lax standards. Modern feminists should be outraged by Frank's objectification of women, discussion of luring very young girls into bed, and enjoyment in photographing nude women.[54] Frank referred to women as "babes" and "broads" and "fine young foxes" and "dykes" and "luscious ripened plums," and blithely made statements like "I have impregnated only three women." He was unapologetic in thrilling over women's private parts, which he described in language too crude and vulgar to repeat here.[55]

Here, too, the story of Frank Marshall Davis is a gut check for liberals. This is a man they would normally have every reason to condemn, and certainly not defend. Frank's perversions would normally be condemned by liberals as sexism. For that matter, liberals should also be offended by Frank's ethnic slurs, from offensive language describing his own race to terms like "the Spanish Jew" and "slant eyed natives."[56]

THE ROOTS OF RAGE

Because of Frank Marshall Davis's sympathies and activities on behalf of such a wretched ideology that killed so many, I harbor few sympathies for the man. I say "few" because there is one abiding compassion I do feel for him: Frank was an African-American who suffered very real racial persecution. Again and again, while researching his early life, I was moved by what he endured. I found myself liking him and rooting for him to persevere and succeed.

As we will see, one particularly awful episode in America's tragic saga with race—the case of the Scottsboro Boys—put Frank on a misguided, crooked track to Communist Party USA. Here, like many on the broader political left, Frank ended up duped into the calloused hands of conniving communists, who exploited race for malevolent Marxist-Leninist purposes.

Tragically, once in the fold, Frank drank deep from the Party's chalice. As he did, his onetime good work to promote racial tolerance was thereafter corroded by the caustic element of communist dogma, which poisoned everything it touched. This meant, among other things, that Frank would toe the Party line in the wildest ways, including advancing the line that Stalin's USSR was absent of racist tendencies. Frank would measure America against the USSR on the matter of race and declare Uncle Sam Stalin's moral inferior. Later still, by the late 1970s, precisely when he interacted with a young Barack Obama, Frank was intensely involved in the one communist front most notorious for exploiting racial divisions in America in order to advance Soviet communism: the American Committee for Protection of Foreign Born. For me personally, it is here, heaped upon the absurdity of his persistent claim of a Russian racial utopia, that most remaining vestiges of empathy for Frank dissipated.

Of course, Frank was misled. As this book will show, his perception of a racism-free USSR was influenced by Paul Robeson, the famous black American entertainer who was a lavish, ludicrous admirer of the Soviet Union. The Soviets duped Robeson badly during an initial 1934 trip to Moscow, with Robeson smitten forever after. They eventually feted him with the "Stalin Peace Prize." The Soviets were pathological liars and manipulators.

While Frank portrayed the USSR as absent of racism, he framed America—and especially Harry Truman and the Democrats—as dripping with racism and every imaginable political malady. In the 1940s and 1950s, Frank employed an early, novel version of the race card, which he employed incessantly in order to advance international communism.

While this was and remains deeply disturbing, I still have never been able to shake my sympathy for what Frank suffered under the Jim Crow era. It is a sympathy I prefer not to shake. It is, I suppose, a healthy sympathy; as healthy as having contempt for the pernicious communist ideology that he supported—an evil that killed over 100 million people throughout the course of Frank Marshall Davis's lifetime.

Despite the many sources identifying Frank as some form of significant influence on Obama—including people who knew them personally, and Obama himself—Obama's supporters and defenders will still attempt to argue that Frank was not a mentor. They will do so for obvious reasons. They do not want their president, a man of the left, to be linked to someone from the farthest reaches of the left: the Communist Party. As with Obama's relationship with Reverend Wright, Bill Ayers, and other left-wing radicals, they do not want their president to be tainted by such a radical association.

That is something I understand fully. Motivations are a revealing thing.

Therefore, let me be clear from the outset: The purpose of this book is not to declare, argue, or insinuate that Barack Obama is a communist and closet member of CPUSA with private loyalties to Mother Russia. My purpose is to show that Frank Marshall Davis—who clearly influenced Obama—was a communist and closet member of CPUSA with private loyalties to Mother Russia.

By the end of this book, readers will have the opportunity to make up their own minds about the exact nature of the Obama-Frank relationship and the degree to which Frank's personal and political views were embraced or at times emulated by young Obama. Given that Obama himself will likely not be commenting on this subject anytime soon, these determinations can be made only by those who have taken the time to consider all of the material.

Growing Up Frank

FRANK MARSHALL DAVIS was born on December 31, 1905. He grew up in Arkansas City, Kansas, which he described as a "yawn town fifty miles south of Wichita, five miles north of Oklahoma, and east and west of nowhere worth remembering."[1] That was a charitable description, given the racism he endured in that little town.

In his memoirs, Frank began by taking readers back to his high-school graduation on a "soft night in late spring, 1923." He was six feet one and 190 pounds at age seventeen, but "I feel more like one foot six; for I am black, and inferiority has been hammered into me at school and in my daily life from home." He and three other black boys "conspicuously float in this sea of white kids," the four of them the most blacks ever in one graduating class. "There are no black girls," wrote Frank. "Who needs a diploma to wash clothes and cook in white kitchens?"[2]

Frank was rightly indignant at this "hellhole of inferiority." He said that he and his fellow "Negroes reared in Dixie" were considered "the scum of the nation," whose high-school education "has prepared us only to exist at a low level within the degrading status quo." And even the education they acquired was often belittling. "My white classmates and I learned from our textbooks that my ancestors were naked savages," said Frank, "exposed for the first time to uplifting civilization when slave traders brought them from the jungles of Africa to America. Had not their kindly white masters granted these primitive heathens the chance to save their souls by becoming Christians?"[3]

Frank would one day rise above the degrading status quo. For now, he lamented that he himself had fallen victim to this "brainwashing," and "ran spiritually with the racist white herd, a pitiful black tag-a-long."[4]

As Frank surveyed the sea of white classmates that soft spring evening, he was glad to know it would be the last time he would be with them. He could think of only three or four white boys who had treated him as an equal and a friend, and whom he cared to remember.[5]

One moment that was unforgettably seared into his soul was an incident when he was five years old. An innocent boy, Frank was walking home across a vacant lot when two third-grade thugs jumped him, tossed him to the ground, and slipped a noose over his neck. He kicked and screamed as the two devils prepared, in Frank's words, "their own junior necktie party." They were trying to lynch little Frank Marshall Davis.[6]

As the noose tightened, a white man heroically appeared, chasing away the two savages, freeing Frank, brushing the dirt from his clothes. He walked little Frank nearly a mile home, then simply turned around and went about his business. Frank never learned the man's identity.[7]

Imagine if that kindly man could have known that that "Negro" boy he shepherded home would one day help mentor the first black president of the United States. It is a moving thought, one that cannot help but elicit the most heartfelt sympathy for Frank, even in the face of his later political transgressions.

Frank's parents apparently informed the school of the attempted lynching, but school officials did not bother. "I was still alive and unharmed, wasn't I?" scoffed Frank. "Besides, I was black."

Frank rose above the jackboot of this repression, assuring the world that this was one young black man who would not be tied down. He enrolled in college, first attending Friends University in Wichita, before transferring to Kansas State University in Manhattan.[8] At Kansas State from 1924 to 1926, Frank majored in journalism and practiced writing poetry, impressing students and faculty alike.

These colleagues were almost universally white. To their credit, some of them saw in Frank a writing talent and were eager to help.

RACISM

Of course, that upturn did not end the racism in Frank's life. Another ugly incident occurred in a return home during college break.[9]

A promising young man, Frank was working at a pool hall, trying to save money to put himself through school. It was midnight, and he was walking home alone. A black sedan slowly approached him. Out of the lowered window came a redneck voice: "Where'n hell you goin' this time of night?"

Frank warily glanced over and saw two white men in the front seat and another in the back. Worried, he asked why it was their business.

"Don't get smart, boy. We're police," snapped one of them, flashing a badge slightly above his holstered pistol. "I'm police chief here. Now, what th' hell you doing in this neighborhood this time of night?"

A frightened Frank explained that this was his neighborhood. He had lived there for years, was home on college break, and was simply walking home from work.

"Yeah?" barked the chief. "Well, you git your black ass in the car with us. A white lady on th' next street over phoned there was somebody prowling around her yard."

Frank asked, "Am I supposed to fit the description?"

The chief found Frank's question haughty: "Shut up an' git in the car!"

They delivered Frank to the woman's doorstep. "Ain't this him?" said the hopeful chief.

The woman quickly said it was not. Frank looked nothing at all like the man she had spotted.

"Are you sure?" pushed the chief. "Maybe you made a mistake."

The lady insisted that Frank was not the suspect, to the lawman's great disappointment.

Frank suspected that the chief was keenly disappointed not to have the opportunity to work him over. "It wasn't everyday they had a chance to whip a big black nigger," said Frank, "and a college nigger at that."

The chief told Frank to get back in the car, where he began interrogating him again, even though Frank was fully exonerated. The chief was not relenting. He was looking for blood.

"Where do you live?" the chief continued. Frank stated his address. The chief turned to his buddies: "I didn't know any damn niggers lived in this part of town, did you?" One of the officers replied: "There's a darky family livin' down here somewhere."

Frank was utterly helpless, at the mercy of men with badges and guns and "the law" behind them. He boiled inside, but could do nothing. He later wrote: "At that moment I would have given twenty years off my life had I been able to bind all three together, throw them motionless on the ground in front of me, and for a whole hour piss in their faces."

RESENTMENT

Frank escaped this incident physically unharmed, released to his home by the police. But he was hardly unscathed. Such injustice understandably fueled a lifelong resentment.

Frank's upbringing, as told through his memoirs, is gripping. His writing is witty, engaging, sarcastic, at times delightful, leaving it hard not to like Frank, or at least be entertained by him. But the wonderful passages are tempered by Frank's numerous ethnic slurs, mostly aimed in a self-deprecating manner at himself and his people, but also directed at others, such as "the Spanish Jew" (never named) whose restaurant he frequented in Atlanta, and, worst of all, by the many sexually explicit passages. One can see in Frank's memoirs the author of *Sex Rebel*, and one can see a lot of sexism, with Frank making constant graphic references to women's private parts (with vulgar slang terms) and referring to women as everything from "white chicks" to "a jane" to a "luscious ripened plum," just for starters.[10] In his memoirs, Frank devoted an inordinate amount of space to his sexual encounters. *Sex Rebel* must have been his chance to more fully indulge his lurid obsessions.

• • •

Of course, Frank also invested his writing talent in noble purposes: advancing civil rights by chronicling the persecutions of a black man. Interestingly, to that end, Frank's memoirs are remarkably similar to Barack Obama's memoirs; the running thread being the racial struggles of a young black man in America.

Frank's memoirs reveal an often bitter man, one who had suffered the spear of racial persecution. His contempt for his culture and society also led to a low view of America. When America is acknowledged in his memoirs, it is not a pretty portrait: "The United States was the only slaveholding nation in the New World that completely dehumanized Africans by considering them as chattel, placing them in the same category as horses, cattle, and furniture." That attitude, wrote Frank, was still held by too many American whites.[11] Thus, his hometown of Arkansas City was "no better or worse than a thousand other places under the Stars and Stripes."[12]

Again, that bitterness is understandable, a toxic by-product of the evil doings of Frank's tormentors. Yet what is unfortunate about Frank's narrative is the lack of concession, smothered (as it was) by resentment, that this same America, no matter the sins of its children, still provided the freedom for Frank to pull himself up and achieve remarkable things, which are manifest as one reads his memoirs.

We also find in those memoirs a resentfulness of religion and God. Frank had been raised by Baptist parents and taught the power of prayer "from infancy." But he felt he did not see results. When blacks were massacred in riots in Tulsa, Oklahoma, Frank knelt at his bedside and "prayed for retribution." When nothing happened to the perpetrators (at least in this world), he was puzzled. The results were the same when a young black mother in the South was burned at the stake while the white mob laughed at her cries. Frank again prayed for divine retribution. "I became deeply depressed," said Frank, "feeling that God had somehow let me down."[13]

Frank was also angry at how every picture he had seen portrayed a white Jesus, "usually blonde," and a blackened devil. If this was so, pondered the young Frank, what could he expect as a black man? He asked himself: Why would a "white Lord" punish his own white, ethnic brothers?[14]

For Frank, this childlike misinterpretation was "tiny at first" but snowballed. He suspected that the Christian religion was a "device" to keep blacks subservient to whites. "Very well," scoffed Frank. "Then I was through with it." [15]

To the contrary, Frank's black contemporaries, and the generation of slaves who recently preceded them, understood the culprit not as God but as men, not a bad Christian religion but bad Christians. Professor Gary Smith, author of an Oxford University Press book on views of heaven, states that black slaves viewed heaven as "the very negation of slavery," a place where they would finally experience the dignity and worth denied on earth. "Admission to heaven would validate their humanity," writes Smith. "Although masters and many other whites defined them as uncivilized brutes or mere commodities, in God's eyes they were valuable, precious human beings for whom His Son died." Smith adds that "many blacks looked forward to heavenly bliss and compensation and divine retribution for their suffering." [16]

There was more to Frank's rejection of God. His grandfather was agnostic, and those seeds, when mixed with Frank's unanswered prayers for retribution, "fell in welcoming soil." (As a parallel to Barack Obama, *Newsweek* described Obama's grandfather as a "lapsed Christian" who likewise did not nurture in him a Christian belief system, nor did Obama's grandmother or mother,[17] with the grandparents at best attending a Unitarian Church known among locals as "The Little Red Church on the Hill." [18]) Frank said that his grandfather "converted me almost immediately." [19] He was easy prey.

Frank began haunting the recesses of the Wichita Public Library, where he imbibed the anti-God writings of agnostics and atheists. This was a pivotal period. By then, Frank was not an immature five-year-old with childlike questions but an eighteen-year-old becoming a man. His break from Jesus Christ was intellectually reinforced.[20]

Overall, Frank said he did not forever physically desert churches, always seeing them as valuable social centers for black Americans who needed them and for addressing problems of everyday living.[21] Did he become a lifelong committed agnostic or atheist? He does not clarify in his memoirs, though he clearly rejected the Christian faith at one point. And as we shall see in his writings in the 1940s and 1950s, he would take pointed jabs at Christians for their supposed *sins* of anticommunism and anti-Sovietism.

Indeed, significantly, among the rancid fruits of this separation from Christianity may have been communism. Herein might be seeds of Frank's eventual turn to Marxism-Leninism, a totalitarian ideology and god that failed, that shackled human freedom to an unparalleled degree. It was President Harry Truman, Frank's eventual nemesis, who remarked that "the seeds of totalitarian regimes" are nurtured by "misery and want." Those seeds "grow in the evil soil of poverty and strife"—of which there was plenty in Frank's life—and "reach their full growth when the hope of a people for a better life has died."[22]

This was Truman's rationale for the benevolent Truman Doctrine and Marshall Plan, which Frank vilified in his columns. So abiding was Frank's opposition to the Marshall Plan that one of the few foreign-policy assessments in his memoirs is his open acknowledgment that he adamantly rejected the Marshall Plan, which he characterized (outlandishly) as a weapon that Truman "aimed directly at the Soviets."[23] Yes, even three or four decades after all the hell that Stalin unleashed after World War II, Frank, in his memoirs, was still convinced that Truman, not Stalin, had spoiled the opportunity for a postwar peace.[24]

But that would come much later. For now, in the 1920s, Frank Marshall Davis was still trying to find himself in this challenging, often cruel world.

CHICAGO—THE FIRST TIME

For about two and a half years in college, Frank worked toward a journalism degree. In those days, however, a college degree was secondary to the training, and Frank would never get a diploma. Young folks did not go to college to party. Frank, like many of his generation, scrapped and scraped to cobble together enough dollars to stay in school long enough to learn a trade, to better himself. He was already writing and impressing his professors, who happily recommended him to newspapers and magazines.

Frank's personal life also underwent turmoil. His mother died in the summer of 1926 from a ruptured appendix not treated quickly. She had divorced in 1906, shortly after Frank's birth, remarrying in 1909. Frank, the twenty-year-old blooming poet, was very philosophical about her death. He described it poetically as a "parting, a period to the sentence, an ending of the chapter, and a final closing of the book." He might be sickened, incensed, horrified at how death comes, but not death itself. There is no way to escape death, he ruminated, so "why weep" at this "eventual rendezvous with this finality?"[25]

So, in 1927, after unsuccessfully looking for writing jobs in Kansas, and as his family bonds severed, Frank sought meaning in Chicago, where—like Obama later—his fledgling career took root.

Frank loved Chicago, finding an acceptance as a black man denied to him in Arkansas City. In his memoirs, he detailed the city vividly, excitedly, particularly his first walk down State Street, with the sweet sounds of jazz emanating from building after building. These scenes are among the most joyous and captivating in Frank's memoir, as he recounts his arrival beautifully and at greater length than any other part of his book. Frank was entranced by Chicago, and entrances others in his characterization. The poet so adored Chicago that he put his love to verse, writing his first long poem on the Windy City.[26]

Frank did not have much experience in journalism, though he had more than most black journalists. He counted himself among the most "professionally trained" (by college education) aspiring black journalists in America. He sought out black newspapers in particular, which, as Frank noted, at that time were almost all Republican.[27] In those days, black Americans overwhelming identified with the GOP, the "party of Lincoln." As Frank noted, not until FDR did this party identification begin to change. Frank himself supported Republican presidential candidates in the 1930s.

Here in Chicago, from 1927 to 1929, Frank launched his career as a professional writer, composing poems and submitting short stories in outlets ranging from *National Magazine* to the Associated Negro Press. He relished the work, calling it "journalitis." In 1927, he secured a full-time post with the Chicago *Evening Bulletin*, a publication he and several other enterprising black journalists launched together, and at a "very good salary" of thirty-five dollars per week. Unfortunately, the *Evening*

Bulletin was a struggle, and it "expired" after only several months, folding up in October 1927.[28]

Here we see an entrepreneurial Frank, another admirable trait that never left him. Frank always worked very hard, busted his rear end, picked himself up again and again. He was the quintessential hardworking American who made his own opportunities, even when the deck was stacked against him. His personal ethic and undeterred individualism were the embodiment of everything communism was not.

Even as the *Evening Bulletin* succumbed, it was an invaluable experience, and Frank continued to look for steady work. Over the next two years, he wrote for (among others) the *Chicago Whip* and the *Gary American* in nearby Gary, Indiana. In August 1929, he left the *Gary American* to return to Kansas State University on a scholarship. Torn between returning to college and returning to the *Gary American*, and alternately doing both, Frank eventually heeded a call, ironically, back in the Jim Crow South—in Atlanta.[29]

It would be in Atlanta that the political Frank began taking form. He would not be there long, eventually returning to Chicago, but long enough to change the course of his political life and philosophy forever.

Atlanta, 1931–32

The Communists Swarm to Scottsboro

IN JANUARY 1931, Frank Marshall Davis's hard work finally paid off when a man named W. A. Scott recruited him to Atlanta for a job as managing editor of the *Atlanta World*, an upstart African-American newspaper.

Scott traveled to Chicago to recruit Frank, telling him that he needed an editor. "Me go South?" asked an incredulous Frank. He had, after all, left the South's racism far behind. He wanted no part of Jim Crow land. But Scott offered Frank thirty-five dollars per week, which, during the Great Depression, was big money. Frank was interested in the dollars and the challenge.[1]

W. A. Scott had started the *Atlanta World* for less than five hundred dollars in 1928. It published twice a week—sporadically. He told Frank he wanted to publish three times per week.[2]

"I was astounded," said Frank of the offer. "I'd never heard of his operations. But if he could live up to his promises, it might be worth risking a trip to the bowels of Dixie."[3]

Frank made the trip, accepted the job, and proceeded to do excellent work. He again worked his tail off, putting in seven-day weeks, ninety to one hundred hours per week, doing everything in the paper, from writing and rewriting every line to scouring every centimeter of layout. The weakest part of the newspaper was the editorial department, which, by Frank's candid estimation, "stank." He had a mandate from Scott to produce a paper that rivaled the respected *Pittsburgh Courier*, arguably America's top black newspaper. Frank quickly turned it into a thrice-weekly paper, and then on March 13, 1932, transitioned it into a daily: the *Atlanta Daily World*.[4]

Key to this success was Frank's taking control of a disorganized and virtually nonexistent editorial department. W. A. Scott was a black entrepreneur, an impressive businessman—bold, brash, daring, a live wire, a man of style and flair, a character. He and his family staffed the paper, and their explosive squabbles were legendary.[5] Frank navigated the family feuds as well as the pages of the paper. He thrived in this freewheeling system that was the antithesis of Soviet communism.[6]

Frank had several different columns to his name at the *Atlanta Daily World*. One was on jazz—a topic he loved as much as poetry, and knew even better. Another was an editorial-page column titled "Touring the World." He also did a brief front-page round-up of the news titled "Jazzin' the News," which was done in a snappy poetic form, usually ten to twelve lines that rhymed. He also wrote the unsigned editorials that represented the position of the newspaper, though it is impossible to know if he wrote every single one of them.

It was the editorial page where Frank slowly emerged as a political animal, but, even then, guardedly. His columns in the *Atlanta Daily World* were mostly about race, and in them Frank weighed in on anything, such as white folks' hair versus Negroes' "straight or kinky hair," or the relative merits of the "Nordic standard of beauty" and the "lighter complexioned Negro."[7] Frank was never lacking an opinion. He could also be sexually and ethnically insensitive, not shy about commenting on a woman's appearance or referring to certain Asian peoples, for instance, as "slant eyed natives."[8]

That Frank's politics began to emerge, and decidedly to the left, was evident in the content. Even then, most editorials were largely nonpolitical—not the unflinchingly pro-Soviet propaganda provided by Frank later in the *Chicago Star* and *Honolulu Record*—even as Frank could be quite strident when dealing with other matters, like race. As Frank later candidly admitted, he vented in his columns and editorials, signed and unsigned. W. A. Scott had warned Frank to "take it easy" editorially, lest he upset some white folks. Frank largely did so, but occasionally another southern racial injustice would propel Frank into editorial rage—or, as Frank put it in one case: "I vomited all my anger in a front-page double-column editorial."[9]

This made W. A. nervous, and he implored Frank: "You gotta be more careful. You can get us all in a mess of trouble with some of these crazy white folks."[10]

One such matter of crazy white folks, which pushed Frank over the edge, was the case of the Scottsboro Boys. What made this case even more volatile was its seizure by communists, who for a decade had been searching frantically for issues to recruit black Americans. Little did Frank know he was about to wade into not only a serious racial injustice but a serious CPUSA campaign as well. As Frank learned, CPUSA intended to use Scottsboro to draw as many black Americans as possible to the communist camp. The case was a crucible for several volatile issues of the day, bringing together southern racism, a dubious justice system, and the desire of the Communist Party to make inroads into the African-American community.

A BRIEF HISTORY OF THE COMMUNIST CARNAGE

Before considering the details of Scottsboro, some crucial background on the communist movement is imperative. By the early 1930s, the global killing machine that was communist ideology was just ramping up. Communism, as vividly noted by Martin Malia, Cal-Berkeley professor and Harvard Ph.D., would generate the "most colossal case of political carnage in history."[11] Through bullets, tanks, the gulag, starvation, mass repression, and more, communism would take the lives of 100 to 140 million people worldwide from 1917—when it took root in Bolshevik Russia—through the end of the twentieth century.[12] That figure equates to more than double the combined death tolls of the two most destructive wars in history: World Wars I and II. It makes the Inquisition, which involved the deaths of thousands, not millions, look like a picnic by comparison.[13] Even Hitler did not approach this level of slaughter.

Worse, communist philosophers and leaders and advocates, from Marx to Lenin to Stalin, desired a worldwide revolution. The headquarters and conductor of the global Marxist symphony would be the Soviet Communist International, the Comintern, established in Moscow in March 1919. The Comintern would oversee the creation and direction of communist parties in every country. "They have a world to win," concluded Marx in the final two lines of his *Communist Manifesto*. "Working men of all countries, unite!"[14]

The American Communist Party was founded in Chicago in the same year as the Comintern: 1919. The Comintern made it clear that members of foreign communist parties—from Europe to America—must give total subservience to Moscow. It stated flatly that those "who reject in principle the conditions and theses put forward by the Communist International are to be expelled from the party." This was the classic "party discipline" that was a trademark of communist parties everywhere. And befitting the militant regime that was its source, the 1920 Comintern congress evoked war rhetoric as central to its mission, stating explicitly in point seventeen of its famous twenty-one-point manifesto: "The Communist International has declared war on the entire bourgeois world."[15]

In turn, members of communist parties around the world, including in the United States, saw themselves as loyal Soviet patriots. As merely one manifestation of this, consider this 1930 exchange between Congressman Hamilton Fish (R-NY) and William Z. Foster, longtime head of CPUSA, who spoke openly of CPUSA's goal of creating a "Soviet America":[16]

FISH: Now, if I understand you, the workers in this country look
  upon the Soviet Union as their country; is that right?

FOSTER: The more advanced workers do.

FISH: They look upon the Soviet flag as their flag?

FOSTER: The workers of this country and the workers of every
  country have only one flag and that is the red flag.

FISH: . . . If they had to choose between the red flag and the
  American flag, I take it from you that you would choose the red
  flag, is that correct?

FOSTER: I have stated my answer.

FISH: I don't want to force you to answer it if it embarrasses you,
  Mr. Foster.

FOSTER: It does not embarrass me at all. I stated very clearly the red
  flag is the flag of the revolutionary class, and we are part of the
  revolutionary class.[17]

The red flag was the flag of American communists. Soviet interests
reigned supreme and held sway over those of any other government or
nation.

It cannot be emphasized enough that American members of the
Communist Party always saw themselves as subservient to Moscow. A
telling document, one of the first that resides in the Soviet Comintern
Archives on CPUSA, was issued from the Chicago convention of September 1–7, 1919. Typed on the letterhead of the newly established
Communist Party of America, at 1219 Blue Island Avenue, Chicago, it
is a brief celebratory salutation to the Comintern from the Communist
Party of America's executive secretary, Charles Ruthenberg.[18] It bears
four simple sentences:

In the name of the Communist Workers of the United States
  organized in the Communist Party of America I extend
  greetings to the Communist Party of Russia.
Hail to the Dictatorship of the Proletariat!
Long live the Russian Socialist Soviet Republic!
Long live the Communist International!

The devotion in this letter speaks for itself. From the outset, American Communist Party members swore a loyalty oath to the USSR.[19]

Moreover, the Communist Party established in the United States was expected to thrive on deceit. This was clear at the first major Comintern congress in Moscow in 1920, which, among the twenty-one requirements for membership, included the extraordinary point three, which called upon communists in every country, including America, to create a "parallel illegal apparatus," which, "at the decisive moment," would seize the day, rising to the surface and taking charge of the revolution. When the moment was ripe, those comrades would assist the masters in Moscow in "performing [their] duty to the revolution." There was no mistaking the clarity of these instructions to American communists, who published these orders in the United States in a document titled "The Twenty One Conditions of Admission into the Communist International." [20]

That devotion to concealment, not only as a tendency but as formal operating policy, would be practiced by the American Communist Party from 1919 to 1989—during the entirety of which period it received direct funding from Moscow.[21]

Finally, crucial to the process of communist concealment and advancement, especially within the United States, was the role of the liberal/progressive dupe. Consider: Communists were always a tiny minority in America, even at the height of Party membership in the 1930s, which peaked at about one hundred thousand members.[22] To advance their agenda, they needed to conceal their pro-Soviet mission. More than that, in their petitions, rallies, and publications, they needed the broader enlistment and endorsement of noncommunists—nearly always liberals/progressives—in order to grant some semblance of legitimacy to their covert objectives. Today we can observe actual Comintern directives ordering American communists to target noncommunist leftists.[23] These documents (far from the only such evidence) show at length how the communist left exploited the softer left, primarily liberals/ progressives; the latter being unaware of the communists' true, full intentions, or often even that the communists were communists. When the communists were correctly accused of being communists—accused, that is, by anticommunists—the liberals/progressives frequently joined the communists in attacking the *anti*communists as paranoid, Red-baiting reprobates.

Unfortunately, communists had their greatest success among "social justice" Christians, especially among three mainline Protestant denominations: the Episcopal Church, the Methodist Church, and Presbyterian Church USA. Herb Romerstein, the veteran investigator of the communist movement, and himself once a communist, when asked which group of Americans were most manipulated by communists, unhesitatingly answered, "liberal Protestant pastors." Romerstein calls them "the biggest suckers of them all."[24]

In Frank's time in the South, this communist penchant for deception, concealment, and subversion found a powerful legal case and rallying point in the most unlikely place: the sleepy town of Scottsboro, Alabama.

THE SCOTTSBORO TRAGEDY

The Scottsboro situation unfolded on March 25, 1931, when two white women, Victoria Price and Ruby Bates, were said to have been raped by nine black teens along the railroad from Chattanooga to Memphis. The boys had hopped a train ride that day, as had the two girls, who were with white boys.

A fight broke out among the black boys and white boys, with the latter tossed off the train. The white boys informed the nearest stationmaster that they had been in a gang fight. At the next stop, a town called Paint Rock, Alabama, a militia/posse took the law into their hands and "arrested" the black boys, transporting them to jail cells in nearby Scottsboro. The charge was that the nine black teens had raped the two white girls.

As news spread, enraged whites gathered outside the jail, ready to form a lynch mob. The governor of Alabama called in the National Guard.

Local authorities promised the seething vigilantes that justice would be hastily served, guaranteeing quick trials and verdicts. On cue, five days later, on March 30, 1931, an all-white jury indicted the nine boys, and the trial began shortly thereafter.

Thus ensued a whirlwind of complications, from miscarriages of justice to incompetence to retractions. The attorneys who defended the boys were judged too old or too drunk. The boys themselves did not always help their cause: One alleged that everyone was guilty except for himself; two others confessed but later withdrew their admissions, saying they had confessed under physical duress; and the remaining six pleaded innocence.

Not helping calm the storm was a racist jury, eager to execute all the boys. Even as the prosecution argued that the youngest should get only life in prison, the whites pressed for the gallows for the entire group.

All were convicted and sentenced to death, but the story was far from over.

A mistrial was declared, appeals were rapidly set in motion, and newspapers began reporting that the two girls were not pure lambs but, rather, Tennessee prostitutes. A second round of trials commenced in March 1933.

In the most sensational development of the second trial, Ruby Bates recanted her earlier testimony, claiming she and Victoria Price had not been raped, and had concocted their story out of fear they might be charged for a federal crime because they had crossed state lines while practicing an "immoral" form of business with the white boys. The prosecution contended that Bates was lying, and had been paid off. The jury again voted for conviction, but the judge vetoed.

SCOTTSBORO AND THE COMMUNIST CAMPAIGN FOR A "SOVIET NEGRO REPUBLIC"

Amid this fiasco, American communists were ready to insert themselves and their agenda. Scottsboro was fully exploited by the domestic and international communist movement. It was an especially attractive situation for CPUSA as it was based not upon untruths but on a very real tragedy.

Communists excelled at "campaigns"; that is, carefully concerted efforts in which they exploited an issue or cause to further their agenda. Such campaigns were a very significant, still vastly unappreciated, tactic vigorously employed by the communist movement throughout the twentieth century. They were conducted with great effect.

The FBI defined campaigns as "concentrated, continuous, and concerted succession of agitation and propaganda activities specifically devised and timed to sway public opinion. All communist campaigns are intended to arouse, influence, and mobilize as many people as possible to further communist goals." Those goals, naturally, included the promotion of the "welfare of the Soviet Union." [25]

The FBI noted that professions ripe for exploitation tended to be clergy, educators, lawyers, scientists, and artists. Prominent personalities were eagerly pursued, especially Hollywood figures and those in entertainment. Communists particularly specialized in campaigns "involving Negroes, workers, trade-unionists, and foreign-born." Campaign issues were either initiated by communists or eventually co-opted, and always involved the formation of front groups to coordinate the agitation. At the end of the campaign, the groups were quickly dissolved, ideally before the public could follow the fingerprints.

The FBI noted, "No other organization has ever engaged in so many diverse, intensive, and extensive campaigns conducted with so much perseverance, deftness, and potency as has the Communist Party, USA." CPUSA was "never without" a campaign of one type or another, and had been responsible for "an inestimable number of campaigns." Communist campaigns, like communist fronts, thrived on deceit. American communists were vigilant in concealing their coordination. They needed to be ever ready to deny their participation.

The chief target audience of these campaigns was gullible liberals/progressives who communists believed could be duped. The dupes were indispensable to success. If the campaigns marshaled only the support of communists, they would be transparent and would collapse under public exposure. The presence of liberal/progressive dupes helped diminish the presence of communists and added credibility to the cause.

The Scottsboro Boys became a full-fledged, intense communist campaign.

Sadly, CPUSA's incursion into the Scottsboro case compounded an already tragic situation, undermining public support for a legitimate civil-rights cause. Civil-rights leaders themselves detected and feared this. They understood that communists were poisoning the well of justice for the Scottsboro Boys.

The timing was tailor-made for CPUSA. From 1928 to 1930, the Comintern had ordered CPUSA to support black causes for freedom and self-determination in the Jim Crow South, in what the Comintern called the "Black Belt."[26] This push to entice black America is one of the most salient features defiling the declassified Comintern Archives on CPUSA.[27]

Only later, under congressional testimony from sources who bolted the Party, did the U.S. government learn about Soviet schemes for black America. In 1922, the Comintern had approved a three-hundred-thousand-dollar subsidy to the American Communist Party for purposes of propaganda among black Americans. In 1925, the Comintern selected a group of twelve black Americans to come to Moscow for training. The most trusted were returned home with more funds for further propaganda.[28]

Among the twelve, Lovett Fort-Whiteman was designated for special assignment at Moscow's prestigious Lenin School. Fort-Whiteman was a force. He founded the American Negro Labor Congress, a mobilization of black workers organized by the Party. *Time* magazine labeled him "the Reddest of the Blacks."[29] No other African-American so impressed the Soviets.

Joining forces with Fort-Whiteman at the American Negro Labor Congress was James W. Ford, who ran as vice-presidential candidate on CPUSA's ticket three times in the 1930s. In 1928, Ford was sent to the USSR for the Fourth World Congress of the Red International of Labor Unions. That same year, Ford attended the Sixth World Congress of the Communist International, serving on the Comintern's Negro Commission. In 1930, he helped organize the Comintern's First International Conference of Negro Workers.[30]

After all that hyperactivity and intense training, Ford was sent back to America in 1932, smack in the middle of the Scottsboro trial. That year, he was elected to CPUSA's Political Bureau and also as vice president of the League of Struggle for Negro Rights.[31]

Ford also received an especially interesting task from his Soviet masters. In 1930, at one of the Comintern conferences, a resolution was passed calling for the creation of a Soviet-directed and -controlled "Negro Republic" among America's southern states.

This, of course, deserves pause. The Soviet Comintern, working through American communists, actually crafted plans to create a "separate Negro state," or a segregated "Negro Republic," in the South. The Soviet goal was to foment an African-American uprising within the South, which, in turn, would join with a workers' uprising in the North. When the revolution was deemed ripe, the two forces would seize and reconstitute America as a Soviet sister state.[32]

Testimony to this Soviet objective was later provided by several former African-American communists, particularly William Odell Nowell and Louis Rosser, under sworn testimony before Congress beginning in November 1939 and continuing through the 1950s. Congress published the testimony in several reports, including a major December 1954 report titled "The American Negro in the Communist Party."[33]

Nowell had joined CPUSA in the summer of 1929, remaining until late 1936. In 1929, he headed to the Motherland as a CPUSA representative. There, he engaged in discussions with the Comintern's "Negro department." He was briefed on the program to organize a separate African-American state in the South. He learned that "the question of the American Negro" had first arisen in 1920 at the Second World Congress of the Communist International. Remarkably, the Bolsheviks were still embroiled in the Russian Civil War, where some seven million men, women, and children perished; it was a struggle for their very survival. Nonetheless, America was too important to set aside. In August 1918, Lenin had paused to issue his "Letter to American Workers," in which he ranted against America's millionaires and imperialists, its profit-seeking "vultures" and "modern slave-owners." "The American workers will not follow the bourgeoisie," Lenin rallied. "They will be with us, for civil war against the bourgeoisie."[34] Lenin was not about to neglect an opportunity with American Negroes.

These talks within the Comintern's Negro department eventually led to the issuing of a resolution from the Comintern's executive committee to CPUSA. The resolution formally established the new program to mobilize black Americans into the southern "Negro republic." Nowell testified that this "Negro state" would be established under control of the Soviet leadership. "The plans were carefully laid out," said Nowell, noting the various contingencies. For instance, if the revolution had not yet unfolded in due course, other emergencies might hasten the timing, such as war or economic depression. Such scenarios, said Nowell, would present "the time to strike; this would be the time to utilize this position to set up a Negro republic in the South." [35]

William Odell Nowell and James W. Ford are just a sample of the many characters tasked by the Comintern and CPUSA with nothing short of a full communist revolution among American blacks.

Another such character was a Party activist named Sol Auerbach, who likewise spent time training in the USSR. Using his Party name, James S. Allen, Auerbach headed south in mid-July 1930 to launch a Party newspaper, the *Southern Worker*, and to agitate for African-American separation into the "republic." [36]

In short, CPUSA, with Soviet support, instituted a major, systemic push to move black Americans away from their beloved party of Lincoln (Republican Party) to the party of Lenin. CPUSA cut loose, splattering the South with flyers sporting photos of Vladimir Lenin under bold headlines like "LENIN Shows The South The Only Way To JOBS LAND and FREEDOM." [37]

When Scottsboro hit in 1931, communists were obviously well prepared; it was a perfect fit for their purposes. And though it was not clear if the boys would ever face execution, the American Communist Party smelled blood and, as many black Americans suspected, perhaps even *wanted* blood. It was a delicious opportunity to place America as a whole on the gallows, and to contrast the evil, racist United States with a Soviet Union of alleged superior morals—Lenin's and Stalin's Soviet Union, where the gulag was running at full, brute capacity.

THE INTERNATIONAL LABOR DEFENSE

As noted by Harvard scholar James Edward Smethurst, an expert on the African-American literary left who has studied Frank Marshall Davis, the Scottsboro Boys became "the cause célèbre of the Communist movement." [38]

Communists seized the case, getting involved in ways that were detrimental to the Scottsboro Boys:

Communists' most visible involvement came with the second trial, as their legal arm, the International Labor Defense (ILD), came to the boys' defense. ILD was established in 1925 as the American section of the International Red Aid, headquartered in Moscow as parent organization to various communist defense groups. The International Red Aid was formed by the Comintern in 1922. Policy decisions within ILD were spearheaded by Robert Minor, a high-level Party official. Later, insiders testifying before Congress, including Carl Hacker, John Lautner, Bella Dodd, and Barbara Hartle, admitted that ILD was "dominated, directed, and controlled by the Communist Party." [39]

ILD's reputation, as Congress later described it, was as "part of an international network of organizations for the defense of Communist lawbreakers." [40] Its largest country operations were in France, Austria, Germany, Holland, and Spain, all operating under Moscow's direction. Its international head was Helen Stassova, a member of the Soviet Central Committee of the Communist Party. [41] ILD was so active that it was investigated by the House Committee on Un-American Activities the first year the committee was established by Democrats.

Testifying to ILD's work was Ben Gitlow, a top early leader of the American Communist Party. Gitlow was one of the original ILD founders in 1925. In October 1939, Gitlow, by then an ex-communist, testified:

> The International Labor Defense is not a defense organization in the pure sense of that term; nor is it a civil liberties defense organization. It is the legal defense organization of the Communist Party and the Communist International in this country, and serves, also, as a highly political and propagandist Communist organization. [42]

As FDR's attorney general, Francis Biddle, put it, ILD was the "legal arm of the Communist Party." President Truman's attorney general, Tom Clark, likewise cited ILD as subversive and communist. [43] Remarkably, ILD's president for a decade was Vito Marcantonio, who became a congressman from New York, and was extremely sympathetic to communism. [44]

AGITATE, AGITATE, AGITATE

As ILD's background emerged in the South during the Scottsboro trial, it badly hurt the boys. ILD brought in two attorneys, Samuel Liebowitz and Joseph Brodsky. Liebowitz was denounced by white southerners as a Jewish-communist-New-York "Yankee." He stepped aside as lead attorney in the third and final round of trials.

In short, communists should have kept away from the case. The boys were not, of course, communists—and would never have been suspected of being so. For a group of desperate boys literally almost dying for support, this was a disastrous association from a PR standpoint. CPUSA's mere presence severely disserved these boys.

But America's communists couldn't care less. They saw the Scottsboro Boys not as fellow communists but as excellent communist propaganda; the boys from Scottsboro were secondary to the boys from Moscow. For American communists, being loyal Soviet patriots, their allegiance and first priority was thousands of miles away from these poor boys.

CPUSA's excitement is evident still today in the Soviet Comintern Archives on CPUSA declassified in the 1990s. Those archives are full of correspondence, newspaper articles, activity reports, flyers, and event announcements on the Scottsboro Boys, as American Party officials proudly beamed their efforts to Soviet officials.[45]

The dates on the flyers, for instance, reveal that CPUSA wasted no time organizing the masses. Almost immediately, communists were protesting and marching, from New York to Chicago, from Philadelphia to Minneapolis to Boston. They transformed the trial into a mass campaign to excoriate the United States and its allegedly phony "democratic" system.

Interestingly, communists inserted the word "workers" throughout their Scottsboro placards, thus revealing their hand as organizers. The excessive use of "workers" in all the flyers must have made the Comintern think twice about ever recruiting the organizers as potential KGB agents. Communists were transparent in their attempt to use the rallies as a recruiting tool. Most of their flyers listed ILD's sponsorship.

And that was just the first round. Another round of Scottsboro-related rallies was initiated only weeks later, just in time for May Day 1931. One promotional flyer in Minneapolis began: "The Negro workers of Minneapolis must unite with the white workers in the celebration of May First, which is the International Labor Day."

MARCHING ORDERS FROM COMRADE BROWDER

These events occurred in that initial 1931 period, precisely when Frank Marshall Davis arrived at the *Atlanta World*, and would persist throughout Frank's time in Atlanta. The entire Scottsboro episode went on for years. For communists, the long, drawn-out legal process was a dream come true. Causes like this gave them life—their dedication to milking this campaign for every drop of agitprop continued for years.

One telling exhibit held today in the Comintern Archives on CPUSA is a January 15, 1936, letter—five years after the initial incident on the train—signed by Earl Browder, general secretary of CPUSA.[46] The heading reads, "To All District Organizers." This was an all-points bulletin to communists nationwide. Browder instructed:

Dear Comrades:

The first Scottsboro verdict is expected in the middle of the week, that is about January 24 or 25—and the verdict is bound to stir up a tremendous reverberation throughout the United States and the world—no matter whether the decision is favorable or unfavorable. In either case, there will be thousands of workers, of Negroes, of trade-unionists, Socialists and middle class people in every city and town who can be reached and drawn into a great mass meeting either in protest against another death verdict, or in reaction to whatever verdict it may be.

We are informed of an important decision made last night by the Scottsboro Defense Committee, which is the new committee recently formed as a united front of:

National Association for Advancement of Colored People,
International Labor Defense,
League for Industrial Democracy[,]

Church League for Industrial Democracy,
Methodist Federation for Social Service,
American Civil Liberties Union.

The decision is that the local bodies of all of these organizations in all cities and towns in the country are asked to act together to hold the biggest possible Scottsboro mass meetings under their join[t] auspices. . . .

It is imperative that you give the full and unstinted help of the Party with the District Organizer taking direct part in helping to make these meetings tremendous successes. . . .

We urge your immediate attention to a telegram sent today by Comrades [Robert] Minor and [Anna] Damon to the I.L.D. representative in your District. Please study the situation carefully and give the wholehearted support of the District leadership of the Party to see that every meeting is a success in your District. . . .

Each of the national headquarters of all of the above-named organizations that are participating in the Scottsboro Defense Committee here in New York is sending instructions to its local representatives in your District to participate with the I.L.D. in putting through the biggest possible meetings.

Comradely yours,
Earl Browder, General Secretary
C.P.U.S.A.

One can still sense the excitement of General Secretary Browder and the American apparatchiks who received their marching orders. Regardless of the verdict, hell would be raised. The verdict was secondary to the greater goal of agitating the working class.

One of the groups named in Browder's letter, the Scottsboro Defense Committee, was the umbrella organization and front group for the communist campaign. The Methodist Federation for Social Service was investigated as a communist front by the U.S. government.[47] It was a hotbed for communist Methodists, fellow-traveling Methodists, and run-of-the-mill "social justice" Methodists, some of them unaware of the full scope of exactly what they were advocating.

THE ROLE OF THE ACLU

Among Methodists mentioned in Browder's Letter was the Reverend Harry Ward, a founding father of the ACLU. Naturally, the ACLU was intimately involved in Scottsboro.

Describing itself as "progressive," the ACLU was founded at almost the same time as the American Communist Party. It was the brainchild of Roger Baldwin, a onetime pro-Soviet communist, though he never joined CPUSA. In 1928 Baldwin wrote a book called *Liberty Under the Soviets*. Likewise, Reverend Ward, a champion of "social justice," himself wrote a book, *The Soviet Spirit*. Published in 1934, it was a virtual valentine to Lenin and Stalin, and was his third book on the Motherland.

The *Daily Worker* and *New Masses* loved Reverend Ward's missive, promoting it in a feature in the January 14, 1945, *Daily Worker*. The *Daily Worker* described Ward as a "ripe people's scholar," a "kindly and wise man," whom communists everywhere were "lucky" to have.[48] In the article, Ward said that "socialism works," described the USSR as "socialist," and described himself as "socialist." The comrades at *New Masses* were so impressed with the Methodist minister's book that they gave away complimentary copies in exchange for a one-year subscription.[49]

Ward, like Baldwin, made trips to the USSR, where he was given the full Potemkin-village treatment by his eager Bolshevik hosts. His seminary, Union Theological Seminary in New York, gave him a one-year sabbatical (1931–32) to go to the Motherland to research and pay homage. A later major congressional report on communist activities in the New York area would feature more references to Ward than any other figure—twice as many as to Earl Browder.[50]

Other early officials of the ACLU included major Party members like William Z. Foster (Browder's predecessor), Elizabeth Gurley Flynn (later recipient of a Soviet state funeral), and Louis Budenz (who later broke with the Party), to name just a few. Communists employed the ACLU to deflect questions from the U.S. government over whether they were loyal to the USSR, were serving Stalin in some capacity, and were committed to the overthrow of the American system.

Another key ACLU member was Clarence Darrow, the wisecracking lawyer who tore into Democratic Party icon William Jennings Bryan in the 1925 "Scopes Monkey Trials," an epic battle over evolution versus creationism. Darrow's name repeatedly appears in the Comintern Archives on CPUSA.[51] Communists greatly appreciated his work against religion and practically revered him for a reason not taught in public schools: Darrow defended them in a series of dramatic incidents and cases that ran from 1919 into the 1920s, when they were being pursued for advocating armed revolution and the replacement of the American system with a "Soviet American republic."

So rampant was the ACLU in aiding and abetting American communists that some legislative committees, federal and state, considered whether it was a communist front. Two reports, one by Congress, released in January 1931, and another released later (1943) by the California Senate Fact-Finding Committee on Un-American Activities, determined that the answer was yes. Both reports claimed that "at least 90 percent of its [the ACLU's] efforts are expended on behalf of communists who come into conflict with the law."[52]

In the case of the Scottsboro Boys, the ACLU was there not to defend communists but to help its communist pals defend (and use) the boys. This was likely the start of Frank Marshall Davis's prolonged exposure to the ACLU and related "civil liberties" groups whose causes he would either join or trumpet in his columns.[53]

THE ROLE OF THE NAACP

When groups like the ACLU (and even ILD) were suspected as communist fronts, the charge elicited the usual counterclaims of "liar" and "witch-hunt" by conniving communists and their duped accomplices on the liberal/progressive left.[54]

The NAACP found itself (at times) lying with these strange bedfellows in the "united front." The NAACP was not, of course, a communist organization. In those days, many of its leaders and supporters were Republicans, including Ben Davis, Sr., whom Frank first encountered when Ben was the owner and editor of the rival *Atlanta Independent*. Frank also met Ben's son, Ben Davis, Jr., the next generation—who became a famous New York City communist councilman who ran for national office on the CPUSA ticket.[55]

At this point, NAACP leaders were in a moral dilemma over whether to accept communist support for their causes, especially in the Deep South, where the NAACP was lacking allies. Some NAACP officials viewed communists as predatory, fearing their cause was being undermined by communist involvement.

Compounding the challenge was that the NAACP, like other mainstream political or social organizations—including the YMCA and the YWCA—found itself targeted for penetration by communists. Given that these communists were usually not forthcoming about their identity, NAACP officials often had a hard time knowing the true intentions of some of their own advisors.

One example of this from the earliest days of the Scottsboro trial, delivered to and filed at the Comintern in Moscow, was an April 19, 1931, note on NAACP letterhead from William Pickens to the *Daily Worker*, flagship publication of CPUSA.[56]

Born in 1881, Pickens was the son of liberated slaves who migrated to Arkansas, where he worked in cotton fields and sawmills and attended a segregated public school. He ended up a Phi Beta Kappa graduate from Yale, becoming an expert linguist. In 1918, he became director of branches for the NAACP.

Pickens's language in his 1931 letter is reflective of someone clearly sympathetic to communism, and writing to offer more than a mere "thank you for your support." Pickens wrote:

I have just seen a copy of the Daily Worker for April 16th and noted the fight which the workers are making, thru I.L.D., to prevent the judicial massacre of Negro youth in Alabama.

Enclosed is a small check for that cause. Please send it to I.L.D., in an enclosed stamped envelope.

The promptness with which the white workers have moved toward defending these helpless and innocent Negro boys, sons of black workers, is significant and prophetic. The only ultimate salvation for black and white workers is their united defense, one of the other. Other causes and movements may do good work, but all other causes are good only as preliminaries to that consummation. The one objective for final security is the absolute and unqualified unity

and co-operation of ALL WORKERS [Pickens's emphasis], of all the
exploited masses.

Whatever the verdict for the boys, concluded Pickens, the ultimate
goal must be "a victory for the workers." He finished his letter to the
Daily Worker: "This is one occasion for every Negro who has intelligence
enough to read, to send aid to you and the I.L.D."

Pickens viewed Scottsboro as a matter of the working class and "exploited masses." He was not only unconcerned about an association
with communists but actually solicited their involvement and sent a personal check.

Pickens left the NAACP in 1941 to join FDR's Treasury Department,
one of the most thoroughly penetrated agencies of the federal government.

"WE WANT NONE OF THAT"

Other black leaders were not quite so taken. They felt they were being
burned by the Reds via Scottsboro. This was evident in a November 23,
1949, NAACP press release that featured a letter by Roy Wilkins, acting
secretary of the NAACP, sent to William L. Patterson.[57] Patterson was
national executive secretary of the communist front, the Civil Rights
Congress, a successor organization to the ILD. Patterson sought the
NAACP's support in another supposed like-minded cause, but Wilkins
had no interest. Citing Scottsboro in particular, Wilkins strongly rejected the offer:

Dear Mr. Patterson:

   *I have your seven page letter of November 14. . . . Although your
letter was not labeled as an open letter, we have since learned that it was
mimeographed and strategically, if not widely, distributed. This tactic is not
either surprising or alarming, and merely tends to confirm our estimate of the
real purpose of the communication.*
   *Without using up seven pages we can say at once that the NAACP
planning committee, which carried out the mandate of our annual*

convention, agreed not to include the Civil Rights Congress on the list of organizations to be invited to participate.

We remember the Scottsboro case and our experience there with the International Labor Defense, one of the predecessors of the Civil Rights Congress. We remember that the present Civil Rights Congress is composed of the remnants of the ILD and other groups. We remember that in the Scottsboro case the NAACP was subjected to the most unprincipled vilification. We remember the campaign of slander in the Daily Worker. We remember the leaflets and the speakers and the whole unspeakable machinery that was turned loose upon all those who did not embrace the "unity" policy as announced by the Communists.

We want none of that unity today. . . .

Roy Wilkins
Acting Secretary

Wilkins was fed up with the so-called *support* of communists.

Similar sentiments were expressed by Herbert Hill, another NAACP official. Writing in the NAACP's flagship publication, Hill detailed instances where CPUSA used the NAACP, cynically advancing Soviet rights under the rubric of civil rights for blacks. "American Communist Party interest in the Negro can be neither genuine nor sincere," wrote Hill. "Quite the contrary. Strategic needs of the party as dictated by Moscow take precedence, not the goals and aspirations of Negroes. Whenever the interests of Negroes come into conflict with the political interest of Russia, the Communists abandon Negroes like rats a sinking ship."[58]

In fact, communists abandoned not only Negroes, but all of humanity. For every Scottsboro boy simply *threatened* with execution—in the end, mercifully, none were executed, though several did hard jail time—there were multiple millions of innocent Soviet men and women in the process of actually being executed.[59]

THE SCOTTSBORO CAMPAIGN DRAWS FRANK

It was Scottsboro that earned the anger of Frank Marshall Davis. And it appears that CPUSA's Scottsboro campaign was what first drew Frank to the Communist Party.

This is evident in several spots throughout Frank's recently declassified FBI file. According to an informant close to Frank in Hawaii, interviewed by FBI special agent Richard B. Stull on June 16, 1950, Frank (in the words of the FBI report) "became interested in the Communist Party in 1931, while he was Editor of the Atlanta Daily World, a Negro newspaper. Subject stated he became interested in the Communist Party mainly because of the Scottsboro case and later because of the Herndon case." "Herndon" refers to Angelo Herndon, another cause célèbre and campaign issue for communists at the time. Frank discussed Herndon in his memoirs—one of the few instances in which he (unavoidably) dared use the word "communist." [60]

This report, as we shall see, makes perfect sense in explaining Frank's initial lurch to the left.

Frank seemed less guarded about Herndon than Scottsboro. "In 1932," wrote Frank, "the Angelo Herndon trial captured world headlines, second only to the Scottsboro case." Frank referred to Herndon as a "young black Communist" who, in "an act of unbelievable courage," had led a march on the Georgia state capitol. He was arrested and faced severe punishment, from a long-term prison sentence to white prosecutors' seeking the death penalty. Frank admitted meeting with Herndon in Chicago, though he offered no further details, including when.

Here, too, communists exploited the situation to bolster the cause of the USSR. This is evident in a June 1934 pamphlet titled "Free Angelo Herndon," published by the *Young Worker*, an arm of Angelo Herndon's own Young Communist League of America. The final four sentences of the pamphlet said it all: "Forward to the freedom of Angelo Herndon! Free the Scottsboro Boys! Forward to a Soviet America and the complete liberation of the Negro people! Join the Young Communist League!" The pamphlet asked for money for the *Young Worker* to benefit "Soviet America."

In his memoirs, Frank acknowledged that Herndon's case had

prompted a "number" of "young Afro-Americans" to join the Communist Party, including Ben Davis, Jr., whom Frank acknowledged befriending in Atlanta at this time. Frank said that he and Ben were often confused not only because of their last names but because they were around the same age and size. Frank also stated that it was Ben Davis, Jr.'s "determined fight for civil rights [that] led him into the Communist Party"—as if the former was a natural precursor to the latter.[61]

Unsurprisingly, riding to Herndon's rescue was, once again, ILD, which defended Angelo Herndon.

By reaching Frank Marshall Davis, CPUSA's Scottsboro campaign may have had precisely the long-term impact that communists had hoped for. Their campaign was a key factor in drawing Frank near the fold.

That reality offers us a whole new perspective on the success of the communists' Scottsboro campaign. Consider: Their target had been black Americans in the 1930s. But history has proven that they were thinking too small. Indirectly, via Frank, they would ultimately reach no less than America's first black president a century later.

In its wildest dreams, CPUSA could never have imagined such a grand success.

3

Frank's Work for the *Atlanta Daily World* (1931–34)

JUST AS SCOTTSBORO coincided with Frank's arrival in Atlanta in 1931, so did the arrival of America's communists. They headed south at the same time as Frank did.

A close look at the contents of the *Atlanta Daily World* in this period, particularly the editorial page that Frank crafted, shows that Frank Marshall Davis began gravitating toward the communist left very early—consistent with the time frame established in his FBI file.

Finding access to old copies of the *Atlanta Daily World* is difficult, but I was able to secure copies of about sixty editions from 1931 to 1932.[1] Starting in December 1931, the end of the year that marked Scottsboro and the move south by Frank and by communists, one can begin to discern Frank's growing attention to the communist movement.

DECEMBER 1931

Readers of the *Atlanta Daily World* the morning of December 11, 1931, would not have missed a page-one, above-the-fold announcement that Spelman College, a local black college, had scheduled Langston Hughes for a lecture. The article noted that, in addition to Hughes's speaking at Spelman on December 16, he would also be at nearby Morehouse College (another black college) for a full week beginning December 9. Readers unfamiliar with Hughes learned only that he was a "young poet."[2]

They would not learn, as Frank well knew, that Hughes—indeed a highly recognized African-American poet—was also a highly recognized African-American communist, vigorous in his politics and his poetry, with his major outlet being the Marxist publication *New Masses*.[3] Yet there was no mention of Hughes's politics in the article.

Such a glaring omission seemed to be no accident. Because Hughes's Spelman talk was ultimately postponed a day, Frank's newspaper followed up with a second front-page article, this time with a photo of Hughes to grab readers. The article raved that Hughes was "recognized throughout the world as a poet of unusual ability."[4]

Again, there was no mention of Hughes's likewise world-recognized politics.

It is not clear if Frank went to hear Hughes at Spelman. In his memoirs, Frank admitted meeting Hughes later (roughly 1935) in Chicago. This led to a long-term correspondence and friendship, though never (in Frank's words) a "really close friendship." They became close enough, though, that Frank for a long time thereafter referred to Hughes as "Lang." "In those days," noted Frank in his memoirs, "Lang was looked upon as a communist."

There was very good reason for that.

Langston Hughes was a loyal Soviet patriot—a fact completely neglected in the two *Atlanta Daily World* headlines. His devotion is evident in one of his most infamous statements: "Put one more 'S' in the USA to make it Soviet," declared Hughes. "The USA when we take control will be the USSA."[5] He urged the Marxist faithful to rise and fight for the "great red flag . . . of the [Communist] Internationale."

Interestingly, immediately upon the end of this tour of the American South, Hughes went directly to Stalin's USSR. There he found his god. "There," wrote Hughes of his Moscow pilgrimage, "it seemed to me that

Marxism had put into practical being many of the precepts which our own Christian America had not yet been able to bring to life."[6] Moved by the Soviet spirit, Hughes penned this poem:

> *Goodbye Christ, Lord Jehovah,*
> *Beat it on away from here, make way for a new guy with no religion*
>   *at all,*
> *A real guy named Marx, Communism, Lenin, Peasant, Stalin,*
>   *worker, me.*[7]

Beat it, Christ. Move over for someone real: Marx, Lenin, Stalin.

This was the real Langston Hughes.

No mention of such revolutionary verse or mind appeared in the plugs for Hughes on the front page of Frank's newspaper that cold December 1931. This signaled a standard practice for Frank that only got worse in his writing/reporting in the decades ahead: the blatant sins of omission when it came to acknowledging hard-core American communists and their true loyalties.

When reading Frank, one always needed to know a lot of crucial background on the communist movement, because Frank rarely injected the "c" word into his reports on prominent figures who also happened to be prominent communists. This inherent deception was the hallmark of being a communist.

Frank did pause to use the "c" word two weeks later in a brief barb in his Christmas column of December 25, 1931. In his "Touring the World" column, Frank provided a Christmas wish list for various people and groups. It was a gentle, tongue-in-cheek piece. He noted of his publisher, W. A. Scott, "A Chrysler that won't damage." For the state of Georgia, he wished: "A definite kind of weather." Then came these two wishes: "The Communists: Either a muzzle or more diplomacy. The N.A.A.C.P: A course on 'How To Be Nonchalant When Embarrassed By the Reds.' "[8]

This was apparently a reference to the NAACP's anger at CPUSA's inserting itself into Scottsboro. That hostility was already palpable, and Frank was watching with keen interest.

SCOTTSBORO REARS ITS HEAD

Two days later, though, the "c" word was conveniently omitted from a December 27 front-page piece on the Scottsboro campaign, in which the *Atlanta Daily World* ran photos of evidence used in the boys' defense by ILD.[9] There was no mention of the communist philosophy that infused ILD.

Perhaps readers noticed and complained, because five days later, on January 1, 1932, the *Atlanta Daily World* ran a huge top-of-the-fold headline that asked: "Will Communists Sacrifice Eights Boys to Propaganda?" With that screaming headline, Frank could hardly be accused of being a shill for the ILD. The corresponding lengthy article noted that sources from the NAACP to Clarence Darrow were concerned over communist involvement in the Scottsboro trial. The article stated that Darrow had "made it plain" that he had "no connection whatever with Communism" and "Mr. Darrow stated that he would not consider entering cases in any connection with any communistic organization."[10] (Recall that Darrow had defended the American Communist Party in major cases the previous decade.)

The article was a news report, not an editorial, but it raised legitimate concerns that "the boys are being sacrificed to Communism." It is not clear who wrote the article, though it could have been Frank, and was at the very least approved by Frank. Frank surely approved the headline, probably crafting it himself.

Frank was likely influenced by the digging of celebrated columnist George Schuyler of the *Pittsburgh Courier*, an influential black conservative. Frank read Schuyler regularly, quoted him in the *Atlanta Daily World*, reviewed his books, knew and liked him, and recalled his work later in his memoirs. As ILD stuck its nose in Scottsboro, Schuyler rushed home from an island off the coast of Africa, where he was writing a book, to eagerly report that he detected in Scottsboro "all the earmarks of a Communist plot." Among the gems Schuyler unearthed was that communists had raised a whopping $250,000 for the Scottsboro Boys' defense, but reportedly used only $12,000 on the boys—for two appeals.[11]

Schuyler quoted a candid Party official who confessed, "We don't give a damn about the Scottsboro boys. If they burn it doesn't make any difference. We are only interested in one thing, how we can use the Scottsboro case to bring the Communist movement to the people and win them over to Communism."[12]

Schuyler concluded: "The record shows that where and when the Communists seemed to be fighting for Negro rights, their object was simply to strengthen the hand of Russia."[13]

BETTER DEAD FOR THE REDS

The *Atlanta Daily World* chimed in on January 6, 1932, with an unsigned editorial, "The N.A.A.C.P. Withdraws." The editorial took sides with the NAACP and against the communists. It lamented that the NAACP's withdrawal from the Scottsboro case left the boys to a "tricky turn of fate." "The youths are now represented solely by the International Labor Defense," noted the editorial, "a Communist organization which has shown by its tactics that saving the lives of these boys is not its major interest."[14]

That was quite a statement, one that could have been written by the most stalwart anticommunist, or by George Schuyler himself. There is a high likelihood that Frank wrote it, given his full control of the editorial department.

Of course, Frank was not a member of the Communist Party at this point, and the plain fact was—as the NAACP noted—that the Party's priority was communist ideology. Even someone sympathetic to communism (as Frank might have been) could see this, or could be critical of ILD's handling of the case. Indeed, the editorial objected less to communism than to ILD's tactics and "blundering methods," especially "the way in which the Reds have alienated the Negro press—a force which kept friendly, might have meant the success of Communism among Negroes."

The problem was not necessarily communism, but the communists themselves.

The editorial then made a stinging point, reflective of George Schuyler's thinking: "The eight boys dead would be as great an aid to Red propaganda as the eight boys set free."

No doubt that was true, just as the execution of the Rosenbergs two decades later precisely served communist interests. If the Rosenbergs were spared the chair, CPUSA and Moscow would have nothing to howl about. If the Scottsboro boys were executed, noted the editorial, communists worldwide could condemn the "white capitalistic legal lynchings."

Moreover, the editorial assailed the Reds' rude treatment of the NAACP. It said that the NAACP had bent over backward to work with ILD, doing everything other than "take out lifetime membership with the Communists." And how did communists respond? With "fresh and vitriolic invectives."

The editorial was spot-on and seemed to match Frank's style of writing. If Frank was the author, he was learning valuable lessons about the cynical conniving endemic to the communist movement. The editorial also showed that, for Frank (if he was the author), civil rights fortunately still trumped political ideology.

At least for now.

CRYING OUT FOR THE COMMUNIST HARVEST

A close reading of Frank's (signed) articles in this period reveals that he was not rejecting communism as a philosophy, even if he was critical of ILD's actions. This was abundantly clear in a striking "Touring the World" column nine days later, January 15, 1932, in which Frank cut loose:

"The gross stupidity, perfect asininity and extreme dunderheadedness of Red management is accountable for failure of black and white workers to flock to the Communist banner in wholesale numbers when the crop almost cries out for harvest. The nation is economically sick today from too many sweets in the days of prosperity; the Reds have offered a medicine sound in its group principles but cannot find patients." [15]

This was a significant statement. There seemed little mistaking Frank's thinking: His beef was not so much with communism but with communists; not the ideology but its managers; not the "sound" medicine of Marx but Marx's "management." This was a common argument by many progressives of the day. For instance, John Dewey, progressive saint of public education, objected not so much to the philosophy of communism but to "Communism, official Communism, spelt with a capital letter." [16]

After expressing his disappointment with communism as run by its managers, and with the American system, he concluded by suggesting that the answer might be a form of "socialism" that mixed the best elements of communism and capitalism. "Socialism, you know, is a sort of halfway station between Communism and Capitalism," wrote Frank. "What the nation needs is a combination of the best points of all three."

"QUESTION OF ECONOMICS"

Frank Marshall Davis continued to chronicle ILD's defense of the Scottsboro Boys, hoping for success for the boys' sake. His newspaper did regular updates on "the Reds'" work on the case. [17] When ILD announced it had spent ten thousand dollars in defense of the boys (without noting how much it had raised and not spent), Frank applauded the news in a headline aside his column. [18]

Frank's newspaper also continued to run procommunist material. In the February 5, 1932, edition came an unsigned editorial that could have been written by Karl Marx himself, and whose contents were at least provided by Marx's disciples. This editorial was titled "Question of Economics Must Be Solved By Negro, Speaker Says."

This was no local speaker. The piece, picked up from the Associated Negro Press service, related a lecture program far removed from Atlanta, all the way north in Philadelphia, hosted by a small group called the Labor Institute, with a speaker named J. B. Matthews. The problem for Negroes in America, according to Matthews, was a "working class problem," based on "imperialism and group exploitation." Said the editorial, "The Negro, according to Mr. Matthews, is particularly handicapped in our economic struggle in America." Matthews argued that the "race problem will not be solved by mere sentimentality, religion and education . . . but that the race must get together as a militant working class group."

• • •

The editorial ended there. What was not said to readers, and likely not discerned by the eighty-year-old Atlantan who survived slavery and the Civil War, was that this was standard Marxist rhetoric and class theory, that the Labor Institute was a communist front, and that J. B. Matthews was a hard-core communist. (Matthews would later undergo a remarkable conversion, becoming one of America's greatest anticommunists, keeping a watchful eye on guys like Frank as Matthews became chief investigator for the House Committee on Un-American Activities.)

Did Frank not know this? Was this another sin of omission?

What is clear is that Frank had misgivings about ILD's handling of Scottsboro. In a March 27, 1932, editorial titled "Red Scottsboro," Frank's *Atlanta Daily World* again hammered the Reds' "blood and thunder activities" and "successful maneuvering" to drive away the NAACP. The editorial smacked the "bungling hands" of communists in exploiting the boys as "nine pawns of Communism." "Dead or alive," the editorial said of the boys, "they will be good material for Communistic propaganda, and that seems to be what this organization wants anyway." [19]

WHICH POLITICAL PARTY FOR BLACK AMERICANS?

Also plain in the pages of the *Atlanta Daily World* was black Americans' search for a political home. The years of 1932–33 constituted a sea change in the demographic makeup of the major political parties. The *Atlanta Daily World* noted this in an unsigned editorial titled "The Sinking Republican Ship," published shortly before the historic November 1932 election that delivered Franklin Delano Roosevelt to the White House. [20]

As the editorial noted, the nation was witnessing a "wholesale defection of Negro voters from Republican ranks in the November elections." In 1932, the Democrats, the party of the white-racist South, had a chance to gather "the largest Negro vote in the party's history." But, cautioned the editorial, this would depend on the Democrats' approach and presidential candidate. It was not yet a done deal.

The editorial assessed that "the Negro has no effective political organization and must cast his ballot where he considers he will be best benefitted."

Not only did Democrats and Republicans alike realize this, but so did another group, with far fewer members, but one that was clearly starving for more: the Communist Party.

Frank Marshall Davis's interest in communist ideology did not escape readers, including those beyond the confines of Atlanta. As he somewhat proudly admitted in the March 24, 1933, issue of the *Atlanta Daily World*, he was one of seven black journalists nationwide surveyed for his opinion on communism, which was to be published in the NAACP magazine, *Crisis*. Frank shared a few of the assessments provided by the seven journalists, but not his own.[21]

Only many years later could one track down Frank's thoughts, published in a book by Herbert Aptheker, the well-known Marxist "theoretician," historian of the Communist Party, and notorious Soviet apologist.[22] Aptheker, ultimately hailed in his *New York Times* obituary as a champion of "civil rights,"[23] dedicated the book to sixties communist radical Angela Davis and to his daughter, Bettina Aptheker, the recognized Marxist-feminist.

Stated Frank: "It is a fact that the Negro, getting the dirty end of the economic[,] social and political stick, finds in Communistic ideals those panacea he seeks." "And yet," Frank quickly lamented, "I believe that were our government adjusted according to Red standards, few members of the kaleidoscopic race would have sense enough to take advantage of it."[24]

Frank regretted that the "panacea" of communism would go undigested by black folks who needed it, and by America as a whole. As for Frank, however, there seemed little resistance.

Remember, Frank did not divulge this more open-minded assessment of communism to readers of the *Atlanta Daily World*, nor did he divulge to them his reasons for suddenly wanting to leave Atlanta. Nonetheless, rather suddenly, Frank Marshall Davis was finished with Atlanta. He left the *Atlanta Daily World* in midsummer 1934, and headed back to Chicago.

Paul Robeson and Progressive Dupes

ONCE FRANK LEFT the *Atlanta Daily World,* and on the heels of Scotts-boro, another profound political influence would tug him further toward the communist left, even as he remained far away from formally joining CPUSA. That influence was Paul Robeson, the celebrated African-American performer, who, as even the *New York Times* conceded, was "an outspoken admirer of the Soviet Union."[1]

In the mid-1930s, Robeson became what I call a "Potemkin Progressive." These were progressives with serious misunderstandings of things Soviet and Stalin, who spread their mistakes on a grand scale. Apart from duped Potemkin Progressives like John Dewey, George Bernard Shaw, the Columbia faculty, and untold numbers of other hoodwinked leftists, Robeson would be the most significant dupe in the life, thinking, and work of Frank Marshall Davis.

In fact, whereas the likes of John Dewey later changed, Robeson swallowed the Stalinist line so completely that he never ceased being an admirer. Robeson's total absorption helps explain how Frank, too, eventually migrated to the furthest extreme of the left.

POTEMKIN PROGRESSIVES

The concept of "Potemkin Progressives"[2] is rooted in the progressive and communist movements of the 1920s and 1930s. To some American liberals/progressives, the *brave new world* charted by the men in Moscow seemed like it might dovetail with the ideals and objectives of the growing progressive movement in the United States. There was a sense that they and the Soviets were traveling a similar path: "fellow travelers" on a shared road toward a better world based on the collective, on redistribution of wealth, on public ownership of "the means of production," on central planning. (The differences were matters of degree.) Some of these progressives traveled to Lenin's and Stalin's USSR, where the Soviets rolled out the red carpet, duping them with phenomenal success.

The statists running the USSR saw a giant opportunity in America's progressives. They hoped to convince them that the Bolsheviks had indeed charted a glistening new world. Soviet officials had many motives; among them, they wanted formal diplomatic recognition of Russia by the United States and the West. Moscow judged that such legitimacy would provide it cover to pursue its totalitarian communist aims not only at home but abroad, with world revolution the ultimate objective.[3]

So, in addition to other forms of propaganda, the Soviet leadership orchestrated carefully managed tours of Potemkin Villages.[4] These were phony areas constructed solely for gullible Western visitors. The goal was to give the false impression that communism was producing a glorious new way of life.

Naturally, these visiting progressives were more than mere "visitors"; they were usually people of impact—educators, academics, journalists, union organizers—encouraged to make the trip (often by communists in the United States) in the hope they would return home with reports of the grand achievements of the communist world, gushing praise for Joe Stalin. And despite their acclaimed sophistication, many did precisely that, swallowing the bait completely.

There to observe the spectacle was Malcolm Muggeridge, the British journalist who became one of the twentieth century's leading intellectual forces and converts to Christianity. At the time, Muggeridge was a man of the left. Unlike his colleagues, however, which included the *New York Times*' Walter Duranty,[5] Muggeridge was not taken by Soviet handlers. He was disgusted by the Soviet regime and its obvious manipulation. He was bewildered by the credulity of his leftist friends, of whom he wrote:

> They are unquestionably one of the wonders of the age, and I shall treasure till I die as a blessed memory the spectacle of them travelling with radiant optimism through a famished countryside, wandering in happy bands about squalid, over-crowded towns, listening with unshakable faith to the fatuous patter of carefully trained and indoctrinated guides, repeating like schoolchildren a multiplication table, the bogus statistics and mindless slogans endlessly intoned to them.[6]

Not only was Muggeridge mystified by such naïveté, but so, too, were Soviet officials. "The almost unbelievable credulity of these mostly university-educated tourists," wrote Muggeridge, "astonished even Soviet officials used to handling foreign visitors."[7]

The visitors were universally "progressives," marveled Muggeridge, united across countries and nationalities only by their common progressivism—"all upholders of progressive causes and members of progressive organizations." Muggeridge recorded: "These fellow-passengers provided my first experience of the progressive elite from all over the world who attached themselves to the Soviet regime, resolved to believe anything they were told by its spokesmen."[8]

Here are just some examples of the ravings of these Western progressives:

Speaking of Stalin, author H. G. Wells expressed awe: "I've never met a man more candid, fair, and honest. . . . Everyone trusts him." Wells said this after meeting Stalin in 1934, the start of the Great Purge, the greatest slaughter in human history.[9]

Wells's fellow socialist, George Bernard Shaw, justified those purges: "We cannot afford to give ourselves moral airs when our most enterprising neighbor [the Soviet Union] humanely and judiciously liquidates a handful of exploiters and speculators to make the world safe for honest men." Shaw was deadly serious about Stalin's "persecution," which "was, I think, justified."[10]

Other such Potemkin Progressives included the ACLU's Roger Baldwin and Harry Ward, Columbia University's Corliss Lamont and John Dewey, and Planned Parenthood founder Margaret Sanger.

Corliss Lamont was the son of New York banker Thomas W. Lamont, chairman and partner at J. P. Morgan, and a giant of Wall Street.[11] At Columbia, Corliss, who was also a top official at the ACLU, had penned his atheist classic, *The Illusion of Immortality*. In 1932, Corliss and his wife shoved off for the USSR. They put their experiences to paper in a horrible 1933 book called *Russia Day by Day*, whose list of outrages is too lengthy to be given due justice here.[12]

Equally embarrassing was Lamont's mentor at Columbia, John Dewey. By the 1920s, a mutual-admiration society had developed between John Dewey and the Bolshevik hierarchy. The Soviets adored Dewey's educational works, quickly translating them into Russian. Yes, Dewey, father of American public education, was also helping to father Soviet public education. The Bolsheviks saw Dewey's ideas for American public schools as perfect for the Soviet communist model. They invited him to Moscow for a "tour," and the professor could not resist. Dewey made his pilgrimage in the summer of 1928, along with twenty-five educators from various universities.[13]

When he returned, Dewey filed a six-part series of reports in *The New Republic*.[14] His dispatches on Russia were loving, lyrical, fulsome in poetic praise of what he experienced. He lauded "the orderly and safe character of life in Russia." "In spite of secret police, inquisitions, arrests and deportations of *Nepmen* and *Kulaks*, exiling of party opponents, including divergent elements in the party," Dewey allowed, "life for the masses goes on with regularity, safety and decorum." The progressive professor proclaimed the Bolshevik Revolution "a great success."[15]

Also impressed was Planned Parenthood matron Margaret Sanger. She sojourned to soak in Stalin's *advancements* for women. "We could well take example from Russia," advised Sanger upon her return, "where birth control instruction is part of the regular welfare service of the government."[16] Sanger enthusiastically reported this in the June 1935 edition of her publication, *Birth Control Review*.

The Planned Parenthood founder was, however, surprised by the explosion in the number of abortions once legalized by the Bolsheviks. She sought to allay fears among abortion opponents, offering this stunning prediction: "All the [Bolshevik] officials with whom I discussed the matter stated that as soon as the economic and social plans of Soviet Russia are realized, neither abortions nor contraception will be necessary or desired. A functioning Communistic society will assure the happiness of every child, and will assume the full responsibility for its welfare and education."

This was pure progressive utopianism, an absolute faith in central planners. Contrary to Sanger's optimism, abortions skyrocketed to seven million annually in the USSR, dwarfing the worst years in America post–*Roe* v. *Wade*.

Margaret Sanger, John Dewey, Corliss Lamont, George Bernard Shaw, and H. G. Wells were not isolated cases among Western progressives. Too many swooned at Potemkin Villages, some permanently. Some, sadly, joined the other side. One of them was Paul Robeson.

PAUL ROBESON'S RED CARPET

Born in April 1898 in Princeton, New Jersey, Paul L. Robeson was the son of a Protestant minister. He attended Rutgers University, where he was a standout athlete. At six feet three and 220 pounds, Robeson was a force not only on the football field but also onstage, where he exhibited a rich singing voice and knack for theater. He went on to attend Columbia Law School.

Columbia was the worst possible choice for Robeson. The university was the single most radical school in America, with a disturbingly strong communist presence. A young man like, for example, Whittaker Chambers, could enter Columbia a devout traditional Republican and leave a raving leftist atheist who ended up a Soviet spy at the center of the most dramatic Cold War case of the twentieth century.

Robeson arrived about the same time as Chambers, yet his hard turn left came a decade later, in the 1930s, as many progressives stood in rapturous awe at the Soviet experiment. Among them, George Bernard Shaw is credited with having helped prompt Robeson, asking him during a 1928 lunch what he thought of socialism. Robeson innocently conceded he had "never really thought about socialism."[17]

Not long after that, Robeson began thinking quite a bit about socialism. After publicly denouncing the "modern white American," Robeson found himself suddenly invited to the USSR, and earnestly accepted. He made the pilgrimage in December 1934.

Robeson's voyage came amid Stalin's notorious famines and Great Purge, but the political pilgrim was carefully shielded from such misery. His gracious hosts rolled out the red carpet, regaling Robeson with (in his words) "nights at the theater and opera," "gala banquets," "private screenings," "trips to hospitals, children's centers," and "factories"—"all in the context of a warm embrace."[18]

It was the typical charade. When communist propagandists find a target, they do not easily relent, whether it is a target they want to demonize or one they want to canonize. In Robeson, they saw usefulness in the latter. And so, that December 1934, the Soviets held a reception in Robeson's honor, at which he was hailed by the emcee with this magnificent introduction: "This is Paul Robeson, the greatest American singer!"

The comrades clapped enthusiastically, as Robeson blushed and bowed. The boys back-slapped and drank until 2:00 a.m. It was a night to remember, a political romance to never forget.[19]

STALIN'S RACIAL PARADISE

Paul Robeson eagerly returned the hugs and kisses. He allowed his hosts to easily convince him that no racism existed in the Soviet Union. Yes, *no racism*. The mere attempt at such a claim was laughable.

Unbelievable as this claim was, the duping of Robeson was thorough. He returned to America marveling that Stalin's boys had abolished racism, along with unemployment and innumerable other ills. This claim is a very important one for this book, in that a soon-to-be close friend of Robeson, who swallowed this whopper hook, line, and sinker, was Frank Marshall Davis, another black American who was at that point merely a liberal/progressive.

In truth, there were very few black people living in Russia. The So-

viets were notorious for lying and fudging all sorts of self-reported statistics: on unemployment, homelessness, crime, prostitution, economic
growth, missiles, military spending, and on and on, from 1917 until the
implosion in the 1980s. None of these statistics were confirmable by
outside organizations, and hardly anyone (not even inside the USSR, as
Mikhail Gorbachev bemoaned) took them seriously.[20] The Soviets' serial
mendacity reflected what Vaclav Havel called "the communist culture of
the lie."

There is no reliable data on blacks populating Russia at the time of
Robeson's visit, but one can be certain it was nowhere near the numbers
in America.[21] Even today, with reliable figures, the number of blacks in
Russia is so low that it does not even register in sources like the *World
Factbook*, as the total is well under 1 percent of the population.[22] By com-
parison, the United States reports 13 percent of Americans as "black."

Moreover, there was no good reason to think that Russians were
more racially tolerant than any other people. Andrew Young, civil-rights
activist and ambassador to the United Nations under President Jimmy
Carter, publicly stated: "The worst racists in the world are Russians."[23]

That is debatable. What is not debatable is the reality that the Soviet
Union was an equal-opportunity oppressor, not singling out for discrimination based on race. The communist regime was just as likely to lock
up and shoot a black person as a white person.

One of the saddest cases in the history of the Cold War was that of
Lovett Fort-Whiteman, a contemporary of Paul Robeson. As noted earlier, Fort-Whiteman founded the American Negro Labor Congress in
Chicago in 1925. A year earlier, Fort-Whiteman traveled to Moscow for
the Fifth World Congress of the Third International, where he excitedly
promised that "Negroes are destined to be the most revolutionary class
in America." A delegate to the Sixth Congress of the Communist International, he was the first black American to undergo Comintern training at the Lenin School.[24]

In 1930, Fort-Whiteman moved to the USSR, proclaiming that he
was "coming home to Moscow." He was living in the Motherland at the
time of Robeson's arrival, and remained there as Robeson left to sing
Stalin's praises back in America. Fort-Whiteman, however, ultimately
found his Moscow audience not quite as agreeable. By the latter 1930s,

he had had enough, and wanted to return to America. The Soviets refused. The freedom to emigrate was one of those American fundamentals that did not exist in the USSR.

Freedom of expression was another. And when Fort-Whiteman dared to gripe about the repression, the onetime loyal Soviet patriot was accused of counterrevolutionary activities and found himself on a one-way, no-return trip to northeastern Siberia—specifically, the frozen hell that was the Kolyma region. He did not last long.[25] In 1939, Lovett Fort-Whiteman died of mistreatment and starvation in the gulag, the full story of his fate unknown for a half century.

In the end, Lovett Fort-Whiteman was a black man treated equally with white men in the Soviet Union: He was sentenced to death.

A JUST PURGE

Fanciful claims about ending racism were not the only phony bill of goods that Paul Robeson bought at the Kremlin's propaganda window. He infamously defended Stalin's purges and even the hideous August 1939 Hitler-Stalin Pact that launched World War II. Robeson remarked that it was acceptable for the Soviets to "destroy anybody who seeks to harm that great country."[26]

That outrageous sentiment was hardly isolated. When Robeson returned from his initial pilgrimage to the Motherland, the *Daily Worker* thrust a microphone in his face, and Robeson glowed about the new world he had discovered. The *Daily Worker* rushed its Robeson interview into print, running it in the January 15, 1935, issue under the headline " 'I Am at Home,' Says Robeson At Reception in Soviet Union."[27]

The Bolsheviks, explained Robeson, using the language of slavery, had been "sons of serfs who are now freed by their own efforts." They were new men, unshackled by Stalinism. Robeson was no Johnny-come-lately to that conclusion. He told the CPUSA organ that he had been studying the USSR for two years before his visit, absorbing himself in the Russian language and regularly reading *Pravda* and *Izvestia*, the totalitarian state's twin mouthpieces.

Robeson had not been "prepared for the happiness I see on every face in Moscow." He had been "aware that there was no starvation" in

Russia—apparently so briefed by "progressive" American friends—but was bowled over by the "bounding life," "endless friendliness," and "feeling of safety and abundance and freedom" he found "wherever I turn." (John Dewey's descriptions were almost identical.[28])

Paul Robeson had discovered sheer equality under Joseph Stalin: racial equality, social equality, cultural equality, economic equality, political equality. When asked about Stalin's purges, which the *Daily Worker* characterized as warranted executions of a "number of counterrevolutionary terrorists," Robeson retorted: "From what I have already seen of the workings of the Soviet Government, I can only say that anybody who lifts his hand against it ought to be shot!"

To shoot such malefactors, said Robeson emphatically, was "the government's duty." How dare anyone oppose "this really free society" run by Stalin, Vyacheslav Molotov, Lavrenti Beria, the NKVD, and the GRU, and regulated by the vast gulag archipelago? Any such villain, by Robeson's estimation, ought to be "put down . . . with a firm hand." Robeson hoped that "they [Soviet authorities] will always do it"—that is, always employ such just executions.

These were Paul Robeson's painful opinions shared with the *Daily Worker*. Given such brutally stated political preferences, is it any wonder that Americans considered Robeson a pro-Soviet, pro-Stalin communist? And yet, many on the American left, in media and academia and Hollywood, from journalists to historians to screenwriters, then and still today, condemned Robeson's accusers rather than Robeson himself.[29] Even as Robeson was careful to avoid publicly admitting joining CPUSA, he expressed an unequivocal preference for what he (and the Soviets) openly called "scientific socialism,"[30] and for the USSR as a literal home as well as a political home.

Robeson told the *Daily Worker* that he felt a "kinship" with the Soviet Union. "I already regard myself at home here," he said, adding that he could not wait to bring his whole family to the USSR for a prolonged stay.

He did just that. The December 1934 trip was his first of many forays among the "freed" masses. A smitten Robeson headed back, enrolling his son, Pauli, in a special Moscow school. There, Pauli basked in the brilliance of sitting side by side and desk by desk with the children of Stalin and Molotov.

PROLIFIC ACTIVITIES

Suitably trained, Paul Robeson spent the next decades flawlessly echoing the Soviet line, even as he refused to tell Congress whether he was a member of CPUSA. Of course, Party membership was totally irrelevant, as Robeson's Bolshevik loyalties were unabashedly clear.

American communists swarmed upon Robeson, and the entertainer hardly batted them away. His involvement with the communist movement was bountiful, giving his comrades copy for their publications and music for their rallies. The invitations flowed unceasingly.

By 1944, when the Democratic-run House Committee on Un-American Activities released its seminal three-volume, 2,166-page "Investigation of Un-American Propaganda Activities in the United States," Robeson's name was among the most cited, listed multiple times across seventy-four separate pages. The report cited Robeson as a member or headliner of thirty communist or front organizations, not to mention a regular contributor to the *Daily Worker* and a contributing editor to *New Masses*—America's two leading communist newspapers.

Paul Robeson had become a communist celebrity.

FROM RUSSIA, WITH LOVE

The love was mutual. In 1952, shortly before Stalin's death, Paul Robeson was awarded the Stalin Peace Prize, which the actor unhesitatingly accepted. The tough-as-nails Robeson was moved to tears.

And when his beloved Stalin perished in March 1953, Robeson was again moved to tears—and verse. He responded with a poetic eulogy titled "To You Beloved Comrade."

Robeson tearfully recalled the moment he had elevated his son at the sight of Stalin. He had waved and cheered with the fawning masses before the presence of their godlike atheist leader. Robeson waxed reverent in describing this "kindly," "good" man of "wisdom," "deep humanity," and "understanding." Stalin's "noble example" and "daily guidance" had left Russians a "rich and monumental heritage," his otherworldly hand at once nurturing, calming, stroking, like a benevolent form of heavenly guidance. The death of the "great Stalin," reported a heartbroken Robeson, left "tens of millions all over the earth bowed in heart-aching grief."[31]

Of course, in reality, Stalin left tens of millions dead in concentration camps all over Siberia, their families bowed in heart-aching grief.

In the mid-1930s, Paul Robeson was just another duped Potemkin Progressive. By the 1950s, he was a shameless lover of Stalin and the tyrant's totalitarian state.

It would take almost a half century more, after Robeson's own death, for Communist Party USA to publicly concede the obvious: Paul Robeson had been a longtime "secret" member.[32] In May 1998, the centennial of Robeson's birth, CPUSA head Gus Hall finally, proudly revealed the truth. Only liberals/progressives were surprised.

All of these facts about Paul Robeson were known by Frank Marshall Davis. Unfortunately, Frank was not among those who denounced Robeson's Soviet statements and sympathies. In his memoirs, Frank was sparse in offering details about Robeson.[33] He acknowledged that he first met Robeson "after arriving in Chicago in 1927," which was remarkably early—earlier than one would expect.[34] Given Frank's politics, profile, and later his professional rise and recognition, it makes more sense that he would have met Robeson after his second arrival in Chicago. Nonetheless, such is Frank's account of when they first met, which would peg the year somewhere between 1927 and late 1930. Where and how they met is still a mystery.

Whatever the answer, the two men would become good friends, with Frank frequently referring to Robeson in his columns. It was Paul Robeson, by Frank's own account, who helped prompt Frank's almost inexplicable sudden relocation to Hawaii in 1948.[35]

In other words, it was the pro-Soviet, pro-Stalin Robeson who helped lead Frank Marshall Davis to Barack Obama—a future president of the United States.

5

Back to Chicago

"Peace" Mobilization and Duping the "Social Justice" Religious Left

A FAVORITE HAUNT OF Paul Robeson and like-minded comrades was Chicago. And that is exactly where Frank Marshall Davis headed upon leaving Atlanta in the summer of 1934. The reasons for Frank's move are not entirely clear, especially given his success turning around the *Atlanta Daily World*. He clearly, however, missed Chicago and its jazz and flair.

Frank's longing for Chicago is felt in his memoirs. He spoke of his return like a kid in a candy store, gliding along the streets, checking the scene, the music. He loved the place. It was a part of him.

By now, he was much more political than when he left Chicago in 1931, and the city offered much in that regard as well, especially from the far left. In the interim, Frank had been exposed to some major African-American communists, from Angelo Herndon (during a visit back to Chicago while in Atlanta) to Ben Davis, Jr., among others.

For a paycheck, Frank went back to the *Gary American* on a part-time basis, but he took a major step up when, in September 1935, he was hired by Associated Negro Press (ANP) as features editor, en route to eventually becoming managing editor. This was an impressive job. Frank would work for ANP for thirteen years. He also published his first book of poetry, *Black Man's Verse*, released in 1935. He was winning acclaim for his work, including a Julius Rosenwald Fellowship for Poetry.[1]

Much of America may have been in a depression, but Frank Marshall Davis's prospects were brighter than ever.

RICHARD WRIGHT

When Frank discussed his return to Chicago in his memoirs, the first two names that popped up were both prominent African-American communists: Langston Hughes (noted earlier) and Richard Wright. As with Paul Robeson, Frank came to know both men well and refer to them on a first-name basis.[2]

Frank met Wright in 1936. Wright was a member of CPUSA who wrote for *New Masses*. He first encountered communists at Chicago's Washington Park, where he met a Party hack named "Sol," whose short stories had been published in a Party publication. Sol pleaded with Wright to attend a literary discussion at one of the Party's John Reed Clubs.[3]

Wright joined the Party around late 1932, early 1933. But as every communist soon learns, however, it took little time for Wright to discover he was dealing with angry brutes. One Chicago communist approvingly told Wright: "The Soviet Union has had to shoot a lot of intellectuals." Wright, an intellectual himself, exclaimed: "Good God! . . . Do you know what you're saying? You're not in Russia. You're standing on a sidewalk in Chicago." Wright learned how the Party was bent on conformity and a lack of individualism, and was no place for anyone, least of all intellectuals. He was "ejected" from the Party in Chicago in 1937 before rejoining in New York that same year, where he had moved to write for the *Daily Worker*. He left the Party permanently in 1940, describing his disenchantment in the huge bestseller *The God That Failed*, which was a profile of Wright and several other prominent ex-communists.[4]

In his memoirs, Frank devoted five full pages to Wright, whom he called "Dick," and liked very much. Frank was proud to know Wright, boasting of their "warm relationship" and the special attention he got from him. When Wright sent galleys of his latest book to Frank for review, Frank beamed, as he did when "Dick" autographed a book with a nice inscription. Frank said years later: "I have never altered my opinion that, as a writer, he [Wright] is by far the most powerful yet produced in black America."[5]

And yet, Frank altered his opinion of Wright in a sudden, blistering departure from his unceasing praise for his warm friend. What had happened? Wright had quit the Communist Party.

"I thoroughly understood his antagonism," averred Frank, with a major "but" loaded in the chamber: "But I thought his resultant series of articles in widely read publications was an act of treason in the fight for our rights and aided only the racists who were constantly seeking any means to destroy cooperation between Reds and blacks."[6]

This stinging reevaluation of a dear friend is the closest thing to a first admission in Frank's memoirs that he had become a devout communist and Party man. It was typical of how the CPUSA faithful treated those who left the church. Dick had committed blasphemy and Frank gnashed his teeth and rent his garments. Frank bitterly explained the sacrilege: "What Dick had done was throw the full weight of his worldwide prestige into a position which, while it gave him emotional release, damaged our battle."[7]

To the contrary, Dick Wright had learned that he was part of a pernicious ideology. Leaving communism, especially amid Stalin's bloody rampage, was the most natural thing he ever did. It was a move on behalf of good and against evil; for the light and against the darkness. Only a hard-core member of CPUSA would think otherwise.

But in Frank's mind, Dick had "dumped his former comrades," and now this comrade was dumping Dick. Frank reviewed Wright's autobiography, *Black Boy*, for ANP member papers, where he "touched upon these matters." After that, said Frank grimly, "I never saw or heard from Wright again."[8]

The dear "Dick" was now the wretched "Wright." He had been excommunicated from the communist church.

OTHER CHICAGO COMRADES AND DOINGS

As Frank recounts this period in his memoirs, the narrative abruptly takes a sharp turn left, more politically strident than at any point theretofore. The period is the latter 1930s, and Frank had not yet actually joined the Party. On a dime, however, his life discussion moved to CPUSA hot buttons, such as the Spanish Civil War, where he opened fire on anticommunists (at the Vatican in particular) for not favoring Spain's communists against Franco's fascists. He blasted America and the Vatican for failing to stop Mussolini's actions in Ethiopia—as if they had the ability—even as the Soviet Union openly provided Mussolini with war supplies (on which Frank was silent).[9] Frank was re-educating himself according to the international communist view of things, the *Daily Worker* line, defiantly tossing away the "brainwashing" he believed he had received in America's "racist propaganda system."[10]

With his new awareness, the names of communists, communist front groups, leftists, dupes, and fellow travelers now rolled off Frank's tongue, with Frank conceding to the reader that his new pals were "militantly leftist" "proletarian writers": the WPA Writers Project, W. E. B. DuBois, the League of American Writers, the John Reed Clubs, the Communist Party.[11]

Even then, Frank still claimed that none of these fiery fighters for the red flag had tried to recruit him to CPUSA, perhaps considering him "too bourgeois" given his hardworking, entrepreneurial past. He had long been privately employed, never on government "relief," nor a front man for front groups. He had even worked on the presidential campaigns of two Republican nominees.

In 1936, Frank spent several months in the publicity section of the "black division" of the Republican National Committee, attempting to sell Kansas governor Alf Landon to an unwilling electorate. He did so at the behest of ANP editor Claude Barnett and "because the price was right." Frank did not seem excited about Landon.[12]

More indicative of his enthusiasm, four years later Frank gave "wholehearted support" to Wendell Willkie, the 1940 Republican nominee. He again joined the publicity staff of the Republican National

Committee, putting in a couple of hours at GOP headquarters at Chicago's Loop.

Modern readers will be taken aback at Frank's stumping for Republican nominees against FDR, but, on closer inspection, it is not a big surprise. For one thing, the parties were very different back then. Today, the vast majority of Republicans in Washington are conservative whereas the vast majority of Democrats are liberal. In the last century, however, there was much more crossover. And certain core social issues that today define a conservative or liberal were nonexistent. A Democrat in the 1930s who advocated gay marriage, gun control, and legalized abortion would have been swiftly taken away to prison or a lunatic asylum as a public menace.

Muddying the waters more is the fact that Wendell Willkie was not a conservative. He went along with most of the New Deal. He was a lifelong liberal Democrat before being persuaded to seek the 1940 Republican nomination. Willkie worked for inclusion of a statement condemning the KKK in the Democrats' 1924 platform, which was rejected. Frank would have greatly respected Willkie for this. Willkie was also an internationalist whom some considered too cozy with Stalin.

Moreover, if Frank had been a communist in 1940, his support of Willkie over FDR would not be a shock for added reasons: By 1940, American communists had been smearing FDR for eight years, dating back to the 1932 campaign. In the immediate weeks after FDR's March 1933 inauguration, CPUSA vilified the Democratic Party icon as a "fascist," "imperialist," and warmongering "dictator," seeking (as one CPUSA flyer put it) "Hunger, Forced Labor, Terror and War." Communists plastered these words on telephone poles, yelled them from street corners, and proudly boasted them to the Comintern. As one May Day 1933 flyer (in Minneapolis) screeched, FDR was "MOVING HEADLONG TOWARD FASCISM AND WAR." A May Day 1933 rally at Chicago's Union Park, no doubt organized by comrades whom Frank came to know, lambasted "Roosevelt forced labor camps"—when, of course, it was Stalin who was constructing forced labor camps. "Billions of dollars are being spent for war," claimed the Union Park organizers, in a typical slander of the new president. "Yet our relief is running out." [13]

American communists did not defend FDR until he allied with Stalin in 1941. Once Joe Stalin became FDR's pal, his "Uncle Joe," American communists[14] embraced the president. Until then, FDR was their whipping boy: a *fascist.*

To his credit, Frank's writings on FDR were not that harsh. He seemed more ambivalent, with tepid support (at best) before FDR's alliance with Stalin. Once FDR allied with Stalin, Frank's position was fully consistent with CPUSA's position. He then cast FDR in a positive light in his columns. It is very telling that only after FDR sided with Stalin, and only after Frank formally joined the Party, did Frank work for FDR's reelection. That did not come until FDR's fourth and final presidential bid. "In 1944," wrote Frank, "I turned down my third opportunity to fatten my purse at the Republican trough and worked at no pay for the reelection for Roosevelt. . . . I was sold on FDR."[15]

But what eventually turned Frank permanently to the extreme left?

Beyond his slow evolution, his Chicago friends and associates were key. One was William Pickens, cited earlier for his appreciative *Daily Worker* letter touting ILD's role in Scottsboro, and the "workers" and "masses." The FBI spent time investigating Pickens, to the point of coming to Frank's office at the ANP building with some questions. After all, Pickens had been hired to work in FDR's Treasury Department, notorious for its closet communists and Soviet spies and sympathizers, including Harry Dexter White and Lauchlin Currie. When the FBI agent asked Frank if Pickens, his old friend, was a radical, Frank scoffed, comparing him to Thomas Jefferson and Ben Franklin and invoking Pickens's alleged love of the Constitution and Declaration of Independence.[16]

That said, Pickens's role in Frank's political evolution is not entirely clear.

Something else, however, appears to have drawn Frank fully into the fold; another communist campaign that purported to care about civil rights.

AMERICAN PEACE MOBILIZATION

Shortly after acknowledging William Pickens in his memoirs, Frank got to World War II. He wanted America out of the war, not desiring black boys to die in another war for Europeans, as they had in World War I. Why should they return to fight the Germans? Had they really gained the promise of democracy Woodrow Wilson had preached? Why was the black man dying for the white man, with little liberation?

These were not unwarranted questions. Frank fumed over the segregation of the armed forces, "a disgraceful policy of longstanding."[17] He wanted black folks to have "a share of the democracy we were asked to defend."[18]

Frank's objection might have been well taken from a race perspective, but not from a security perspective. Hitler's vandals were at the gates. And, either way, his stance just happened to dovetail with CPUSA's stance. Here again, Frank walked directly into—or, this time around, perhaps deliberately aided—another CPUSA campaign, one that apparently snagged him as a soon-to-be registered, full-blown Party member.

What was CPUSA's position on Hitler's war in Europe?

CPUSA and the Soviet Comintern cooked up a singularly contemptuous campaign. The umbrella organization for the new campaign was an antiwar group called the American Peace Mobilization. This front publicly pushed President Roosevelt to accommodate Hitler; that is, neither go to war against the Nazis nor aid allies under assault by the Nazis. When FDR did otherwise, aiding Britain, for instance, the comrades demonized him as a bloodthirsty warmonger. They did this relentlessly, never hesitating to smear this iconic liberal/progressive president.

Why did communists take this position? Because, in August 1939, Hitler signed a nonaggression pact with Stalin, known as the Hitler-Stalin Pact or Molotov-Ribbentrop Pact. In other words, Stalin and Hitler had become allies, with the Soviets even providing material support to the Nazi war machine. This meant that CPUSA and its members, as loyal Soviet patriots, had to take the same position. For American communists, this meant they suddenly could no longer oppose Hitler, as they had been doing throughout the 1930s.

And so, consequently, the American Peace Mobilization angrily demanded (among other policy positions) no U.S. Lend-Lease money to the Brits, even as they were being savagely bombed by Hitler's *Blitzkrieg*.

This appeasement of the Führer was a bitter pill for American comrades to swallow, especially Jewish-American communists. Many fled the Party, turning instead to Trotsky (Stalin's nemesis), or leaving communism altogether. As for the faithful communist ringleaders who remained, and filled the ranks of the American Peace Mobilization, they took Stalin's stance. They blindly saluted their flag—the Soviet flag—no matter the consequences.

The stance of the American Peace Mobilization changed dramatically on June 22, 1941, when Hitler betrayed Stain and invaded the USSR. With that, the American *Peace* Mobilization immediately changed its name to the American *People's* Mobilization, and became fanatically prowar, pro-British, pro-Lend-Lease. Incredible, yes, but true. The ringleaders cleverly retained the acronym: it was still the "APM." Now, however, "peace" was no longer part of the equation.

How could anyone be so naïve as to not see through this? Surely, this transparent political mutation was simply unbelievable. The comrades knew this would be a tough sell. Nonetheless, they took their orders, unquestioningly obeying (as George Kennan described it) "the master's voice."[19]

A telling testimony was the reaction of Henry Winston, black communist and head of the Young Communist League, home of Angelo Herndon. "When the news of [Hitler's] attack came over the air," said a breathless Winston, "many of our young comrades were coming home tired and ready for a good sleep. Yet, these comrades . . . sat up all night eagerly waiting until the headquarters would be open, ready for activity in the fight to crush Hitlerism . . . to smash and wipe Hitlerism from the face of the earth."[20]

The comrades had been antiwar when Stalin had been allied with Hitler. But now *their* country—that is, the Soviet Union—had been attacked. They were, in effect, Soviet exiles merely taking up residence in America. The American communist movement wanted immediate American entrance into a war against Nazi Germany.

Comrade Winston addressed an emergency two-day "enlarged meeting" of the Young Communist League, urging a broad coalition "among the masses" to defend their beloved USSR. "The new situation," explained Winston, "tremendously increases our responsibility and calls for the greatest amount of heroism and courage on the part of each and every one of our members. It calls for a readiness to sacrifice even to the point of death."[21]

To the point of death. America's communists had their Pearl Harbor. The American Peace Mobilization changed its stripes overnight, revealing itself as a shameless communist front.

As the House Committee on Un-American Activities—bear in mind, an eternal demon of liberals/progressives—later noted, the American Peace Mobilization was "one of the most seditious organizations which ever operated in the United States." This "instrument of the Communist Party line" was "one of the most notorious and blatantly Communist fronts ever organized in this country." This was also the conclusion of Tom Clark, President Truman's attorney general.[22]

And yet, this seditious front, which tried to stop America and its Western allies from resisting Hitler, had tremendous success recruiting liberals/progressives, especially turn-the-other-check "social justice" Christians. So omnipresent was the Religious Left at American Peace Mobilization rallies that the perfectly duped *New York Times* described the group not as a communist front—the word "communist" never once appeared in the *Times'* article—but as a "group of clergymen."[23]

WANTED: "SOCIAL JUSTICE" SUCKERS

That switch from American Peace Mobilization to American People's Mobilization came in late June 1941. We need to back up and observe how this unfolded and when and where it involved Frank and his friends.

One of the communists' more productive hunting expeditions for liberal/progressive dupes was the gala rally held by the American Peace Mobilization in New York City from April 5 to 6, 1941, meticulously organized in close coordination with CPUSA and the Comintern.[24] In promoting the event, the mobilization generated a formal statement addressed "To all Friends of Peace and Liberty," where the Soviet patriots warned "fellow Americans" that they were in great danger.[25]

In great danger from whom? Not from Hitler—this was *before* Hitler invaded the USSR—but from capitalism and, worse, from the fiendish

FDR. "This is not a war to wipe out the evils of Hitlerism and tyranny," explained the American Peace Mobilization. "It is not a war to defend democracy. It is a war to line the pockets of corporate interests." It was FDR who was the cretin conspiratorially commandeering this capitalist cabal. The warmongering Roosevelt was itching to "drag America more deeply into this war. . . . To get us into total war against the will of the people."[26]

FDR could not do this alone, according to the Reds' propaganda. He was working in tandem with another saber-rattling scoundrel: Winston Churchill.

With a straight face, the closet comrades attempted to convince liberals/progressives that "total war" was being pursued not by Hitler against Britain, but by the "British Empire"—the "warring empire"— and by "the American people" (read: FDR) supplying Britain with aid. America, claimed these self-professed peaceniks, needed to "Get out and stay out of World War II"; they needed to stay out of "Britain's war."[27]

To say this was the world turned upside down is a colossal understatement. In truth, Britain was being savaged by Hitler's total war.

And yet, the signers lined up to sign the mobilization's *antiwar* resolution, "Let our foreign policy wage peace!" with the Reds finding their biggest suckers among Christians from the mainline Protestant denominations, especially Episcopalians and Methodists. The overall chairman of the American Peace Mobilization was the Reverend John B. Thompson. Of the eighty signers of the formal resolution, nearly 20 percent, or one in four, carried the title "Reverend" in front of their name. Shockingly, there was even a rabbi on the list, Rabbi Moses Miller, chairman of the Jewish Peoples Committee.[28]

The difficulty today is figuring out who on that list was a liberal/ progressive dupe and who was a communist duper secretly affiliated with CPUSA. The eighty signers included known communists and communist sympathizers like U.S. Congressman Vito Marcantonio (D-NY) and Theodore Dreiser (the two vice chairmen of the American Peace Mobilization), plus well-known Reds like Abe Flaxer, Fred Field (a self-described "progressive" and heir to the Vanderbilt fortune), and Donald Henderson. Most of them successfully hid their true colors, in-

cluding Henderson, who was close to Harold Ware, architect of the infamous "Ware cell" that had penetrated FDR's Agricultural Adjustment
Administration.[29]

The April 1941 rally featured carefully crafted breakout sessions
appealing to "social justice" and civil rights, bearing names like "The
Church and the War," "The Negro People and the War," and "Civil
Rights in Wartime."[30]

But the New York event was not all stuffy politics. Entertainment was
interwoven into the show. A communist musical troupe, "The Almanacs," was brought in. The group's headliners were (at varying times)
Pete Seeger, Woody Guthrie, Burl Ives, and Will Geer, among others,
some of them duped liberals/progressives and other hard-core Party
members, with Pete Seeger a proud member of Henry Winston's Young
Communist League and Woody Guthrie a CPUSA supporter, if not a
member.[31] Nearly all their "folk ballads" ripped FDR and his pursuit
of "unjust war," with titles like "Get Out and Stay Out" and "Franklin,
Oh Franklin." Other renditions, like "Jim Crow," were targeted at black
Americans.

The marquee musical name was none other than Paul Robeson. If
there was a major pro-Soviet event held in New York City, with an unflinchingly pro-Stalin platform, one could count on Robeson to be
there to supply an energetic performance.[32]

Filled with enthusiasm and purpose, the patriots concluded the day
by joining in unison in a banner "American People's Chorus." Waving
the stars and stripes, these apostles of peace finished the day with a
teary-eyed, lump-in-the-throat "Battle Hymn of the Republic."[33]

FRANK'S INVOLVEMENT

How did Frank drift into this orbit? The answer is simple: Chicago. Everything was rooted there.

We can now see this starkly in a document declassified from the
Soviet Comintern Archives on CPUSA.[34] The document is an April 2,
1941, memo prepared by Comrade "T. Ryan," Tim Ryan, also known as
Eugene Dennis, a longtime American communist and major Comintern
operative. Ryan/Dennis prepared the memo for Georgi Dimitroff, head

of the Comintern. The two directed the New York City rally. Six pages long, the document opened by stating flatly that the American Peace Mobilization "was organised on the initiative of our Party in Chicago in September, 1940 at a national anti-war conference representing approximately 12 million working people." Who filled the ranks? Participants ranged from "progressive labor, youth, farm and Negro movements" to "Progressive Protestant church organisations." Ryan/Dennis was in awe at the Party's success in organizing this coalition, especially a "committee of 800 progressive Protestant ministers."

The dominant word in the document was not "communist" but "progressive." Communists knew where to find their suckers. It would be hard to get public recognition for a rally composed strictly of well-known or suspected communists. The Reds needed to draw progressive sheep to the slaughter.

The group organized another major Chicago meeting in November 1940, just two months after the September 1940 conference highlighted by Ryan/Dennis. Here, the Reds employed racial discrimination as their tactic for opposing the war—tailor-made for Frank. This gathering was called the First Illinois Conference of the National Negro Congress, held at the YMCA the weekend of November 9–10, 1940, on the corner of Thirty-eighth and Wabash streets in Chicago.

And it was attended by Frank Marshall Davis.

The event was billed as "Negroes and National Defense." Listed on the event letterhead was national officer Max Yergan, a well-known YMCA figure and communist,[35] as well as various Religious Left leaders, especially black pastors from the Chicago area. Among the short list of select endorsers was Frank Marshall Davis, whose name also appeared on the letterhead, just above the name Robert Taylor, a very interesting figure with striking contemporary relevance.

Robert Rochon Taylor was the first African-American head of the Chicago Housing Authority. His wife, Dorothy, born in Berkeley, California, was active in Planned Parenthood, undeterred by—or not knowledgeable of—Margaret Sanger's championing of racial eugenics.[36] Robert R. Taylor also appears in the major 1944 congressional report "Investigation of Un-American Propaganda Activities in the United States."[37] On pages 609 and 2,100 of the voluminous report, Taylor was flagged for his participation in the "Arrangements Committee" that organized the July 1939 Chicago Conference on Race Relations. Congress investigated this conference because of the presence of nationally known communist figures, including William Patterson, a leading black communist who was also on the Arrangements Committee—and a very close friend of Frank's.

We do not know if Robert Taylor was a dupe or a duper, a liberal/ progressive being exploited by communists or an exploiter himself. One thing we do know is that Robert Taylor was the maternal grandfather of Valerie Jarrett, who today is the single most influential member of President Barack Obama's inner circle.

The *New York Times* calls Valerie Jarrett Barack Obama's "old hometown mentor," "closest friend in the White House," "all-purpose ambassador," "skillful envoy," "emissary," the "ultimate Obama insider," and "guardian" of Obama's "authenticity."[38] The *Washington Post*'s Dana Milbank describes Jarrett as Obama's "longtime mentor and friend" and "the real center of Obama's inner circle," with ties to the president that are "deep and personal," holding a "position of unparalleled influence over the president."[39] Obama himself calls Jarrett one of his "oldest friends," who is "like a sibling to me . . . I trust her completely." As for Jarrett herself, she says of her and Obama: "We have kind of a mind meld. And chances are, what he wants to do is what I'd want to do."[40]

And chances are that Jarrett's and Obama's forebears, Robert Taylor and Frank Marshall Davis, also did what the other wanted to do, including attending the CPUSA/Comintern-organized "antiwar" rally in Chicago in November 1940.

The promotional material for the November 9–10 event charged that "Negroes and the whole American population are being called upon to 'sacrifice for national defense.'" Black Americans, the conference organizers urged, should not send their money, their bodies, or their bonds to support this "wave of war hysteria" by FDR and his corporate cronies. They should not be "bludgeoned into situations against their best interest." The powers-that-be in Washington were pining for "another war," contrary to the well-being of the poor masses.

The flyers for the conference used five categories to appeal to black Americans: the war, discrimination, "restrictive covenants," lynching, and poll taxes. The words "communism" or "Soviet Union" never appeared. It was classic communist deception.

That is no surprise given that the event was sponsored by the National Negro Congress, which usually marched in lockstep with CPUSA and the Comintern. The National Negro Congress was organized in Chicago on February 14, 1936. As testified by William Odell Nowell, the ex-communist who in Moscow had been enlisted in plans to establish a Soviet-directed "Negro republic" in the South: "We received communications from the Central Committee of the Communist Party to establish a branch of the National Negro Congress." Just four months later, Earl Browder, in his report to the ninth convention of CPUSA, declared that the National Negro Congress had "found the correct road to a broad unity of the varied progressive forces among the Negro people and their friends." Comrade Browder heartily encouraged "Communists and all progressives . . . to give it their energetic and steadfast support." "Communists," Browder triumphed, "have earned an unchallenged place" in the National Negro Congress.[41]

The National Negro Congress would later be identified by Congress as a communist front.[42]

Frank would later play a central part in such efforts, personally marshaling together both black communists and noncommunists under the same National Negro Congress roof. Frank's goal, according to one historian, was to create "a progressive program for blacks." Communists would be enlisted in this "progressive" project. Not only should blacks not be afraid of communists, Frank instructed his friends at the National Negro Congress, but they should embrace them "as the salvation" of the organization.[43]

Among these communist and progressive partners, Frank Marshall Davis duly agitated against U.S. involvement in World War II and rejected aiding Britain against Germany—the Party line of the American Peace Mobilization. He urged that "Negroes" resist "the wave of war hysteria."

While Frank may have been impressed by the American Peace Mobilization's charade, one civil-rights leader who was not was the NAACP's Roy Wilkins, still seething over how communists had hijacked Scottsboro. Wilkins had watched communists exploit blacks then, and now he saw it happening again in the face of Hitler's terror. Soon enough, Wilkins knew, communists would send blacks to the back of the bus: "They abandoned the fight for Negro rights on the ground that such a campaign would 'interfere with the war effort,' " noted Wilkins. "As soon as Russia was attacked by Germany they dropped the Negro question and concentrated all effort in support of the war in order to help the Soviet Union. During the war years the disciples of the extreme Left [communists] sounded very much like the worst of the Negro-hating southerners."[44]

Roy Wilkins was exactly right. He would have no part in this latest communist campaign. But Frank Marshall Davis had no such reservations; he was firmly on board.

6

War Time and Party Time (1943–45)

Frank with CPUSA and the Associated Negro Press

FRANK MARSHALL DAVIS was increasingly involved in events sponsored or covertly organized by the communist left. His willingness to sign his name to various Red-affiliated activities easily caught the attention of Democrats who ran the investigative committees on Capitol Hill. By 1944, Congress's compilation of "Un-American Propaganda Activities in the United States" flagged Frank as a member of at least three known or suspected communist fronts, including Youth for Democracy and the League of American Writers. Congress hardly caught everything Frank did, however, even missing his involvement in the November 1940 "anti-war" conference by the National Negro Congress.[1]

Nonetheless, as America finally went to war, Frank Marshall Davis finally turned to the Communist Party, crossing the threshold from progressive to communist. Though Frank had been extremely negative about his brethren fighting for America against Hitler, he was gung ho about the Soviet Union going to war against Hitler. In fact, he was so inspired that he put his feelings into verse, writing a poem titled "To the Red Army."[2] Frank urged:

> *Smash on, victory-eating Red warriors!*
> *Drive on, oh mighty people's juggernaut!*
> *Grind into spreading dust the Nazi killers!*
> *Since your soil is the land they wanted*
> *Assure their murdering millions*
> *Of remaining there forever;*
> *Stake a permanent claim for each*
> *To hold his blood and bones and ruptured dreams*
> *Beneath your dark and dripping dirt.*

In this ode to Stalin's tanks, Frank exhorted the Soviets to show the West's "rich industrialists" and political "experts" what communism could do:

> *Show the marveling multitudes*
> *Americans, British, all your allied brothers*
> *How strong you are*
> *How great you are*
> *How your young tree of new unity*
> *Planted twenty-five years ago*
> *Bears today the golden fruit of victory!*

If only Frank had been so patriotic about American entry into the battle against Hitler. Then, Frank had been downright angry, insisting black Americans think twice about serving Uncle Sam. As for Uncle Joe, however, Frank seemed ready to sell war bonds.

FRANK'S BREAK TO CPUSA

While considerably more subtle, Frank's break to CPUSA is evident in his memoirs, even as he carefully avoided saying he had joined the Party.

That departure became apparent as Frank described a period during "the opening years of the war" when "I immediately started writing a weekly column of editorial comment for ANP members." For America, the opening years of the war were 1942–43; Frank started that weekly column in September 1943. With the time frame established, Frank then offered his most candid statement on his willingness to "join hands" with communists, but not before an attempt to frame anticommunists in the federal government as suspicious of his support of "free speech" and racial tolerance. He wrote:

> I resolved to join hands with others seriously interested in curing the disease of American racism. . . .
>
> But when two or more of you get together you become a threat even though you speak only in whispers. Two or more automatically become a conspiracy which endangers "Our Way of Life;" and those agencies, such as the FBI or House Committee on Un-American Activities . . . now begin hounding you as dangerous radicals. . . .

This was Frank's explanation for why the federal government took interest in his activities: because he was interested in fighting racism, and not for anything related to his communist activities. And this, claimed Frank, got him labeled a "communist." He went on:

> From now on I knew I would be described as a Communist, but frankly I had reached the stage where I didn't give a damn. . . . The genuine Communists I knew as well as others so labeled had one principle in common: to use any and every means to abolish racism. From now on, I would join hands with anybody going my way. . . .
>
> Thus I worked with all kinds of groups, I made no distinctions between those labeled Communists, Socialist, or merely liberal. My sole criterion was this: Are you with me in my determination to wipe out white supremacy?[3]

And it was this, according to Frank, that "had attracted the special attention of the House Committee on Un-American Activities." And so be it: "I would accept any resultant citation as an honor, for it would indicate I was beginning to upset the white power structure."

Frank's statement deserves no empathy or attempt at understanding. His charges were plainly outrageous. As will be seen in the chapters ahead, what attracted the House Committee on Un-American Activities was Frank's blatantly pro-Soviet writings, not anything he wrote on race. It was Frank's scathing words on Churchill and Truman and the Marshall Plan and much more—not Scottsboro or lynchings—that got him noticed. Frank's attempt to paint his accusers as motivated by racism is irresponsible. It was deeply divisive. And yet, Frank flung these race charges in self-defense for forty years, especially in his commentaries, always insisting it was the alleged racism of congressmen, not his pro-Soviet communism, that raised flags in Washington.

It is also an outrage for Frank to assume that to work against racism meant joining the political party of Marx, Lenin, Stalin, Mao, Fidel, Pol Pot, Kim Il-Sung, and Kim Jong-Il. One wonders: How has the NAACP managed to fight racism for one hundred years without flying a red hammer-and-sickle from building headquarters?

Countless millions of people, if not billions, have combated racism without becoming card-carrying communists.

Frank maintained that "the genuine Communists" he knew shared in common "one principle": to abolish racism. This, too, is misleading, as Frank listed "only a handful of genuine Communists" whom "I knew personally." He named four of them: Ben Davis, Jr., Angelo Herndon, Richard Wright, and William L. Patterson. Yes, all four of these men were black communists who fought for civil rights; but four people are not exactly a representative sample. What about the millions of black Americans who wanted to abolish racism but were not communists?

Frank was using race to cover a much deeper interest in communist philosophy. It was an interest that soon turned into something much more formal.

"I HAVE RECENTLY JOINED THE COMMUNIST PARTY"

While the pages of Frank's memoir make it more evident that he had officially joined the Party, he still did not dare provide an unequivocal admission, refusing his accusers the satisfaction, even in words published posthumously in 1992, five years after his death. For direct evidence, we would need to wait another decade.

Then, at last, came a smoking gun. The source was John Edgar Tidwell, a University of Kansas professor and Frank Marshall Davis biographer, the preeminent authority on Frank's writing and career. Tidwell is no conservative; his interest in Frank was literary. A fair-minded scholar, Tidwell has no expertise in Cold War history, and has not delved into the dark dealings of American communists and their duplicitous work for Stalin's Comintern. Tidwell tends to exonerate Frank by criticizing the likes of Congressman Martin Dies, the Texas Democrat who headed the House Committee on Un-American Activities, for his "notorious" "persecution and 'Red-baiting' of socialists and pro-labor radicals."[4] Tidwell goes easy on the communist threat, adding further credibility to his evidence on Frank's Party membership.

Tidwell's most important work on Frank was released in 2002, titled *Frank Marshall Davis: Black Moods, Collected Poems.* In it, he provided the key statement on Frank's joining CPUSA: "Sometime during the middle of the war [World War II], he [Frank] joined the Communist Party." In the introductory pages, Tidwell produced the smoking gun: a letter by Frank to a woman named Irma Wassall, a poet from Wichita, Kansas.[5]

Frank had opened up to Wassall, whom he liked for romantic as well as professional reasons. When he described the first time he laid eyes on Wassall, Frank, as usual, had trouble containing himself, vividly describing the contours of her body. She was a "gorgeous doll," "exquisitely lovely," "exotic," "positively stunning."[6]

Frank writes this in his memoirs, but was more circumspect when it came to his attempts to lure Wassall politically. As Tidwell shows, Frank appeared to be attempting to recruit Wassall to CPUSA. In his letter to Wassall, Frank confided:

> I've never discussed this with you and don't know whether you share
> the typical American uninformed concepts of Marxism or not, but I
> am risking such a reaction by saying that I have recently joined the
> Communist party.[7]

There it was: the rarest admission by Frank; perhaps the *only* admission in writing. Frank Marshall Davis had recently joined the Communist Party.

He explained to Wassall that communism was "the only movement that is actually conscious of social evolution and the meaning of various forces at play in the world today." As a "matter of fact," he added, in a very revealing piece of political-biographical information, he had "leanings in that direction since I was in college."[8]

That particular line is eye-opening, as most indications suggest Frank's interest began in Atlanta in the early 1930s, with Scottsboro and Herndon—which Frank's declassified FBI file affirms. To imagine he was interested while in college, in the mid-1920s, is quite surprising. That interest may be rooted in those visits to the library when the young Frank began looking through atheist (and presumably other) literature.

The remainder of Frank's admission to Wassall is no surprise. And Frank obviously understood it was a "risk" to concede this in writing, but he did so for purposes of reaching out to Wassall, albeit in a private letter never intended for the public eye.

As Tidwell rightly notes, this letter proves that "despite Davis's public denial of his [communist] activities," the Senate's and FBI's suspicions were not based "solely on supposition." The "historical record" vindicates those suspicions.[9] As Tidwell subsequently reported in later works, Frank "became a closet member of the Communist Party."[10]

One important question that the letter leaves unanswered is a precise date. As Tidwell notes, the letter is not dated, which is common in the real world of biographical research. It was apparently especially common in Frank's letters, to the point that Tidwell inserted a "Note on the Text" that discussed Frank's undated letters.[11] My estimate is that the letter was written around 1943–44. It seems no earlier than 1943 and no later than 1945.

My overall estimate is that Frank joined the Communist Party in 1943.

Further confirming my timeline are details in Frank's FBI file, which show that Frank had been identified as a member of the Dorie Miller Club of the Communist Party in Chicago in 1944 and had been elected to the Communist Party convention that same year. As noted by Herb Romerstein, convention members were required to have been Party members for at least one year. This would date Frank's membership no later than 1943.[12]

"MY ATTITUDE TOWARD RUSSIA"

In his memoirs, Frank gave hints about why he went to the other side. "Since those smeared with the Red brush were accused of 'taking orders from Moscow,'" he wrote, "I should explain my attitude toward Russia."[13]

Frank admitted that his attitude on Russia had "shifted as time passed." He lamented that he, like "most readers" of the "general press," especially the "pathological screams of hate" by the Hearst press, had been "brainwashed" on the dangers of Bolshevism. But then he started to learn different. He heard about "the official policies of the Soviet Union and its determination to stamp out discrimination."[14]

This, of course, was the ludicrous line of Paul Robeson. Nonetheless, Frank bought it—and then some. "Russia had no colonies," averred Frank, "and was strongly opposed to the imperialism under which my black kinsmen lived in Africa."[15]

Here, Frank revealed *himself* to be a victim of brainwashing—not by the "general" or Hearst press but by the communist press. The reality is that Soviet Russia wanted to colonize the world with pro-Soviet dictatorships, and had done so first in Eastern Europe in the late 1940s and then methodically throughout the Third World, from Asia to Africa, until its dying days. Most alarming, Frank wrote this in memoirs written in the 1970s. By then, no one should have been under any delusions about Soviet expansion.

And yet, Frank had obviously been fully hoodwinked: "I considered Red Russia our friend."

That said, he also claimed, in what seemed an indirect admission of Party membership: "I never uncritically accepted party positions."[16] Frank clung to his independence—independence expected to be sacrificed at the altar of the Kremlin.

One position Frank did not accept without argument was the August 1939 Hitler-Stalin Pact.

For the record, it is very significant—and disturbing—that Frank joined the Party after, rather than before, the Hitler-Stalin Pact. Numerous American communists joined CPUSA during the Great Depression in the early 1930s, but fled the Party like the plague after Stalin betrayed them by signing this pernicious pact with Hitler. For Frank to join *after* the pact is a striking display of his commitment.

Frank made sure he addressed this in his memoirs, mercifully conceding that he had "felt betrayed" by Stalin. But he apparently got over the betrayal easily. "So the Russians were as hypocritical as the rest of the white world!" he wrote. No surprise, he shrugged: "after all, since the Russians were white, what else could you really expect?"[17]

FRANK AT THE ASSOCIATED NEGRO PRESS

Frank's subsequent procommunist, pro-Soviet work, delving into issues far beyond race and into the realm of foreign policy, was manifest in his commentaries for the Associated Negro Press. ANP was an impressive operation, gathering the best material from black journalists and writers, a clearinghouse for good product. "ANP prided itself on mirroring black activities everywhere," stated Frank "I still marvel at the comprehensiveness of our operations."[18]

Frank wrote a lot of copy for ANP. My interest is his commentaries on world affairs during World War II, precisely when he joined CPUSA. He swore that loyalty oath to Soviet communism, and that loyalty was palpable in his columns, which were more political, more communist, and more pro-Soviet than at any other time in the prior two decades of writing.

OUT OF THE CLOSET

Frank began his "Passing Parade" column with a bang, not shying away from showing full sympathy toward communism, enough to be an outright Party member.

In "Defeats of the Home Front," February 23, 1944, Frank hailed "our glorious ally, the Soviet Union." As Frank framed it, the USSR, and specifically Stalin—whom Frank singled out by name at least twice in columns in this period[19]—was seeking "unity" and "cooperation" at Big Three conferences with FDR and Churchill. He painted a picture of a USSR committed to internal harmony as well as external. He described Stalin's state as a bastion of tolerance, one giant rainbow coalition arching from Leningrad to Siberia. "The Soviet Union has every type of person, from blonde to black," reported a straight-faced Frank, who had never been there.

A second example of Frank's pro-Soviet writing from this period was an article titled "If It's Red It's Dangerous," May 10, 1944. Frank thanked the Soviet Union, "which has saved us and the rest of the world from the Nazi menace." The USSR had thus demonstrated to Americans "that most of what had been said in the past about the Reds was wholesale lying, with generally increasing knowledge of the truth about the Soviet system."

Of course, this was a major stretch at best. That the USSR was fighting for its survival against Hitler's onslaught—in a war Stalin helped launch—did not suddenly mean that Soviet communism was good, or that previous reports in the American press regarding mass arrests and persecutions and deaths and the Red Terror and the Great Purge and the gulag and the war on religion and the abolition of private property and the banning of speech and press and assembly and emigration had been wholesale lies.

A third example of Frank's sympathies was a February 9, 1944, column, "Check Your Dagger, Mister?" in which he hailed decisions made at the Tehran Conference by Stalin, Roosevelt, and Churchill, which "ought to set the pattern for our group thinking." Frank finished the column with a rather halting assessment: "even the sorriest ignoramus among us ought to know that there is no element in our population more desirous of completely eliminating fascism at home and abroad . . . than are the Communists."

That was not a consensus opinion.

But the most telltale column by Frank in this period was a September 17, 1943, piece titled "Ben and the Reds," concerning his old Atlanta

friend Benjamin J. Davis, Jr. In this column, Frank accurately presented
Ben Davis as "associate editor of the *Daily Worker*" and "county chairman
of the Communist Party in New York." Ben Davis, noted Frank, was running for New York's city council. Frank was writing to endorse the CPUSA
candidate, referring to him on a first-name basis: "Ben may not win, but
I don't believe Harlemites can elect a more honest and fearless fighter."

Frank shared details of his long friendship with Ben, dating back
to Atlanta. He told readers that the two of them had often been mistaken for each other. Frank portrayed Ben as a principled communist
of conviction, battling reactionary anticommunists. He presented this
as a virtue. "Believing firmly in the Communist doctrine," wrote Frank
of Ben, "he renounced easy gold for manhood. He became an avowed
Red in open defiance of the witch hunters and went all the way with
young [Angelo] Herndon, fighting to eventually win him freedom in
the United States Supreme Court."

"Maybe we ought to get more savvy [*sic*] about the Communists anyway," nudged Frank, closet member of CPUSA. "A social system that
can mold Russia from a huge weakling in twenty-five years to what is
today the strongest and most united nation in Europe, a people who
has borne the full brunt of the terrible Nazi war machine and has flung
it back, must have something fundamentally sound."

With such statements, we can see why Frank began earning suspicions he was a communist, openly celebrating the "fundamentally
sound" Soviet system. And yet, if anyone dared entertain that thought,
Frank was ready to smack him down:

> You have probably noticed here at home that practically every so-
> cial advance made under the Roosevelt regime has been labeled
> "Red." You may have noticed also that practically everybody who
> yells, "Communist," is himself anti-Negro or anti-labor, that when-
> ever a white person makes a bold and determined fight for full ra-
> cial equality and justice, he is painted as a "dangerous radical taking
> orders from Moscow."

Frank perfected this dishonest defense over the next decade and a
half, claiming that anyone suggesting he was a Red was nothing more

than a racist Red-baiter. It was these reactionaries, insisted Frank, who had "hoodwinked the public into believing that Communism is something despicable and its followers as unshaven anarchists who want to seize the government and murder everybody who has a dollar left from the following payday." As an example, Frank listed "men like Martin Dies," the Texas Democrat who headed the House Committee on Un-American Activities.

Frank went further still, admitting he had read CPUSA's constitution . . . but merely out of curiosity:

> Out of curiosity I have read the constitution of the Communist Party of the United States of America, adopted in 1938 and amended in 1940, and certain sections ought to set at rest the minds of those who believe the Reds are anarchists, whether you believe or disagree with their general theories.
>
> Says Section 10 of Article VI on "The Party's Rights and Duties of Members."
>
> "It shall be the duty of party members to struggle against the national oppression of the Negro people; to fight for complete equality for Negroes in all phases of American life and to promote the unity of Negro and white toilers for the advancement of their common interests." . . .
>
> As I was saying, I think Ben Davis, Jr., would make a good councilman. He's got to have the interests of the ordinary people at heart, people like you and me, to be a Communist.

With comments like this, stated boldly and publicly—with far more yet to come—it remained difficult to believe that Frank Marshall Davis was just an ordinary liberal.

TARGET: WINSTON CHURCHILL

Frank's harshest pronouncements in this period were saved for Winston Churchill. His assessment of the legendary prime minister was out of sync with that of other Americans not only at the time, but through the ages; Americans still consider Churchill a great hero, a national treasure to the United States as well as the United Kingdom, and even "the man of the century." That, however, was not exactly the way Frank thought about him.

Frank wrote three articles for ANP contrasting Churchill with Henry Wallace.[20] Churchill, of course, was the world's preeminent anticommunist, whereas Wallace, FDR's vice president, was America's preeminent dupe for communists. While Churchill was toasted for his anticommunism, Wallace was roasted for his horribly pro-Soviet, pro-Stalin comments. Wallace's remarks were so bad that Democrats demanded he be expelled as FDR's running mate. That, too, was not exactly Frank's thinking.

Frank kicked off his three-part series "Churchill or Wallace World?" with this jaw-dropper of an opening:

> Two influential leaders of the United States and Great Britain, Vice President Henry Wallace and Prime Minister Winston Churchill, are moving in opposite directions toward a postwar world. Wallace wants peace and security for all the people in a universal brotherhood of nations; the only people Churchill gives a rap about are the white people of the British Empire[. . .] [A]nd America[,] he thinks, ought to use strong[-]arm tactics to bludgeon all other countries into submission.[21]

Now, there was a sentence bound to grab readers' attention.[22] For Frank to charge that "the only people Churchill gives a rap about are the white people of the British Empire," and that Churchill wanted America to join him in bludgeoning "all other countries into submission," was staggering. Needless to say, this was very much a rare opinion on Churchill, alien to anyone's thinking about his ambitions in World War II. It was Churchill's country that had been attacked. The only place this kind of shocking opinion could be found was in the communist press.

Frank bemoaned that Churchill envisioned a postwar U.S.-U.K. alliance that excluded the USSR. Churchill desired a two-nation alliance of "the United States and Great Britain" because of "a pattern for Anglo-American world domination, for super-imperialism." Frank foresaw

America aiding Britain in greedily "divid[ing] up Asia and the Pacific islands as they see fit" and establishing "semi-fascist governments all over Europe." He warned not of a Soviet menace but of "Anglo-American imperialist domination."

And who, along with Churchill, would relish such imperialism? In Frank's world, American capitalists were licking their chops: "Big business, of course, would like to see it. You know, big business such as Standard Oil."

Part two of Frank's Churchill-Wallace series continued with those same themes, with no apologies:

> Last week I stated that the postwar world envisioned by Prime Minister Churchill is obviously Anglo-American imperialism and global control, whereas that desired by Vice President Henry J. Wallace is one of peace and security obtained by a universal brotherhood of all nations.
>
> I am against the Churchill conception because I honestly believe that it can but lead to a bigger and greater war. If America and Great Britain alone intend to dominate the world, they are going to have their supremacy challenged by other nations led by the Soviet Union and China.
>
> There can be no plan for permanent peace that does not call for a coalition between the Big Four nations—Britain, America, Russia and China.
>
> The last member of the Big Four is the Soviet Union, against which certain powerful and vocal forces in this nation are carrying on a war of their own. This is caused by the growing admiration of Americans for the amazing power of this great country, which had been lied about so much in the United States before World War II; the fear that Russia wants to foist her system of government upon the world, and the fact that the attitude of the "private enterprise and monopoly" democracies was to a large extent responsible for the present global conflict.

Here was another dose of Frank's belief that Stalin's Russia was a "great country" that had been unfairly maligned by American miseducation. Also, in a perfect refrain of the Stalinist-Leninist line, he did not blame the Hitler-Stalin Pact but capitalism (at least in part) for helping create the current war.

In the third and final installment of "Churchill or Wallace World?" Frank desired the "kind of world cooperation and brotherhood envisioned by Henry J. Wallace and other advanced humanitarians of the day." This would be an America working not alone with Great Britain but with "the Soviet Union and China in formulating a world program of international cooperation and democracy for all humans," one that would constitute "the century of the common man."

Henry Wallace was, according to Frank, a "great humanitarian," "trying to bring this nation to see the necessity of creating a postwar world without exploitation or inequality."[23]

Frank finished his three-part series by posing the choice between Churchill and Wallace in stark terms: "How about it? Are you willing to outtalk the imperialists, the isolationists, and the fascists: Or would you prefer World War III?"

WILD FOR WALLACE AND WILLKIE

In addition to stumping for Henry Wallace, Frank was partial to Wendell Willkie. As previously noted, he wholeheartedly supported Willkie's Republican presidential bid in 1940. He had always liked Willkie for reasons of race, appreciating his "verbal lashings of Jim Crow and discrimination."[24]

In the interim, Willkie had given Frank yet more reason to like him: In 1942, Willkie made a stop in Moscow, part of his 1941–42 world tour, which he chronicled in his best selling book, *One World*.

The Soviets gave Willkie a warm welcome. Stalin threw a huge banquet in his honor. Almost the entire Politburo was present. Willkie stood up and down at least fifty times for vodka toasts during the evening, and still managed to walk to his car at the end of the night.[25]

From this developed something of a minor pen-pal relationship between Willkie and "Uncle Joe." Henry Luce's *Time* magazine ridiculed the apparent affection, calling Willkie and Stalin "good friends" in a July 1943 piece titled "Politicians and Love."[26]

This potential Russian romance further endeared Willkie to Frank. In his December 22, 1943, column, sarcastically titled "Let's Go Fascist!" Frank wrote: "Do you know that Willkie thinks this ought to be one world, and that race discrimination ought to end?" There was "no Republican candidate . . . in the running who has the awareness of Willkie, his approach to world problems, his savvy of the necessity of world cooperation and unity to win the war and the peace," nor one who possessed Willkie's record "on the race question."

Frank was quite upset at Republicans for leaning to New York governor Tom Dewey as their 1944 presidential nominee. What was Dewey's major liability? For Frank, it was his opposition to Stalin. Frank called Dewey "an opportunist who has come out for an Anglo-American alliance which automatically excludes China and the Soviet Union."

Frank posed Governor Dewey as the anti-Willkie and anti-Wallace candidate. In a July 19, 1944, column, "We Need Wallace," Frank fumed that the "forces which shoved Wendell Willkie out of the Republican picture" were the "same forces" pushing Wallace away from FDR. Who were they? "They are the reactionaries, the America Firsters, the labor baiters, and the Negro haters," Frank wrote with the calm of a flamethrower. "These, the handmaidens of fascism, took complete possession of the Republican Party. Governor Tom Dewey is the stooge of Herbert Hoover, the high priest of monopoly and big business and skybusting profits and breadlines."

Frank was likewise upset with Democrats for dumping Wallace. This almost certainly had (from the outset) soured Frank on Harry Truman, Wallace's replacement and FDR's running mate in 1944. In urgently demanding "We Need Wallace," Frank contended that failure to renominate Wallace would be a "serious setback," not just to America but to the "people of this planet." "The issue of Wallace's re-nomination transcends party politics," Frank urged. "There is no other known prospective running mate for Roosevelt who can compare with Wallace."

Frank Marshall Davis's ideal presidential ticket would have been Wallace and Willkie. Otherwise, he feared the "Signposts to Fascism" (November 3, 1943, column) he believed were being erected all over America. "I don't like what's happening," he snarled. "The signs point towards a determined effort to create fascism in areas which heretofore had some semblance of genuine democracy."

Who could stop this fascist march? In Frank's mind, only Wallace and Willkie.

Frank's columns for the Associated Negro Press ran only until July 1944—not even a full year. One must wonder if his pro-Soviet, procommunist line created a fuss at ANP's offices. Surely the editorial folks received a letter or two concerning Frank's verbal hand grenades tossed at Winston Churchill.

But Frank was fearless. And he was suddenly more political than ever, as if he could not contain his love for his ideology.

Years later, in his memoirs, he shared his view on certain major Party issues of the time. Notably, he rejected the concept of a separate, segregated "Negro republic" or "Negro nation" in the so-called southern Black Belt. Here, said Frank, "Stalin's definition of nationhood" would not work. He believed that "Stalin's criteria in the Soviet Union had no practical relevancy among us souls who couldn't care less about Stalin's views, and that at that time the prevailing goal was complete integration, not separation into a black nation."[27]

This is an important statement because it showed Frank was willing to reject Stalin's position on an issue, which Party members did not do—at least not openly. Of course, this was not openly. This rejection came in his memoirs decades later, long after Stalin's death. Similarly, Frank had criticized Stalin in a poem published in his 1937 collection, *I Am the American Negro*. But here, too, he was not a Party member at that point.[28]

In his public writings, as a formal Party member, Frank obeyed the Party line, not questioning Stalin. To be a member of CPUSA was to be unwaveringly pro-Soviet and pro-Stalin—period. American communists who refused to salute Stalin left the Party, becoming lower-case "c" "communists" in ideology/philosophy only, or followed Trotsky or some other communist leader. CPUSA members, on the other hand, devoutly followed Stalin, and many adored him with reverence commensurate with the cult of personality he and the Kremlin carefully cultivated and demanded.[29]

Though I have seen no evidence of Stalin worship by Frank, I found him to be a fully loyal foot soldier. Even four decades later he remained fully convinced that Stalin wanted peace after World War II, only to be spurned by Harry Truman.[30] We will see this stance from Frank unceasingly over the next few chapters.

With the war ending, Frank bemoaned "the American way," which he seemed to see as synonymous with racism, a view he held from the 1940s until his dying days. "As the victorious white army liberated various parts of Europe from the Axis," Frank remembered bitterly in his memoirs, "they had begun to replace European fascism with 'the American way of life' and its tradition of racism."[31]

Frank's perception of America's place in the world was not exactly the Shining City on a Hill. He looked at America and squinted and blanched. He saw not a beacon of freedom, a light shining unto the captives, but an emergent imperial force to be tamed only through a nurturing alliance with Stalin's Russia. As Frank watched that alliance crumble—a collapse he blamed squarely on America—he became even more strident in his writings.

Over the next three years, Frank got intimately involved in a number of communist causes, fronts, and organizations. It all boiled over when he finally began to uncork his opinions in a bolder enterprise: a full-blown pro-CPUSA newspaper of his own lead and editorship: the *Chicago Star*. The city of Chicago was a veritable communist cornucopia, and Frank Marshall Davis was ready to feast.

The Latter 1940s

Frank and the Chicago Crew

DURING THIS POST WORLD War II period, Frank Marshall Davis thrived in Chicago's Communist Party circles, affiliating himself with all sorts of explicitly communist groups and fronts.

Among them was the Abraham Lincoln School, located on the top floor of a building in the heart of Chicago's Loop.[1] Frank first hooked up with the school in 1944, the same year Congress listed it as "communist."[2] Run by well-known Party members like Frank's good friend William L. Patterson, the school was notorious for its Marxist instruction. The *Chicago Tribune* labeled it the "little Red school house."[3]

Frank taught a History of Jazz course at the school and also served on the board of directors.

In one of his classes, Frank encountered a pupil named Helen Canfield, nineteen years his junior. Their interest went beyond music.

Helen worked for a group called American Youth for Democracy. On October 17, 1943, the Young Communist League of Angelo Herndon and Henry Winston had gathered in New York for a national convention. The league decided to go underground, re-emerging seven months later with a new name: American Youth for Democracy. The *new* group featured the likes of Paul Robeson and Langston Hughes. Frank himself was now a formal "national sponsor" for American Youth for Democracy.[4]

Helen Canfield was a kindred spirit. She was also a Party member. This we know today, as Frank's declassified FBI file discloses her as a member of the Chicago-based Paul Robeson Communist Party Club and as having CPUSA membership number 62109.[5]

None of that was mentioned by Frank in his memoirs, but his interest in Helen was not trivial. They married in May 1946.[6]

FRONTS AND AFFILIATIONS AND "FIGHTING PROGRESSIVES"

In later describing the people in his life during this period, Frank was less than honest. He wrote that he could not begin to remember all the meetings he chaired, speeches he gave, or books he reviewed. As an example, he said: "Once when the great historian Dr. Herbert Aptheker came to Chicago for a series of lectures, I chaired his appearances on three consecutive nights in as many sections of Chicago."[7]

What Frank did not note—and Aptheker is not listed in the index of his memoirs—is that this "great historian" was among the most celebrated communists in America, widely known as the Party's "theoretician." Aptheker was longtime editor of CPUSA's theoretical journal, *Political Affairs*. That Frank was granted the honor of chairing all three of Aptheker's appearances is a clear sign of how influential he had become within the Party.

In his memoirs, Frank recounted these and other duplicitous names and associations, never hinting that they were communist. He also simultaneously took nasty jabs at the FBI and House Committee on Un-American Activities for their supposed Red-baiting paranoia and Keystone Cops clumsiness. His goal, of course, was to attempt to discredit their interest in his activities.[8]

That was no easy deflection.

In this same period, Frank signed up with the Chicago Civil Liberties

Committee, whose mere title reflected a common tactic by American communists to seize the banner of "civil liberties." This allowed them to defend themselves with the very U.S. Constitution—specifically, the First and Fifth amendments—that the USSR spurned and which would be the first thing crushed in the establishment of a "Soviet American Republic."

By forming groups with titles invoking "civil liberties," communists easily duped liberals/progressives. Those liberals/progressives could then be counted on to help cast anticommunist accusers as "fascists" opposing fundamental civil liberties like freedom of thought and speech.

Frank served on the board of directors of the Chicago Civil Liberties Committee, and was eventually named its vice chairman.[9] The chairman was Ira Latimer, a man whose name appeared eight times in Congress's 1944 "Investigation of Un-American Propaganda Activities in the United States."[10] That is eight times more than Latimer was listed in the index of Frank's memoirs.

Frank also mentioned his interaction with Mike Quill, whom he called "a fighting progressive," and who likewise eluded any mention in the index of his memoirs. Again, that was not an omission Congress would make: Quill, identified by ex-Party members as a member of CPUSA, was so active with communist groups that Congress's "Investigation of Un-American Propaganda Activities in the United States" listed Quill in its index fifty-five times.[11]

Frank also finally mentioned Paul Robeson in this part of his memoirs.[12] A member of every communist front under the sun, Robeson rubbed shoulders with Frank in numerous capacities, including through the Chicago Civil Liberties Committee.

And there was one more familiar name serving with Frank on the board: Robert R. Taylor, grandfather of Valerie Jarrett, top advisor to President Barack Obama.[13]

CIVIL RIGHTS CONGRESS

The Chicago Civil Liberties Committee immediately affiliated itself with William Patterson's Civil Rights Congress. So did Frank.[14] In 1947, Frank joined the board of the Civil Rights Congress, eventually becoming a highly active member.[15] In his memoirs, Frank mentioned only that he worked with the Civil Rights Congress, nothing more.

In fact, the Civil Rights Congress (CRC) was a notorious communist front, fitting the definition so precisely that it was ordered by the Subversive Activities Control Board to formally register as a "Communist-front organization" under the Internal Security Act of 1950. That order was provided by President Truman's attorney general, Tom Clark—whom, not coincidentally, Frank would excoriate in his columns as a wild-eyed racist and fascist. Clark listed the Civil Rights Congress as both communist and subversive, as would the House Committee on Un-American Activities under both Democratic and Republican chairmen.[16]

It is revealing how quickly both the Justice Department and Congress pursued the Civil Rights Congress and how quickly Frank joined. The group came into being at a meeting in Detroit in April 1946, the by-product of a merger between ILD, the National Federation for Constitutional Liberties, and the National Negro Congress—all of which were labeled as communist fronts by the U.S. government. The CRC was to be ILD's successor as the Party's legal defense arm, established by CPUSA to use civil rights as the primary vehicle for defending Party members, Party leaders, Party positions, and the Party itself. This included Party members who broke the law or were suspected of serving Soviet interests.[17]

For the record, ILD's procommunist work had become so overt that even liberals/progressives were aware of its private loyalties. Before Attorney General Clark, it had been designated as communist and subversive by FDR's attorney general, Francis Biddle. Biddle was an Ivy League–educated progressive, a Harvard Law grad who worked for Supreme Court Justice Oliver Wendell Holmes. He represented the United States as a judge at the Nuremberg Trials. It would have been pretty hard for Frank and his comrades to denounce Biddle as a fascist.

The Civil Rights Congress had come so rapidly upon the government's radar that, just a year after its founding meeting in Detroit, the House Committee on Un-American Activities produced a full report, titled "Civil Rights Congress as a Communist Front Organization." Rarely does the opening line of a congressional report include the words "militant skullduggery," but this one did. Especially notable is the uncanny resemblance between Frank Marshall Davis's rhetoric and the incendiary Civil Rights Congress language documented in the congressional report. There was a perfect consistency in the carefully crafted talking points and the disciplined communist propaganda and agitation. This applied equally to all Civil Rights Congress comrades, from the leadership to the fieldworkers. Their accusations were one and the same: America was headed toward "fascism"; "imperial America" was under siege by "approaching stormtroopers" and by the "racist" "un-American Committee" and its "Hitlerite tactic of Red-baiting"; anticommunism was inherently "racist" and was "destroying our democracy"; a "LYNCH TERROR STALKS AMERICA" (words printed on a Civil Rights Congress flyer); Americans were being plunged into a "new world war"; and on and on it went. Like Frank, the Civil Rights Congress assailed Winston Churchill, protesting and picketing Churchill's historic March 1946 visit to America, during which he courageously and correctly warned the world of a Soviet "Iron Curtain" descending upon Europe.

One Civil Rights Congress pamphlet warned of the "Fascist offensive . . . on our lives and liberties . . . on the minds of our children" commencing in America, including the alleged "Hitler's white supremacy technique . . . of gun, whip, and rope." One statement issued from CRC headquarters in New York claimed, "We are getting a taste of the divide-and-conquer technique which in Germany led to fascism, to the human slaughterhouse at Dachau and Maideneck—and to World War II." [18]

And who was the front man for this new American-Nazi state? Democratic President Harry Truman. Even something as routine as Truman's statement on a threatened railroad strike—mild compared to FDR's railroad actions—was hastily converted into headlines like this one from a Civil Rights Congress press release: "Truman bill means fascism in America." [19]

This was classic communist agitprop. And this was also exactly the way Frank wrote his columns.

It is critical to understand that the Civil Rights Congress sprang from the American Peace Mobilization campaign by communists before World War II. That fact makes the group's incredibly inflammatory rhetoric about American "fascism" and "Nazism" and "Hitlerism" even more painfully outrageous and hypocritical; after all, it had been the American Peace Mobilization that once urged America not to resist Hitler, even with mere Lend-Lease aid. On the surface, these comrades seem inconsistent, until you realize that their allegiance was not to America but to Stalin's USSR.

In its report on the Civil Rights Congress, Congress found forty-three individuals in prominent posts in both the CRC and American Peace Mobilization, including Frank's friends Langston Hughes, Paul Robeson, Michael Quill, Ira Latimer, Howard Fast, the Reverend William Howard Melish, and Max Yergan—the National Negro Congress president who had been an organizer of the original American Peace Mobilization event, "Negroes and National Defense," held in Chicago in November 1940. Also listed were the likes of Hollywood writer Dashiell Hammett and the ACLU's Reverend Harry Ward, one of the Civil Rights Congress's honorary cochairmen. Hammett, a closet CPUSA member, was the well-known lover of the scowling Stalin apologist Lillian Hellman. Hammett was one of the largest financial contributors to the Civil Rights Congress.[20] Also intimately involved were the ACLU's Elizabeth Gurley Flynn, *Crucible* author Arthur Miller,[21] and Hollywood's so-called commissar, John Howard Lawson, the most rabid of the Hollywood Ten.

Of the thirty-four individuals guiding CRC policies, Congress knew twelve as outright CPUSA members, and most of the remainder as suspected ones.[22]

As for Frank's involvement, he was not only active in the Civil Rights Congress but a member of its national board.[23] He was particularly involved in its campaigns to defend Paul Robeson and Howard Fast.

In Congress's investigative report on the CRC, Frank was listed twice, both times as a signer/sponsor of statements and petitions. One of these was a March 3, 1947, statement denouncing President Truman and "the Un-American Activities Committee." Also signing that statement were W. E. B. DuBois, Dashiell Hammett, John Howard Lawson, Arthur Miller, Harry Ward, and thirty-three others. The other statement was a May 20, 1947, petition protesting Congress's alleged infringement on the rights of American communists; it accused certain congressmen of following the "Hitler pattern" and leading America "down the road

to fascism." Among these signers with Frank—who again included Lawson, Miller, Ward, plus the usual gaggle of progressive pastors—were
two notable new names: Harvard professor Archibald Cox (later of Wa-
tergate fame) and Margaret Sanger.[24]

Sanger's presence is especially intriguing. The Planned Parenthood founder is a saint in the liberal/progressive church. Ignored by
liberals/progressives, however, are a few aspects of Sanger's story that
bear on Frank's keen interests in race: Sanger was a racial eugenicist
whose work included a "Negro Project"; she spoke to a 1926 KKK rally
in New Jersey; she wished to rid America of what she termed "human
weeds" and "morons" and "imbeciles"; and she wanted birth control for
what she openly called "race improvement."[25]

Frank Marshall Davis was lying with some strange bedfellows. The vagaries of the political left had united him with some unlikely souls. One
wonders whether Frank ever met Margaret Sanger; if so, did he question the liberal/progressive heroine about her views on retarding the
birth of Negroes? No organization in history has slaughtered as many
unborn black Americans as Sanger's Planned Parenthood.[26]

THE PACKINGHOUSE WORKERS—AND VERNON JARRETT

Also among the Civil Rights Congress's activities during this period was
a May 1947 effort of 550 union officials protesting what the *Daily Worker*
called "the House Un-Americans [who] are spearheading the drive
of big business against labor 'in the name of hunting Communists.' "
Among the unions represented were the United Packinghouse Workers
of America, whose lead signatory was Chicago's Herbert March.[27]

Frank was intimately familiar with this particular union, which
Chicago communists grabbed by the horns and reincarnated as a
communist-controlled group called Citizens' Committee to Aid Packing-
House Workers. A surviving April 12, 1948, document printed on committee letterhead and found by researcher Trevor Loudon lists Frank
both as a committee member and as being among the small group of
journalistically inclined individuals who composed the committee's publicity committee.[28] Joining Frank in both capacities was Vernon Jarrett.

Vernon Jarrett would become a major name in Chicago, as well as nationally. He wrote syndicated columns for the *Chicago Tribune* before joining the *Chicago Sun-Times*, where he served on the editorial board. When Jarrett died in May 2004, he was hailed in a *Washington Post* obituary titled "Vernon Jarrett, 84; Journalist, Crusader."

The *Post*'s tribute neglected to note that in his youth Jarrett had been elected to the Illinois Council of American Youth for Democracy, the CPUSA youth wing. That occurred in June 1946 at the group's national convention.[29] He also wrote for the left-wing *Chicago Defender*. He was buddies with Paul Robeson (and Robeson's son), and, decades later, would emcee a Paul Robeson Citywide Centennial Celebration in Chicago in April 1998.[30] In any of those capacities, Jarrett could have worked with Frank Marshall Davis.

That was far from the end to the links between Vernon Jarrett and Frank Marshall Davis. In 1983, Jarrett's son, Dr. William Robert Jarrett, married a young woman named Valerie Bowman. Valerie Bowman became Valerie Jarrett, who today is Barack Obama's top advisor.

In April 1948, Vernon Jarrett and Frank Marshall Davis put their minds together for the Packing-House Committee at 4859 South Wabash Avenue in Chicago. "The duty of this Committee," declared their statement, "is to give publicity to . . . the plight of the workers." In doing so, the pair put their pens together defending Chicago's oppressed proletariat. Today, their political heirs, Valerie Jarrett and Barack Obama, put their minds together at a much more prestigious address: 1600 Pennsylvania Avenue.

THE CANTER FAMILY—AND DAVID AXELROD

Collaborating with those minds in the Oval Office is David Axelrod, who, in another bizarre twist of political fate, also has ties to this same Chicago crowd and period.

No single person is more responsible for making Barack Obama president than David Axelrod, right down to the words "hope and change."[31] The *Los Angeles Times* calls Axelrod "the man behind Obama's message," the "keeper" of the message in an image-based campaign in which "message is everything."[32] The *New York Times* dubbed him "Obama's Narrator."[33] The *Times* noted that it is Axelrod "who sits closest to the Oval Office" as the "president's protector, ever close at hand."[34] *Politico* refers to Axelrod as Obama's "pillar." Both men told the *New York Times* that they "share a worldview."[35]

For Axelrod, that worldview began in New York under his mother, Myril, who worked for a self-styled "progressive" daily called *PM*. The newspaper ran from 1940 until 1948 and was funded by Chicago-based millionaire Marshall Field of the Marshall Field department-store chain, a progressive dupe extraordinaire. *PM* was a political battleground within the American left, penetrated by communists who attempted to hijack the newspaper to advance the Stalinist line. Among the most popular writers at *PM* was I. F. Stone—hailed by liberals for decades as the "conscience" of journalism[36]—but who we now know was once a paid Soviet agent.[37]

Axelrod's true mentorship began in Chicago. He enrolled at the University of Chicago in the fall of 1972, majoring in political science and writing for the student newspaper. He soon secured a nice job as a very young political columnist for the *Hyde Park Herald*, a weekly local paper. Through his work at the *Herald*, Axelrod met David Canter and his partner Don Rose—two men who would mentor him and help set him on a path leading to Barack Obama and, eventually, the White House.[38]

David Canter was the son of Harry Jacob Canter, who in the 1920s embraced every progressive/communist cause under the sun, from the Scottsboro Boys to Sacco-Vanzetti. In 1929, Harry Canter was convicted for radical activities and served a year in jail.[39] While his family today describes his work as "progressive,"[40] the truth is that Harry was secretary of the Boston Communist Party. In 1930, he ran for governor of Massachusetts on the Communist Party ticket.[41]

Harry Canter was so *progressive* that, in 1932, he got a special invitation to Stalin's USSR, which he eagerly accepted, taking along his entire family.[42] Fluent in Russian, he taught printing techniques to the Bolsheviks, translating major volumes of Lenin's writings.[43]

In 1937, Harry and family suddenly left Moscow and landed in Chicago. David Canter, now fourteen years old, had been nurtured in the USSR under Stalin's collectivization, mass wealth redistribution, and five-year plans. Like David Axelrod, whom he would mentor eventually,

David Canter attended the University of Chicago, writing for the college newspaper and other publications. He eventually edited the Packinghouse Workers Union newsletter, titled *Champion.*[44]

Like his father's, David Canter's politics became especially bold—and pro-Soviet. He was eventually subpoenaed to testify before the Democrat-run House Committee on Un-American Activities, where he refused to answer any questions about past or present membership in the Communist Party.[45] Represented by George Kleindorfer, an ACLU attorney, Canter pleaded the Fifth Amendment from start to finish.[46]

In one line of questioning, Canter was told that Carl Nelson, a Chicagoan who was a member of the Communist Party, had testified under oath that Canter, too, was a Party member. Canter refused to answer.[47] The committee was especially interested in an operation called Translation World Publishers, a publishing endeavor that seemed unusually pro-Soviet, and was created by David Canter and his co-owner, LeRoy Wolins, a well-known communist. Among other intriguing details, the committee had evidence that "the Soviet Government advanced to Translation World Publishers . . . the sum of $2,400" for a specific set of books to be produced. This was a stunning item. Was David Canter's publishing house being subsidized by the Kremlin? Canter refused to answer.[48]

Regardless, the committee concluded that Translation World Publishers was "an outlet for the distribution of Soviet propaganda" and was "subsidized by Soviet funds and was created by known Communists to serve the propaganda interests of the USSR."[49] Canter, according to the committee, had thereby failed to comply with the provisions of the Foreign Agents Registration Act.[50] To clarify: This is the same man who directly mentored David Axelrod.

In addition to the Packinghouse Union connection, the Canter family was also very much acquainted with the *Chicago Star* (more on this later), and both Frank and Harry Canter taught at the Abraham Lincoln School. Harry taught the Monday evening class, 8:45–10:15 p.m., titled "Wartime Trade Union Problems." The Wednesday evening class, "Trade Union Leadership," was team-taught by Frank's pals Herbert March and Ernest DeMaio. As we will see, DeMaio founded the *Chicago Star* with Frank.[51]

Again, the overlapping orbits are fascinating. Think about the relationships: Frank mentored Obama. The Canter family mentored David Axelrod, who helped get Barack Obama elected president. Vernon Jarrett's daughter-in-law is Valerie Jarrett. Robert R. Taylor, Frank's "anti-war" and "civil liberties" pal, was Jarrett's grandfather. Valerie Jarrett and Axelrod became Obama's top two presidential advisors.

The ghosts of Chicago's frightening political past are alive and well in Washington today.

WILLIAM PATTERSON

Also among these 1940s Chicago comrades was a husband-and-wife team, headlined by a man who was a close communist mentor to Frank: William and Louise Patterson.

Louise T. Patterson served on the Citizens' Committee to Aid Packing-House Workers as one of the group's five officials as well its assistant treasurer. A self-styled "progressive" professor, Louise was the spouse of William T. Patterson, and was omnipresent in Chicago radical circles. She was district president of the International Workers Order.[52]

William T. Patterson's communist faith was so unwavering that even his entry in Wikipedia—which typically portrays communists like Patterson as mere progressives hounded by a fanged Joe McCarthy—described him as "a leader in the Communist Party USA."[53]

Patterson was a member of the Central Committee of CPUSA. He attended the 1928 Sixth Comintern Conference in Moscow, where the "Negro Soviet Republic" was adopted. There are conflicting accounts of Patterson's role in that discussion, though he apparently opposed the separatist policy and advocated a type of integration, believing the Party could recruit enough blacks to create an internal power base throughout the South.[54]

Patterson got intimately involved in the Scottsboro case. Recall that it was Patterson who had angered Roy Wilkins, acting secretary of the NAACP. He became arguably the most prominent face at the International Labor Defense. In the organization's letterhead, his name appeared only below that of Vito Marcantonio, the Red-friendly congressman from New York, with Marcantonio listed as president and Patterson as vice president.

Patterson worked closely with the Lincoln School, the National Negro Congress, and the Packinghouse Union.[55] In his memoirs, Patterson said that the idea of setting up the Abraham Lincoln School was encouraged by "black friends" at the *Chicago Defender*, where Frank and Vernon Jarrett both worked at the time. Patterson took the train to New York to further discuss the idea with CPUSA general secretary Earl Browder and youth-wing leader Henry Winston. They approved. He also consulted Paul Robeson, who, said Patterson, became one of the school's "staunchest supporters."[56]

Given this whirl of Red activity, the Pattersons decided to move closer to Chicago's Washington Park to stay atop the action. There, they became even more political, engaging in what Patterson called "weekly forums and free-for-all debates," including gatherings with "Black Nationalists, Muslims, Communists."[57] In 1949, Patterson became national executive secretary of the Civil Rights Congress. "I determined to follow the course established by the ILD," he explained.[58]

Even Frank could not help but identify Patterson as a communist when referring to him in his memoirs.[59] But Frank did not bother with further details, nor does the index bother to list Patterson's name.

Nonetheless, Frank and Patterson were extremely close, working arm in arm from the Lincoln School to the Civil Rights Congress to the Packing-House Committee to various lectures and symposia.[60] Herb Romerstein describes Patterson as a "close friend and mentor" to Frank, an appraisal confirmed by Frank's FBI file.[61] He was clearly a political mentor to Frank.

But Patterson's mentorship did not end with Frank. He yearned to mentor young folks, especially black communists, and he hoped to do it on the consecrated ground of the glorious Motherland. That dream was hampered, however, by the U.S. State Department, which, fearing Patterson to be a potential security/espionage threat, had denied him a passport. For this, communists—with a dependable echo chamber of liberals/progressives—labeled U.S. officials "fascists" and "Nazis" and "racists."

Under pressure, the government relented in 1960. That summer, Comrade Patterson arrived in Leningrad, en route to Peking (to meet with China's Reds), and then back to Moscow. Once back home in Moscow, he sought to enroll African-Americans in what he wished would be a modern Lenin School. Among them was his daughter, Mary Louise.

As Mary Louise later reported, Patterson made plans, presumably on CPUSA's behalf, with the Kremlin's "People's Friendship University." "My dad had worked out an arrangement for a new university in Moscow, People's Friendship University, to take five African American young people," wrote Mary Louise, the only one of the five to actually enroll. She entered the university in September 1960, the year it first opened its doors, and studied medicine. She would continue her studies in other Soviet outposts, including Cuba, leaving the USSR as a doctor in 1968.[62]

People's Friendship University became better known as the "Patrice Lumumba Friendship University," a Kremlin grooming school for Third World revolutionaries.[63] This university, the third largest in the USSR, has schooled some of the world's leading terrorists. Distinguished alumni include Iran's Supreme Leader Ayatollah Ali Khamenei and Palestinian leader Mahmoud Abbas, whose doctoral thesis became a book titled *The Other Side: The Secret Relations between Nazism and the Leadership of the Zionist Movement.*[64] According to Abbas, "only a few hundred thousand Jews" were killed in the Holocaust, and mostly through Nazi-Zionist collusion. Other proud alumni include Carlos the Jackal, Mohamed Boudia, and Henry Ruiz, Nicaraguan Sandinista commander and economic planner-in-chief.[65]

Among this band of rogues, Mohamed Boudia was a top figure in the Popular Front for the Liberation of Palestine (PFLP), one of the core branches of the PLO. He was in charge of PFLP terrorist operations in Europe, placed there by the KGB, where he worked with Soviet-backed terror cells in East Berlin. There he also worked with the Black September organization. Among Boudia's most dastardly acts—which involved Mahmoud Abbas—was the brutal murder of Jewish Olympians in the 1972 Munich massacre.[66]

Such is the sordid legacy of the People's Friendship University, championed by Frank Marshall Davis mentor William Patterson.

8

The *Chicago Star*

Comrades, "Progressives," and Soviet Agents

THE BOLDEST EXPRESSION of Frank's communist politics was yet to come: the *Chicago Star*, known by locals as the "*Red Star*."[1]

In his memoirs, Frank offered conspicuously little on the *Chicago Star*—three cursory paragraphs in a 373-page book. He called it a "cooperative weekly newspaper" that was "financed by a number of CIO and AFL unions, progressives, liberals, and ghetto dwellers." No mention of "communists" to be found.[2] His biographer, John Edgar Tidwell, described the newspaper as a "citywide labor weekly."[3]

In truth, the *Chicago Star* was a weekly publication that was unabashedly communist and unerringly toed the CPUSA/Soviet line. Its scope was not Chicago but the wider world, with labor interests based on communist interests. It included contributors who were closet members of CPUSA, and some who were literal Soviet agents.

Frank cofounded the *Star*, served as executive editor, was a member of its board of directors, and wrote a weekly column titled "Frank-ly Speaking." The sixteen-page newspaper debuted July 6, 1946, and its launch around the July 4 holiday was no coincidence, as Frank sought to identify the *Star* with the Stars and Stripes; that is, with the principles of the American Founders. It would be a "modern Declaration of Independence" by new "spiritual descendants . . . of 1776."[4]

This invocation of the American Founding by Frank was absurd, but it was a common tactic by American communists.[5] "It seems to me," Frank wrote, "the time has come for a new Declaration of Independence, to be implemented at the polls by the plain people such as you and I, which will remove the chains forged about us by the big money boys and their mouthpieces."[6]

THE *STAR*'S STAFF

One "big money boy" to whom Frank did not object was William Sennett, one of the *Star*'s enablers, who also served as its general manager. As Tidwell noted in his biography, Sennett helped "found" the *Star* with Frank. There is, however, a lot more to the story.

In an April 1947 article on the *Star*, a Hearst reporter consulted Congress's investigative reports on American communists. The reporter noted that while there was "no William Sennett listed in the House Committee reports," there was "on page 288 of the report . . . a Bill Sennett of Chicago. He is declared a Communist Party organizer."[7]

It was for such reasons that Frank, American communists, and liberals/progressives generally deemed the "Red-baiting Hearst press" rude, crude, vulgar, and downright simplistic and stupid. Such reporting was judged unacceptable.

Never mind, of course, that the Hearst press was right. The Hearst reporter had referred to Congress's 1944 "Investigation of Un-American Propaganda Activities in the United States." Not only was Bill Sennett listed on page 288 as "Chicago, C.P. organizer," but he was also named among a lengthy list of Americans who directly helped Spain's communists in the Spanish Civil War. Some of those Americans actually took up arms in Spain; others helped the Comintern secure passports or worked directly as Soviet agents.[8]

In addition to Sennett, Tidwell listed Ernest DeMaio as a founder of the *Star*.[9] Sennett was cited only once in Congress's "Investigation of Un-American Propaganda Activities in the United States"; Ernest De-Maio appeared eleven times. (DeMaio was first cited directly under the name of Jack Conroy, a regular in the communist press, from the *Daily Worker* to *New Masses*—who happens to appear in a 1936 photo standing next to Frank in Frank's memoirs, where the caption identifies Conroy only as a "writer."[10]) DeMaio, president of an electrical workers union, was a common face at front activities, from the American Peace Mobilization, to the Lincoln School, to *Daily Worker* happenings, to the Joint Anti-Fascist Refugee Committee (along with Paul Robeson), to the Friends of the New Masses in Chicago (with Frank and William and Louise Patterson), to even serving as a speaker at a March 1941 banquet honoring CPUSA godfather William Z. Foster.[11]

Also neglected by Frank in his memoirs, and missed by both his biographer and the wily Hearst press, were two other members of the five-man board of directors of the *Chicago Star*: William Patterson and Grant Oakes. Had the Hearst press learned of Comrade Patterson's presence at the *Star*, it would have had quite a scoop. As for Grant Oakes, he was an official with the metal workers and farm-equipment workers union, and, like DeMaio, was listed throughout Congress's investigative report—eleven times, as a member of many of the same fronts and activities.[12]

For the record, all five names comprising the *Star*'s board were learned through the astute investigative work of the Senate Fact-Finding Committee on Un-American Activities of the California legislature. This California committee was keen on the communist threat because of the infiltration by communists in Hollywood. In 1949, it issued its "Fifth Report of the Senate Fact-Finding Committee on Un-American Activities." The report listed communist publications that constituted the movement's "press network." Beginning with the *Daily Worker*, *Political Affairs*, *People's Daily World*, *Soviet Russia Today*, *Masses & Mainstream*, and the other usual suspects, the committee also listed the *Chicago Star*.[13]

Beyond the confines of California, at the federal level, the Democrat-run Senate Judiciary Committee referred to the newspaper as "the Communist-line Chicago Star."[14]

SOVIET HARD-LINERS, SYMPATHIZERS, AND AGENTS

And communist-line it was. Frank shared the *Star*'s spotlight with a number of notable Reds. Top contributors included pro-Soviet reporter Johannes Steel and an op-ed-page trio of Frank, Howard Fast, and Claude Pepper.

Fast was a well-known Hollywood writer and novelist. In 1953, he would be feted with the Bolsheviks' illustrious Stalin Prize, an honor he shared with Paul Robeson (1952 winner). Fast wrote for every issue of the *Star* and had top billing with his "State of the Nation" column.

Featured alongside Frank and Fast was America's most left-leaning U.S. senator, Florida's Claude "Red" Pepper.[15]

Ironically, it was precisely at this time that Pepper, in addition to writing for the *Star*, also wrote legislation to implement socialized medicine in America.[16] He was the Senate's leading such advocate, a man against whom the American Medical Association was embroiled in what members described as a "terrific fight" to stop a federal takeover of health care.[17] Pepper had a powerful perch to enact change; he was chairman of the Senate Subcommittee on Wartime Health and Education.

That information was well-known, but what few knew at the time was the supporting role played by Pepper's chief of staff, Charles Kramer.

Kramer was born Charles Krivitsky in New York in 1906. In 1933, he was hired as an economist by FDR's Agricultural Adjustment Administration, a magnet for collectivists and central planners. That same year, Kramer secretly joined CPUSA. The Soviets quickly began recruiting him, and by the end of World War II, Kramer was working for the KGB.[18]

As he worked for Senator Pepper, Charles Kramer, official Soviet agent, secretly handed over important information to the USSR. His code name, believe it or not, was "Mole."[19] His transgressions were so serious that on May 31, 1946, FBI Director J. Edgar Hoover personally wrote a letter directly to President Truman on Kramer, highlighting him "as a known Soviet espionage agent operating within the U.S. Government," who had been unusually influential in Pepper's work, from foreign policy to domestic policy. According to Herb Romerstein, Kramer, as staff director of Pepper's subcommittee, wrote the bill to establish a National Health Program—socialized medicine.[20]

When subpoenaed by the FBI and House Committee on Un-American Activities, Kramer refused to answer questions. He had learned well what to do in the face of such accusations: denounce your accusers as Red-baiting lunatics and declare yourself a "progressive." When the *Chicago Star* was up and running, Kramer and his boss, Senator Pepper, proclaimed themselves to be Henry Wallace "progressives."

Such were Claude Pepper's unique connections while writing for Frank's *Chicago Star.*

At his death, the *New York Times*—which noted none of this background—hailed Pepper as a "champion of the elderly," a "fiery fighter of elderly rights," and a "liberal." The *Times* longingly noted that the great Pepper had been literally pictured alongside another great: "Paul Robeson, the noted black progressive."[21]

Yes, *progressive.*

Also contributing to the *Star* was Lee Pressman, another Soviet agent and a close colleague of Charles Kramer. Pressman was a Harvard Law colleague of Alger Hiss, the most notorious of Soviet spies.

Pressman was likewise hired into FDR's AAA, where he, too, headed one of its infamous communist cells and secretly joined CPUSA. As noted, these cells were started by Harold Ware upon his return from Moscow. Ware initiated them as "study groups" of federal-government employees. Intended to influence policy, they morphed into full-scale spy rings, with Pressman and Hiss both organizers.[22]

In 1935, Pressman was hired by no less than Harry Hopkins as general counsel to FDR's Federal Employment Relief Administration, which later became the Works Progress Administration. Hopkins, of course, was FDR's right-hand man, so dear to the president (and first lady) that he literally lived in the White House. Hopkins was FDR's chief confidant, privy to the president's most confidential discussions with Churchill and Stalin. FDR delegated Hopkins to consult with Stalin one-on-one. Some Cold War researchers, including Herb Romerstein, believe Hopkins was a Soviet spy—specifically, "Agent 19" in the Venona Papers.[23]

In 1936, Lee Pressman left the government to become general

counsel of the CIO labor union. As Romerstein has noted, this move revealed how crucial the CIO was to CPUSA. Consider that the Party was willing to let Pressman leave the spy ring inside FDR's administration.[24]

Frank's *Chicago Star* happily gave Pressman a platform, covering a speech he gave to the CIO on the alleged dangers of the Taft-Hartley law. The *Star* also published a guest column from Pressman direly warning that the House "Un-American Committee" was a "charter for fascism" intended to "establish fascist control" of America.[25]

By the time of these writings, Pressman, whose KGB code name was "Vig," had been covertly assisting Soviet intelligence (both the KGB and GRU) for a decade and a half. Publicly, Pressman put on another face. He masqueraded as a proud "progressive," joining the presidential campaign of Henry Wallace and becoming the principal author of Wallace's pro-Soviet platform.[26]

Another contributor to Frank's newspaper was I. F. Stone, who wrote for *PM* with David Axelrod's mother. Like Pressman, Stone was promoted by the *Star* in a news article and also granted a guest column where, not coincidentally, he positioned himself as a simple progressive taking on the "Un-American" Committee.[27]

In truth, Stone (like Lee Pressman), was not just progressive, he was a spy, having served the Kremlin as a Soviet agent beginning in the late 1930s.

Such was the crew who made up the pages of the *Chicago Star*. And this roster of sordid names is an extremely abbreviated list culled from fifteen hundred pages of newspaper print reviewed for this book, some four hundred plus of which are in my possession.[28]

This was no "cooperative" "citywide labor weekly." This was a Chicago-based communist publication that was effectively working for Moscow.

9

Frank's Writings in the *Chicago Star* (1946–48)

THE *CHICAGO STAR*'S contributors list alone is indicative of the politics of both the newspaper and Frank Marshall Davis. But to get the full feel for how radical Frank's politics had become, one needs to read his columns from July 1946 through September 1948, as the Cold War was heating up. It is in these columns that we see a Frank not merely from the left but from the left's furthest extremes, even as he and his comrades attempted to cloak their Marxist-Leninist-Stalinist loyalties under the banner of progressivism.

"PROGRESSIVE" STAR

In its July 6, 1946, kickoff editorial, titled "The Star is Born," which would have been written, or at least approved, by Frank, the *Star* vowed to combat "American imperialism," the "Red-baiting . . . weapons of fascism," and "the big money boys and the high priests of rising American fascism." With sights set on President Truman and other resisters of Stalin's Russia, the *Star* bemoaned "those forces in America who work night and day to condition this nation for an atomic bomb attack on our great ally of less than a year ago"—the Soviet Union.[1]

Historical context is crucial here: By this point, it was President Truman, along with ex–prime minister Winston Churchill—who had recently come to America to warn of a Soviet "Iron Curtain" descending across the European continent—leading the opposition to Joseph Stalin. Truman's resolve grew between the time of Churchill's speech in March 1946 and the final edition of the *Star* in September 1948, three months into the Soviet blockade of Berlin. As Truman's steadfastness stiffened, CPUSA members everywhere took aim.

In so doing, America's Reds co-opted the "progressive" label, claiming to be merry liberals, whom they hoped to dupe and bring along in condemning Truman and advancing Stalin. In fact, the *Star* was not beyond begging liberals/progressives to come to the table. "Liberals, Where Are You?" pleaded one desperate *Star* headline, looking to its reliable cache.[2]

Frank's newspaper repeatedly retreated to the progressive label, calling for "progressive legislation" and for "candidates committed to a progressive program." It was a fitting sign of what was to come, as the *Star* described itself as "progressive" throughout its blatantly communist existence.[3]

Communists were ecstatic over the progressive presidential candidacy of Henry Wallace during this time. He was the best they could hope for at the ballot box. He became their adopted candidate and their point man for firing at Harry Truman, and many CPUSA operatives became major operatives in Wallace's Progressive Party, including Paul Robeson, who became cochair.[4]

As for the *Chicago Star*, it was on fire for Henry Wallace throughout its twenty-six-month existence, essentially serving as Chicago's flagship publication for the '48 campaign. It is telling that, at one point, the *Star* ran "A Statement from Stalin" supposedly supporting Wallace's presidential bid. This, in the *Star*'s mind, was the ultimate endorsement for its man—like a blessing from the pope.[5]

Wallace attracted a dedicated mix of closet communists and progressive dupes, with the latter including a glistening parade of oblivious Hollywood celebrities ranging from Katharine Hepburn to Gene

Kelly, who were suckered again and again by Hollywood screenwriters Dalton Trumbo and John Howard Lawson.[6] The *Star* trumpeted this celebrity support while defending Hollywood communists (like Trumbo and Lawson) summoned to testify for their extensive support of Soviet causes. The *Star* cast these accused communists as innocent lambs slaughtered by the high priests of McCarthyism. When Lawson returned from testifying in Washington, where Congress had presented a vast array of evidence, from his unprecedented list of front memberships to his CPUSA card number (47275), he stopped in Chicago. When he did, the *Star* helped portray the Stalinist as a *progressive*. Lawson's November 1947 talk in Chicago, sponsored by the Civil Rights Congress, was promoted in the *Star* as an address on "civil rights."[7]

So it was: Communists publicly hoisted not the Soviet hammer and sickle—the symbol held in their hearts—but the banner of American progressivism. In his first editorial, Frank Marshall Davis urged "cooperation of all progressive forces from liberals to Communists; of all religions; of Negroes and whites; and of all minority groups."

Still, the communists' duplicity was easily detectable. Only the most breathtakingly naïve liberals/progressives could not discern the obvious. Positioned immediately under the kickoff editorial was an item not run in the typical "citywide weekly": a small piece headlined "Communists in election drive," underscoring the bid for Illinois State Senate by Claude Lightfoot, Communist Party. Lightfoot was the first CPUSA candidate in Illinois since William Patterson in 1940, noted the newspaper excitedly. Lightfoot needed signatures.

It is somewhat ironic that here, in this first issue of the *Chicago Star*, Frank Marshall Davis was stumping for a communist candidate for Illinois State Senate from a district very near to that later won by a young Illinois politician named Barack Obama.

"I HONOR THE RED NATION"

In his new "Frank-ly Speaking" column, Frank wasted no time frankly expressing his admiration for Stalin's Russia. In his July 20, 1946, "A-Bombs for Russia," Frank offered his first of numerous claims that Stalin's Soviet Union had abolished racism—an assertion he could have heard only from friends like William Patterson and Paul Robeson. "As a Negro," Frank wrote, "I salute the Soviet Union for in less than a generation abolishing a discrimination and racism as crippling as anything that ever happened in Mississippi."[8] He added: "I admire Russia for wiping out an economic system which permitted a handful of rich to exploit and beat gold from the millions of plain people who had to live a hand-to-mouth existence. As one who believes in freedom and democracy for all, I honor the Red nation."

Yet, as Frank hailed Stalin's state for its alleged freedom and democracy and equality and tolerance, there was something else he neither honored nor saluted: the American "Big Money Boys" and "prostitute press [that] brazenly solicits public hate for our former ally." According to Frank, it was anticommunists like William Randolph Hearst and Henry Luce of *Time* magazine who "have gotten drunk on printers' ink and rant and rave against the Soviets," and ditto for anticommunists like John Foster Dulles, Cardinal Francis Spellman, ex-communist Max Eastman, Pennsylvania governor George Earle—a Democrat who tried to convince FDR that the Soviets had committed the Katyn Woods massacre against the Poles[9]—and the boys at the National Association of Manufacturers. It was these "hate evangelists" and the millions they supposedly misled that, by Frank's estimation, longed to "knock out Russia" by bombing it back to the Stone Age.

He torched those who opposed Stalin. And those who suspected Frank and friends of Soviet sympathies were denigrated as loathsome racists.

Frank unsheathed that sword in his August 24, 1946, column, titled "Our International Klansmen."

"The Ku Klux Klan is international," started Frank. "Maybe you hadn't thought of it this way, but there's a strong similarity between the Negro people of America and the rising peoples of the rest of the world. The forces supporting racism and attacks on Negroes are the same forces seeking to wreck the new Poland, Yugoslavia and China and who want to get tough with Russia."

Amazingly, but predictably given his Soviet loyalty, Frank was attempting to argue that "the new Poland, Yugoslavia and China"—all being savagely overtaken by totalitarian dictatorships—were part of a rising tide of freedom. Those who claimed otherwise—that is, those telling the truth about the communist takeovers of these unfortunate nations—were the equivalent of international Klansmen.

What was the abiding goal of these anticommunist racists brewing and exporting their American brand of hate?

"All of this is for the retention of the American way of life," Frank fumed, using that phrase with contempt, "for that glorious and cherished thing called Private Enterprise."

This "International Klan knows what it wants," he raged. In Frank's mind, these home-brewed hatemongers wanted to turn "the Polish people and the Czechs, the Yugoslavs and the masses of China" away from the one benevolent, democracy-desiring, multiracial hand that would feed and nurture them: the USSR.

NEEDED: "PROGRESSIVE" LEADERSHIP

Frank continued these themes throughout the summer and fall, with the help of like-minded contributors such as Howard Fast, Claude Pepper, and Johannes Steel. Frank blasted Truman and Churchill and Hearst and J. Edgar Hoover and the "un-American Committee" and outspoken ex-communists;[10] he hammered "American fascists" (that is, anticommunists) looking to "engineer" a "Reichstag fire" in Washington; he eviscerated Wall Street and Standard Oil and "Big Business" and America's "dividend diplomats"; he promoted Wallace and Stalin; and he consistently pushed for communist victory in Poland, Czechoslovakia, Yugoslavia, Turkey, Greece, and wherever he could. The democratic forces that opposed communists in any of these nations were handily derided by Frank as "fascist-monarchists." Employing the absurd language of the Kremlin, CPUSA, and international Marxist movement, Frank constantly referred to the nations behind the Iron Curtain as "the new democracies."

In Asia, Frank urged defeat of Chiang Kai-Shek and his Nationalists, who were trying to spare China the unprecedented bloodletting of Mao Tse-tung. Even in Japan, Frank condemned U.S. policy, writing: "Gen. MacArthur today is bolstering the dictatorship of the Japanese big money gang that has made a career of hating Russia."[11] Yes, even

Japan, embarking upon the greatest turnabout of any nation in modern history, from the belligerent Bushido code of the Rape of Nanking to a wondrously peaceful free-market democracy, earned Frank's enmity for not going Russia's way.

Understanding Frank's position on a particular issue or country was not difficult: One merely needed to know the position of Stalin and Molotov and the Kremlin. His *Chicago Star* never veered a centimeter from Moscow's Red star, always locked into the Soviet orbit.

Frank gazed toward that Russian horizon and saw no gulag, no suppression, no death, no banning of fundamental freedoms, and certainly no Iron Curtain. In fact, the *Chicago Star* that fall of 1946 launched a subscription drive with an ad campaign blasting the *real* "Iron Curtain." And what was that? It was a "journalistic IRON CURTAIN," an "Iron Curtain American press style." This was not a Soviet Iron Curtain, of course, but an American "Iron Curtain" by an anticommunist press that crassly portrayed Stalin's USSR as a malevolent place. To breach that Iron Curtain, the *Star* wanted *your* (capitalist) dollars.[12]

Frank's newspaper was an odd duck, requiring full knowledge of the Soviet stance for a reader to have any understanding of where the *Star* was coming from. For example, side-by-side headlines in the *Star*'s international section on October 5, 1946—"Urge U.S. support for Poland" and "Is Greece a new Franco Spain?"—carried entirely different meaning in the *Star* than in the typical newspaper. The bad guys were always those opposing Soviet-backed communist forces.

To understand Frank's newspaper also required understanding the nuances of the communist tactics of concealment and deception. For instance, one issue included a full-page guest article on page 16 by Henry Wallace, titled "Needed: A Progressive Congress." As usual, communists were wearing the "progressive" label. And anyone who suspected otherwise was, well, a "Wall Street dictator."

"Have you been Red-baited lately?" Frank asked in his October 12, 1946, column. "Has anybody called you a Communist this week?" That is what happens, he lamented, "if you consider yourself a progressive." Such "Red-baiting" belonged "in the same fascist arsenal from which comes labor-baiting, Jew-baiting, Negro-baiting and Catholic-baiting."

Frank repeated this exact same line of defense in his October 26 column, a virtual cut-and-paste. He parroted this defense constantly, unceasingly, column after column, editorial upon editorial, article upon article, week after week, to the point of pure sophistry. It was almost impossible to get through a Frank column or *Chicago Star* copy without painfully enduring, again and again, the patently dishonest contention that they were innocent civil-rights-crusading progressives being hounded by reactionary, racist, goose-stepping Red-baiters. That thread was interwoven throughout the very fabric of the *Star*, as if it was mixed into the ink—right alongside ads for every Soviet/communist cause under the sun.[13]

SOVIET CURES, REPUBLICAN EVILS

Frank's November 9, 1946, article, which yet again mocked "the American way of life," sat adjacent to a large ad plugging a coming Chicago appearance by William Z. Foster, CPUSA national chairman, with musical entertainment by Woody Guthrie.

The January 11, 1947, issue featured an "Exclusive Star Interview" with a Soviet scientist reportedly on the verge of a cure for cancer.[14] If only America would stop its hate, urged Frank, the Soviets were ready to save humanity.

To the contrary, who was looking to drive a stake into the heart of humanity? The *Star* answered in the same January 11, 1947, issue: It was Republicans in Congress seeking tax cuts. In an article on page 8, titled "GOP would 'spare rich' with 20% tax cut plan," the *Chicago Star*, sounding remarkably like President Barack Obama and the Democrats in 2010–12, accused Republicans of "phony" tax cuts that hurt the poor and padded the pockets of "millionaires" and the "corporation executive." The rich were not paying their fair share. What was needed, according to Frank's *Star*, was a more "fair" and "equitable" tax code that did not benefit millionaires.

TRUMAN DOCTRINE

What really exploded Frank's *Star* was President Truman's historic announcement of his Truman Doctrine.

On March 12, 1947, in front of a joint session of Congress, Truman announced his plan, which sought $400 million in essential aid to Greece and Turkey to try to stem the rapid advance of Soviet communism:

> This is an investment in world freedom and world peace. The assistance that I am recommending for Greece and Turkey . . . is only common sense. The seeds of totalitarian regimes are nurtured by misery and want. They spread and grow in the evil soil of poverty and strife. They reach their full growth when the hope of a people for a better life has died. We must keep that hope alive. The free peoples of the world look to us for support in maintaining their freedoms.

Beyond the humanitarian aspect, the principal motivation for this action was to keep Greece and Turkey from falling to communism and becoming Soviet satellites: from going the way of Eastern Europe, where the Iron Curtain was sealing quickly. In Truman's words, the Truman Doctrine and its soon-to-come ambitious successor, the Marshall Plan, were "two halves of the same walnut."

Stalin lusted for a "Red Mediterranean," or, at least, for access to the sea at some point along the Mediterranean coast. He was optimistic about Greece, Turkey, Italy, all of which had strong indigenous communist movements, and perhaps even Israel—where Prime Minister David Ben-Gurion was perceived as pro-Bolshevik,[15] and which Stalin had supported with arms during the May 1948 war. The Kremlin hoped at least one of these nations would become a Soviet satellite or ally. Greece and Turkey seemed especially ripe.

The USSR and international communist movement immediately began a campaign to demonize the Truman Doctrine, and Frank pounced, even before the *Star* as a whole could launch a special issue. On the March 15, 1947, op-ed page, sandwiched between columns by Howard Fast and Senator Pepper, Frank smoked off a piece titled "Democracy—for export."

Bear in mind that the Party line had been that Stalin (not America) was setting up "democracies," especially in nations like Poland, Czechoslovakia, and Yugoslavia. That Harry Truman would come along and provide $400 million in aid for genuine democracy, in Greece and Turkey specifically, sent communists like Frank into a flaming tailspin.

"We seem to be shipping it everywhere," Frank began sarcastically, as though America's understanding of "democracy" was a joke. "We've got some for Korea," he sniffed. He mockingly added that America also had some "democracy" for Japan and the Philippines. And yet, howled Frank, Americans looked "with disfavor on the new peoples' governments in the Balkans." This was Frank's twisted description of communist (nondemocratic) Yugoslavia, which was falling into the iron grip of a dictatorship by Marshall Tito that would touch parts of five decades.

Frank framed the communist world as the real bearer of freedom and democracy. He ridiculed America's bipartisan attempts to export democracy: "President Truman—bless him!—sent the world renowned apostle of democracy, Saint Herbert Hoover, abroad to survey the field and determine how we can lather it on Germany in particular. He and the great crusader, John Foster Dulles, now have it all worked out." Dulles would become secretary of state under Republican president Dwight Eisenhower. Frank also zinged Truman's secretary of state, George Marshall, calling him the new "shipping clerk for American democracy."

Like CPUSA, Frank wanted America to stay out of the democracy business and leave it to Stalin, allowing the Russians to install "new peoples' governments" worldwide, just like the Kremlin was doing in Poland and Czechoslovakia and Yugoslavia and every other spot planted with the Red flag. Only then would there be justice. What was needed was not the hypocritical "American way" but the unimpeachable *Soviet* way.

Frank especially wanted America to quit sticking its nose in West Germany. That, of course, was precisely the Soviet position as well. Stalin and his foreign minister, Molotov, wanted West Germany prostrate, starving, leaving a vacuum to be filled by the unclean spirit of Marxism-Leninism now consuming East Germany.

For now, though, Greece and Turkey formed the arc of the current crisis for American communists, requiring all hands on deck for churning Soviet propaganda. And just as the American left has done in recent decades, Frank and his comrades tried to pose America's interest in Greece and Turkey and the Middle East as motivated by oil. "Greece must be kept 'safe' so that none may sever the pipeline of democracy to Turkey, Iran and the Near East," Frank explained, using the language of oil: "That's quite oil right, isn't it?"

The communist line was issued in bright red: America didn't give a damn about democracy in this region. She merely wanted the damned oil. All this democracy talk was bunkum.

Frank was angry again. "I am proud of our distance democrats," he mocked. "There is something touching and noble about our . . . unselfish desire for democracy." If America's democrats wanted democracy, they should stay home and let Stalin lead. "The Soviet Union," he noted, "holds the absurd idea that democracy ought to begin at home." With the USSR abolishing racism, unemployment, inequality, and all else, it had the moral authority to export its vision abroad; America, on the other hand, did not.

"FACTS ON THE GREEK CRISIS"

Frank's opening salvo was a signal of the firing brigade to follow. Right on cue, the entire March 22, 1947, edition of the *Star* was devoted to debunking "Truman's Plan." The cover of the newspaper featured a poor Greek woman barefoot outside her mud hut, holding one shoeless child in front of another hunched behind her. The caption decried "Truman's proposal to furnish arms to the reactionary Greek dictatorship." These Greeks, said the caption, live in "unspeakable poverty" and "grope for a democratic and more fruitful life." To attain that life, they needed nothing from America—certainly not aid. America needed to stay out of Greece's business.

The *Star's* front page asked several probing, rhetorical questions, all aimed at Truman: "Who threatens the freedom of Greece? What's behind the Truman proposal? Is the Greek gov't worthy of support? What is the solution to the Greek crisis?" After those teasers came one more headline targeted at Truman: "His plot to ban Communists."

Chiming in on the editorial page was the triumvirate of Howard Fast, Frank, and Claude Pepper, with the senator giving the view from Capitol Hill. "We want to see democracy there," said Senator Pepper, whose position was undoubtedly directly influenced by Charles Kramer, the secret Soviet agent, "but not outside money poured in to maintain a disputed king or to pull British chestnuts out of the eastern Mediterranean fire."[16]

The *Star* had outlined its position on the Truman Doctrine and Greece very clearly: America needed to stay away from Greece, which was a monarchical-fascist government, a "legalized tyranny" guilty of "Nazi collaboration."[17]

The only saving grace for anticommunists bothered by this unrestrained Soviet propaganda was the *Star*'s transparent bias, fully revealing the newspaper's underlying loyalties. To cite just one example from one issue, it was not uncommon to find a headline like "Truman plan for Greece hit by rising protests" right alongside a full-page ad from CPUSA general secretary Eugene Dennis and Chicago CPUSA state chairman Gil Green.[18]

At least the reader would have no delusions about the real motivations of the *Star*, even as its editor, Frank Marshall Davis, instinctively blasted anyone who had the audacity to think the good folks at the *Star* might be communists. Such readers were unregenerate/un-American monarchical-colonial-racist-fascists—"like Hitler," explained Frank.[19]

FRANK'S USEFUL IDIOTS: "SOCIAL JUSTICE" PASTORS

As was standard practice, Frank and other communists sought out Religious Left pastors in their assault on the Truman Doctrine. Just as with the American Peace Mobilization, they would sing "Blessed are the peacemakers!" They would contend that they opposed U.S. aid to Greece and Turkey (especially military aid) because they desired peace; they wanted to stop war.

There would be no talk of the Red Army subduing cities from East Berlin to Warsaw to Prague to Sofia to Bucharest to Budapest to Belgrade, of coups and political murder, of executing pastors, of rampant human-rights violations, of the two million rapes by Soviet soldiers in East German territory alone.[20] The communists knew how to stick to a script, and they knew how to push the buttons of progressive Protestant pastors. This would be a matter of "social justice."

Not only were atheistic communists master manipulators in mobilizing the Religious Left, but certain self-styled "progressive" ministers were actually closet communists themselves, a fact they concealed from their trusting brethren. Within less than a month of Truman's announcement of his plan, the Reds had organized Christian ministers into action, led by Frank's friend the Reverend William Howard Melish and by the Reverend Professor Walter Russell Bowie of New York's Union Theological Seminary, a faculty colleague of the ACLU's Reverend Harry Ward. Melish was chairman of the National Council of American-Soviet Friendship, a communist front, and Bowie was a top official. The reverends were particularly successful in drawing in pastors from the United Methodist Church, Presbyterian Church USA, the Episcopal Church, and the Unitarian Church.

Once up and running with a statement from the pastors, the communist press responded in kind. "U.S. ministers denounce Greece-Turkey plan," exclaimed the excited headline in Frank's *Chicago Star* of April 12, 1947. The *Star* celebrated, "Nearly 200 leading churchmen of 30 states have asked for the rejection of President Truman's request for financial and military aid to Greece and Turkey." The *Star* quoted the seekers of social justice: "Such a division of the globe into two armed camps . . . seems to us a dangerous misreading of history."

There was no mention of the USSR's being one of these two camps, or of its being responsible for the division into camps—nor even of its dividing Europe. Scales covered the pastors' eyes as they squinted in vain for contours of a Soviet Iron Curtain. Joe Stalin, it seemed, had turned the other cheek. Unfortunately, sighed the pastors, the same could not be said for Harry Truman, a naked militarist seeking economic dominance. The *Star* reported: "Expressing distrust of the President's foreign policy because it 'would abandon true moral leadership in favor of reliance on naked military and economic power,' the churchmen said it would 'actually frustrate and inhibit' the spread of democracy."[21]

Directly above the *Star*'s story on the churchmen was a glimmer of light that had been hidden under a bushel. That glimmer emanated from the former vice president whom Harry Truman had once replaced: Henry Wallace, pro-Soviet leader of the progressives. " 'Truman endangers peace'—Wallace," screamed the *Star* headline, quoting Wallace.[22] The article reprinted a Wallace speech to the Progressive Citizens of America in New York:

> We are here tonight because we want peace.
> We are here tonight because we mean to have peace.
> We are here tonight to state that the Truman Doctrine endangers
>   peace.

Wallace said that America's soldiers "did not win one war to fight another." The *Star* appreciatively ran that line, knowing it would be effective among antiwar liberals/progressives, especially the Religious Left. "Before an overflow crowd of 25,000 [at] New York's Madison Square Garden," the *Star* gushed, "Henry A. Wallace charged that Pres. Truman's program of military aid to Greece and Turkey may lead to a new war."

A DIRECT LINE TO THE KREMLIN

Rounding out the *Star*'s team taking on the Truman Doctrine was an unimpeachable source. On page 6 of its special issue was a final word straight from the horse's mouth: Vyacheslav Molotov. The *Star*'s Johannes Steel had secured an exclusive interview with the Soviet foreign minister.

The interview focused on America's desire to help West Germany and Greece. Molotov advised that the United States stay out of both countries. Steel asked: "How can democracy best be restored in Greece?" The Soviet foreign minister answered: "The best way is the rejection of foreign intervention in the internal affairs of Greece."[23]

This was the Soviet canned response from the post–World War II period through the Brezhnev and Andropov and Chernenko regimes in the 1980s. It meant *America* should remove itself from these nations' "internal affairs," but the Soviet Union should not. The tactic, of course, was intended to enable communist overthrow. The "internal affairs" maxim was spurious, although, in 1947, it was fairly new and had mass appeal, especially when draped in the mantle of avoiding military conflict.

The interview with Molotov is significant for another reason as well. It underscores the political associations and standing of Frank Marshall Davis at this time. Consider: It is quite remarkable that one of Frank's regular reporters, Johannes Steel, could get an exclusive interview with Foreign Minister Molotov, Stalin's right-hand man. In April 1947, Molotov was one of the most influential men on the planet. If Frank's top reporter, who wrote for nearly every issue, could access Kremlin sources like Vyacheslav Molotov, then Frank had a direct line to the Soviet Central Committee.

That is no minor point. The Kremlin constantly sought influential CPUSA members as formal KGB agents; every member was a potential recruit. Surely, Frank would have been at least considered for recruitment by Moscow, especially as he, more than Johannes Steel or anyone else at the *Star*, excoriated the "un-Americans" opposing Stalin's Soviet Union and American communists in every issue. He was very vocal with a very public platform. Beyond that, Frank had a coterie of close associates—from William Patterson to Paul Robeson, among others—who had long been intimate with CPUSA and the Comintern, and who had traveled frequently to Moscow for political work and even training.

To think that Frank would have not been at least considered by KGB recruiters would be very surprising, if not naïve.

SOVIET COMMUNISM: A CHRISTIAN AND RACIAL PARADISE

In July and August 1947, Frank wrote back-to-back pieces insisting, "The evidence of logic and history should align the deeply religious with believers in socialism and communism." Frank proclaimed that a genuine Christian should be a genuine communist. And given that most Christians in America were anticommunist and anti-Soviet, he questioned whether America was really a Christian nation. True Christians, Frank declared, "should be working together as one" with communists.[24]

Frank was irate with the Roman Catholic Church, which more than any other institution had fiercely opposed communism spiritually and intellectually since the mid-1800s, including through a blistering 1937 encyclical that defined communism as a "satanic scourge."[25] In 1947, leading American Catholics like Cardinal Francis Spellman and Bishop Fulton Sheen were annihilating the communist philosophy in churches, in print, on radio, and on TV—with Sheen's weekly TV program being among the most widely watched in the country. Communists were not happy about this. "The Catholic hierarchy," sneered Frank, had launched a "holy war against communism."[26]

And how wrong this was, judged Frank. Communism and Christianity were natural friends, not foes.

Frank did not bother with any of the innumerable infamous statements on religion from Marx and Lenin and communists generally, describing Christianity as everything from silly superstition to a form of venereal disease that must be eradicated.

The Soviet Union was, of course, officially atheist. Marx dubbed religion the "opiate of the masses" and opined that "Communism begins where atheism begins"—a statement that Fulton Sheen often repeated.[27] Vladimir Lenin said far worse. Speaking on behalf of the Bolsheviks in his famous October 2, 1920, speech, Lenin stated matter-of-factly: "We do not believe in God." He insisted that "all worship of a divinity is a necrophilia."[28] Lenin wrote in a November 1913 letter that "any religious idea, any idea of any God at all, any flirtation even with a God is the most inexpressible foulness."[29] "There can be nothing more abominable than religion," wrote Lenin to Maxim Gorky in January 1913.[30] Along with Trotsky, Lenin created groups like the League of the Militant Godless, which was responsible for the dissemination of antireligious propaganda.[31] This institutionalized hatred and bigotry continued to thrive under Lenin's disciples.

Frank, however, was not interested in those facts. He wanted American Christians to pay reverence to the greater glory of the USSR, which, in his mind, was not a nation blowing up churches, gulaging the religious, shooting priests, locking up nuns with prostitutes—declaring nuns "whores to Christ"[32]—and pursuing what Mikhail Gorbachev later correctly described as a "war on religion."[33] On the contrary, Frank went so far as to write columns exonerating communists in their vicious persecution of leading Church figures like Archbishop Aloysius Stepinac, a classic communist show trial and disinformation campaign. Toeing the Soviet line, Frank dismissed Stepinac's persecution as a "lie" and "propaganda."[34]

Beyond religion, Frank continued to uphold the USSR as the apotheosis of racial tolerance. The Soviet Union, he persisted, had "abolished racism and color prejudice." Just as Christian Americans should look to Soviet communism for religious salvation, black Americans should look there for racial salvation.

To further the point, the *Star* did an April 26, 1947, "salute" to Paul Robeson, which included an exclusive column provided by Robeson, titled "Credo of an American." This came in addition to its many ads promoting Robeson's appearances in Chicago.[35] Frank himself wrote columns venerating Robeson as no less than a "modern Moses" persecuted by assorted pharaohs and "fascists" ranging from the "un-American Committee" to the American Legion to the National Association of Manufacturers, the last a favorite whipping boy of the *Star.*[36]

MORE AND MORE FRANK

This book could fill its pages with outrageous snippets from the *Chicago Star* from 1947 to 1948. A few brief, final examples are worth highlighting:

Frank repeatedly blasted "the American way," and even ridiculed the notion of Horatio Alger, which he denounced as a "myth."[37] Frank's vision of America was not the Reaganesque image (Ronald Reagan believed in Horatio Alger) of a "tall, proud city" set on rocks, "wind-swept, God-blessed," sea to shining sea.[38]

The *Star* also frequently reported on the packinghouse workers union organized by Frank and Vernon Jarrett.[39] In an illuminating column, Frank candidly stated that he wanted to flat-out nationalize the packinghouse industry, as well as impose national price controls and a federal tax on the rich and their "excess profits." "I'm so un-American right now," wrote Frank, "that I want to see price controls clamped back on this minute, a new and stronger excess profits tax put into operation, and the whole packing industry nationalized."[40]

For Frank, "Wall Street" and "profits" were dirty words.[41]

Frank and his *Star* comrades constantly had General Motors in their sights. The *Star* had no fear of Stalin erecting an Iron Curtain,[42] but it was apoplectic at what it called "G.M.'s iron curtain" and "General Motors' Hitlers."[43] The *Chicago Star* carried headlines claiming that GM itself was a "branch of U.S. imperialism."[44] Frank saw GM as a sinister force, and would be unrelenting in his anti-GM crusade for years to come.[45]

Frank had also turned on the GOP. The Republican Party was portrayed in the *Star* as in bed with the wealthy, as "sparing the rich," as "soaking the poor," as against health care for the needy. "GOP 'purge' at County Hospital may take toll of lives," screamed one front-page headline.[46]

Overall, the *Chicago Star* was so openly communist that it took on a Marxist educational mission, with full-page discussions like "What is Communism?" in which those tasked to provide answers were the likes of CPUSA chairman Gil Green—not exactly J. Edgar Hoover.[47] Other educational features included a multipage analysis of "May Day—born in Chicago," where May Day was treated more sacredly than Christmas.[48]

Frank and his newspaper also continued to hammer Harry Truman, with *Star* headlines like this: "White house to white hoods: KKK hails Truman's policy as its own."[49] And this: "Peace hope flares; Truman douses it."[50] Or this page-one bulletin: "TRUMAN KNIFES HOPE FOR PEACE."[51]

Frank also never hesitated to add new names to his anticommunist blacklist, expanding it from Hearst and Luce and Truman and Marshall to Hollywood anticommunists like Robert Taylor, Adolph Menjou, and Ginger Rogers. For her crime of anticommunism, Frank judged sweet, dancing Ginger guilty of "hatred."[52]

Speaking of hatred, the photos of Frank accompanying his columns, which carried titles like "I've Had Enough,"[53] never showed him with a smile. That was fitting, in accord with his style and tone. He came across as a very angry man, and not just about race—where his anger was justified—but on just about everything. Gone was the occasionally fun and witty Frank of the *Atlanta Daily World.* As Frank signed on to CPUSA, he acquired the endemic hostility and vitriol that permeated its membership. Communists were notorious for being miserable people; in the pages of the *Star*, Frank was no exception.

One can only wonder if there was unease in Frank's conscience. His newspaper, because it carried the flag of the Soviet Central Committee, took horribly immoral positions on foreign policy, from supporting or denying communist coups in Hungary[54] and Czechoslovakia,[55] to launching a war against the Marshall Plan,[56] to, believe it or not, even excusing the Soviet blockade of Berlin.[57] In one all-inclusive column, Frank slapped "little White House Harry," again ridiculed "the American way," and celebrated that the "Hungarian democrats" (read: Soviet-supported communists) had "kicked out" the nation's "fascist plotters" (read: Soviet resisters).[58]

Might Frank's conscience have been bothered by all of this? He was, after all, excusing a great evil.

If it was, Frank Marshall Davis gave no indication in his words, though his unsmiling countenance spoke volumes. The frown and snarl betrayed a true believer seemingly ready and willing to toe the Soviet line no matter what immorality it ordered.

10

Frank Heads to Hawaii

THE SEPTEMBER 4, 1948, issue of the *Star* quietly announced that the newspaper had been sold to something called the Progressive Publishing Co. It would be renamed the *Illinois Standard.*[1] Frank's communist conscience was apparently not so red that he was beyond selling the *Chicago Star* for some capitalist dollars as it slowly tanked.

Was this decision dictated by the Party? A look at the board of directors, officers, and stockholders for the *Illinois Standard* reveals the usual suspects who served or contributed to the *Chicago Star*. Bill Sennett stayed on, but there were also new members of the board, some especially notable given today's politics. They included Harry Canter, whose family would mentor David Axelrod, the man who would get Barack Obama elected president.[2]

For the record, Harry Canter was no stranger to the *Chicago Star*. He is listed in the April 28, 1947, edition, wishing "May Day Greetings" along with other "Friends" of the *Star*, and in the May 15, 1948, "Inside Labor" column. Canter, organizer for the Chicago Typographical Union, Local 16, was a candidate for delegate to the International Typographical Union's ninetieth convention. Frank's *Star* spotlighted Canter as a "leader in the fight against the Taft-Hartley Act" who "calls himself a 'non-partisan Independent-Progressive.'" That would be a *progressive* who happened to have run CPUSA in Boston and worked in Moscow as a Soviet translator and editor.

Frank, nonetheless, was packing his bags. In a rather extraordinary twist, he was heading all the way to Hawaii.

Did the Party line include an order to Frank to relocate to Hawaii? That question begs to be answered, as Frank Marshall Davis, suddenly, on a dime, uprooted and absconded from his beloved adopted city of Chicago for a far, far away place he had never visited, or ever previously mentioned in his vast volume of writings.

Frank adored Chicago. He had thrived there, was respected, and was proud of the prestige he had acquired. He had come into his own, establishing himself professionally, personally, politically, culturally. Racially, he was comfortable there, and nothing mattered to Frank like race. "Chicago was in his blood," his biographer wrote.[3] He was not only read there but listened to—literally. He hosted a nightly jazz program on WJJD, spinning records for a city that was a global mecca for this uniquely American (and African-American) music. He emceed events, both musical and political. He taught.

Why in the world would Frank Marshall Davis leave this? Here, Frank's memoirs are sparse and unsatisfactory. Quite abruptly, he noted that his wife, Helen, one day in the summer of 1948, read an article about Hawaii in a "woman's magazine." The place sounded "wonderful." "I suggested we investigate," recalled Frank. "We decided to go there in December and stay two or three months, long enough to miss the worst of another Chicago winter; if we liked it, we would live there permanently."[4]

Frank said he, too, consulted a bunch of magazines. Soon, he was taken with the idea. "When I learned the islands were free of snakes, I was automatically sold."

And so, just like that, Frank Marshall Davis left everything he had established in the Windy City, a perch from which he achieved national recognition in journalism, poetry, music, and Communist Party politics.

Speaking of such politics, Frank did add one other enlightening piece to the Hawaii puzzle:

"I had also talked with Paul Robeson," he added, "who the previous year had appeared there in a series of concerts sponsored by the International Longshoremen's and Warehousemen's Union (ILWU), the most powerful labor organization in the territory. Paul enthusiastically supported our pending trip." Frank then added two more very revealing names: "I also wrote to Harry Bridges, head of the ILWU, whom I had met at the Lincoln School. He suggested I get in touch with Koji Ariyoshi, editor of the Honolulu *Record*, a newspaper that was generally similar to the Chicago *Star*."[5]

In this one paragraph, we get closer to a fuller explanation of Frank's Hawaiian dreaming. Like the words "communist" and "CPUSA," neither Harry Bridges nor Koji Ariyoshi is flagged in the index of Frank's memoirs. In fact, Bridges and Ariyoshi—like Robeson and Frank—were secret Party members. And the ILWU, *Chicago Star*, and *Honolulu Record* were all either Party organizations or manipulated by the Party to further the Soviet/communist agenda.

KOJI, HARRY, THE ILWU, AND THE *HONOLULU RECORD*

Koji Ariyoshi was, to put it mildly, a highly suspicious agitator. He was a member of the executive board of the Communist Party of Hawaii. During World War II, he served as an officer in the U.S. Army and as a representative of FDR's Office of Wartime Information, one of the most penetrated agencies in the federal government.[6] In visits to the Far East, Ariyoshi was in contact with Chinese communists, including Mao Tsetung himself.[7] The Party assigned him to work with the Red Chinese in Yenan, dispatched there for special training in propaganda methods.[8]

Ariyoshi was also editor of the *Honolulu Record*.[9] As reported by the Democrat-run Senate Judiciary Committee in a 1957 report titled "Scope of Soviet Activity in the United States," the *Honolulu Record* was founded in 1948 by leaders of the Communist Party of Hawaii. Those leaders realized the limited popularity of CPUSA organs far removed from the islands, such as the *Daily Worker* and the Los Angeles–based

People's World. Seeking to "broaden their sphere of influence" in Hawaii (in the words of the Senate report), they created their own weekly.

That action came from a resolution adopted at the territorial convention of the Communist Party of Hawaii held at Hauula and Kuliouou Beach in April 1948. With that, the *Honolulu Record* was established in August 1948.[10]

The launching of the *Record* occurred at precisely the same time that Frank claimed his wife had been reading women's magazines and struck a sudden interest in Hawaii. Even more coincidentally, Frank landed a full-time job at the weekly, seamlessly resurrecting his "Frank-ly Speaking" column from the *Chicago Star*—from Chicago's communist publication to Hawaii's communist publication. He wrote for the *Record* from May 1949 through 1958, almost the entirety of its existence.

Frank was hired by Koji Ariyoshi, who, not long after Frank's arrival, was among seven Honolulu defendants identified as communists and convicted under the Smith Act for "conspiring to teach and advocate the overthrow of the government by force and violence."[11]

Also intimately involved was Harry Bridges, who was more infamous than Koji Ariyoshi, even as Bridges is hailed as a "progressive" hero by modern liberals such as former Democratic House Speaker Nancy Pelosi (D-CA). "I rise today to pay tribute to Harry Bridges, arguably the most significant labor leader of the 20th century," Pelosi said in a House floor tribute to Bridges a decade after his death. "Today we can all hold our heads high and be proud of Harry Bridges' legacy."[12]

Bridges ran the ILWU, which Pelosi referred to as "the most progressive union of the time."[13] In fact, the ILWU was widely recognized (including among Democrats and the labor movement) as one of the most communist-penetrated and -controlled unions of the time. The ILWU was expelled from the CIO for faithfully adhering to the Communist Party line.[14] Bridges's communist connections and meanderings were so obvious that the U.S. government repeatedly tried to deport him to his native Australia. Bridges battled them, insisting, with the eager help of liberals/progressives, that he was an innocent lamb ravaged by McCarthyite wolves. (Pelosi described it as a "persecution.")

We now know that Bridges was so high up in the Party that he served

on the Central Committee of the American Communist Party. The
Kremlin itself approved the appointment, as it always had, and specifically did so in 1938 when CPUSA—as standard operating procedure—
sent to Moscow a list of names for the Central Committee. One of those
names, as declassified Comintern documents show, was listed as "Rossi
(Bridges)—CP USA Central Committee member and president of the
Longshoremen's and Warehousemen's Union." [15]

Harry Bridges's ILWU was fully behind the *Honolulu Record*.[16] As the
Senate Judiciary Committee noted, based on sworn testimony from
Jack Kawano, a member of the executive board of the Communist Party
of Hawaii, the Party "instructed its members to get the ILWU behind
the *Honolulu Record* and urged the union to buy subscriptions and ads.
Every cell of the Communist Party was instructed to designate someone
to handle the ads and subscriptions in the union for both the *People's
World* and the *Honolulu Record*." [17]

The ILWU's support was critical, as it had some thirty thousand
members. As the Senate report stated, "Operating through representatives within the ILWU, Communist Party leaders arranged for wide
union support of their publication." Jack Kawano testified: "The *Honolulu Record* got all the help from the ILWU through the communists
in it." [18]

The ILWU's communist kingpin, Harry Bridges, got plenty of help
in return from Frank Marshall Davis at the *Record*. In one of his first
columns for the *Honolulu Record*, sarcastically titled "How to Become a
Communist," Frank protested that any poor soul "who wants enough
money to eat regularly, have sufficient clothes and a decent roof above
his head is a 'dupe' who 'has been tricked by the Communist leadership
of the union [Harry Bridges' ILWU].' " [19]

Frank claimed that accusations against Harry Bridges were simply
"vicious hate propaganda directed against the ILWU and the working
people." Those maligning Bridges as a communist "subversive" were
merely using that "loud cry" as a grotesque tactic to divide the world
among the rich and poor, greedily carving themselves a spot among
the wealthy class at the expense of the common man. This was "a device used by the haves to block the onward march of the have-nots and
maintain the status quo." It was a "divisive Big Business weapon of Red-

baiting," directed squarely at the backs of "working people." Innocents like Bridges "will be labeled Marxists," regretted Frank, because "they want higher pay and better working conditions." Frank asked sarcastically, "See how easy it is to become a Communist?"

Frank, of course, was employing this argument not only to defend Bridges, but also to defend himself and other accused communists. "So long as I believe that my cause is just," Frank vowed to his readers, "I shall not be halted by name-calling."

Just as at the *Chicago Star*, Frank took this posture throughout his columns for the *Honolulu Record*. In a July 7, 1949, column, Frank insisted: "I don't know about you, but I personally am tired of the wolf cry of Communism raised by those in power to justify their refusal to grant equality, whether to a territory, a minority group, or an individual. And I am not alone in this stand. Increasing numbers of Americans are becoming angered when they are thrown the same old smelly Red herring each time they ask for a helping of democracy."

JACK HALL

One other intriguing figure in this plot was Jack Hall, second only to Harry Bridges in ILWU prominence.

Born in Wisconsin, Hall's activism flourished in Hawaii. As stated in his bio at the ILWU website, Hall "made Hawaii his home port in 1935 and began working with other mainland and local labor activists to build a democratic labor movement in Hawaii."[20] This was precisely the same period when the Anglo-American Secretariat of the Comintern held a meeting in Moscow (February 17, 1935) on the "Hawaiian Question," where the Soviets decided to make a concerted effort to flood the area and start a base of operations on the islands.[21]

Jack Hall became international vice president of ILWU and was arguably the top person in organizing and building the union in Hawaii. Like Koji Ariyoshi, Hall was convicted under the Smith Act for advocating "the overthrow of the government by force and violence." Along with six members of the Hawaiian Communist Party, Hall was found guilty in 1953, fined five thousand dollars, and sentenced to five years in prison, the maximum penalty under the law. (Hall appealed the conviction to the Supreme Court and eventually won on the grounds that it was unconstitutional.)[22]

In his memoirs, Frank mentioned meeting Jack Hall immediately upon his arrival in Hawaii in 1948. He hailed how "organized labor led by the ILWU with Jack Hall at the helm" was struggling to break big business's "iron grip" on the island. Frank referred to the Smith Act investigation of Hall and Ariyoshi as resulting from "McCarthyism" and a "witch hunt atmosphere" led by "rabid supporters of the status quo, mainly reactionary whites." "The whole episode," sniffed Frank, "was completely ridiculous in the first place."[23]

OTHER HAWAII MOTIVATIONS

Frank described his new job at the *Honolulu Record* as unpaid—or at least not paid by the *Record*. As Frank put it, the *Record* itself "did not have the financial resources to add me to its payroll."[24]

So, how could Frank afford the move? He was not wealthy. He could not possibly have completely uprooted his family without a steady income. Someone, or some group, must have paid him, whether the ILWU, the Communist Party, or some other source. As noted by one observer, the simple answer is that the Party must have offered Frank a deal he could not refuse.[25]

And, in fact, Frank's FBI file seems to provide that answer. On page 2 of the Chicago portion of the file, record number 100-15799, are two reports on Frank's employment status for 1949. The first is a March 23, 1949, report from the bureau's Honolulu office, stating that "DAVIS has under consideration an offer to take some unspecified position within the International Long Shoremen and Warehousemen Union–CIO in Honolulu which would put him 'on easy street' if he succeeded in obtaining this position." The second item is a November 13, 1949, report stating that "FRANK MARSHALL DAVIS and his wife were going to leave for Honolulu where DAVIS would be employed by the International Long Shoremen and Warehousemen Union–CIO."

Still another document from the file is an "F.B.I. Teletype," a transmission sent to the Honolulu office from the Chicago office via bureau radio. The date remains redacted, though the message was received at

9:41 p.m. (presumably Hawaii time), and would have been sent in late 1948 or early 1949. This report stated that "DAVIS MAY TAKE EMPLOY-MENT IN HONOLULU WITH LONG SHOREMAN UNION."

The FBI was on to Frank. The only flaw in the bureau's reporting was that some of its sources were late on Frank's thought process, arrival, and start of employment. He arrived in Honolulu in December 1948 and began writing for the *Record* in May 1949.

Nonetheless, as the file indicates, it appears it was indeed the ILWU, and thus likely the Party itself—which together had launched, operated, and funded the *Honolulu Record*—that greased Frank's arrival in Honolulu. Davis was now on easy street.

SOVIET MOTIVATIONS

Frank's arrival in Hawaii was, in a general sense, forecast by Ichiro Izuka, a Hawaii-born Japanese-American who had been a communist. In 1947, shortly before Frank's arrival, Izuka alerted his fellow citizens to the machinations of this "conspiratorial Party," which clandestinely worked "against the welfare of the people of my native islands." The Party fed on character assassination, on "libel," on deception, on "hate [as] a weapon." "The Communist Party in Hawaii is a secret, underground organization," Izuka noted. "It works in the dark—fears the light of day."[26]

Frank was a member of that conspiratorial Party. And yet, the historical background to Frank's arrival is even more disturbing.

Even the most erudite students of Cold War history are generally unaware of the Soviet interest in Hawaii before the territory became part of the United States in August 1959.[27] Hawaii was, in fact, on Stalin's radar, a reality that the Kremlin kept close to the vest, as did CPUSA and the Comintern cronies who provided its marching orders.

As alluded to earlier, this was evident way back on February 17, 1935, when the Anglo-American Secretariat of the Comintern held a meeting in Moscow on the "Hawaiian Question"—a meeting we have learned about only through recently opened Soviet archives.[28] It was through the Anglo-American Secretariat that the Comintern micromanaged the American Communist Party. Among the seventeen attendees at the meeting, the two most important players were "I. Mingulin," the head of the Anglo-American Secretariat, and William Schneiderman, an American agent of the NKVD. Schneiderman, who went by the alias "Sherman," was the American Communist Party's representative in residence in Moscow, whose job was to pass information between the two sides, delivering orders from the Soviet Communist Party to the American Communist Party.[29]

Schneiderman was later made head of the Communist Party of California, the closest American port of interest to the Hawaiian theater of operations. He was instructed by Mingulin to draft a message to the American Party on the Hawaiian Question. Mingulin, in turn, had the confidential dispatch delivered to American communists. The Comintern ordered that a clandestine Communist Party apparatus be set up in Hawaii, given the islands' increasing international significance, particularly vis-à-vis U.S. foreign policy, which was diametrically opposed to Stalin's foreign policy.

The Soviet aim in Hawaii was as anti-American as imaginable. This is immediately apparent in the follow-up document of July 7, 1935, simply titled "Letter to the CPUSA on Hawaii."[30] Whereas many Hawaiians longed to become a part of the United States, and would eventually get that statehood, the Comintern document argued that a "growing discontent of the masses of the population in the Hawaiian Islands" was the result of "the regime of colonial oppression and the exploitation of American imperialism with its policy of militarisation of the Hawaiian Islands."[31]

To take advantage of this alleged discontent among the masses, the "Letter to the CPUSA on Hawaii" deemed it "essential" that American communists "give every possible assistance to the development of the mass revolutionary movement in Hawaii, so that the foundations will be laid for the formation of a Communist Party as the leader of the emancipation movement in Hawaii." A truly emancipated Hawaii, in their eyes, would be a communist Hawaii, a satellite in the Soviet orbit, serving as a vital strategic base to spread Marxism-Leninism into Asia.

To get there, the Comintern and CPUSA decided to begin placing communists in Hawaii. The Kremlin commanded the American Party to "raise the slogan of 'Right of Self-determination of the Peoples of Hawaii, up to the Point of Separation.' "

Communists were direly needed in Hawaii to agitate and advance specific Soviet policy goals, including "the withdrawal of the U.S. armed forces" from the islands. Among the "political slogans" of the "Hawaiian revolutionary movement," ordered the Comintern, should be an exhortation to join the "struggle against the yoke of American imperialism" in order to advance "revolutionary tasks in Hawaii." [32]

As any student of World War II understands, the U.S. forces cited in these documents, and namely the base at Pearl Harbor, were crucial to the security of the United States, as the Japanese made painfully clear on December 7, 1941.

Mingulin and Schneiderman strategized on getting communists onto the mainland to agitate against the U.S. government and to promote the Soviet line wherever they could. This goal remains so explosive—so utterly contrary to American interests—that portions of the Comintern Archives on this subject (those in Moscow) have been resealed. American researchers—specifically, Herb Romerstein—were, however, able to obtain copies of some of this correspondence in Moscow during the brief period when the window was open.

The document on the February 17, 1935, meeting concludes with this edict expressing the plan of action: "Responsible for Commission: Com. Sherman." This meant that Comrade "Sherman," that is, William Schneiderman, would be in the field gathering recruits. [33] And this was where the likes of Frank Marshall Davis could become agents of interest, agents of influence, agents of change.

"YELPING STALINISTS" AND THEIR PROGRESSIVE DUPES

It was into this Red milieu that Frank waded in 1948.

Upon leaving Chicago, Frank had signed a petition urging Congress to abolish the House Committee on Un-American Activities and calling upon President Truman to effect the immediate release of communist Gerhart Eisler—two parting shots on behalf of the Party. When he got to Hawaii, Frank sought out the NAACP. As in Chicago, he searched for "civil rights" groups where he could make a splash.

It took little time before members of the local branch of the NAACP became suspicious. Some NAACP members called him "Comrade Davis," and were irritated at how he "sneaked" into meetings "with the avowed intent and purpose of converting it [the local NAACP] into a front for the Stalinist line."

Noncommunist liberals like Edward Berman, a local civil-rights activist who supported the Hawaii branch of the NAACP, did not view Frank as an ally. Berman recalled a meeting when "one Frank Marshall Davis, formerly of Chicago (and formerly editor of the Chicago Communist paper, the *Star*), suddenly appeared on the scene to propagandize the membership about our 'racial problems' in Hawaii. He had just sneaked in here on a boat, and presto, was an 'expert' on racial problems in Hawaii."[34]

Berman, a Caucasian, wrote to the NAACP's Roy Wilkins, emphasizing the racial unity and harmony in Hawaii: "There is no segregation here." Berman knew right away that the likes of Frank had come to agitate, to "create a mythical racial problem here." Such were "their tactics."[35]

Berman warned Wilkins that the "influx of this element" had "frightened away . . . scores of Negro members." He feared that the goal of the communists was nothing short of "destroy[ing] the local branch of the NAACP." Berman went so far as to urge that "only by a reorganization with a policy that will check this infiltration, can we hope to get former members back into a local NAACP branch."[36] Berman had good reason to be nervous. He had already seen precisely this happen to an organization close to his heart, the Hawaiian Association for Civil Unity, and saw it unfolding again with the local NAACP.

Berman was troubled at how Stalinists, among whom he apparently included Frank Marshall Davis, duped liberals/progressives into the Soviet line. "We are going to have to have the authority over here," he wrote. "Otherwise you'll have a branch exclusively composed of yelping Stalinists and their dupes—characters who are more concerned about the speedy assassination of Tito [in Yugoslavia] than they are about the advancement of the colored people of these United States."[37]

Frank wasted no time searching out liberal/progressive dupes. Immediately, he helped mobilize the Hawaii Civil Liberties Committee

(HCLC), precisely as he had done in Chicago with the Chicago Civil Liberties Committee, in which he served on the board and as vice chairman. Just as in Chicago, he right away affiliated the group with William Patterson's communist Civil Rights Congress. Even before his first *Honolulu Record* column, Frank was working with the HCLC. By May 1949, he was speaking at the group's events.[38]

As in Chicago, the HCLC would fly the flag of civil liberties and the Bill of Rights, with the hidden purpose of advancing not the American Constitution and way of life but the Soviet Constitution and way of life. And Frank did it well. Ten years after his arrival, the U.S. Congress would refer to the HCLC, this "ostensible civil-rights group," as "the most effective sounding board for communism in the Territory of Hawaii."[39]

Frank in the *Honolulu Record* (1949–50)

Target, Harry Truman

FRANK'S WEEKLY WRITINGS in the *Honolulu Record*, beginning May 1949, unerringly echoed the Soviet line pushed by Stalin's USSR and the international communist movement. That reality is immediately apparent upon even a cursory glance at his columns from 1949 to 1950, when the Cold War was in full force, with Iron Curtains erect in Europe and hot wars exploding in faraway places like North Korea. What is also apparent is the degree to which Frank eviscerated President Harry Truman and American foreign policy generally, especially concepts like the Marshall Plan—which were hailed everywhere except Moscow and CPUSA headquarters. Any U.S. policy that opposed the USSR or its goals was a moving target for Frank, and he did not hesitate to fire the cannons.

Consider the Marshall Plan, which will surface many times throughout this chapter: Everyone understood the Marshall Plan as an unparalleled act of American generosity. Here was Uncle Sam clothing and feeding not only all of Europe, but the German nation that had killed millions, including America's own soldiers. Never in U.S. history had so many boys been ground up in a foreign war, and at the hands of Hitler's hordes. Imagine a nation gracious enough to bandage and bathe such an enemy. And yet, America, after the war, did just that.

Could anyone accuse such a nation of malice?

Well, communists did just that. Their house organ, the *Daily Worker*, was rife with attacks on the Marshall Plan, deriding it as a "billion-dollar empire scheme" that was "taking over various parts of the world." The plan was not about democracy and saving Europe from starvation but about "imperialist expansion and dollar diplomacy." Truman was employing the plan "to launch political and economic war," to foster "chaos, civil war and world unrest."[1] As the *Daily Worker* approvingly noted in a quotation from Foreign Minister Molotov, Americans should not "impose their will on other states" and "interfere with their sovereignty."[2] America should stay out of Europe.

Stalin ordered Molotov to walk out of the Paris Talks where leaders discussed the plan; thus, America's communists joined the Kremlin in boycotting and blasting the plan.

By 1040 50, Truman and team grappled with the Russian Bear at every turn, from Berlin to Budapest to Pyongyang. Harry Truman painfully learned he could never trust Stalin. The Red Army was brutally swallowing up territory, and Stalin (as Truman often complained) methodically broke every promise he made to Truman and Roosevelt.

MARSHALL PLAN: SLAVERY AND WHITE IMPERIALISM

As the Soviet Union gobbled up Europe and rounded up innocents, Frank was certain who the bad guy was: Uncle Sam. More specifically, it was Harry Truman and Secretary of State George Marshall—the men standing in Stalin's way.

In his first column for the *Record*, titled "How Our Democracy Looks To Oppressed Peoples," Frank took aim at the Marshall Plan with a line of attack identical to that used by Stalin, Molotov, and the entirety of the Kremlin and Soviet International Department. He pointed the finger at imperialism and aggression in one direction only: the United States.

"For a nation that calls itself the champion of democracy," he scoffed, "our stupendous stupidity is equalled [sic] only by our mountainous ego." He insisted, "Our actions at home and abroad are making American democracy synonymous with oppression instead of freedom."

Frank was unrelenting in his attacks on the Marshall Plan throughout this period. It was, in sum, an evil program to "help maintain European empires at the expense of exploited dark colonial peoples."[3]

Frank's angle, like that of the Kremlin and CPUSA, of *Pravda* and the *Daily Worker*, would both widen and sharpen, cutting at the heart of good intentions in Europe: America's postwar plans were not about liberation, but slavery; not about rescue and democracy, but imperialism and neocolonialism. As Frank explained it, the thrust behind Harry Truman and George Marshall and Uncle Sam was, believe it or not, a not-so-veiled form of racism.

"Four years ago, we had the opportunity for world leadership," wrote a saddened Frank. "This was near the end of World War II, a global conflict for freedom and liberation." But what happened? "But before the guns grew cold, we interpreted freedom and liberation to be the exclusive possession of the imperialist governments of Europe. I have watched with growing shame for my America as our leaders have used our golden riches to re-enslave the yellow and brown and black peoples of the world."

Frank pointed to "yellow" people living under Chiang Kai Shek's anticommunist Kuomintang regime in China. Communists were zeroed in on this corner of the globe, as China was the world's most populous country, and was under intense threat in 1949 by an indigenous communist movement poised to quickly turn this vast nation Red and make it a vital Soviet ally. According to the communist line, America, rather than backing Mao and his alleged freedom fighters, was supporting the oppressors in China—that is, the anticommunist government.

This was a scandalous line infamously pushed by pro-Mao forces in America. Some Republicans charged that such forces were scheming within the Truman administration; they would later accuse the Truman administration (fairly or unfairly) of "losing China."

The communist line on Mao was pushed by Frank Marshall Davis. "With our usual genius for suppressing the common people, we backed the oppressors in China," he argued. "We poured in a Niagara of cash to the corrupt Kuomintang, thus insuring the enmity of millions of Chinese who thereby faced a harder fight for freedom and the end of feudalism."

What was the vehicle for this reinvigorated feudalism? The Marshall Plan. "As the colonials see it," Frank explained, "the Marshall plan is a device to maintain what they call 'white imperialism,' and no manner of slick phrases can convince them otherwise." The plan was a disgusting "oppression of non-white peoples everywhere," a slavery purchased by Secretary of State Marshall's "billions of U.S. dollars . . . to bolster the tottering empires of England, France, Belgium, Holland and the other western exploiters of teeming millions of humans."

In Frank's narrative, the West as a whole was reinstituting slavery. It was being brought back by liberals, by Keynesians, by the Labour Party, by dirty Democrats; specifically by Clement Attlee and the Labour government in Britain and Truman and the Democrats in America.

Of course, Republicans were complicit as well. Frank blamed a "bipartisan foreign policy" and "bi-partisan coalition" busily unleashing "crimes" being "committed in the name of democracy." This bipartisan cabal had "wrecked the civil rights program" in America, and was now seeking slavery around the world.

The Marshall Plan was imperialism, repression, slavery, racism.

THE ANTI-TRUMAN AND HIROSHIMA CAMPAIGNS

During this period, Frank's columns were more consistently anti-Truman than at any other time in his writing. This was consistent with the anti-Truman campaign pushed by communists. Related to that campaign was another communist push to frame Truman and the United States generally as loathsome killers of innocents via the dropping of atomic bombs on Hiroshima and Nagasaki.

Both of these related campaigns, with Truman at the center, were later commented upon by Lieutenant General Ion Mihai Pacepa, a Romanian who was the highest-ranking intelligence official to defect from the Soviet Bloc, and who today is an American citizen. "The communist effort to generate hatred for the American president began soon after President Truman set up NATO and propelled the three Western occupation forces to unite their zones to form a West German nation," said Pacepa.

Pacepa and his fellow propagandists were tasked to shift leftist Europeans' "hatred for Hitler over into hatred for Truman—the leader of the new 'occupation power.' " Western Europe's angry left "needed a tangible enemy, and we gave them one." That enemy, said Pacepa, was Harry Truman: "In no time they began beating their drums decrying President Truman as the 'butcher of Hiroshima.' "

Even so, getting people to turn against Truman would seem a tall task, given that most Western Europeans were still grateful to America and its president for having restored their freedom. But that was not true for leftist Europeans. Europe, said Pacepa, "had strong leftist movements that we secretly financed." "They were like putty in our hands."[4]

Pacepa did this because it was his job, but it did not come without considerable guilt. He knew the campaign was a lie. He was a Romanian stuck in the new Soviet Communist Bloc. He and his family lived and suffered under communism. His father had hung a framed picture of Harry Truman in their home.

Naturally, CPUSA, being composed of loyal Soviet patriots, followed their orders as well, orchestrating a domestic campaign to demonize not merely Harry Truman but all of America for using the atomic bomb. This campaign was especially hypocritical given that Stalin had enthusiastically supported Truman's decision to deploy the bomb when informed at Potsdam in July 1945. And why wouldn't he? Truman's decision saved the lives of countless Russian soldiers, sparing them a deadly land invasion. (Millions of Russians were stationed in Manchuria, ready to invade the Japanese mainland.) No matter, once the war was over, and the Cold War on, the Soviets and CPUSA portrayed the use of the bomb as an unnecessary, barbaric, ruthless, imperial-colonial abomination by a wretched America seeking to dominate the globe and launch World War III.

Sadly, but predictably, this campaign was successful in duping liberals/progressives. In February 1947, Progressive Citizens of America held a major rally at the embassy auditorium in Los Angeles. The introduction was provided by duped liberal/progressive actor Gene Kelly. The large screen onstage flashed photographs of Hiroshima before and after the bomb, with rolling footage of the dead and maimed interspersed with images of overflowing hospitals. This was a predominantly Hollywood group, as the film industry was a significant target of the Reds. On the ballot that evening for election as executive board members of Progressive Citizens were closet, card-carrying CPUSA members like screenwriters John Howard Lawson and Dalton Trumbo, right alongside gullible liberal/progressive celebrities such as Edward G. Robinson, Humphrey Bogart, John Garfield, Gregory Peck, Lena Horne, Melvyn Douglas, and Gene Kelly.[5]

Youth were also a very popular communist target. Among other venues, the Hiroshima campaign reared its head at the various Soviet-orchestrated World Youth Festivals, which were major propaganda pushes by communists. There, the Soviet and Communist Bloc delegations organized events like "Hiroshima Day,"[6] focused explicitly on convincing wide-eyed Americans (including an unusually high number of leftist students) that their country had committed a sin of unparalleled inhumanity in Japan.

In short, this campaign was remarkably successful, to the point that many of the anti-Truman/Hiroshima arguments promulgated by communists in the 1940s are still heard today, especially at American universities. And Frank Marshall Davis was one of those honing the argument.

HELL-BOMB HARRY

In a February 9, 1950, piece titled "Onward with the Hydrogen Bomb," Frank wrote, "When we dropped the atom bomb on Hiroshima, we believed the world was ours." Frank interpreted: "Having defeated the Axis powers on the battlefront, we were ready to show the Russians who was boss of this world."

By this account, America was guilty not merely of cruelty against Japan in dropping the bomb, but also cruelty against Joe Stalin. It had been "the combined efforts of our nation and the Soviet Union working closely together to curb the greatest threat to civilization the world had ever known" (it had indeed), but Uncle Sam, Frank argued, turned on the good Soviet leadership, unable to satiate his lust for violence.

Frank contended that it was not only a lust for power driving this colonial-imperial American ambition but also greedy capitalism. The Truman administration manufactured "crises" so rapidly "that a new one is shoved in front of us before we can examine yesterday's." And these things, Frank sighed, were done with stunning hypocrisy, as Americans claimed they "love peace" while "rattling our atom bombs."

Frank then juxtaposed this apparent American phoniness with the genuine love of peace by the men in Moscow—by "Uncle Joe," as Frank referred to Stalin in this column. This was a brotherly love that, supposedly, Truman and crew flagrantly ignored:

But we, too, love peace, said the men in the Kremlin. . . . [L]et's get together, talk this thing out and settle our differences amicably so that we can all go about the business of making the world safe forever from another war. Peace we want above all else, said Uncle Joe in messages to America.

While the hopes of our people rose at these words, our dividend diplomats recoiled in horror. If the ideological conflict between our side and the Soviets was brought to an end, what would happen to our giant corporations getting fat contracts to make materials of war and products for the anti-Communists of Europe? . . .

But ours is a resourceful land. Unless we have a threat better than the other fellow's, the crisis making business might go bankrupt, thus forcing us to cut our war budget, and you know what that would do to the incomes of the poor millionaires. Therefore, we will create a hydrogen bomb to shake at Russia, and then we can keep on making shiny new crises on a mass production basis. After all, there's always the chance that the American people will agree to war—for the sake of peace, of course!—while we have an H-bomb and before the Soviets can make one of their own.

But if the Soviets steal enough secrets . . . and get an H-bomb at the same time or even before we test ours, we shall have reached another stalemate, and the boys will have to think up a weapon guaranteed to destroy everything—that is, everything, not marked with the Stars and Stripes—in one global explosion.

Peace, it's wonderful!

According to Frank, Harry Truman had authorized hydrogen bomb research not because he feared Stalin getting it first—which, in fact, was Truman's primary motivation—but because of the same consuming greed and lust for power that had driven him all along, from his use of the bomb against Japan in August 1945 through his pursuit of the Marshall Plan in June 1947.

TRIGGER-HAPPY TRUMAN'S "PROGRAM FOR WORLD WAR III"

Throughout his columns in 1949–50, Frank Marshall Davis ramped up his vitriol at the Democratic president, portraying him as trigger-happy Truman, eager to launch World War III against the USSR and its affiliated "new democracies," a phrase he persisted in using to describe the captive nations choking under the jackboots of the Red Army.[7]

Especially harsh was Frank's August 4, 1949, column. He depicted Harry Truman as part of an American propaganda machine "aimed to deceive the American people into supporting a new world war, if need be, to bail Big Business out of a depression."

Again, this was the Soviet line, stated with exacting precision. Stalin, in his alarming February 1946 Bolshoi Theatre speech, enraged the free world—especially Truman advisors Paul Nitze and George Kennan—when he contended that capitalist countries had started World War II in order to generate money for big business. The charge was sickening in its hypocrisy, given that it was Stalin himself who had helped start World War II via his pact with Hitler.

In Frank's column two weeks later, he stepped up the attack. He roasted "the double-talking Truman administration with its program for World War III." Frank lumped together the Marshall Plan and the Truman Doctrine. Together, the two constituted a new form of colonial slavery: "The Truman doctrine in Greece and Turkey and then the Marshall Plan," he wrote, were "based upon the continuation of colonial slavery by the ruling classes of Western Europe." And regrettably, at the root of all of this was the almighty dollar—a "dictatorship of Big Business."[8]

In his next piece, Frank sounded a call that would resound unto the political left for generations to come, and that had been used by the American Peace Mobilization in opposing U.S. involvement in World War II. He protested that he would not die for Big Oil: "I have no desire to give my life to maintain high profits for Standard Oil. . . . I shall not help England and France keep millions of my colored brothers in Africa and Asia in colonial slavery. Yet that is what our dividend diplomats ask of you and me when they demand our support of the bi-partisan Marshall plan, Atlantic pact and a shooting war, if necessary, to bail us out of depression."

Once again, Frank brought China into the picture, urging *imperialist* America to dump Chiang's Chinese nationalists. Of course, this would result in a communist takeover of China, which, at the time of this article, was perilously close to becoming reality. Frank urged the Truman administration and Congress to divert money from Chiang to more worthwhile endeavors like inner-city poverty: "Billions poured down the rat-hole in China to aid the corrupt Nationalist regime of Chiang Kai-shek could have completely eliminated the slums in a number of major American cities, not only providing decent housing but employment in the construction of this housing."

This was a very strategic policy position. Communists were licking their chops to secure a military advantage for Mao and his minions. Here, Frank used the ruse of domestic poverty programs to divert money from anti-Mao forces. His pro-Mao position was masked as charity for the inner-city poor in America.

But Frank went even further, suggesting not only that America abandon Chiang but that it, instead, trade with a "Liberated China"—meaning Mao's Red China—along with the so-called democracies of the Soviet empire: "Trade with Russia, Eastern Europe and Liberated China should be demanded, thus creating additional jobs in U.S. industry and halting lay-offs." And as such trade was sought with Eastern Europe, Frank advised, "We must reject all war alliances such as the Atlantic pact" and "fake 'recovery programs' such as the Marshall plan," with Western Europe.

What Frank really wanted was U.S. aid (in the form of trade) to Stalin's Russia, to Mao's China, and to the Communist Bloc, while opposing U.S. aid to the noncommunist democracies of Western Europe (which, of course, were actual democracies) and to Chiang's China. This was nothing short of a prescription for communist dominance of the world. The Kremlin could not have laid out a clearer plan.

Frank's demands were so in lockstep with Moscow that it defies the imagination that liberals/progressives could ever begin to try to claim, or want to claim, that he had been unfairly maligned as a communist. It seems especially naïve given that liberals, in defending Frank, provide cover for a man who lied mercilessly about Harry Truman, a great American, a great president, and a great Democrat—not to mention the great men in Truman's administration, such as George C. Marshall. Worst of all, Frank Marshall Davis perpetrated these lies on behalf of Joseph Stalin and Mao Tse-tung, the two greatest mass murderers in human history.

TRUMAN'S BID TO "RULE RUSSIA"—AND RACISM

In his September 1, 1949, column, Frank suggested that America, under President Truman, was actually seeking to rule Russia. In fact, this alleged conspiracy was such a certainty that Frank wrote of it almost as an assumption. "It has also been asked how the U.S. expects to rule Russia when the federal government can't rule Mississippi," he asked rhetorically.

And yet, this was nothing compared to another propaganda dagger that Frank was continuing to sharpen: namely, that anticommunism was a veiled form of racism.

This was part of Frank's attack on Truman specifically. His contempt for Harry Truman ran so deep that he could not even bring himself to credit Truman's wonderful progress on civil rights, including desegregating the military, which he had done in 1948 by executive order. Truman had even issued a call for federal antilynching legislation, a move that a decade earlier would have spared the Scottsboro Boys. Nonetheless, Frank claimed that Truman merely "talked a good civil rights program," giving "token support."[9] In fact, going back to his days at the *Star*, Frank had mocked Truman's work on civil rights.[10]

This was very unfair. Normally, Frank would have applauded a president for such civil-rights actions. But in this case he had to take this position because it was the position of the Soviet Union, a country to which he had pledged his loyalty. To credit Truman on race would have also credited America on race. America had a soiled past of slavery and discrimination, and there was no way that communists, from Moscow to New York to Chicago, were going to give up that gem of a propaganda point—no matter the truth.

12

Frank in the *Honolulu Record* (1949–50)

Other Targets, from "HUAC" to "Profits" to GM

HARRY TRUMAN REMAINED a target in Frank's columns at the *Hono-lulu Record* throughout 1949–50. But the Democrats' man in the White House was not Frank's only concern. Other adversaries came into the crosshairs, from anticommunists at the House Committee on Un-American Activities to anticommunist Christians, whom Frank por-trayed as modern-day Pontius Pilates for their supposed sins and ingrati-tude to Stalin for helping stop Hitler. And, speaking of Hitler, Frank engaged in one of the most hideous communist/Soviet gambits of the late 1940s: the totally unfounded allegation that American policymakers were seeking to hand West Germany back to the Nazis.

Within Frank's widening enemies list, we can also discern the broader CPUSA campaign to undermine public support for "HUAC," a deliberately misordered acronym that framed the committee as the "House *Un-American* Committee"—claiming that the committee it-self was un-American. I counted forty-three examples of Frank's using the word "un-American" at the *Honolulu Record* in just 1949–50 alone.[1] This anti-"HUAC" campaign—in which the American left was not shy about labeling certain (anticommunist) Americans "un-American"[2]— was an intense campaign led by (among others, at various times) CPUSA, the *Daily Worker*, communist fronts masquerading as "progressives," the ACLU, and especially an ACLU splinter group called the National Emergency Civil Liberties Committee (NECLC).[3] The NECLC was headed by Columbia University's Corliss Lamont (an earlier noted Potemkin Progressive) and by self-proclaimed "progressive" I. F. Stone, the secret Soviet agent and liberal icon who contributed to the pages of Frank's *Chicago Star*.[4] The goal of this "Operation Abolition" was simple: to smear and discredit the House Committee as un-American.

This well-organized effort built upon a larger "anti-anticommunist" campaign that the American left still advances to this day. That push had been so forceful that the Democrat-run Senate Judiciary Committee eventually held hearings and published a report titled "The New Drive Against the Anti-Communist Program." This anti-anticommunism, which was especially prevalent at the *New York Times*,[5] was extremely effective in stirring liberals/progressives into action.

It was incredibly ironic that after two decades of being duped by Stalin and his secret supporters, America's liberals/progressives—led by the likes of the ACLU and NECLC—were alarmed not by the duped liberals/progressives or procommunists who defended Stalin as he massacred tens of millions, but by *anti*communists who tried to tell the truth about Stalin, his murderous state, and his secret supporters in America. And Frank helped make that happen.

ANTICOMMUNISM IS RACISM—AND FASCISM

In his *Honolulu Record* columns, Frank reinvigorated his efforts to equate anticommunism with racism. This was a tactic obviously aimed at self-interest and self-preservation.

Throughout the Cold War, and even post–Cold War, CPUSA maligned what it dubbed "the racist, McCarthyite forces of evil" and the

"fascist House Un-American Activities Committee."[6] This was an obscene accusation from a generation that had faced the Nazis. And yet,
as is typical of the American left, opponents were transmogrified into
political monsters: "racists," "fascists," "*Nazis.*"

Frank was one of the flamethrowers.

It is sad that Frank leveled claims of racism to advance the Soviet/
Stalinist line. It was not how he started his career. Charging racism to
defend the Scottsboro Boys was a just cause; charging it to defend the
Soviet Union was completely unjust.

In his columns for the *Honolulu Record* from 1949 to 1950, Frank
used the word "racist" ten times. In only one column[7] was the charge
not coupled with a shot at Harry Truman's foreign policy; at Truman's
attorney general Tom Clark, who sought out communist subversives
(and whom Frank ripped six separate times); or at racist southern Democrats on the House Committee on Un-American Activities. Even when
a certain southern Democrat might have merited the charge, Frank's in-
dictment fell flat because it was almost always embedded within a larger
Party-line cover for Stalin's international ambitions. There were countless racists in America in Frank's time, but Frank just happened to focus
on those tasked with investigating American subversives loyal to Stalin.
During this period, Frank's charges of racism were almost always political and twisted into the ideological context of the CPUSA line. And, for
that matter, so were his charges of "fascism."

Frank fired the "fascist" bullet thirteen times during columns in this
period, and again mostly toward "domestic fascists" (his words) trying to
stop communist subversion.[8] So hand in hand were Frank's accusations
of fascism and racism that in one column he blasted what he called "fascist racism."[9] In the sentence in which he used that term, Frank mentioned World War II, Hitler, and the racism of the South—all obviously
appropriate—but could not help but toss in Congressman John Rankin
(D-MS), a racist, segregationist southern New Deal Democrat who was
a member of the House Committee on Un-American Activities. Even
if the likes of Rankin generally merited the denunciation (he did), it
seemed that Frank could not separate such charges from his wider goal
of prodding the Party line.

This particular column condemning "fascist racism" was actually written as a wider defense of Paul Robeson, whom Frank had hailed in his very first piece for the *Record*, in which he persisted in arguing that the USSR had abolished racism.[10] Robeson had said black Americans would "never go to war against Russia." Frank brought in W. E. B. DuBois to Paul's defense, referring to him not as a professing member of CPUSA,[11] but as a "world famous scholar and a founder of the National Association for the Advancement of Colored People."

In another example, Frank flung the racist label for Party purposes in his November 24, 1949, column, linking anticommunism to KKK membership.

"For many years the Ku Klux Klan has been virtually inactive," he wrote. "But recently the groups have come alive. . . . They are trying at present to unite all under a single leadership with the slogan of 'Fight Communism to Maintain White Supremacy.' . . . To reaction, any attempt to change the status quo of discrimination is Communistic."

That Frank was employing this creative angle to protect himself was very clear in his columns going forward. "If you fight too hard for civil rights," he wrote two weeks later, in a December 8 piece, "you are likely to be branded a communist." Frank directly implied that this was why he was being branded with the "c" word—not because he was crusading for communism but because he was crusading for civil rights. "I, personally, have no intention of letting the cry of 'communism' sidetrack me from my goal of complete civil rights as guaranteed by the Constitution," he said stoically. "The fight for absolute equality will continue. . . . I want civil rights for all people, and I shall not rest until that goal is achieved."

As transparently phony as this defense was, it has been picked up by Frank's defenders and is still used today. It is amazing that when Frank is mentioned in sympathetic Obama biographies today, he is upheld as a civil-rights crusader who was hounded by merciless anticommunists.

This was a maneuver by Frank to shield not only himself, but other African-American communists. He did so in columns on Ben Davis and Henry Winston.[12]

On Winston and Ben Davis, Frank wrote: "Negro Americans are concerned about the growing attacks upon their rights, but they are also anxious about the growing assaults upon the liberties of many other groups. . . . Anyone who dares to think for himself and to say what he thinks is in danger of being fired from his job, branded as a Communist subversive, and thrown in jail." [13]

That was hardly the case with Winston and Ben Davis, who for decades had been very well-known communists. No one questioned whether they were Party members. Regardless, Frank contended that mere suspicions of the two men meant that "freedoms guaranteed by the Bill of Rights are now, once more, in serious danger." Worse, he believed, "There is no hope for Negro freedom if the liberties of our country are now snuffed out behind anti-Communist hysteria." [14]

Anticommunism, by this narrative, was destroying the rights of black Americans. Like the Marshall Plan, it was undermining freedom itself, complicit in a new form of slavery, with black Americans shackled. The only hope for the stars and stripes was the hammer and sickle—under which racism did not exist.

Frank was quick to provide precisely such a reminder in his column two weeks later, on September 15, 1949. He again insisted that "racism is a serious crime" in the Soviet Union. In the USSR, "discrimination against colored peoples . . . has ended." He called upon Robeson for evidence: "In Paul's own words," noted Frank, "what he admires most about the Soviet Union is the abolition, by strict law, of racism and jim crow, the doctrine of equality regardless of color or race, and human dignity for all." [15]

"Paul," said Frank, had been treated so well in the Soviet Union, but was being pursued, hounded, discriminated against in America— especially by Harry Truman's racist administration. Frank highlighted the harassment of Robeson at an event in Peekskill, New York, that is infamous among the American left, as angry protesters showed up to denounce Robeson's appearance. [16] Interestingly, while liberals/ progressives today portray this event as evidence of "McCarthyism" run amok, with the mob motivated by racism and anti-Semitism, Frank pointed the finger not at Joe McCarthy but at Harry Truman and the boys—given that, again, it was Truman making policy against Stalin.

In August 1949, Robeson had headed to Peekskill to perform on behalf of William Patterson's communist front, the Civil Rights Congress. He had recently uttered his statement about how black Americans would not fight for America in a war against the USSR—an assertion that Robeson would spend the rest of his life addressing.[17] Specifically, at the Soviet-sponsored World Peace Conference in Paris earlier in the summer, Robeson had declared that it was "unthinkable" that American Negros "would go to war" against the Soviet Union on behalf of an America that oppressed them. He heralded the USSR as brimming with "human dignity" and America as fascist-minded.

Liberal historians dutifully scramble to cover for Robeson, claiming he was misquoted, or that the wire dispatch provided by the Associated Press and broadcast from Paris was somehow inaccurate. They ignore Robeson's careful statement at a "Welcome Home Rally" in New York on June 19, 1949, where he clarified: "I said it was unthinkable that the Negro people of America or elsewhere in the world could be drawn into war with the Soviet Union. I repeat it with hundredfold emphasis: *they will not.*" Robeson said it was unjust to go to war against the USSR or "with the people of China and the new democracies."[18]

Americans, including black Americans, were understandably upset with Robeson's remarks. In Peekskill, a mob showed up to denounce Robeson. But for the American left in general, the protesters themselves became the focus of anger, not Robeson or his remarks.

True to form, Frank Marshall Davis, thousands of miles away, wasted no time unloading on the protesters. Reaching for Nazi metaphors, he described Robeson's Peekskill detractors as a cross between "white storm troopers" and the "Ku Klux Klan." The mob was "aroused" into "a lynching spirit." Worse, Frank reported, "not a single policeman or state trooper was on hand to maintain law and order."

Was the lack of law and order the fault of local authorities? One would figure. But to American communists, blaming local authorities had limited utility; it was not helpful in the global struggle. So communists recast the fracas within the struggle between Stalin's USSR and Truman's America. Frank blamed the Democrats in the Truman White House for the mistreatment and failure to control rioters in Peekskill.

According to his logic, it was the fault of Truman's attorney general, Tom Clark, who identified the Civil Rights Congress as subversive.

Frank had Clark's guilt on good authority: the *New York Times*. "The mob of white veterans who planned the terror say they did so," Frank wrote, "according to the *New York Times*, 'mindful of the fact that former Attorney General Tom Clark had labelled [*sic*] the Civil Rights Congress as a subversive organization.' This was interpreted as government sanction for violence."

Frank believed that Clark and Truman had incited Americans, drawing a bull's-eye on the chest of this noble "civil rights" organization. According to Frank and his fellow travelers, labeling the Civil Rights Congress as subversive had been "interpreted as government sanction for violence," and the "young white storm-troopers" in Peekskill, "operating under Ku Klux Klan direction," had simply responded in kind.

That had been Paul Robeson's conclusion. "It's clear now who uses force and violence," Frank quoting Robeson as saying. "Let it be equally clear who advocates its use. The money crowd pulls the strings, right up to the White House. President Truman talks a good game of civil rights, but that's just talk. He gives the lynchers the green light."

In all, said Frank Marshall Davis, this was a new form of fascism overrunning the Red, White, & Blue, a Democratic Party fascism. It was "fascism, American style," with "the silent backing of President Truman, Democrat."

ANTICOMMUNISTS: THE NEW PONTIUS PILATES

Anticommunists were deemed not only racist and "un-American"; they were also, by Frank's reckoning, un-Christian—betrayers of Jesus Christ.

In several columns from this period, Frank Marshall Davis hammered anticommunist Christians for the *sin* of being anticommunist. Their anti-Sovietism was simply un-Christian. In the process, Frank made use of left-wing Christians, some of whom were duped "social justice" Christians and some of whom were actually closet communists (yes, *communist* Christians).

In a July 7, 1949, piece, Frank used the case of the Reverend Thomas

S. Harten. He described Harten as "for many years one of the most noted Negro pastors." Frank neglected to mention that Harten was a member of the general assembly and board of the radical, communist-infiltrated National Council of Churches and an especially active supporter of the communist candidacy of Ben Davis.[19]

Frank quoted the pastor: "I say to America that before she preaches to Russia or to any other nation, she must remove the mote from her own eye, and clean up the dirt in her own backyard." When Harten gazed from his pulpit in the direction of Stalin's state, he saw no mote there at all.

Sadly, said Frank, Harten was another victim sacrificed at the altar of anticommunism. Anticommunists were no less than Pontius Pilates seeking to crucify poor Reverend Harten. Harten, however, was ready for martyrdom, if such was necessary to stop Christians from criticizing Stalin's utopia. According to Frank, the likes of the good Reverend Harten "feel their cause is just and are ready to face crucifixion, if need be, for what they believe in. They have no fear of the Pontius Pilates."

Washington's anticommunists had washed their hands, and now Reverend Harten would carry his cross all the way to Calvary.

In resurrecting Harten's case, Frank was bidding for the biggest dupes of all: the Religious Left.

In his column from September 22, 1949, "Cold War in Church," he listed several radical preachers on the far-left fringes. They publicly called themselves "social justice" progressives, but their lengthy record with communist fronts suggested otherwise. They were, in fact, among the most prominent, longest entries in the investigative compilations put together by J. B. Matthews, the famed former-communist-turned-government-investigator who served as director of research for the House Committee on Un-American Activities—and who once had been approvingly cited by Frank's *Atlanta Daily World* in 1932, back when Matthews was a "working class" hero.[20]

Among the names of "progressive" pastors Frank listed in his column, few appeared as many times in Matthew's compilation of over fourteen hundred radical Protestant Episcopal rectors as John Howard Melish.[21] And it was John Howard and his son, William Howard, who were the focus of Frank's "Cold War in Church" column.

John's son, William Howard Melish, was chairman of the National Council of American Soviet Friendship (NCASF), a well-known front that, for two decades, had undergone constant name changes under advisement by the Comintern. In a major investigation of NCASF, Congress noted that the group's officers and board of directors tended to be "functionaries and members of the Communist Party." It took positions "invariably and markedly pro-Soviet and, except during the war years, anti–United States Government." NCASF's "primary purpose," explained Congress's report, was to "advance and promote the objectives of the Soviet Union for the Communist Party behind a facade of being independent of the Party and interested only in developing friendship between the Soviet Union and the United States."[22]

Aside from pro-Soviet work for NCASF, William Howard was also a frequent contributor to the *Daily Worker*, *New Masses* (in which he had a column), and the front-group publication *Soviet Russia Today*, not to mention numerous petitions and other work.[23]

Frank did not bother to share such critical information on Melish with *Honolulu Record* readers. To the contrary, he described NCSAF as "nonpolitical," and attacked Truman's attorney general for having listed the front group as a "subversive" organization.

And then there was the senior Melish. "Remember the name of the Rev. Dr. John Howard Melish, rector of the Church of the Holy Trinity, Episcopalian, in Brooklyn," began Frank. "If civilization survives the threat of World War III, future generations will remember Dr. Melish as one of the great martyrs of 1949 in the fight against the flood-tide of American fascism."

Who was stoning this saintly man of the cloth?

It was the devils in the Truman administration. Frank declared John Howard Melish "a victim . . . of a Truman administration that talks like an angel and acts like the devil."

Referring not to the KGB but to America's "thought control police," Frank maintained that the bipartisan policies of the Truman administration and congressional Republicans were "aimed against such Negroes as Paul Robeson, who think American democracy could learn about race relations from Russia, against such labor leaders as Harry Bridges, who oppose Taft-Hartley and the imperialistic Marshall plan, and against such pastors as Dr. Melish, who believe the Soviet Union and the U.S. can live peacefully in the same world. This is pro-fascist ideology, pure and simple."

And for that, said Frank, John Howard Melish was being vilified. Melish's crime was that "he believed in applied Christianity," and "refused to join in the anti-Communist hysteria."

Worsening Melish's plight, by Frank's account, was that his son, William Howard, was "working toward friendly postwar relations between the Soviet Union and the U.S.," which he had done with the "blessings and advice" of his father. The younger Melish "saw that the future of the world would largely be shaped by how these two powerful wartime allies got along in peace," and he "believed it was up to the Christian church to lead in this field."

But unfortunately, sighed Frank, who two decades earlier gave up God, Christians were not listening; they were consumed by anticommunist hysteria. Christians were bearing false witness to Stalin.

In fact, of course, American Christians correctly understood that the Soviets were the most relentless, vicious persecutors of Christians anywhere on the planet. No ideology in history was as ruthlessly anti-religion as communism. Communists worldwide generated Christian martyrs by the thousands, an unceasing bloody stream flowing from St. Petersburg to Peking.

Frank raised the stakes even higher in his next column, "Challenge to the Church," September 29, 1949. He doubled down, not only posing anticommunism as un-Christian, but postulating that communism is *friendly* to Christianity.

Frank imagined Judgment Day, where anticommunist Christians would be called to account for their transgressions: "On your Judgment Day, when the Lord will ask you for an account of your stewardship, will you have to say, 'Lord, they were a pack of wolves'? If God will then ask you, 'My son, did you do all you could to humanize these wolves, to Christianize them, to teach them My Way?' will your answer be, 'Lord I was too busy Redbaiting'?"

And the Catholic Church especially deserved a good scourging. "The Christian churches, and the Catholic Church in particular," Frank preached, "are making a grievous error in their shortsighted belief that the major enemy of Christianity is Communism."

The great irony is that no communist in Moscow would have agreed with Frank, and the late Lenin would have laughed him out of the country—or thanked him for his efforts.

Not only was Soviet Russia not antireligious, said Frank Marshall Davis, but it had saved the world from Hitler's "anti-Christian paganism." Really, Christians worldwide should pay homage to Stalin. Instead, they were blinded by their anticommunist bigotry.

Frank wrapped up this uniquely sordid piece by yet again using the "American way of life" phrase, but this time not cynically. He concluded that in this "Challenge to the Church," as well as in places like Peekskill, New York, where Paul Robeson had endured "stormtroopers," it was not Russia or Robeson who was on trial, but "the American way of life," and, more so, the Christian faith itself.

AMERICA'S RE-NAZIFICATION PROGRAM

A particularly outrageous piece by Frank appeared in the May 18, 1950, *Honolulu Record*. It stands out as a very important, insidious illustration of where American communists stood on postwar Germany: in accord with orders from Moscow. And yet again, Frank's target was the Democratic Truman administration.

When World War II ended, the Soviet objective was to keep Germany down and divided, with the hopeful goal of the entirety of Germany going communist. The communist movement hoped to foment enough discontent in West Germany to drive it into the communist camp.

Right on cue, Frank Marshall Davis ripped West Germany in a piece mockingly titled "Our New 'Democratic' Partner." "We have the amazing spectacle of the foreign ministers of the United States, Great Britain and France formally announcing that Western Germany is being brought in as a full fledged partner in the alliance of the 'western democracies' against Russia," he wrote. "If there had been a sincere effort to democratize Western Germany, I would feel much better about it."

Frank argued—with no evidence whatsoever—not only that American officials were insincere about democratizing West Germany, but that they were permitting (if not enabling) a return of Hitler's Third Reich. "It is a known fact that many honest American officials have quit their posts in disgust over the way in which Western Germany is being handed back to the Nazis." Frank insisted that the Truman administration's policy of de-Nazification was "one of the big jokes of the 20th century."

Frank claimed that the American public had "gradually forgotten in five years" the horrors of the gas ovens of Dachau and Buchenwald. "And as the memory of these atrocities faded, so did our denazification."

As Frank was writing, the Russians were actually taking over Nazi concentration camps like Buchenwald, which was renamed Soviet Special Camp No. 2.[24]

Frank maintained that American officials were trying to make an enemy not out of these new Nazis but out of Stalin: "Stalin has been built up as a greater menace than Hitler," Frank said. "Jail doors have been opened and Nazi leaders have been almost invited to take up business at the old stand."

Here again, Frank alleged that this was the product of a racist-fascist-imperialist-capitalist conspiracy between Democrats in the White House, Republicans in Congress, and wicked Big Business on Wall Street: "The big industrialists who financed Hitler have been handed back their factories and the old school ties with Wall Street are almost as strong as they ever were."

What kind of West Germany was America trying to help to its feet? According to Frank Marshall Davis, "It is the Germany of the master race theory. . . . The fascists we sought to exterminate in World War II as 'the greatest threat to mankind the globe has ever known,' are now our partners. . . . '[W]hat d'you say we kiss and make up?' "

Frank figured this was a natural alliance desired by bigoted anticommunists on "the un-American committee." "This alliance with a revived Nazi Germany," he wrote, "may please such persons as John Rankin of Mississippi and John Wood of Georgia, two past and present chairmen of the un-American committee whose ideas on race parallel those of

Adolf Hitler." Frank believed that Rankin and Wood were not merely run-of-the-mill, redneck Democratic Party racists, but "upholders of master race theory of the Nazis."

Frank Marshall Davis did not mince words: If America, and especially anticommunists at "HUAC," wanted to see Nazis, they should look in the mirror.

DOMESTIC DEMONS AND ANGELS

Frank was not writing only about foreign policy during this period. There were also plenty of domestic enemies to target.

In a column dated August 25, 1949,[25] Frank again went after the Marshall Plan and its "colonial slavery," the Atlantic Pact, Uncle Sam's "dividend diplomats," "Red-baiting" members of "HUAC," and his usual targets, but he also backhanded several economic bogeyman, from "Big Business and Big Brass," to "high profits for Standard Oil," to "corporation profits" and "profit sheets."

Most interesting, given its applicability to today—specifically to modern economic thinking by President Barack Obama, liberals/progressives, and the Occupy Wall Street movement—were Frank's thoughts on the economy. Frank fretted over looming layoffs and the possibility of another Great Depression. He wrote of the need for "higher minimum pay," a "living wage," and to rid America of the problem of "huge funds" finding their way into "Wall Street" and "into the pockets of our gigantic trusts and monopolies."

"Instead," Frank said, "money should be spent for the benefit of the people instead of the corporations." And tax money, he urged, "should be used for public works projects," and especially "increased social security benefits, health insurance, education and low-cost housing." Frank had in mind *stimulus* of a solely public-sector type. The goal was not for business or Wall Street or individual businessmen and corporations to stimulate the economy, but for "taxes" to be redistributed by the federal government.

Most salient here was Frank's suggestion of using tax money for "health insurance." Was Frank advocating government health care, or socialized medicine? He did not expand on his thinking, though he clearly wanted to redistribute money from "Wall Street," "corporations," and their "huge funds" to such public purposes.

Frank did not like "Big Business," as he showed in a revealing January 26, 1950, column, "Free Enterprise or Socialism." He perceived an America on the verge of another Great Depression, with a "virtual dictatorship of Big Business" being the culprit.

In particular, Frank did not like General Motors. He was indignant at GM's profits, which he felt were too high. Frank believed, or at least wanted to suggest, that the U.S. government, "Big Business," and "dividend diplomats" were in bed together, pining for war with the Russians in order to make profits for the Daddy Warbucks who were the real powers behind the throne in America. In a subhead titled "Tentacles of Big Business," Frank cut loose:

> Alfred Sloan of General Motors announced that his gigantic company made a profit last year of $600,000,000, more than any other corporation in history. Over the years, General Motors has swallowed up or knocked out car manufacturer after car manufacturer so that today less than a handful of competitors remains. Free enterprise, eh?
>
> Obviously, a business that can show a profit in one year of $600,000,000 is in a position to control government. When we remember that the directors and major stockholders of one industry also shape the policies of banks and other huge corporations, it is easy to see that the tentacles of Big Business control just about everything they think they need to insure continued profits. . . . The control of our wealth and government by the giant corporations and the flight of aircraft are accomplished facts.
>
> For many years now we have been living under the virtual dictatorship of Big Business which all but drove us to ruin in 1929. . . .
>
> Government policy is fixed in Wall Street and transmitted through the corporation executives who have been appointed by Truman to high federal office. OPA was killed, the Marshall Plan launched and the nation placed on the brink of war economy—so

that such firms as General Motors could make $600,000,000 profit while unemployment skyrocketed.

Frank finished with a remarkable (if not completely predictable) statement, given his far-left view of government and economics:

As for free enterprise, it doesn't live here anymore. At the same time we have manufactured a national horror of socialism. Meanwhile, the dictatorship of the monopolies is driving us down the road to ruin.

And so, with still rising unemployment and a mounting depression, the time draws nearer when we will have to decide to oust the monopolies and restore a competing system of free enterprise, or let the government own and operate our major industries.

Frank did not bother explaining which option he preferred. Given that he was obviously a man of the far left, a communist, even a member of CPUSA, it seems certain that he would have favored the option of letting the government own and operate America's major industries.[26] The Soviets and Stalin and Lenin and Mao and all communists favor nationalization of industry as the centerpiece of their philosophy, with Marx repeatedly demanding "factories and instruments of production owned by the state."[27] A communist nationalizes; the state takes over industries. Paul Robeson, while refusing to answer whether he was a communist, nonetheless told the Senate (May 1948) that he favored nationalization of "public necessities," "such industries as coal, railroads, etc."[28] No one reading Frank's columns would be under any illusions that he advocated anything but nationalization.

Two weeks later, in a February 9, 1950, piece, Frank again went after GM, asking rhetorically: "With no brink-of-war economy, how could General Motors make $600,000,000 in one year in the face of rising unemployment? What would our generals and admirals think? No, real peace is an expensive luxury that the big stockholders and professional soldiers can't afford."

Frank continued to call out these alleged obscene profits by the automaker. He cited the $600,000,000 figure four times in these two columns. He did not like General Motors.

It would be easy to picture Frank Marshall, if he were president of the United States, nationalizing GM. It probably would have been the first company in line to be nationalized.

That task, of course, would be left to another president many years down the road. And in a strange twist of fate, it would be done by the only president whom Frank Marshall Davis just happened to get the opportunity to mentor.

13

Frank and the Founders

THERE IS AN illuminating theme in Frank's columns that merits our attention, both for its historical relevancy and for contemporary interest: Communists lifted the language and symbols of the Founding. This is something that the progressive movement, too, has done for decades, and that has been recognized and documented by certain conservative scholars.[1] But unrecognized by both scholars and the general public is the degree to which communists did the same. America's Reds attempted to argue that they were the new revolutionaries, the inheritors of Jefferson and Madison and Washington. They quoted the Founders and the Founding documents, from the Declaration and Constitution to Ben Franklin and Tom Paine. When they were not invoking the Declaration's inalienable rights to advance their Marxist-Leninist ideology, they were appealing to the Constitution and Bill of Rights (First Amendment, Fifth Amendment) to counter and denounce accusers who suspected them of Soviet sympathies and potential espionage. They did this constantly, consistently, from the founding of the American Communist Party in 1919.

Frank was among them. Trying to determine the number of times that Frank did this in his columns is difficult, though during a short window of 1949–50 alone, I counted seven examples of Frank in the *Honolulu Record* citing the "Founding Fathers," primarily Thomas Jefferson and George Washington; one case of his pointing to the Declaration of Independence; two instances in which he invoked the Declaration's inalienable rights of life, liberty, and the pursuit of happiness; over thirty references to "liberty" or "freedom"; and nearly seventy citations of the First Amendment, the Bill of Rights, or the words "Constitution," "constitutional," or "unconstitutional." As to the last, Frank was not shy about declaring something unconstitutional. "That, it seems to me, is unconstitutional," he pronounced without hesitation.[2]

To hitch his (red) star to the wagon of the American Founders was old hat. Frank did so in his first column for the first edition of the *Chicago Star*. Yet there seemed to be an upsurge in such efforts during the Hawaii period, no doubt because Congress was investigating his comrades (and was on his trail as well). As Congress accumulated evidence, America's communists did what they did best: spun propaganda. Because Congress was looking into activities promoting a Moscow-directed "Soviet American Republic," American communists wrapped themselves in the American flag. As the insightful British commentator Alistair Cooke put it, upon observing the conniving tactics of Hollywood's communists in this period, they were "down-the-line communists coolly exploiting the protection of the First and Fifth Amendments to the Constitution."[3]

Taking a close look at this phenomenon is important for understanding the far left in America over the last hundred years. This is a valuable teachable moment for Americans in understanding just why their system, as devised by their Founders, is so special and worth knowing and remembering and preserving. Courtesy of Frank and friends, this is a civics lesson to be absorbed not merely for the sake of the past, but also for our future.

YOU SAY YOU WANT A "REVOLUTION"?

American communists frequently hoisted the banner of the American Revolution, often for the purpose of duping liberals/progressives. Communists engaged in this distortion unhesitatingly and with great success.

American communists co-opted the American Founding from the very onset of the revolution—that is, *their* revolution. Consider the case of Louis Fraina:

Fraina is credited as the first communist editor in the United States. His role in creating the American Party is evident in a letter located in the Comintern Archives on CPUSA, declassified for viewing. The letter was dated "Chicago, Illinois, November 24th, 1919," and addressed "To the Bureau of the Communist International." Sent by the leadership of the American Communist Party, it is signed by "International Secretary, Louis C. Fraina."[4]

The letter began, "Comrades: As International Secretary, I make application for admission of the Communist Party of America to the Bureau of the Communist International." Noting that the Communist Party of America had been officially organized in Chicago on September 1, 1919, Fraina and his comrades were filing their official application. The close to the seven-page letter makes abundantly clear to whom and what American communists were loyal:

> The [American] Communist Party realizes the immensity of its task; it realizes that the final struggle of the Communist Proletariat will be waged in the United States, our conquest of power alone assuring the world Soviet Republic. Realizing all this, the Communist Party prepares for the struggle.

American communists saluted the Soviet Comintern, the "world Soviet Republic," and a Marxist "World Revolution"—not the America of the Founding Fathers, which they looked to conquer and replace. Documents like this were never intended for the public eye, and in fact were locked up in Soviet archives for eight decades until the end of the Cold War and the USSR.

Fraina and his colleagues used very different language when communicating to the American public. Fraina applied not the language of the Bolshevik Revolution but that of the American Revolution; he and his comrades were the modern revolutionaries whom Uncle Sam now needed, picking up the torch from Thomas Jefferson. Before the American Communist Party was founded in Chicago that September, Fraina had already launched a publication called *Revolutionary Age*. The title sought to capture the spirit of the American Revolution, as did its place and date. Fraina's *Revolutionary Age* set sail in Boston on July 5, 1919, the day after America's birthday.

By Fraina's framing, America was on the verge of another Tea Party—with Vladimir Lenin the gracious host.

Once readers cracked open Fraina's publication, they discovered something totally unlike the *Federalist Papers*. Fraina's revolution devoted itself to the overthrow of what the Founders had founded, calling for a "dissolution and collapse of the whole capitalist world system" and "world culture," to be "replaced by communism." His publication advocated "an international alliance of the Communist Party of the United States only with the communist groups of other countries, such as the Bolsheviki of Russia." These, said Fraina's *Revolutionary Age*, would be the principles to be adopted by the comrades at their convention in Chicago in September—a convention bearing no resemblance to the Constitutional Convention in Philadelphia.[5]

And yet, communists harped on this theme of "revolution" to uphold themselves as the modern inheritors of the American Revolution.

THE CURIOUS CASE OF CLARENCE DARROW

To that end, a curious case of abusing the Founding for such perverse purposes was that of Clarence Darrow. Because of his work in the "Scopes Monkey Trials," Darrow is a liberal/progressive icon. Liberals love Darrow, immortalizing him as a brilliant defender of civil liberties, "tolerance," and "reason," in contrast to Bryan (a three-time Democratic Party presidential nominee), whom they portray as a slack-jawed fundamentalist.

American communists likewise greatly appreciated Darrow's work against religion in the Scopes Trials. Darrow was the toast of the movement for his yeoman's work countering God and exposing the silly "superstitions" of Bryan and his merry band of narrow-minded, slow-witted Christians. Frank was a big fan. His *Chicago Star* glowingly profiled Darrow.[6]

Another reason for the communist reverence of Darrow is a lesson not taught in schools: Darrow defended *them*, and particularly communist leader Ben Gitlow, beginning with a series of dramatic cases that ran from 1919 into the 1920s, when they were being pursued for advocating armed revolution and the replacement of the American system with a "Soviet American republic." They were being challenged by Democratic attorney general Alexander Mitchell Palmer.

Darrow, a member of the ACLU and a dependable progressive dupe, argued that not only were American communists *not* loyal to the USSR, but they were the embodiment of the American Revolution. "For a man to be afraid of revolution in America," Darrow protested to the court, "would be to be ashamed of his own mother!" He scoffed: "Revolution?" What was more quintessentially American? These American Bolsheviks were modern incarnations of John Adams.

As if that were not offensive enough, Darrow, atheist champion, invoked the Almighty on behalf of this exalted revolution: "There is not a drop of honest blood in a single man that does not look back to some revolution for which he would thank his God that those who revolted won." It was as if the Hand of Providence, after blessing the American Revolution, was now guiding the Bolshevik Revolution and its consecrated American counterpart, anointing Lenin and Trotsky and Stalin and the NKVD—and the American Communist Party.

Tellingly, these words from Darrow are cited in the 1940 autobiography of Ben Gitlow, who recalled Darrow's defense with a measure of embarrassment, as Gitlow by then had fled the communist movement. It was quite a conversion. Gitlow had twice run as the Communist Party's candidate for vice president of the United States, and had even served on the Comintern's Executive Committee. After a long silence, Gitlow emerged to testify before Congress (1939) and to write two major books, *I Confess* (1940) and *The Whole of Their Lives* (1948), in which he laid out CPUSA's relationship with Moscow, its "fanatical zeal" for the Soviet Union, its continuing pledge of "ultimate victory over the capitalist world," its espionage and acceptance of funding from Stalin's regime, including subsidies for the *Daily Worker*, and much more.

TOM PAINE: COMMUNIST REVOLUTIONARY

One of revolutionary America's most inspiring manifestos was Thomas Paine's *Common Sense*, published in January 1776, seven months before the Declaration of Independence. It was the most influential pamphlet of the Revolution, stirring in its message, profound in its pronouncements, and extremely effective in stoking the embers.

Paine comes under criticism by many sources today, including conservatives who have faith-based misgivings about the man.[7] Nonetheless, *Common Sense* embodies the heart, soul, and spirit of the American Revolution. Thus, it is obviously the antithesis of the *Communist Manifesto*. No reasonable observer would link Tom Paine to Vladimir Lenin. The two figures were revolutionaries, but similarities abruptly end there.

Leave it to America's comrades to make that link. In fact, the worst such abuse was committed by an American communist extremely close to Frank Marshall Davis: Howard Fast, Stalin Prize winner and arm-in-arm associate with Frank on the *Chicago Star* op-ed page.

In 1943, Fast published a book called *Citizen Tom Paine*.[8] Fast set the stage by opening with a quotation from Dr. Benjamin Rush, another brilliant mind of the American Revolution: "There is nothing more common than to confound the terms of *American Revolution* with those of the *late American War* [italics original]. The American war is over, but this is far from being the case with the American revolution. On the contrary, nothing but the first act of the great drama is closed."

Fast's message was consistent with what American communists like Louis Fraina had been preaching since 1919. The American Revolution needed to be continued, extended into an American *Bolshevik* Revolution—even as Fast carefully avoided the word "Bolshevik."

His message was also unmistakable to those who watched such things with an interest in, and with an oath to protect, American security. In other words, Congress was among the intensely interested readers of *Citizen Tom Paine*.

In 1947, Congress published its report on the Civil Rights Congress as a communist front. The report devoted space to Fast's book on Tom Paine. "This book is a fictionalized, sugar-coated, but thinly disguised exposition of Communist theory and practice," concluded the report, "including the advocacy of overthrow of government by force and violence." The report noted that the book's "clear implication is that we must carry over the revolutionary tactics used against the British Government in colonial times as described by Mr. Fast, to the present against our own Government."[9]

It was not simply Fast's interpretation that bothered Congress. What concerned congressional Democrats and Republicans alike was that Fast's book was used in public schools. Some school boards caught on and stopped using the book, including New York's board of school superintendents. For superintendents to balk in New York City, home of CPUSA, Columbia University, and more communists than any other city in America, meant blood, and the Reds responded with calculated rage.

Leading the battle was the Civil Rights Congress, which, of course, included Fast's colleague at the *Chicago Star*, Frank Marshall Davis, and whose leader was *Star* board member and Frank pal William Patterson. The Civil Rights Congress responded by issuing a March 11, 1947, press release demanding that Fast's book be restored to public schools. The *Daily Worker* dutifully carried that demand in its March 20, 1947, issue.[10]

So did the *Chicago Star*. As a sign of just how interconnected Frank, the *Star*, and the Civil Rights Congress were, the *Star* fired off an editorial well before the Civil Rights Congress press release. Published February 22, 1947, the editorial was derisively titled " 'Dangerous' Tom Paine."

"It took place in 'our most civilized city,' " began the editorial, which would have been written by Frank, or at least approved by him and his editorial board. "It was an act of political and cultural barbarism that throws us back to the darkest ages and to the days when Hitlerism turned out the lights in our modern world."

There it was again: "Hitlerism." It was Frank's customary flair for understatement. The editorial called the New York superintendents' action "more than stupidity and backwardness." It was "fascism." More than that, "this is a kind of treason."

Imagine: Here were American Bolsheviks, secretly pledged to Stalin, who had even sought to accommodate Hitler when Stalin did, who swore an oath to a world Soviet republic, who wished to conquer America on behalf of the Comintern . . . and they were accusing *anticommunists* of treason.

Frank's newspaper sought to mobilize Chicagoans, urging the Windy City's Reds to send "several thousand" letters to the New York board of school superintendents.

HOLLYWOOD'S "FIRST AMENDMENT" CRUSADERS

Frank's *Star* gave extensive coverage to another telling case of communists tapping America's Founding. The sucker was the Committee for the First Amendment, the biggest bunch of duped liberals/progressives ever to appear in Hollywood.[11]

By late 1947, Congress discerned that communists were trying to infiltrate the motion-picture industry. Screenwriters like John Howard Lawson, Dalton Trumbo, Alvah Bessie, and Albert Maltz assured their liberal/progressive friends that they were like them. These congressmen investigating their loyalties to Stalin's Russia were "fascists," heirs to Hitler. Their trusting friends believed them, reflexively taking the side not of anticommunists telling the truth to America but of procommunists lying on behalf of Stalin's state.

The accused screenwriters rallied liberals/progressives to their side in a PR campaign that framed the congressmen as Nazi stormtroopers and, on the flip side, painted themselves as the living embodiment of Alexander Hamilton. They appealed to good old-fashioned American civil liberties, wrapping themselves in the flag. Predictably, they got the support they sought.

In October 1947, a group of high-profile liberal/progressive actors, writers, and producers organized a major public-relations trip to Washington to defend their accused "friends," who had been summoned to testify before the House Committee on Un-American Activities. After consulting with the accused, the celebrities changed their group's name from the confrontational "Hollywood Fights Back" to the commendable "Committee for the First Amendment." It was a savvy PR move. Right on cue, the self-professed Constitution lovers at the *Daily Worker* joined in, headlining the campaign as a "Bill-of-Rights Tour."[12]

The liberal/progressive stars enlisted in the communists' clandestine cause ran into the hundreds, from Katharine Hepburn to Henry Fonda to Gregory Peck to Myrna Loy to Paulette Goddard. Roughly two dozen lent more than their signatures, volunteering to head to Washington. That troupe included some huge faces: Danny Kaye, Ira Gershwin, Judy Garland, John Garfield, Sterling Hayden, Gene Kelly, Burt Lancaster, John Huston, Philip Dunne, Billy Wilder, and the headliner couple of Humphrey Bogart and Lauren Bacall.[13] There was an understanding that Congress's questions were "un-American" and did not merit a response.[14]

There was also an assumption that the accused were innocent; that they were crusaders for the American way.

When the celebrities got to Washington, they got quite a surprise. Congress presented stacks of evidence: CPUSA registration rolls, *Daily Worker* articles, *New Masses* bylines, news clips, front-group memberships, party applications, forms, cards, checks, cash, and even numbers. For each of the accused, Congress listed not only membership in dozens of notorious front groups but Communist Party membership numbers: John Howard Lawson, number 47275; Dalton Trumbo, number 47187; Alvah Bessie, number 46836; Albert Maltz, number 47106.

The Committee for the First Amendment felt stunned and betrayed. Humphrey Bogart snapped: "You f–ers sold me out!"[15]

FRANK THE "JEFFERSONIAN"

All of these examples—from Louis Fraina to Clarence Darrow to Howard Fast to the Committee for the First Amendment—are important background to better understand Frank Marshall Davis's tactical invocation of the Founders.

Recall that in his kickoff "Frank-ly Speaking" column for the *Chicago Star*, "Those Radicals of '76," Frank claimed himself and his comrades as the true "spiritual descendants of . . . 1776." Preaching a mantra of "change," Frank averred: "If history teaches us anything, it teaches that any fundamental change advancing society is spearheaded by strong radicals." These were radicals, presumably, like Jefferson and John Jay and . . . Lenin and Stalin.[16]

Speaking precisely the language of the Marxist dialectic (without naming Marx), Frank noted that all radicals of "past and present" "anticipate the logical course of history and lead humanity on its way." "So it was in 1776; so it is today." Like "this nation's forefathers in the 18th century," exhorted Frank, it was time to "force into effect a modern Declaration of Independence."

On this occasion, Frank invoked the Declaration positively—even if inappropriately. A year later, however, in his July 5, 1947, *Chicago Star* column, he was bitter, fuming over the Truman Doctrine and Marshall Plan. He referred to the Declaration in more bellicose (but still handy) terms, calling it a "militant document" whose inalienable rights, further defined in the Constitution, included free speech and free assembly, "which J. Edgar Hoover would deny to Americans who don't like the Big Money Boys."[17]

Frank's piece on the *Star* op-ed page that day sat underneath a lead column by Howard Fast, titled "These are the times . . ." It was an excerpt from Fast's *Citizen Tom Paine*. "These are the times that try men's souls," Paine had beautifully written. Now, Fast and Frank and friends were overlaying Paine's soul-trying time upon Stalin's soul-denying time.

Frank persisted in this practice from Chicago to Hawaii.

As for Frank, he presented himself in the finest American/ Jeffersonian tradition. In his March 2, 1950, *Honolulu Record* column, "Left of Center," he referred to himself as "left of center in the best American tradition." He quoted Jefferson: "The tree of liberty must be refreshed from time to time with the blood of patriots and tyrants. . . . I hold that a little rebellion, now and then, is a good thing, and as necessary in the political world, as storms in the physical."

In this instance, Frank apparently openly advocated political rebellion, including the literal blood of "patriots and tyrants," in order to fertilize and grow the tree of "liberty." This might indeed sound quintessentially Jeffersonian, but only if one's barometer was Philadelphia circa 1776, certainly not Leningrad circa 1917. And if Frank and other

Communist Party members were modern incarnations of Jefferson and Jay, then who were the enemies?

The enemies, the "un-Americans," were anticommunists in groups like the House Committee on Un-American Activities, which was, by extension, libeling and defaming great *patriots* like Frank Marshall Davis, Howard Fast, John Howard Lawson, Dalton Trumbo, Albert Maltz, and Alvah Bessie. As Frank put it, "We have descended to such a low level in our history that a person becomes cannon fodder for the un-American committees merely by repeating the words of Lincoln and Jefferson."

By Frank's narrative, the accused communists were being hounded not for their efforts on behalf of the *Communist Manifesto*, but for their patriotic advocacy of *Federalist* 10.

Needless to say, Karl Marx and the American Founders had nothing in common.

In the *Communist Manifesto*, Marx expressed revulsion for all sorts of fundamental rights and things, from religion to morality to the family to free enterprise, and, most of all, for private property. Marx's rejection of private property is the common thread throughout the *Manifesto*: "The theory of the Communists may be summed up in the single sentence: Abolition of private property."[18] That is the essence of communism, which Marx returned to repeatedly in his treatise.

Of course, as the American Founders understood, abolishing private property is contrary to human nature, to what Jefferson called the "Laws of Nature and of Nature's God." To banish private property is to violate the most innate precepts of all peoples, from the cave to the courthouse. Such thinking shatters Judeo-Christian thinking, Western philosophy, the beliefs of the ancient and modern worlds, Cicero, Aristotle, Augustine, Aquinas, Sophocles, Francisco de Vitoria, John Locke, Jefferson, Old Testament, New Testament, Moses, Jesus Christ, just for starters. All human beings are entitled to certain inherent, inalienable rights, and men and governments have no right to deny those rights to anyone. They cannot deny what the Creator has endowed us with. It is a truth so obvious, agreed the Founders, that it is "self-evident."

What is the job of government at its essence and most fundamental?

As Jefferson put it in the Declaration, "That to secure these Rights, Governments are instituted among Men." The Founders' view was that governments exist to help human beings secure basic rights that are theirs because the Creator conceived them. Governments and men cannot dare take them away.

Marx and his disciples took them away, and violently, beginning with the right of private property and then on to all the full sweep of First Amendment freedoms, from religion to press, speech, assembly, and more. There was no greater mass murderer of civil liberties than communism. Moreover, in communist societies, the God that endowed us with those rights was Himself targeted. For communists, it was elemental to obstruct the very fountainhead from which all rights flow; they even took the right to life—the first and most fundamental of all freedoms, without which no other freedoms can exist.

And to imagine that communists invoked these same American Founders? It was obscene. But American communists did just that. Frank Marshall Davis was one of them.

14

1951–57

Frank on Red China, Korea, Vietnam, and More

FRANK CONTINUED TO write for the *Record* throughout its existence. His articles from 1951 to 1957 reiterated themes and stances in his writings dating back to the *Chicago Star*—but with a twist corresponding to the changing global landscape. By this point, Eastern Europe was firmly in the Soviet camp. Frank's propaganda work for that region could cool—as could his work regarding Western Europe. There, the crucial intervention of the Truman Doctrine and Marshall Plan ensured that nations like Greece, Italy, France, and West Germany—and onward into Turkey—were secure from the communist threat. Frank's shameless agitation in that area bore little fruit.

With that, the communists turned to Asia.

The action was in places like China, where Mao Tse-tung and crew had taken over in October 1949, commencing a bloody rampage that would lay waste to some 60 to 70 million lives by 1969. It was also in Korea, which was being divided into a communist north and noncommunist south, along with a brutal war from 1950 to 1953 that involved America, China, and the Soviet Union. And it was in Vietnam, which, at that early point, was degenerating into a shooting war between French colonialists and Vietnamese nationalists/communists.

Among these, consider the Party line on Korea: CPUSA and the global communist movement tried to portray South Korea as the aggressor, even as Stalin had ordered North Korea to attack South Korea, precipitating the war. This communist distortion on the Koreas was so transparently dishonest that even Henry Wallace had enough, issuing an August 1950 statement resigning from his Progressive Party because he felt the party "should support the U.S. and the U.N. in the Korean War."[1]

Throughout Asia, communists worldwide portrayed other communists as innocent nationalists defending themselves against colonialism/imperialism. That was the Party line.

Given his passionate anticolonialism and procommunism, even if misdirected, Frank Marshall Davis was an excellent choice to write a regular weekly column for a Hawaii-based communist organ seeking to advance communism in colonial regions of the world.

Frank had arrived in Hawaii, deep into the Pacific and Asian horizon, just as communism in Asia was exploding—and, as noted, was hired (fittingly) at the *Record* by Koji Ariyoshi, an Asian communist.

Frank railed against British and French colonial-imperial interests in Asia, Africa, the Middle East, and everywhere. This was the mantra of communists worldwide. It served their aims and interests, providing a pretext for the Soviets to "liberate" those peoples—liberate them with the *caressing* hand of Marxism-Leninism. In the Soviet Union's case, the concerns about colonialism were insincere; in Frank's case, they were not insincere, given that he genuinely hated colonialism. This hatred, however, was misguided when he sided with Soviet aims. As Ronald Reagan later put it, the "Soviet empire" was fully engaged in its own "colonial policy" for all of Eastern Europe and beyond; the Kremlin was pursuing *communist* colonialism/imperialism.[2] Harry Truman called it "imperialistic communism."

WE WANT WAR!

From 1951 to 1957, Frank fired away from the pages of the *Honolulu Record*. Once again, Harry Truman was a target, remaining in the White House until the arrival of Republican President Dwight "Ike" Eisenhower in January 1953.

In January 1951, Frank wrote a piece railing against Truman's State of the Union Address. By this point, Truman was the Truman of history. Six years into his unexpected presidency, the former farmer and haberdasher from Independence, Missouri, had gotten some rude life lessons from Joe Stalin. Truman had initially hoped Stalin might seek peace, but he quickly learned that Stalin and the men in the Kremlin were political gangsters. In his State of the Union Address, Truman said he was willing to consider negotiating "honorable settlements" with Russia but that America "will not engage in appeasement."

Congress roared with approval. Frank roared with indignation. He was convinced Uncle Joe wanted peace, and Truman wanted war. Frank reported: "Our nation, which through its official spokesmen in Washington, repeatedly says it wants peace, is busy girding for full war mobilization, according to President Truman in his State of the Union message to Congress Monday."[3]

This "according to" was how Frank began his column. He was most concerned that the United States might resist North Korea's regime. As Frank and his comrades argued, this was a regime that aspired to create one giant Korean "democratic republic"—allied with Stalin's Russia and Mao's China. America, Frank insisted, parroting the line of the Soviets—not to mention the Chinese, the North Koreans, CPUSA, and communists everywhere—should stay out of Korea. Korea should be allowed to emerge according to its own Russia-friendly specifications, not America's specifications. "One concludes that the Washington idea of an 'honorable settlement' in Korea would be the complete crushing of the North Koreans and the emergence of a Korean republic shaped to our specifications," wrote an angry Frank. "Conversely, you get the idea that if a united Korea friendly to Russia is allowed to appear, that is 'appeasement' and we will not accept it."

In his next sentence, Frank applied this thinking to Vietnam: "That seems to be the pattern elsewhere in the world. If the French can crush the people of Viet-Nam and restore their colonial grip on these Asians through a puppet ruler, that apparently is an 'honorable settlement.' "

Again, by this same narrative, the Western nations (America included) should not be *meddling* in Vietnam's internal affairs. As for Soviet or Chinese involvement, Frank and communists everywhere failed to portray that as meddling of any kind.

Frank's agitation on this issue is significant, especially given the historical big picture. Consider:

Americans do not appreciate that Vietnam began unraveling long before the 1960s. Soviet agitation started in the 1920s under a Comintern operative named Mikhail Borodin. Known as "Stalin's Man in China," Borodin sized up Vietnam. There, Borodin would seek his masters' ambitions with help from some friends, including an international agent known as Lee Suei.[4] "Lee" was the future Ho Chi Minh, godfather of Vietnamese communism. Through a complicated process, Ho, by September 1945, was able to install an anticolonial, independent, communist government in Vietnam. By 1946, after many twists and turns, he was engaged in armed conflict with French forces.

Frank was writing for the *Record* in the thick of this battle, which ended in May 1954 with the French defeat at Dien Bien Phu. In July 1954, a treaty divided Vietnam at the seventeenth parallel, with the north remaining communist. Millions of Vietnamese escaped south. Five years later, in May 1959, Ho and his forces, with the backing of the USSR and Mao's China, invaded South Vietnam. The seeds of the Vietnam War were in place.

Frank's angle was that no one needed to worry about the Russians; it was only hysterical warmongers in Washington who were worried about Russia. Everyone else in the world, including the Vietnamese and the Koreans, liked and trusted the Russians. It was Washington that was banging the war drums. "We just must have war!" screamed Frank.[5]

According to Frank, Americans were "determined" to "give a war, by golly, even if nobody comes but ourselves." He claimed, "We are being induced to develop a kind of national unison tremble as we sit behind bolted doors in fear that any moment now, Uncle Joe will send over a few of his fly-boys to drop bombs down the chimney." This was pure hysteria, reserved to Americans alone: "So far as I can determine," esti-mated Frank, "we are the only nation worrying about a war with Russia."

The Koreans were not worried; the Vietnamese were not worried. Only aggressive, war-hungry Americans were.

Worse, added Frank, America was gassing up the tanks while Stalin and the Soviets, "according to New York Times correspondents," were producing not bombs and war material but "more and more civilian goods." America was manufacturing war, while Stalin was manufactur-ing food for the masses and seeking peace. And yet, fumed Frank, "our own hate-Russia crowd will themselves make such drastic steps that a new world war will be immediately ignited. . . . This is the dead end street down which we are racing." America was itching to "start using our stockpile of war material on the Russians," including "the terror of atomic bombs and bacteriological warfare."

That last line deserves pause: According to Frank Marshall Davis, Washington was poised to use not merely atomic weaponry on its peace-making Russian friends, but even biological weapons.

More than that, Washington was gearing up to end all of civilization: "Yes," lamented Frank, "we plan to give a war. And whether or not we know it, we also plan to write *finis* to civilization!"

TRUMAN'S "CROWNING ACT": KILLING "ALMOST THE WHOLE WORLD"

In Frank's portrait, behind all of this was a raving, raging devil of a man named Harry Truman.

Frank narrowed in on Korea. He commented on the uproar over the Truman-MacArthur controversy, during which President Truman fired General Douglas MacArthur for going too far into Korean-Chinese ter-ritory. Frank framed the controversy as no big deal: He boiled it down to a willingness to "have a full-scale war with China and Russia" a "little today" under MacArthur or a lot later under Truman. Indeed, sniffed Frank, "all the noise is over the matter of timing."[6]

Besides, said Frank, with the Truman Doctrine, which had been a warm-up to the Marshall Plan and the Atlantic Pact, America had al-ready begun "liquidating communists." Korea was merely a logical genocidal progression of American policy. It was only a matter of time before America's belligerent anticommunists invaded the friendly confines of lands like China and Russia, where the leaders just wanted peace.

Frank was certain he had Harry Truman pegged: "Could it be he does not realize that the killing of a few thousand Greeks yesterday paves the way for killing a few million Asians today and then, as a final crowning act, killing almost the whole world tomorrow?"

It was sad, grieved Frank. "The People of China have begun to shape their own destiny." That is, the Chinese under Mao. The Red Chinese, like the communists who had taken over Poland, Czechoslovakia, Yugoslavia, and all of Eastern Europe, constituted the world's "people's democracies."

Frank insisted that America was not about democracy but fascism— a betrayal of the vision of her Founding Fathers. "Instead of making American democracy synonymous with freedom," explained Frank, "as the Founding Fathers intended when the 13 colonies threw off the yoke of British exploitation, we are making American democracy the twin brother of oppression and fascist domination."[7]

If Uncle Sam's advocacy of this were not bad enough, America was also exporting white supremacy. "A nation which has white supremacy as its internal policy would obviously support white supremacy internationally," figured Frank. "It is quite consistent for us to block the attempts of non-white peoples in the rest of the world to get freedom and equality."[8]

RED CHINA: TRUE FREEDOM

Frank saw Mao's Red China, like Stalin's Russia, as a kind of Shining City—certainly when compared to the rot that was the United States of America. Given the choice between America and Red China, what sane person would ever choose America? For that matter, what Chinese person would ever choose America?

Such was Frank's argument in a June 19, 1952, piece titled "Those 6,000 Chinese Students."

Frank teed off on an editorial in the main Hawaiian daily, the *Ho-*

nolulu Star-Bulletin, that had noted the plight of some six thousand recently graduated Chinese students who had been attending American universities. Those students now faced a perilous return to China—that is, the new Red China under Mao. Frank, though, saw no peril whatsoever, and mocked the *Star-Bulletin* for its America-centrism. Frank practically howled when the *Star-Bulletin* observed that if these Chinese students returned to China "they will lose their freedom."

Quite the contrary, said Frank, calling this brand of thinking "cockeyed." To Frank, the decision was a no-brainer: If the Chinese students went home to the brave new world of communism, they could become a "trained Chinese doctor or dentist or teacher or scientist," but if they stayed in America they were destined to "wash dishes or scrub floors for white folks in democratic Chicago or New York."

The students had a choice: "America versus going to Red China?" For Frank Marshall Davis, the decision was laughably simple: Red China.

Similarly, another notably pro–Red China column by Frank ran on October 10, 1953, titled "Trade With China." Frank argued for U.S. trade with China not only for economic reasons but also for political reasons—that is, reasons of "democracy." "The people chose," said Frank of the Chinese people's "choice" of the unelected Mao and his ravenous single-party communist dictatorship. A frustrated Frank pleaded: "Wake up, Washington!"

Throughout his *Honolulu Record* columns, Frank went full throttle on Red China, urging U.S. trade, diplomatic recognition, and admission to the United Nations. His pleas came just ahead of Mao's disastrous Great Leap Forward (1957–60), which killed more people more quickly than Stalin and Lenin accomplished in the previous forty years combined.

Frank had nothing but respect and admiration for "the new Chinese democracy."[9]

HANDSPRINGS AND HELL-BOMBS FOR UNCLE JOE

While Frank saw Mao's China as a glistening jewel, the USSR remained his beacon, his guiding light.

The 1953 New Year's Day edition of the *Honolulu Record* looked to a new year and a new presidential administration. Democrat Harry Truman was out. Republican Dwight Eisenhower was in. Frank assessed the coming year and prospects of U.S.-Soviet peace under Ike.

This particular column is an important illustration of the trust Frank placed in the person of Joe Stalin, whom he singled out for his peaceful intentions. "Several days ago Josef Stalin told the New York Times that he would like to confer with Eisenhower on ending both the Korean and cold wars and easing tensions between the U.S. and the Soviet Union," reported Frank. "Since this is what we profess to want, both the outgoing and incoming Presidents should have turned handsprings. Instead, they turned coy." [10]

Frank took Stalin's offer at face value, as if the Soviet tyrant was indisputably a man of peace. At this point in Stalin's rule, with only three months remaining until his death, he was responsible for the deaths of tens of millions of Soviet citizens, with some estimates as high as 60 to 70 million. [11]

Frank had no doubts about Stalin's olive branch. To the contrary, he was palpably displeased that "our leaders raised the immediate cry that the Russian premier was 'insincere' " and that Stalin was "trying to hoodwink" America. Frank Marshall Davis completely disagreed. The hoodwinking was coming from Washington.

Frank even framed Stalin's Warsaw Pact military alliance as a defensive response to "neutralize those nations arrayed against her." [12] He viewed NATO not as a defense against the Soviets but an offensive act of aggression by the United States—precisely the propaganda line of the Kremlin. "NATO," declared Frank, "is aimed at Russia." [13]

This enormous amount of goodwill and unwarranted charity Frank extended to Stalin was nonexistent when it came to U.S. officials. He was sure that "the brass in the Pentagon can hardly refrain from ordering 'preventive action' tonight on Moscow with the H-bomb." [14] He was also sure that George Marshall's successor at the State Department, Secretary of State John Foster Dulles, was yearning to drop the H-bomb on the Chinese. "Dulles & Co. are apparently aching for an excuse to launch a nuclear nightmare of mass murder and extermination against the Chinese mainland," reported Frank authoritatively. "After all, we have a huge stockpile of A-bombs and a quite workable H-bomb, which in the past have been used quite successfully against Orientals, including fishermen who got too close." [15]

Here, Frank was referring to the atomic bomb dropped on Japan and the infinitely more powerful and destructive H-bomb—or hydrogen bomb, also known as the Hell-bomb—that America tested in the Pacific, including (on one occasion) too close to nearby Japanese fishermen. Frank judged that Dulles was "aching" to nuke Orientals with such bombs—just as he figured the Pentagon was itching to pulverize Russians.

Frank also maintained that Dulles's charges of Chinese "acts of aggression" and delivery of arms and advisors to Vietnamese communists were trumped-up baloney, just as had been the case in Korea. The people of Vietnam want "freedom and independence from the yoke of French imperialism," added Frank, but Washington was standing in the way. Why? Because of capitalist greed: "Our leaders have decided that economic control of this area rich in natural resources must be maintained by what is called the 'free world.' "

Uncle Sam's nefarious plan for Vietnam, according to Frank, was twofold: 1) to allow France to continue to rule Vietnam "under our thumb," or 2) to allow Americans to "work ourselves into a position of direct domination." [16]

Frank looked to Washington and saw nothing but dollars and hell-bombs. He looked to Moscow and saw nothing but equality and olive branches.

ON THE POPE, SANTA, AND UNIVERSAL HEALTH CARE

Aside from headlines like communism in Asia and negotiations with Stalin, Frank chimed in on numerous other subjects of worldwide and domestic interest.

In his June 11, 1953, column, "Dupes, Blood and a Pope," Frank curiously found himself allied with Pope Pius XII, one of the most stalwart anticommunists of the twentieth century. The reason? Pius XII opposed the execution of Julius and Ethel Rosenberg, charged with giving atomic secrets to the Soviets. Of course, Pope Pius XII opposed the execution because he was consistently loyal to his Church's teachings against capital punishment. Frank Marshall Davis opposed the Rosenbergs' execution because he was consistently loyal to the Kremlin.

In a column for Christmas 1953, he wrote a parody of Santa Claus being persecuted by McCarthyite witch-hunters for daring to bring Christmas to kids in the Soviet Union. Frank's fictional Red-baiting senator attacked "this spy here, Santa Claus, alias Kris Kringle, alias Saint Nicholas."[17]

This piece was another novel outrage, considering Christmas was banned throughout the communist world—as Frank should have known. It was banned not by Joe McCarthy and his anticommunists but by Joe Stalin and his communists. The war on Christmas prevailed as standard operating procedure from Bucharest to Havana. An auspicious, symbolic starting point was a December 25, 1919, order from Vladimir Lenin, issued in his own writing to the Cheka, the brutal secret police: "To put up with 'Nikola' [the religious holiday] would be stupid," scowled Lenin in a surviving handwritten document. "The entire Cheka must be on the alert to see to it that those who do not show up for work because of 'Nikola' are shot."[18]

Yes, *shot.*

The jolly fat man in the red suit was being persecuted not by anticommunist U.S. senators but by God-hating, Christmas-hating communists.

Quite apart from St. Nick, Frank's July 21, 1955, column has crucial modern relevance in light of President Obama's dramatic changes in national health-care policy. Frank called for taxpayer funding of universal health care. "I would rather see my tax dollars go to insure health care for everybody," he stated.[19]

Frank Marshall Davis's *Honolulu Record* columns in the 1950s covered his usual gamut of interests, but he gave special attention to the spread of communism in Asia. And ultimately, Frank got what he wanted: communism in China under Mao, in North Korea under a father-son combination of Kims, in Vietnam under Ho. But he also got far more than he bargained for; indeed, a most sordid legacy:

In China, it is a legacy of 60 to 70 million dead, with a Lao-Gai gulag system and vast human-rights repression. In North Korea, it is the decay of millions dead under madmen Kim Il-Sung and Kim Jong-Il; an unprecedented violation of basic civil liberties; and the terror of North Korean prison camps like the horrendous Camp 22, where entire families of North Korean dissidents are executed together in gas chambers, and where newborn babies are killed by prison guards who stomp on their necks.[20] In North Korea, it is a Stalinist dystopia that from 1995 to 1998 produced an unrivaled famine that saw the starvation of 2 to 3 million people out of a population of 20 million.[21] In Vietnam, it is a legacy of five hundred thousand to one million South Vietnamese political slaves who underwent forced "re-education" from 1975 to 1986. Millions of Vietnamese fled to the jungles or the water. From 1975 to 1982, a "Boat People Exodus" ensued, with thousands to millions heading for the high seas, leaving behind all possessions in search of freedom. Hundreds of thousands drowned in the process.

None of this was "democracy." Freedom was as absent in Asia as it had been in Eastern Europe. The communist "democracy" canard was yet another deadly lie.

These tragic developments in Asia unfolded throughout the decades ahead. For now, Frank's writings continued to get him noticed in Washington. In fact, he finally earned himself a special invitation to Capitol Hill. There, at the U.S. Senate, Harry Truman's fellow Democrats had some intriguing questions for Frank Marshall Davis.

15

Mr. Davis Goes to Washington

IT IS NO surprise that these columns in the *Honolulu Record*, on top of everything Frank had written for the *Chicago Star* and elsewhere, got read not so much by Joe Six-pack but by the boys in Washington. The Democrats running the committees at the U.S. Capitol wanted to talk to Frank, with things reaching a boiling point in late 1956 when he was summoned to Washington to testify on a decade and a half of work and association with communists, communist fronts, and communist causes.

BLACK AMERICANS REJECT CPUSA

Before examining Frank's testimony in December 1956, it is worth pausing to consider a major congressional report released not long before Frank was called to testify. In December 1954, Congress issued a report titled "The American Negro in the Communist Party."[1]

After decades of attempts by the Comintern and CPUSA to recruit African-Americans, foment revolution among them—even create a separate "Negro republic" under Soviet command in the American South—

communists had utterly failed to attract black Americans. Citing figures collected by the FBI and inserted into the *Congressional Record*, federal investigators found that of 5,395 leading members of CPUSA, only 411 were black. This was merely 7.6 percent of top membership, far below the percentage of black Americans in the population as a whole. As the *Congressional Record* stated, "The fact that only 411 Negroes were found in this select group is strong evidence that the American Negro is not hoodwinked by these false messiahs."[2]

Like other groups of Americans whom communists desperately attempted to organize—Pittsburgh steelworkers, West Virginia coalminers, the (later) blue-collar Chicago "greasers"[3]—black Americans told communists to take their hammer and sickle and stick it.

After all that hard work by Frank, Paul Robeson, Langston Hughes, Angelo Herndon, Henry Winston, and other African-American comrades, blacks were not going red. The hopes and dreams of black American communists were as dashed and dead as the corpse of Lovett Fort-Whiteman slowly decomposing in a frozen, lonely outpost of Siberia. No wonder Frank was furious at Richard Wright for becoming a staunch anticommunist. As Frank knew, Wright further undermined the Red cause.

As the congressional report noted, everyday black Americans figured out what Frank and his college-educated colleagues had not: Communists had always "betrayed the Negro's cause whenever it was expedient." Communist intentions had one consistency: "to use the American Negro . . . in bringing about the real aim of the Communist, a proletarian revolution." Communists would exploit black Americans to the point of literally segregating them.[4]

Compelling testimony to this was provided by Louis Rosser. Rosser was drawn into the Party in the early 1930s precisely because of its civil-rights campaigns, like Scottsboro. An African-American, he came in via the Young Communist League of Herndon and Winston. He remained in the Party for twelve years.

Rosser testified that in 1932 CPUSA persuaded a group of renowned left-wing black intellectuals to visit the USSR. Though Rosser did not name names, Langston Hughes was almost certainly one of them, given that Hughes admitted heading to Moscow in 1932 immediately after his southern tour, which had been promoted by Frank (twice) on the front page of the *Atlanta Daily World*. According to Rosser's sworn testimony, one purpose of the visit was to enlist the select group of black Americans into making a motion picture. The movie would have highlighted the persecution of American blacks—in contrast to Stalin's *racial utopia*—and would have been exhibited in Africa and Asia.[5]

Rosser also testified to the Comintern's "Negro republic" project. He had inside knowledge, having personally attended the 1938 World Congress of the Communist International.[6] He emphasized the lack of unity among African-American communists over precisely this project. Many of them "accused the Party of attempting to segregate the Negroes once the revolution is had, and they have also accused them—said that if the Negro would rebel in the South, the rest of this country would shoot them down like a bunch of dogs. So you can see it is a tactic of the Party."[7]

What, exactly, was the tactic? To abandon black communists once the revolution was under way and allow them to be shot like dogs? Such would have been a quintessentially Stalinist approach, perfected in the USSR among various disposable groups, from kulaks to priests.

Rosser had seen enough. By World War II, he had bolted the Party—just when Frank was joining.

Rosser added one more especially notable chapter to his story. It involved the final push from the Party for Rosser and, ironically, the final draw for Frank: World War II and the American Peace Mobilization.

Rosser observed that as groups like the NAACP called for a "double V program" during the war, meaning victory both at home and abroad, CPUSA wanted victory not for America but for the USSR. He was disgusted at how "Communist Party policy changed abruptly upon Stalin's alliance with Hitler in 1939 . . . and the party instructed its members to make every effort to sabotage the United States defense mobilization." This included sabotaging industries that provided income for black workers, which CPUSA had theretofore championed. Rosser was appalled at how American communists, who had vigorously opposed Hitler, suddenly urged black Americans to refuse to be drafted into the military and even to refuse donating blood to the Red Cross.[8]

Rosser's jaw dropped when CPUSA flip-flopped yet again, becom-

ing militantly prowar the minute Hitler's Germany invaded Stalin's Soviet Union. All these things, said Rosser, "caused me to break with the
party."[9] He realized that CPUSA members were not loyal to America but
to the USSR. Millions of other black Americans agreed.

FRANK TAKES THE STAND

Louis Rosser spoke enthusiastically when called to testify before Congress. He was no longer a true believer. He refused to be hoodwinked
by false messiahs. He wanted the world to know about this betrayal of
black Americans by communism. He wanted Americans of all races to
know that members of the Communist Party were un-American; they
were pro-Soviet.

As for Frank Marshall Davis, he was of a different mind altogether.
When called to Capitol Hill to testify, he refused to condemn or even
admit his communist past—or say anything at all.

It was December 1956. Democrats controlled the U.S. Senate, and
included intense anticommunists like Senator John F. Kennedy (D-MA),
Senator Pat McCarran (D-NV), and, among others, Senator Thomas
Dodd (D-CT), father of recent-day Senator Chris Dodd (D-CT). Some
of the best work investigating pro-Soviet activity by American communists was done by the Senate Judiciary Committee, led by James Eastland
(D-MS), and including (at various points during the 1950s) Democrats
Pat McCarran, Thomas Dodd, Sam Ervin (D-NC), and Philip Hart
(D-MI), plus top Republicans like Everett Dirksen (R-L) and Arthur Wat-
kins (R-UT). Within the Judiciary Committee was the Senate Internal
Security Subcommittee. The 1956 Senate Judiciary Committee and Sen
ate Internal Security Subcommittee (Eighty-fourth Congress) were both
chaired by Senator Eastland. It was that subcommittee that on December
5–6, 1956, held continued hearings on the "Scope of Soviet Activity in the
United States," under which Frank Marshall Davis appeared to testify.[10]

Frank's testimony turned out to be very brief, consuming merely a
page and a half of text among thousands of pages from the overall hearings. He was questioned by Senator Watkins and by Chief Counsel Robert Morris.

Frank's attorney during his questioning was a woman named Harriet

Bouslog, who herself was a closet CPUSA member. Since 1943, Bouslog had been legal counsel for Harry Bridges's ILWU, serving both its Washington and Honolulu offices. Bouslog was also a member of communist fronts ranging from the National Lawyers Guild to Frank's Hawaii Civil Liberties Committee.[11] She, too, like all communist lawyers, was adept at invoking the American Founders' documents to defend communists and their concealed Soviet loyalties.

And with that, the questioning of Frank Marshall Davis began. It was December 5, 1956, high noon. Here is the official transcript of the exchange:

> **MR. MORRIS:** Give your name and address to the reporter, Mr. Davis.
>
> **MR. DAVIS:** Frank Marshall Davis, 47-388 Kam Highway.
>
> **MR. MORRIS:** Mr. Davis, when did you come to Honolulu?
>
> **MR. DAVIS:** In 1948.
>
> **MR. MORRIS:** 1948. Where were you born?
>
> **MR. DAVIS:** Arkansas City, Kansas.
>
> **MR. MORRIS:** What has been your education?
>
> **MR. DAVIS:** Let's see. Through high school and a year at Friends University.
>
> **MR. MORRIS:** Where is Friends University?
>
> **MR. DAVIS:** And at Kansas State College. This is at Manhattan, Kansas.
>
> **MR. MORRIS:** You are a columnist, are you not, for the Honolulu Record? (The witness consults with his attorney.)
>
> **SENATOR WATKINS:** Just a minute, Counsel. Did he ask you anything before you started to talk?
>
> **MRS. BOUSLOG:** Yes; he did, Senator.
>
> **SENATOR WATKINS:** I couldn't see his lips move.
>
> **MRS. BOUSLOG:** He had his back to me.
>
> **SENATOR WATKINS:** I have noticed the tendency, however, for counsel, not only in this hearing here but in the hearings on other days, before the witness could even open his mouth, to start to advise him. That amounts to what we call coaching the witness and it is not permitted in this committee. . . . Now, to

have an attorney present to advise a witness, in this hearing, is a
privilege that is granted. It is not a right.

MRS. BOUSLOG: I regard the fact that my client has the
constitutional right to counsel—

SENATOR WATKINS: Oh, certainly, but not to be coached as to the
testimony he shall give in the proceedings.

MRS. BOUSLOG: He turned to me and asked for my advice, and I
gave it to him.

SENATOR WATKINS: I have been watching this very closely, ever
since these hearings out here began, and obviously the witnesses
have asked for advice in many instances, but obviously the
witnesses never had time to make their requests for legal advice
before counsel has begun to give advice. I just warn you. That
is all.[12]

Senator Watkins's lack of patience with Frank's attorney was not
unjustified. In both Senate and House committees, legislators had
grown weary of attorneys they suspected or knew were closet members
of CPUSA. These communist lawyers had sworn an oath to a Marxist-
Leninist ideology headquartered in Moscow, which operated under a
"constitution" that was the antithesis of the U.S. Constitution. Three
years after this exchange, Congress released an entire report solely on
the phenomenon of communist lawyers and their subservience to the
international communist movement. Bouslog was one of the attorneys
flagged in that report.[13]

After this back-and-forth, attorney Morris took over from Senator
Watkins and continued the questioning of Frank:

MR. MORRIS: We have information, Mr. Davis—did you answer the
question, or did you invoke the privilege of the—

MR. DAVIS: No; I decline to answer that, on the basis of the Fifth
Amendment.

MR. MORRIS: We have information and evidence you were a
member of the faculty of the Abraham Lincoln School in
Chicago. Is that information accurate, Mr. Davis?

MR. DAVIS: I decline to answer that, also on the same grounds.

MR. MORRIS: Mr. Chairman, the Abraham Lincoln School was one of the Communist schools.

Are you a Communist now, Mr. Davis?

MR. DAVIS: Same answer.

MR. MORRIS: I have no further questions at this time, Senator. I ask that you order the witness to stand by.

SENATOR WATKINS: Stand by. . . .

MR. MORRIS: That concludes the testimony of Mr. Davis. . . .

SENATOR JOHNSTON: Thank you. Any other questions?

MR. MORRIS: No, Senator.

SENATOR JOHNSTON: There are no questions. The witness will be excused at this particular time.

MRS. BOUSLOG: Thank you, Senator.[14]

Frank Marshall Davis was off the hook, compliments of the Fifth Amendment of the U.S. Constitution. He had been saved from self-incrimination by the American Founding Fathers. Countless American communists loyal to Stalin were so protected. Had they been put on "trial" in Stalin's USSR, they would have never had such blessed protections; they would have been railroaded to Siberia or simply executed on the spot. At best, they might have been treated to a show trial.

Frank, to put it mildly, did not like this Democrat-run committee, and made his disapproval quite clear. The big question asked of Frank, "Are you a communist now, Mr. Davis?" was posed by Chief Counsel Morris. It elicited from Frank a mere "Same answer."[15]

That was to say: no answer.

The Senate nonetheless listed Frank as connected with several communist fronts: the Abraham Lincoln School, American Youth for Democracy, Chicago Committee for Spanish Freedom, Civil Rights Congress, League of American Writers, and the National Negro Congress.[16] The documentation of Frank's doings continued to stack up, with other congressional committees, including the Democrat-run House Committee on Un-American Activities, publicly printing, in both January 1957 and December 1961, a list of "communist" or "subversive" organizations, as compiled almost exclusively by attorney generals of Democratic presidents, and pursuant to law instituted through several presidential executive orders. Reading the list is like revisiting the stops along Frank's professional life from the 1940s through the 1950s.[17]

Among the various forms of documentation, the Senate Judiciary Committee published (in 1957) "Part 41-A, Appendix III," a subreport of its comprehensive investigation, "Scope of Soviet Activity in the United States." This subreport focused on subversive activities in Hawaii, the product of extended 1953–55 investigations by the Commission on Subversive Activities of the Territory of Hawaii. That report, on pages 2,698 and 2,801, listed Frank Marshall Davis as "an identified member of the Communist Party," as well as detailing Frank's work with "the Communist-line *Chicago Star*," the Communist Party–established *Honolulu Record*, and several of Frank's front groups.[18]

THE ANTI–JOE MCCARTHY

There is a fascinating coda to the story of Frank's testimony before the Senate Judiciary Committee.

The left today will want to frame the questioning of Frank as symptomatic of a 1950s-era McCarthyite witch-hunt; indeed, some liberal journalists and Obama biographers and other defenders have done precisely that. In truth, as noted, Frank's December 1956 testimony took place before a Senate committee run by Democrats. But even more interesting—and contrary to any possible claims of McCarthyism— is that the senator who directly questioned Frank was Arthur V. Watkins.

Why is that so interesting? It was Arthur Watkins, a Utah Republican, who spearheaded the very committee that pursued Senator Joe McCarthy.

In other words, Frank was hardly being questioned by McCarthyites. He was being questioned by arguably the nation's top anti-McCarthyite. It was Watkins who was the namesake of the 1954 Watkins Committee, the special Senate committee that censured Joe McCarthy. Watkins chaired the committee, and even had McCarthy expelled from the room during one heated confrontation. McCarthy personally denounced the Watkins Committee as an "unwitting handmaiden" (that is, dupes) of international communism.[19]

The work of the Watkins Committee, which included two months of hearings and deliberations, prompted the entire U.S. Senate on December 2, 1954, to vote to "condemn" McCarthy by a vote of sixty-seven to twenty-two. It was this move of censure that was the final straw in McCarthy's career, and arguably even his life—certainly his public life and influence. He died two and a half years later, a broken man.

That censure of McCarthy by Watkins came two years before Frank's testimony to Watkins. Watkins was hardly a McCarthyite.

Any modern-day Obama defender who attempts to portray Frank Marshall Davis's appearance before the Senate Judiciary Committee as victimization at the hands of McCarthy's witch-hunters is utterly ignorant of the facts. Joe McCarthy was not a member of that committee. By then, McCarthy was disgraced, his ultimate undoing coming at the hands of the Watkins Committee—*named for the Senator Watkins who questioned Frank Marshall Davis.*

And by the time the Senate in 1957 publicly declared Frank "an identified member of the Communist Party," Joe McCarthy was dead.

Also intriguing was the possible cooling effect that this appearance before the Senate had on Frank. In what seems an unlikely coincidence, immediately after returning from testifying in Washington, Frank wrote his most reasonable foreign-policy column in at least a decade and a half.

In the column, titled "An Atrocity Is An Atrocity," and published in the December 20, 1956, *Honolulu Record,* Frank juxtaposed the two violent militant excursions the world had just witnessed in Eastern Europe and the Middle East: The Soviets invaded Hungary while Israel, France, and Britain went to war with Egypt over the Suez Canal. Normally, one would expect Frank to somehow defend the Soviet indefensible, especially as there were CPUSA members who shamelessly did just that.

This time, however, Frank condemned the Soviet action. To be sure, he was not exactly harsh. But, to be fair, he did not give the Soviets the moral high ground. In both Hungary and the Suez, the aggressors were "equally murderous," said Frank, and "an atrocity is an atrocity"—"the French and the British were at least as murderous as the Russians."

One can pick at Frank's analysis, easily arguing the Soviet action was worse than the conflagration in the Suez. Suez, after all, was a battle among militaries; in Hungary, the Soviets mowed down unarmed freedom fighters by the thousands. For Frank Marshall Davis, however, this was progress.

16

Frank versus "the Gestapo"

FRANK MARSHALL DAVIS also attracted the attention of the FBI, which he referred to in his memoirs as "the J. Edgar Hoover Gestapo."[1] As an old man, an angry Frank could not restrain himself from continuing to characterize his well-deserved opponents as Nazis; old habits die hard. Frank portrayed his FBI investigators as motivated not by his pro-Soviet work but by an oppressive penchant to "harass" "those demanding democracy at home."[2]

Frank said he first drew the FBI's notice way back in 1937 "when I joined with others in speaking my mind," specifically via his involvement with the League of American Writers. He figured that "a huge dossier" was "compiled on me because of my activities during World War II," and was "confident this dossier arrived [in Hawaii] as soon as I did."[3] Frank was sure the FBI had Honolulu agents watching his every move.

Frank never had access to what we have now; namely, his six-hundred-plus-page FBI file, which was only recently declassified. That file is tremendously revealing and includes evidence that the FBI was indeed watching his every move. The FBI began watching him not in 1937 but during World War II; not when he was speaking his mind and "demanding democracy" but when he joined CPUSA. The monitoring stepped up when Frank moved to Hawaii.

FRANK AND THE SECURITY INDEX

Among the most sensational assertions in the FBI file are claims that Frank, in Hawaii, had been observed repeatedly photographing shorelines with a telescopic lens. This is contained in an August 15, 1962, report filed by an FBI agent listed as "Mr. Petit," with a file number of 100-5082.

The alleged incident took place the first full year of Frank's move to Hawaii. The source was an informant who witnessed Frank at Manners Beach on September 17, 1949, "photographing large sections of the coastline with a camera containing a telescopic lens." The informant (in the words of the FBI report) "stated that DAVIS spent much of his time in this activity. He said this was the third different occasion DAVIS had been observed photographing shorelines and beachfronts. Informant advised that it did not appear he was photographing any particular objects."

What should we make of this?

The implication, which has been picked up by conservative commentators, particularly Cliff Kincaid, Trevor Loudon, and Jack Cashill, is that Frank might have been photographing shorelines and beachfronts "possibly for intelligence purposes" (as Loudon puts it).[4] As Kincaid says, "This information suggests the possibility of espionage or some other form of illegal activity."[5]

Frank's defenders will vehemently disagree, pointing to his lifelong interest in photography—albeit usually photographs of objects or nude women. And they certainly have a valid point. Frank was fascinated by photography. He had long been a photographer. Why wouldn't he want to take pictures of the gorgeous Hawaiian beaches? This is a perfectly reasonable assumption.

That said, once we combine Frank's expertise and interest in photography, his expertise and interest in Soviet communism, his formal

membership in CPUSA (which made him an immediate target for Soviet recruitment), his long association with men who traveled to and
served the USSR (some as actual Soviet agents), his paid work for Harry
Bridges's ILWU, and much more, he became a natural recruit to do a
job like photograph shorelines for foreign intelligence, especially as he
already wrote propaganda for the Soviet line.

The FBI had to err on the side of caution. The agency leaned toward
a negative interpretation of Frank's photographic fascination with Hawaiian shorelines. The first page of Mr. Pettit's August 15, 1962, report
noted that Frank's name "is being retained on the Security Index at this
time."

To be listed on the federal government's Security Index meant that
one was deemed dangerous to national security and could be detained
or arrested in the event of a national emergency. Trevor Loudon puts
it more bluntly: "This meant Davis was marked for immediate arrest
should war break out between the United States and the Soviet Union;
an honor reserved for the most dangerous subversives."[6]

This is obviously a matter of monumental importance in the career
of Frank Marshall Davis. And it was not a onetime thing. It continued
over years. Frank's continued placement and recertification on the Security Index is the most salient thread (along with his Party membership) in his FBI file. It dated back to at least 1951, as evidenced by a
January 4, 1952, document in his file.

FRANK AND THE AGENT

Juxtaposing Frank's FBI file with his memoirs poses some intriguing
subplots. In one section of his memoirs, Frank described an encounter
he had with FBI agents in Honolulu. He did not share the date.

Frank was leaving a shop in a neighborhood away from downtown
Honolulu. He was approached by a man who had parked and waited for
him behind his station wagon. The man showed Frank his FBI credentials and asked to talk. "My first reaction was to tell him to go to hell,"
said Frank. On second thought, Frank agreed to meet in a public park
at noon one day.[7]

When Frank arrived, the man greeted him, along with another agent who clutched a briefcase throughout the conversation. Frank figured the briefcase probably contained a small tape recorder. The conversation was carried on amicably, with Frank impressed that they parted "without visible rancor." They also parted without much information.

The agent knew about Frank's Party membership and activities, but Frank was giving away nothing. "I know you're not a member of the Communist Party now," the agent said, apparently with evidence Frank had by then left CPUSA—though, in truth, Frank's membership would have ceased because the Hawaiian branch of the Party disbanded and went underground. The agent inquired: "Would you mind telling me why you decided to quit?"[8]

It was the second time the agent had tried that approach. "Listen," Frank reiterated, "I've never told you I ever was a member. How, then, can I tell you I quit? Really now, that doesn't make sense."[9]

It was an obviously well-rehearsed response. Frank did not deny that he was a Party member. He simply told the agent he never told him he was a member.

Here was Frank, writing his memoirs, long after the fact, and he still was not budging. Frank Marshall Davis, so long as he lived, would not give his critics the satisfaction of a confession.

Apparently, however, Frank did say a little more than what he recalled in his memoirs. We know this because the episode was carefully recorded in his FBI file.

According to the FBI's report, Frank had been contacted on August 2, 1963, at his car on Waikamilo Road. Frank agreed to set up an appointment. They met three weeks later, on August 26, at Kapiolani Park, Honolulu. The agents' names were Robert F. Ryan and Leo S. Brenneisen, the latter of whom had followed Frank for quite some time. The account prepared by Brenneisen squares with Frank's account, with Frank telling the agents (in the words of the report) that "little could be gained from the interview." Asked if he was a Party member, Frank told the agents "that as far as he knew, there was no Communist Party in existence in Hawaii."

Frank was asked "why and when he had broken with the Communist Party." According to the report, "DAVIS then went on at length to state that he had never gone on record as having been a member of the Communist Party, and he, therefore, did not see what could be gained by answering that question."

Notably, the FBI report reveals that Frank did declare that the Communist Party in Hawaii had gone "out of existence since 1955 or 1956." Other records in the FBI file (and elsewhere, including congressional investigations) agree, with some sources suggesting the Hawaiian Party went underground in 1952, when Congress began to hotly pursue local communist organizers. The death knell would have come by 1956, when Nikita Khrushchev's revelations of Stalin's "crimes" and "terror" and "personality cult" devastated Party members from New York all the way to Hawaii.

So the best Frank would admit to the agents that August day in 1963 was that the Hawaiian Party had broken up. As Agent Brenneisen entered in a separate summary page of Frank's FBI file, "DAVIS has always been vociferous in criticism of Government prosecution of Communists, and there appears to be no likelihood he might cooperate with the FBI."[10]

None, indeed. Frank Marshall Davis would go to his grave without telling the feds a damned thing.

Finally, Frank's FBI file shows another piece of remarkable Party information. As the Hawaiian Communist Party went underground, its members infiltrated the Democratic Party, the start of a long march by American communists. This tactic coincided with the collapse of Henry Wallace's Progressive Party.

The comrades would continue to masquerade as "progressives," except this time from within the Democratic Party. This arguably helped foster a tectonic shift within the Democratic Party, moving it away from the party of JFK, Harry Truman, and (at one time) even Ronald Reagan, to the party of Ted Kennedy, Nancy Pelosi, and Barack Obama.

The FBI file reported details from an informant, provided in April 1950, stating that "members of the subversive element in Honolulu were concentrating their efforts on infiltration of the Democratic Party through control of Precinct Clubs and organizations." These communist subversives were pushing "their candidates in these Precinct Club elections." According to the informant, on April 6, 1950, one such candidate, Frank Marshall Davis, was elected "assistant secretary and delegate" to the Territorial Democratic Convention in his particular Precinct Club—the Third Precinct of the Fifth District. Frank, in fact, attended that convention on April 30, 1950.

The Reds' infiltration and internal subversion of the Democratic Party were on.

And it would be as a "Democrat" that Frank would one day influence a future Democratic Party president.

17

American Committee for Protection of Foreign Born

REGARDLESS OF THE status of the Hawaiian branch of the Communist Party, Frank Marshall Davis remained engaged in radical politics.

Frank also suffered serious personal turmoil when he and Helen divorced in 1970, after twenty-four years of marriage and five children together—four daughters and a son. They had struggled for a long time. Frank's FBI file includes claims that Frank once intended to divorce Helen as far back as May 1957.[1]

The FBI file also records something quite striking related to Frank's continued radicalism throughout the 1970s; it documents his involvement with a notorious communist front, the American Committee for Protection of Foreign Born (ACPFB). The file makes several references to Frank's membership in ACPFB—or sponsorship of events—dating back to at least 1959.

ACPFB AGITATORS

ACPFB's radicalism predates Frank's. The group had been so extreme in the 1930s that the Democratic Congress's "Investigation of Un-American Propaganda Activities in the United States" (published in 1944) devoted a lengthy fifteen-page section just to ACPFB, atop innumerable added references elsewhere.[2] Key members that far back included Langston Hughes and Paul Robeson, plus the usual assemblage of duped liberals/progressives, ranging from the thoughtful theologian Reinhold Niebuhr, to the great Orson Welles, to famed movie actor Edward G. Robinson, who later sheepishly admitted, "I was duped and used. I was lied to. . . . The Reds made a sucker out of me."[3] Frank never made any such admission.

As the congressional report noted, ACPFB "was founded by the Communist Party in order to exploit racial divisions in the United States for its own revolutionary purposes." From the outset, it had been closely linked to International Labor Defense. The founding of ACPFB came well before ILD took up Scottsboro, with seeds dating to at least 1923 and Charles Ruthenberg, founder of the American Communist Party.[4]

The primary intention of ACPFB (concealed from the general public) was to protect and defend foreign communists who came to America and agitated for the Comintern. The group's explicitly Soviet goal was to aid and enable agitprop artists to operate inside the United States.[5] The core objective was to prevent deportation of these foreign-born communists living in America. One such figure was German communist Gerhart Eisler, who became a major CPUSA campaign cause, and whose name was omnipresent throughout Frank's *Chicago Star*. Another was the Australian-born Harry Bridges, whose ILWU buttered Frank's bread when he arrived on the island and wrote for the ILWU-controlled *Honolulu Record*.

Few communist fronts so directly served Soviet interests. Beyond this core mission defending foreign communists and Comintern operatives, ACPFB expanded into all sorts of added agitation and propaganda, especially those that were race-based.

No other front so perfectly matched Frank's interests and public work. ACPFB's modus operandi was to polarize Americans along racial lines in order to advance the Soviet agenda. Few American communists did this as vigorously and viciously as Frank Marshall Davis, never hesitating to denounce anticommunists—from Harry Truman to Tom Clark—as warmongering, bomb-dropping, white-hooded racists. Not coincidentally, ACPFB was designated as a subversive group by the office of President Truman's attorney general, Tom Clark, pursuant to Executive Order 10450.

It is also no surprise that ACPFB remained the one group Frank embraced through the final stages of his life.

FRANK AND THE ACPFB

It is not clear exactly when Frank joined the New York–based ACPFB, though, as noted, his FBI file reveals an association back to at least the 1950s. His membership in the 1970s is unmistakable: Frank's name is listed on the group's letterhead.[6]

In fact, the names on the ACPFB letterhead, from fellow travelers to liberal/progressive dupes to hard-core Party members, read like a Who's Who of Congress's "Investigation of Un-American Propaganda Activities in the United States," including the ubiquitous Hugh DeLacy, Jerome Davis, James Dombrowski, Scott Nearing, and, among others, Hollywood screenwriter Albert Maltz.[7] Names on the letterhead with special relevance to this book or modern politics include Harriet Bouslog, the ILWU/Hawaiian attorney who defended Frank before the Senate Judiciary Committee; the Reverend William Howard Melish; Professor Curtis D. MacDougall; Henry Foner; and George W. Crockett, Jr.[8]

Among these names, a few merit special attention:

In the mid-1940s, Hugh DeLacy had been elected to Congress as a Democratic member from Washington State, specifically the Seattle area. DeLacy was later identified by John Abt as one of two closet CPUSA members successfully elected to Congress—the other being Minnesota congressman Johnny Bernard, who, incidentally, taught with Frank at the Abraham Lincoln School.[9] (Abt, for the record, was the celebrated attorney and activist, and a member of the "Ware cell" within FDR's AAA, along with Soviet agents Lee Pressman and Charles Kramer.[10]) To repeat: Hugh DeLacy was identified as a communist congressman. According to Abt, DeLacy was a CPUSA member while he was a member of Congress.[11]

DeLacy and Frank were old comrades. They likely first met when DeLacy was elected a national officer of the American Peace Mobilization in Chicago on September 2, 1940—along with Paul Robeson, Langston Hughes, Richard Wright, and liberal/progressive dupes like Carl Sandburg.[12] DeLacy had been a member of every imaginable leftist front group, from ILD, to the National Council of American Soviet Friendship, to the Harry Bridges Defense Committee, to the Citizens Committee to Free Earl Browder.[13] He was also a major union director, helping organize the American Federation of Teachers.

None of this extraordinary work was noted in DeLacy's August 1986 obituary in the *New York Times*. The *Times* described DeLacy as a "Progressive Party activist."[14]

Joining DeLacy at ACPFB, and in Congress, was George Crockett, listed on the ACPFB letterhead as "Judge George W. Crockett, Jr." This is the same George W. Crockett, Jr., who, in November 1980, would be elected to the U.S. House of Representatives as a Democratic congressman from Detroit, Michigan. In Congress, he became an outspoken member of the Congressional Black Caucus.

Crockett graduated from Morehouse College in 1931, precisely when Frank was at the *Atlanta Daily World* and plugged the Morehouse appearance of Langston Hughes. If Frank had not by chance met the young Crockett then, he later knew of Crockett's legal work in 1949 defending American communists Ben Davis, Jr., Gus Hall, Eugene Dennis, and others on trial for violation of the Smith Act. Frank wrote a *Honolulu Record* column cheering Crockett and the eleven accused communists he defended.[15] Crockett became national vice president of the procommunist National Lawyers Guild.

Upon his death in September 1997, the *New York Times* hailed Crockett as a "civil rights crusader" and "civil rights warrior" who battled for "racial justice" and who "had no interest in communism"—even though Crockett (as the *Times* grudgingly acknowledged) described the Communist Party as "the conscience of America." Congressman Crockett, the *Times* lamented, had suffered "hysterical denunciations from right-wing groups."[16]

Also on the ACPFB letterhead was Henry Foner. Henry was the uncle of Eric Foner, the Columbia University professor and president of the American Historical Association who, after 9/11, said of President George W. Bush, "I'm not sure which is more frightening: the horror that engulfed New York City or the apocalyptic rhetoric emanating daily from the White House."[17] When the American Council of Trustees criticized Eric Foner for this remark, the Columbia historian knew whom to blame: Joe McCarthy. The criticism smacked of "McCarthyism," explained Foner in a cover story for *The Progressive*. He was a victim of "blacklisting," and predicted "loyalty oaths" just around the dark corner.[18]

(One person not worthy of blacklisting, in Eric Foner's view, is Iranian madman Mahmoud Ahmadinejad. When Columbia's president, Lee Bollinger, blasted Ahmadinejad before his speaking at the university in September 2007, Foner joined the faculty in a "statement of concern" over the "strident tone" of Bollinger's remarks. It smacked of the tone of "the Bush administration's war in Iraq."[19])

Joining Henry Foner in archived ACPFB documents was his brother, Moe Foner.[20] Both Henry and Moe were listed in ACPFB documents as union heads, with Henry the president of the Fur, Leather, and Machine (FLM) Workers Union.[21]

ACPFB's agitators engaged in many radical-left campaigns in the 1970s. A popular one was to frame the U.S. Internal Security Act as a congressional attempt to erect "concentration camps" in America. "Such camps," charged ACPFB literature, with dramatic cartoon renditions, "are already provided for in the McCarran Internal Security Act of 1950."

This act had been named for Senator Pat McCarran, an intensely anticommunist Roman Catholic Democrat from Nevada. It required CPUSA and affiliated subversive front groups to register with the Office of the Attorney General, among other steps. Its constitutionality was challenged. The American left protested the act vigorously, with communists leading the way among liberals/progressives. McCarran often joined forces with another steadfast anticommunist Democrat, Pennsylvania congressman Francis Walter, longtime head of the House Committee on Un-American Activities, whom the Left today denounces as "reactionary and racist."[22]

Senator McCarran died in 1954. For ACPFB, however, the Internal Security Act remained a vampire ready to rise from the grave at any moment. Under its black cape was the ultimate horror: the threat of deportation of foreign-born communists.

ACPFB cast the Internal Security Act as a reincarnation of no less than Nazism itself. ACPFB envisioned a vast sea of concentration camps—akin only to *Nazi* concentration camps, with Soviet camps never mentioned—installed nationwide to detain "dark-skinned persons."[23] ACPFB portrayed the act not as anticommunist and anti-Soviet but as anti-immigrant and antiminority. At this particular time, ACPFB latched on to Haitian refugees to further conceal its procommunist mission.

As usual, the self-described "progressives" at ACPFB succeeded in drawing the Religious Left from dependable national groups like the National Council of Churches to small local congregations like the Friendship Baptist Church in Miami, Florida.[24]

ABE FEINGLASS

A separate book could be written simply on the names that shared the ACPFB letterhead with Frank Marshall Davis. To cite just one added example, consider Abe Feinglass.

Frank would have worked with Abe back in Chicago. Abe was prominent at the extremely busy Illinois State Office of ILD, side by side with Frank's good friend William Patterson. He was a member of the State Advisory Board of the Illinois chapter of ILD, with loyalties dating back to the Scottsboro campaign.

Abe was flagged by Congress for his vocal public efforts as a vigilant defender of CPUSA kingpin Earl Browder. He was also noticed for his active role in Chicago events organized by the American Peace Mobilization. For Abe, unlike Frank, that "peace mobilization" involvement was a worse sin given that he was Jewish. Many Jewish-American communists bolted Stalin with the signing of the Hitler-Stalin Pact, which precipitated World War II and Hitler's genocide against Jews.[25]

Abe was present at Chicago's La Salle Hotel on June 29, 1940, for a noontime event, "A Call to the People of Chicago to Keep America Out of the War." The event was organized by the Chicago Peace Congress, a communist front whose chief members included William Patterson, Herbert March of the Packing-House Workers Organizing Committee, and Ira Latimer, Frank's pal at the Chicago Civil Liberties Committee. This was, in essence, a preliminary to the launching of the American Peace Mobilization in Chicago a few months later. Sadly, this Hitler-appeasing event included several Jewish leaders among the nearly fifty sponsors. At this time, Abe was international vice president of the CIO's Fur, Leather, and Machine Workers Union—later headed by Henry Foner.[26]

The comrades at the *Daily Worker* happily promoted the June 1940 "peace" conference. The CPUSA organ framed the conference not as motivated by an allegiance to Stalin but as a protest "to the Wall Street–Washington war makers."[27] It was a joint cabal between Wall Street and Roosevelt.

At ILD's Illinois office, Abe and William Patterson and crew demanded an end to the "Dies Committee"—that is, Democratic congressman Martin Dies's House Committee on Un-American Activities. The group blasted "reactionary Democratic and tory Republicans" manipulated by the greedy "hands of Wall Street" in order "to smear red-paint on every individual and group who is working for *progress* [emphasis added] in America."[28]

Again: the classic communist gambit to mask pro-Soviet ambitions under the banner of American progressivism.

ABE AND FRANK AND CANTER—
AND JOHN KERRY AND DAVID AXELROD

The winding path of Abe Feinglass's comings and goings and interminable involvement with innumerable communist fronts could be threaded throughout this book, but a couple have special relevance for modern politics.

Feinglass, suspected by some as a potential Soviet agent of influence,[29] was active in Vietnam protests organized by Mobe, New Mobe, and other radical organizations. These rallies were penetrated and often organized by communist ringleaders, some with close personal connection to the KGB, Vietcong, Communist Bloc, and other international plotters. Omnipresent at these and related rallies, from the Columbia University shutdown to the Days of Rage in Chicago to the sabotaging of the 1968 Democratic National Convention and more, were sixties revolutionaries who later re-emerged in 2008 as Progressives for Obama: Tom Hayden, Jane Fonda, Mark Rudd, Carl Davidson, Thorne Dreyer, Daniel Ellsberg, Richard Flacks, John McAuliff, Jay Schaffner, and more. They also included top pro-Obama "progressives" like Bill Ayers and Bernardine Dohrn. Among them, Tom Hayden, in an amazing irony, wrote both the founding Port Huron manifesto for Students for a Democratic Society (SDS) in 1962 and also the founding manifesto for Progressives for Obama in 2008.[30]

Abe Feinglass was older than the sixties flower children, but he was more than supportive of their antiwar (and often anti-American) activities.

In one notable episode, flagged recently by several bloggers, one can view a photo of Feinglass standing to the left of John Kerry, future Democratic presidential nominee, as Kerry addressed the People's Coalition for Peace & Justice Demonstration on April 24, 1971—another event widely suspected of having KGB fingerprints.[31] This was one of the infamous moments of John Kerry, a Vietnam vet, undermining the war effort, which, when resurfacing in 2004, arguably undermined his bid for the presidency.[32]

In the 1940s, Abe had been a common face in the pages of Frank's *Chicago Star*. Among other instances, he was pictured on the *Star*'s cover at an April 1947 rally and also addressing ten thousand union brothers at the 1948 May Day rally at Union Park.[33] Abe was a mainstay through the literal final issue of the *Star*, where his name appeared among the stockholders of the Progressive Publishing Co. that purchased the *Star* and renamed it the *Illinois Standard*.[34]

In fact, that list of stockholders, officers, and owners of the *Star*-turned-*Standard*, published in the September 4, 1948, issue, which billed the *Illinois Standard* as a "liberal" and "progressive" newspaper, had many interesting names.[35] Among them was Curtis D. MacDougall, also a member of ACPFB, and the notable Harry Canter.

Recall that Harry Canter and his son, David, were active in Chicago left-wing politics in the 1940s—fresh from returning from Moscow, where Harry had a full-time position for the Soviet government. The Canters' work included the Packinghouse Workers Union, where they would have met Abe Feinglass, who, among his many hats in the movement, also headed the communist-controlled Amalgamated Meatcutters and Butcherworkmen's Union. Recall, of course, that Frank Marshall Davis and Vernon Jarrett both worked for the communist-controlled Citizens' Committee to Aid Packing-House Workers.

Harry and David Canter remained active in Chicago newspapers and radical politics. David would mentor David Axelrod, who would become President Barack Obama's top political advisor, whose White House influence was rivaled only by that of Valerie Jarrett, daughter-in-law of Vernon Jarrett.

Once again, today's political family at 1600 Pennsylvania Avenue, from Barack Obama to Valerie Jarrett to David Axelrod, can be traced back to the political family of Chicago in the 1940s, from Frank Marshall Davis to Vernon Jarrett to Robert Taylor to Abe Feinglass to the Canters and on and on. The names are many, and hard to keep track of, but they are all eerily connected.

That White House reunion, however, would come later, in November 2008. What is most important about Frank's ACPFB activity is that it occurred as late as the 1970s, precisely when he met a young man named Barack Obama.

18

When Frank Met Obama

AS FRANK PERSISTED in his political extremism, he came into contact with a family that provided a most unexpected rendezvous with history.

A decade earlier, a family of three had relocated to Hawaii from Washington State, specifically, the Seattle–Mercer Island area. Just like Frank, they originally hailed from Kansas. They were Stanley and Madelyn Dunham and their teenage daughter, Stanley Ann—named after her father. The politics of the Dunhams were very much anchored on the left, especially those of Stanley, whose FBI files have been reportedly destroyed.[1]

The family moved to Hawaii shortly after Ann graduated from high school in June 1960. That fall, Ann enrolled at the University of Hawaii. There she met a twentysomething Kenyan named Barack Obama, whose politics were rooted on the socialist/communist left.[2] Barack was the first African student at the University of Hawaii, an elite member of the first airlift of Kenyan students brought to study at American universities through a program launched by Kenya's Tom Mboya, a mentor to the senior Obama.[3]

In a jarring circumstance, Ann and Barack met in a Russian language class. Sympathetic liberal biographers have predictably shrugged off the interest in Russian as simply a charming curiosity about a nation dominating headlines. No doubt, though, their choice of study was at least in part a reflection of political interests.[4] As one sympathetic biographer, Sally Jacobs, could not help but note, "Obama had an abiding interest in the Soviet Union."[5]

Jacobs has published the preeminent biographical work on the senior Obama. Among those she quotes is Naranhkiri Tith—a prominent native of Cambodia. Tith was a classmate of Barack at the University of Hawaii and came to know him well. The two had frequent, spirited debates about many subjects, including communism, an ideology that would ravage Tith's native land, where the killing fields of Pol Pot's Khmer Rouge slaughtered 1 to 2 million (or more) out of a population of 5 to 7 million in just four years. An economics major, Tith was vehemently anticommunist.

"Obama and I were on opposite poles," says Tith, who became a professor in international economics at the prestigious Paul H. Nitze School of Advanced International Studies at Johns Hopkins University. "I did not believe communism could save the world. It was too good to be true and I gave examples of what I had seen. Obama senior was the opposite. He was always glorying about how communism had liberated Africa and Cuba. He had no idea what communism was all about. For him, communism was going to save the world. Capitalism was going to collapse."[6]

In his Introductory Russian class that fall of 1960, the senior Obama found a receptive audience in Ann Dunham. An atheist with the radical-left politics to match his own, Dunham questioned the American way. As Sally Jacobs put it, Dunham was given to inquiries like: "What was so good about democracy? What's so bad about communism? And why was capitalism so great?"[7]

Ann Dunham and the senior Barack Obama were politically and romantically compatible. Frank Marshall Davis would not meet their child for another decade, but one wonders if he encountered Barack senior earlier, possibly through mutual political circles.

To cite just one possibility, on May 13, 1962, Barack senior spoke at a Mother's Day "peace rally" at Honolulu's Ala Moana Park. The senior Obama urged a reduction in U.S. military spending—precisely as the Soviet Union was installing nuclear missiles in Cuba. Joining Obama at the rally were Frank's friend Jack Hall and other ILWU organizers. So proud is the ILWU of this piece of history that photos of the senior Obama at the rally are today posted at the website of Hawaii's ILWU local 142.[8]

It is very possible that Obama senior would have rubbed shoulders with Frank through some ILWU-backed event. More than that, Frank, in his memoirs, made a passing comment on the presence of African exchange students at the University of Hawaii, some of whom (in Frank's words) "wreaked havoc among co-eds at the university." Frank shared this observation with his usual chest-thumping, admiring the "local studs" who were "frantic to bed a soul sister" or some "lush" "local dolls." Frank even pointed to a "student from Kenya" who "split leaving two pregnant blondes."[9]

Ann Dunham was not blonde, but some observers have understandably wondered whether this particular characterization might apply to Barack Obama senior, who, at least, fits Frank's profile of a Kenyan/ African exchange student who met and impregnated a university girl.[10] And if Frank did not meet the senior Obama directly, he certainly would have heard all about him later from the Dunhams.

Those who met Barack senior described him in ways that would have struck a chord with Frank, right down to the sound of his voice and the tenor of his politics. In the words of Janny Scott, Ann Dunham biographer, Barack senior's "booming baritone brought to mind Paul Robeson."[11]

Robeson, oddly, offers another intriguing connection, or notable degree of separation: In the 1930s, Robeson met Jomo Kenyatta, the founder of the Kenyan nation, and a giant in the life of Barack senior. Robeson and Kenyatta met in England, becoming not only good friends but roommates, sharing a flat in London.[12] Kenyatta likewise spent time in the USSR; he studied economics at Moscow's "Stalin Communist University" for two years beginning in 1933—with the Comintern furnishing and paying for his housing.[13] Later in London, he was defended by the same attorney who defended Gerhart Eisler—whose cause Frank and the *Chicago Star* and ACPFB championed. In an April 1953 profile, the *New York Times* referred to Kenyatta as a "Soviet-trained terrorist."[14] Under Kenyatta's leadership, some Kenyans went to Moscow's Patrice Lumumba University for training—the favored school of William Patterson.[15]

Kenyatta's career was no mystery to the son of Ann Dunham and Barack senior. In his memoirs, *Dreams from My Father*, the junior Barack Obama mentioned Kenyatta at least a dozen times, almost always in relation to his father.[16]

FRANK IN *DREAMS FROM MY FATHER*

The long, winding roads and uneven, interconnected paths in the lives of Frank Marshall Davis and Barack Obama are varied and complex—but rarely irrelevant.

So, with this background, we come to the critical moment in this history, and the central questions: When and why and how did Frank Marshall Davis eventually come into the life of the young Obama, and what was the nature of that relationship?

Before examining the testimony and research of others, we first should consider Obama's own accounting of that relationship, which he provided at length in his bestseller, *Dreams from My Father*, originally published in 1995.[17]

Given what we now know about Frank, Obama was wise avoiding the use of Frank's full name anywhere in his book, which happens to not include an index. Obama, however, could not expunge Frank altogether. He could not have been so dishonest and disrespectful as to not include Frank in the recounting of his life, even as Obama was no doubt well aware of Frank's problematic political past. That admission from Obama seems obvious in *Dreams from My Father*, where he talks at length of "Frank." It is here, in *Dreams*, that we can glean more about Obama and Frank than from any other source.

Frank first appears in Chapter 4. Significantly, Obama set up Frank's entrance with a telling discussion on the lack of a black male role model in his life:

Away from my mother, away from my grandparents, I was engaged
in a fitful interior struggle. I was trying to raise myself to be a black
man in America, and beyond the given of my appearance, no one
around me seemed to know exactly what that meant.

My father's letters provided few clues. They would arrive sporadically. . . . From time to time he would include advice, usually in the
form of aphorisms I didn't quite understand. . . . [H]is letters would
find their way into the closet.[18]

Longing and searching for role models, Obama noted that his
grandfather had a number of black male friends, mostly poker and
bridge partners. He would let "Gramps" drag him along to some of their
card games. "Whenever they saw me they would give me a jovial slap on
the back and ask how my mother was doing," recalled Obama. Once it
was time to play, however, these men "wouldn't say another word except
to complain to their partner about a bid."

And yet, said Obama, "There was one exception, a poet named Frank
who lived in a dilapidated house in a run-down section of Waikiki." Frank
stood apart from Obama's grandfather's black male friends. None of
those friends had given Obama much, if any, attention—nary a word.
Frank, we are told, was different.

In his memoir, Obama introduced Frank by pointing to a void that
Frank could fill. He was struggling to find his place, and to find someone to guide him. He was not physically "away" from his mother and
grandparents, but he was disconnected, "trying to raise" himself. He was
mired in an "interior struggle," particularly as a "black man in America." In that struggle, he had no father figure; he had only his biological
father's letters, which did not help at all. The letters offered some advice, some aphorisms, but were deep-sixed in the closet.

All of that prefaces Frank's arrival. Obama continued the narrative,
describing Frank:

He [Frank] had enjoyed some modest notoriety once, was a contemporary of Richard Wright and Langston Hughes during his years in
Chicago—Gramps once showed me some of his work anthologized

in a book of black poetry. But by the time I met Frank he must have been pushing eighty, with a big, dewlapped face and an ill-kempt gray Afro that made him look like an old, shaggy-maned lion. He would read us his poetry whenever we stopped by his house, sharing whiskey with Gramps out of an emptied jelly jar. As the night wore on, the two of them would solicit my help in composing dirty limericks. Eventually, the conversation would turn to laments about women.[19]

Women will "drive you to drink," Frank told Obama, and "drive you into your grave."

The young boy was intrigued by the old man, by his knowledge, his experiences. When he left Frank's house, Obama felt different. "I was intrigued by old Frank, with his books and whiskey breath and the hint of hard-earned knowledge behind the hooded eyes," wrote Obama. "The visits to his house always left me feeling vaguely uncomfortable, though, as if I were witnessing some complicated, unspoken transaction between the two men, a transaction I couldn't fully understand."

Obama admitted, cautiously, to knowing that Frank "had enjoyed some modest notoriety once." What was that notoriety? Obama answered in the same sentence, when he cited none other than the Chicago influences of Richard Wright and Langston Hughes, who, as Obama surely knew, were both well-known black communists. Also, Obama's grandfather was clearly familiar with Frank, perhaps even owning one of Frank's books on poetry.

Frank read some of that poetry to Obama and his grandfather. Obama's account of those readings suggests repeated visits that were not short, extending well into the evenings. "He would read us his poetry whenever we stopped by his house," recalled Obama. He did this "as the night wore on."

Of course, for Frank, that poetry, like his writings, could be quite political.

Obama carefully avoided any mention of discussion of politics and history, no doubt for the same reason he avoided mentioning Frank's full name. But it would be naïve to think there was never any discussion of politics and history, or that Obama would be unaware of Frank's highly political history, especially as Frank and Stanley Dunham continued to pour down the whiskey.

In fact, as Obama related, there were "books," and there was also "hard-earned knowledge," which is an interesting phrase, surely signifying more than knowledge of women and dirty limericks. The knowledge Frank had long shared in his writings was political, with a lot of knowledge of communism, the Communist Party, the Soviet position, and his advocacy thereof.

Obama was "intrigued" by Frank, who did not ignore him, unlike Stanley Dunham's other older black male friends. Frank talked to Obama, over extended "visits" (plural) and evenings, sharing his knowledge, and Obama listened. He was different from the other older gentlemen, and worth Obama's time; indeed, so much so that Frank stuck with Obama years later, in the future president's memoirs.

So worthy was Frank of Obama's time and mind that Obama returned to him, both in real time as a young man in Hawaii and eleven pages later in *Dreams*. Though his precise age at this stage in his narrative is unclear, Obama was old enough to drive a car.

Obama had not seen Frank in a while—three years, to be exact—though neither had any trouble immediately recognizing the other. Obama had continued to struggle and search, which brought him struggling and searching for Frank. Obama was prompted by an unsettling exchange with his grandparents, with his grandmother apparently bothered by the fact that an aggressive panhandler was not merely aggressive, but black. Obama sought Frank for answers:

> That night, I drove into Waikiki, past the bright-lit hotels and down toward the Ala-Wai Canal. It took me a while to recognize the house, with its wobbly porch and low-pitched roof. Inside, the light was on, and I could see Frank sitting in his overstuffed chair, a book of poetry in his lap, his reading glasses slipping down his nose. I sat in the car, watching him for a time, then finally got out and tapped on the door. The old man barely looked up as he rose to undo the latch.

Frank asked the teenager if he wanted a drink. Obama nodded and watched Frank grab a bottle of whiskey and two cups. Obama told Frank about the incident with his grandparents and the panhandler:

I told Frank some of what had happened. He nodded and poured us each a shot. "Funny cat, your grandfather," he said. "You know we grew up maybe fifty miles apart?"

I shook my head.

"We sure did. Both of us lived near Wichita. We didn't know each other, of course. I was long gone by the time he was old enough to remember anything. I might have seen some of his people, though. Might've passed 'em on the street. If I did, I would've had to step off the sidewalk to give 'em room. . . .

Obama reached for the bottle of whiskey, pouring himself some more, as Frank's eyes slowly closed while leaning against his chair. "You can't blame Stan for what he is," said Frank quietly. "He's basically a good man." The conversation continued:

Frank opened his eyes. "What I'm trying to tell you is, your grandma's right to be scared. She's at least as right as Stanley is. She understands that black people have a reason to hate. That's just how it is. For your sake, I wish it were otherwise. But it's not. So you might as well get used to it."

Frank closed his eyes again. His breathing slowed until he seemed to be asleep. I thought about waking him, then decided against it and walked back to the car. The earth shook under my feet, ready to crack open at any moment. I stopped, trying to steady myself, and knew for the first time that I was utterly alone.[20]

Here, Obama was counting on Frank. He left unfulfilled, which is not to say Frank did not deliver. Quite the contrary, what Frank leveled was a sobering punch to the gut. Obama never forgot the exchange, and it sunk firmly enough to endure in his memoirs.

If Obama had earlier felt disconnected, "away" from his white mother and grandparents, now he felt even more so. And, even as he left and the aging communist passed out in his overstuffed chair, he could now identify with Frank more than ever. Frank left a lasting impression that brought Obama closer to him than to his grandfather, the only other person who might have been considered a mentor.

With that, Obama ended Chapter 4 of his memoirs, though he returned to Frank's counsel and understanding again and again. When writing about Frank, Obama biographers, like David Remnick, curiously stick mainly to this particular passage, without proceeding on.

In fact, Frank's influence on Obama was far from over, as Obama returned to "Frank" eleven times in the remaining pages of his memoir, with scattered meaningful references throughout the remaining text. Frank remained a thread in the life and mind of Obama.

The next mention of Frank in *Dreams* came from Obama's college years, specifically fall 1979 at Occidental College in Los Angeles. Despite being ignored by certain Obama biographers, this may be the most instructive Frank-related passage in *Dreams from My Father*, fully reflective of the old Frank. Obama wrote:

> I had graduated without mishap, was accepted into several respectable schools, and settled on Occidental College in Los Angeles mainly because I'd met a girl from Brentwood while she was vacationing in Hawaii with her family. But I was still just going through the motions, as indifferent toward college as toward most everything else. Even Frank thought I had a bad attitude, although he was less than clear about how I should change it. What had Frank called college? An advanced degree in compromise.

Here again, Obama thought of Frank. His mind raced back to the last time he had seen him, just a "few days" before Obama left Hawaii. Frank had asked him what he expected to get out of college. When Obama said he "didn't know," Frank shook his head.

> "Well," he said, "that's the problem, isn't it? You don't know. You're just like the rest of these young cats out here.
>
> All you know is that college is the next thing you're supposed to do. . . ."

He studied me over the top of his reading glasses. "Understand something, boy. You're not going to college to get educated. You're going there to get trained. They'll train you to want what you don't need. They'll train you to manipulate words so they don't mean anything anymore. They'll train you to forget what it is that you already know. They'll train you so good, you'll start believing what they tell you about equal opportunity and the American way and all that sh-t."[21]

Not quite prepared for that diatribe, the young Obama asked: "So what is it you're telling me—that I shouldn't be going to college?" He described Frank's response: "Frank's shoulders slumped, and he fell back in his chair with a sigh. 'No. I didn't say that. You've got to go. I'm just telling you to keep your eyes open.' " Frank, said Obama, "made me smile. . . . In some ways he was as incurable as my mother, as certain in his faith, living in the same sixties time warp that Hawaii had created."[22]

Here was Obama at Frank's side again, seeking him out, taking in his counsel, absorbing his hard-earned knowledge, this time on college specifically, though, as always, also on life in general. He saw Frank just before leaving for Occidental, with the old CPUSA stalwart again making a lasting impact.

Thereafter, their conversation was not so much about college but rather what Obama would get from college for his larger, longer life. And there, finally, Obama's pages let down the guard and allowed the political Frank to erupt—with words that just happened to be used by Frank in communist organs like the *Chicago Star* and *Honolulu Record*.[23] They were bitter but choice words: Frank's continued disparaging use of the phrase "the American way," here referred to as "the American way and all that sh-t."

Thanks to Obama (unintentionally),[24] we can see a consistency in Frank traversing four decades, dating back to his columns in the 1940s and 1950s. In the *Star* and the *Record*, Frank likewise demeaned the very notion of "the American way," though style guidelines and editors and protocol and manners of the day ensured he would not refer to the American way as "sh-t." This was the bitter, old-school Frank, blasting the unimpeachable American way of life.

"I'm tired of being beaned with those double meaning words like 'sacred institutions' and 'the American way of life,' " growled Frank in the *Chicago Star* on November 9, 1946, "which our flag-waving fascists and lukewarm liberals hurl at us day and night."

Obama's next mention of Frank in *Dreams from My Father* might seem minor on the surface, but it is somewhat telling.

It was 1983. Obama had finished college. He made a pivotal decision, post-Occidental, post-Columbia, to become a community organizer. Here, Obama provided readers a life assessment at that point in his journey. He paused to acknowledge the major names on his path that served as meaningful markers. He did not list many names, focusing on those with the most impact. Frank is mentioned as one among only a handful of people, and fewer still among nonrelatives:

> In 1983, I decided to become a community organizer. . . .
>
> Now, with the benefit of hindsight, I can construct a certain logic to my decision, show how becoming an organizer was a part of that larger narrative, starting with my father and his father before him, my mother and her parents, my memories of Indonesia with its beggars and farmers and the loss of Lolo to power, on through Ray and Frank, Marcus and Regina; my move to New York; my father's death. I can see that my choices were never truly mine alone—and that that is how it should be, that to assert otherwise is to chase after a sorry sort of freedom.[25]

Frank stands out as a continuing influence, a person who had an effect on Obama that was lasting. He was one of the core people in Obama's life who guaranteed that Obama's choices had never been truly his alone but involved the contributions of others.

Later in the book, Obama returned again to Frank. This time, it was when he landed in Chicago, where, of all things and people that might enter his mind, he thought of Frank. In fact, Frank Marshall Davis was literally the first face that Obama imagined upon arriving in the Windy City: "I imagined Frank in a baggy suit and wide lapels, standing in front of the old Regal Theatre, waiting to see Duke or Ella emerge from a gig."[26]

Young Obama seemed spellbound by this "seductive siren" (Frank's words) that was Chicago.[27] Remarkably, Obama arrived in Chicago at almost precisely the same age that Frank had.[28]

Even then, in Chicago, Frank was far from finished in Obama's life. In Obama's very next chapter, Frank was back. Ironically, this time Obama referred to the dilapidated public-housing projects that harkened back to Valerie Jarrett's kin. He wrote of "the Chicago Housing Authority— the CHA—as a patronage trough; the subsequent mismanagement and neglect. It wasn't as bad as Chicago's high-rise projects yet, the Robert Taylors and Cabrini Greens, with their ink-black stairwells and urine-stained lobbies and random shootings."[29]

For the record, these involved not only Valerie Jarrett's grandfather, but Jarrett herself. She was embroiled in the funding, mismanagement, and ultimate demise of these projects. It was this sordid saga that brought the controversial (and, later, indicted) Tony Rezko into the lives of Jarrett and a young Senator Obama—the first big scandal of Obama's political career.[30]

In this chapter, Obama included a vivid discussion of Chicago and its politics and problems. Obama was struggling again, grappling with despair and the challenges of race, culture, poverty, and politics. He again visualized Frank. What would Frank do? What would Frank think? Obama recorded:

> Words jumbled up in my head, and for a moment I was gripped with panic. Then the panic gave way to anger. . . . I suddenly remembered what Frank had told me that night back in Hawaii, after I had heard that Toot was scared of a black man.
>
> That's the way it is, he had said. You might as well get used to it.[31]

That is exactly what Frank had said. In this moment of frustration, exasperation, Obama retreated, for better or worse, to one of Frank's enduring nuggets of wisdom. It seemed to help. It did not solve the problem, but it seemed to help.

And still, Obama's recollections of Frank in *Dreams* were not over.

In Chapter 11, he wrote warmly of embracing his African sister, Auma, at the airport. Auma was in Germany, studying. The brother and sister talked about life and about race. They related their mutual struggles as black persons in white environments. Obama then again recalled "the black men I knew," listing four of them, with Frank first. Obama "had learned to respect these men for the struggles they went through, recognizing them as my own."[32]

Frank's struggles had been Barack's.

In Chapter 14, as Obama returned himself and the reader to Chicago, so, too, did he return to Frank. Here, Obama wrote philosophically, almost lyrically, about "escape." As he did, he escaped to Frank, twice; on each of those occasions, he listed Frank first, ahead of other influences, including his own father:

> It always came down to a simple matter of escape. An escape from poverty or boredom or crime or the shackles of your skin. Maybe, by going to law school, I'd be repeating a pattern that had been set in motion centuries before, the moment white men, themselves spurred on by their own fears of inconsequence, had landed on Africa's shores, bringing with them their guns and blind hunger, to drag away the conquered in chains. That first encounter had redrawn the map of black life, recentered its universe, created the very idea of escape—an idea that lived on in Frank and those other old black men who had found refuge in Hawaii. . . .
>
> The relationship between black and white, the meaning of escape, would never be quite the same for me as it had been for Frank, or for the Old Man.[33]

Frank reappeared as a symbol, influence, theme throughout Obama's life and career, with Obama always mindful of Frank across varied contexts. Obama's final references came in Chapter 16, and again they were instructive. This is the final stage of Obama's book, Part Three, titled "Kenya," in which he movingly reached out to his dead father. This is where Obama sealed the dreams of his father, and thus the title of the book. And yet, Frank is there, too. Obama wrote:

> It was the same dilemma that old Frank had posed to me the year
> I left Hawaii, the same tensions that certain children in Altgeld
> might suffer if they took too much pleasure in doing their school-
> work, the same perverse survivor's guilt that I could expect to expe-
> rience if I ever did try to make money and had to pass the throngs
> of young black men on the corner as I made my way to a downtown
> office.[34]

This may be Frank's most lingering impact, most permanent to
Obama's lifelong accomplishments. Frank had warned Obama that
"they" would give him a nice "corner office" and "fancy" dinner invitations while he left behind his race and people.[35]

Consider: No matter what happens to Barack Obama from here
on, he will always be incredibly accomplished, unsurpassed, and unprecedented. He is the most successful black American ever. If major
achievements had identified Obama with Frank up to this point, in an
autobiography published in 1995, before becoming a state politician let
alone rising to U.S. senator, imagine the intense identification Obama
must feel with Frank now as he sits in the White House as leader of
America and the free world.

In all, there are approximately twenty-five hundred words in the passages relating to Frank in *Dreams from My Father*. *Dreams* features twenty-
two specific references to "Frank" by name and far more via pronouns
and other forms of reference. Frank surfaces repeatedly from start to
finish, from Hawaii to Los Angeles to Chicago to Germany to Kenya,
traversing time zones and all parts of the globe with Obama, from the
1970s to the 1980s to the 1990s. Throughout, Frank is with Barack, an
abiding part of his journey, one of the most consistent themes in his
sojourn—by the future president's own account.

Bear in mind, as noted at the start of this book, that Ronald Reagan mentioned his mentor, Ben Cleaver, not once in his memoirs, and
Hillary Clinton mentioned Don Jones only a handful of times. In other
words, the litmus test for mentors is not how often they are cited in a
memoir—though, in Obama's case, Frank is certainly cited much more
than usual. But, no matter the word count or the number of references,
one thing is clear: *Dreams from My Father* illustrates the strong, endur-

ing influence of Frank Marshall Davis in Obama's life, career, and much more.

FRANK MEETS OBAMA: OTHER TESTIMONIES

Obama's own accounting is the best source on Frank's influence, but it is short on many details. David Remnick, in *The Bridge*, the definitive biography of Obama, cites sources who knew Frank, Obama, and Stanley Dunham, and who claim Frank and Obama met in the early 1970s. Remnick's account is valuable, provided by no less than an eyewitness to the first meeting: Dawna Weatherly-Williams, a close friend and next-door neighbor to Frank, so close that she called Frank "Daddy."[36]

That initial introduction was no small thing, notes Weatherly-Williams. It had been eagerly anticipated by all sides, including Frank, suggesting the opportunity that Frank rightly saw in Barack. Upon first seeing the well-dressed young man with his grandfather, Frank said, "Hey, Stan! Oh, is this him?"

Weatherly-Williams detailed the moment: "We were all grinning like idiots, me and Frank and Stan, because we were thinking that we know this secret about life and we were going to share it with Barry." That "secret," though not clearly specified by Remnick, seemed to be about life for someone half black and half white, which was not only Obama's racial makeup, but also that of Frank's children.[37]

Weatherly-Williams next provided an especially important first-person observation of Frank's influence on Obama. "Frank was also a great listener, which may be why Barack liked him, too," she said. "I am sure he influenced Barack more than Barack is saying. About social jus tice, about finding out more about life, about what's important, about how to use your heart and your mind."[38]

Remnick followed up Weatherly-Williams's account with another noteworthy piece of information on the Frank-Obama relationship, further demonstrating that this was not a mere matter of a little boy who sat around watching Frank and his granddad drink whiskey and swap dirty limericks. Remnick wrote, "As a teenager, Obama called on Davis on his own, driving along the Ala Wai Canal to the Jungle."[39]

The Jungle was a kind of bohemian community in Waikiki where Frank lived. As Remnick described, drawing from Obama's memoirs, the teenage Obama drove there to talk, to have substantive discussions with Frank well into the evening. Frank told Obama things about his maternal grandfather and the delicate issue of race within his own family. He said that when it came to the racism of whites inflicted upon blacks, "black people have a reason to hate." [40]

Not surprisingly, given his biases, Remnick mentioned no other issue discussed between Frank and Obama beyond race, avoiding Frank's extreme-left political views like the plague. He did, however, say, "Davis, by Obama's own accounting, made the young man feel something deep and disorienting." [41]

As we shall see, David Remnick, like Obama himself, sugarcoated Frank Marshall Davis's role in Obama's life. Amazingly, he concluded that introducing young Obama to Frank was "one of the more thoughtful and consequential things that Stanley did in his role as surrogate father." [42]

And when, exactly, did Stanley provide that introduction?

One journalist who dug into that specific question is Toby Harnden of the *London Telegraph.* In a two-part profile he traced the meeting to as early as 1970. Harnden likewise quoted Weatherly-Williams, though more freely than Remnick did. "He [Frank] knew Stan real well," Weatherly-Williams told Harnden. "They'd play Scrabble and drink and crack jokes and argue. Frank always won and he was always very braggadocio about it too. It was all jocular. They didn't get polluted drunk. And Frank never really did drugs, though he and Stan would smoke pot together." [43]

Speaking about mixed-race experiences, Weatherly-Williams told Harnden what she told Remnick: "Stan had been promising to bring Barry by because we all had that in common. Frank's kids were half-white, Stan's grandson was half-black and my son was half-black. We all had that in common and we all really enjoyed it. We got a real kick out of reality." [44]

Weatherly-Williams informed Harnden that Frank was introduced to Obama "in 1970." [45] Through further research, Harnden narrowed the meeting to "the autumn of 1970." [46] Harnden said the young Obama spent the previous three years in Indonesia with his mother and her second husband, Lolo Soetoro, and returned to Hawaii shortly after his mother gave birth to her second child, Maya, in 1970. Thus, he was living with his grandparents, Stanley and Madelyn Dunham, when he first met Frank.[47]

If this timeline is accurate, then Obama knew Frank not merely for a few years, but a full decade—or throughout the entirety of his adolescence.

Harnden affirmed that Stanley had identified Frank "as someone who could help the boy solve the puzzle of how he, brought up by white people, could relate to a future as a black man." Harnden reported that Obama's "visits to Davis were irregular, but he nevertheless gravitated there at moments of doubt."[48]

It is clear from these accounts that the Obama-Frank relationship is certainly not inconsequential. Frank Marshall Davis was a decisive influence in the life of the young Barack Obama. So much so that he could not escape frequent mentions throughout Obama's memoirs, even as an older and more politically savvy Obama surely understood the risk of repeatedly invoking a closet CPUSA member pursued by Democratic committees in Washington. Frank is interwoven through the filament and fiber of *Dreams from My Father*, there with Obama—even with the aid of Obama imagining him there—from Hawaii to Chicago and more.

Among those stops, one in particular merits special reflection in further understanding the Obama-Frank relationship: an eighteen-year-old Barack flew from Hawaii to the shores of California, enrolling in college and initiating a historic trek that would change not only his life but the life of the country as well.

When Obama Leaves Frank

Occidental College

IN SEPTEMBER 1979, Barack Obama began classes at Occidental College in Los Angeles, moving into a single-room dormitory at Haines Hall Annex, which he shared with two other students.[1]

As noted, a visit to Frank was one of the final things Obama did before heading to Occidental.[2] Frank was not exactly enthusiastic, barking at Obama that he would get "an advanced degree in compromise," wined and dined and patronized, and would leave his "people behind." "Well-paid" and "well-trained," the young man would learn all about "the American way and all that sh-t."[3]

It seems hard to imagine that Frank thought Obama would be indoctrinated in "the American way." American universities have been citadels of liberalism, especially during the post-Vietnam, post-Watergate malaise of the late 1970s, and Occidental was certainly not bucking the tide by teaching Reagan conservatism. In fact, American exceptionalism did not seem to be in the curriculum at Occidental, and definitely was not what Obama took away.

In Chapter 5 of *Dreams from My Father*, Obama chronicled his arrival at Occidental College. He informed readers that he had applied and been accepted to "several respectable schools," though he did not list any of them, nor did he give reason why he chose Occidental, other than settling there "mainly because I'd met a girl from Brentwood while she was vacationing in Hawaii with her family." This tells us little, and Occidental has not been forthcoming in revealing Obama's records, including denying my request. One wonders if Frank might have provided a letter of recommendation, which would be appropriate, given Frank's credentials in the African-American literary world—though given Frank's attitude, a recommendation seems less likely.

It is telling—again reflective of Frank's mentoring role—that in addressing Occidental, Obama immediately cited Frank's input. He did so at great length: The next seven paragraphs of his memoirs are extended quotations from Frank, as the seventy-three-year-old card-carrying communist ranted against the American system and American way.[4]

Obama then proceeded to write about the campus. After discussing issues of race and a girl named Joyce, he hinted at his political discussions and political philosophy—and that of like-minded associates. "I chose my friends carefully," Obama stated. "The more politically active black students. The foreign students. The Chicanos. The Marxist professors and structural feminists and punk-rock performance poets. We smoked cigarettes and wore leather jackets. At night, in the dorms, we discussed neocolonialism, Franz [*sic*] Fanon, Eurocentrism, and patriarchy. When we ground out our cigarettes in the hallway carpet or set our stereos so loud that the walls began to shake, we were resisting bourgeois society's stifling constraints. . . . We were alienated."[5]

Marxists, poets, politically active minority, and foreign students; Obama carefully sought them out. Neocolonialism, Eurocentrism, resisting *bourgeois* society, alienation; Obama felt them. Politics, poetry, cigarettes; Obama's atmosphere was pervaded by them.

They all ring of Frank. These were topics and sentiments Frank carried and coddled through decades. Among them, colonialism dominated his writings in Hawaii: The word "colonial" or "colonialism" is used seventeen times in Frank's *Honolulu Record* columns from 1949 to 1950 alone, and in the context of Eurocentrism.[6]

On that, Obama's citing of Frantz Fanon cannot be dismissed. Fanon (1925–61) was a Martinique-born French political philosopher, radical, and revolutionary who wrote on colonialism, particularly regarding Africa, and was widely read by Marxists and so-called critical theorists. He was intensely, militantly anticolonial. He portrayed (not always incorrectly) white colonialists as rapists and pillagers and looters who had enriched themselves on the backs of black Africans. It would be hard to imagine Frank Marshall Davis not reading Fanon, or at least not knowing of him, especially given Fanon's popular 1960s work, *The Wretched of the Earth*, which Frank would have heartily endorsed.[7]

After this, Obama's *Dreams* moved quickly and insignificantly through Occidental and on to Columbia University, to which he transferred in 1981. Occidental gets only one more mention in the entire book. Even less is said of Columbia, though Obama recorded that he attended "socialist conferences" at New York's Cooper Union.[8]

Interestingly, in Obama's memoirs, as in Frank's memoirs, the professional and political animal does not really emerge until Chicago. When it does, in Chapter 7 of *Dreams*, Obama employed the word "change" seven times in the opening paragraphs, including the need for "change in the White House, where Reagan and his minions were carrying on their dirty deeds." Obama perceived an America that needed a "change in the mood of the country." Ronald Reagan's "morning in America" needed a change.[9]

That is a mesmerizing insight into young Obama's political mind. Consider: Even among liberal academics and journalists, both at the time and today, there is a consensus that among President Reagan's greatest impacts was his dramatic change in the mood of the nation, and decidedly for the better, lifting up America and restoring its sagging morale.[10] As the cynical Reagan biographer Edmund Morris agreed, Reagan had "changed the mood overnight."[11] That was one thing about Reagan that conservatives and liberals, plus millions of Reagan Democrats, came together and applauded. Obama wanted to change the mood that Reagan changed. *To what*, one might ask?

That *change* would come later. For now, Barack Obama, age eighteen, was enrolled at Occidental College, a period vitally instructive regarding Frank's continued impact.

JOHN DREW'S TESTIMONY

A contemporary of Obama at Occidental was John Drew, who described the college as so far to the left that he and others called it (approvingly) "the Moscow of southern California." Drew was a Marxist, and, remarkably, knew Barack Obama as a fellow believer.

Drew today refers to himself as the "missing link" between Hawaii/ Frank and later radical/communist associates in Obama's orbit in Chicago, including the infamous Bill Ayers. Drew had been a student at Occidental before moving on to earn his Ph.D. at Cornell, ultimately becoming a professor at Williams College, where he taught economics and political science. I have come to know Drew well, and have repeatedly pressed him on details of his experiences with Obama. I have reviewed with him various material on Obama's relationship with Frank Marshall Davis. Drew has even exchanged emails with Mark Davis, son of Frank, and attempted to liaison between Mark and myself—attempts that proved unsuccessful.

I first wrote up Drew's account for the online conservative publication *American Thinker*, which considered the material with an open mind and after careful fact-checking by the editor-in-chief, Thomas Lifson. Lifson is a former Harvard professor, having taught in Harvard's sociology department and business school after receiving three graduate degrees there. He did visiting professorships at Columbia University and other colleges. Lifson is a former liberal, a onetime sixties antiwar activist raised in a devout progressive home in Minnesota. My article on Drew in *American Thinker*, titled "Obama's Missing Link," includes an audio link to my interview with him on the Glen Meakem program,[12] which listeners can click and listen to and judge Drew's credibility themselves.[13]

"I see myself as a missing link between Barack Obama's exposure to communism with Frank Marshall Davis and his later exposure to Bill Ayers and Alice Palmer in Chicago," Drew told me.

Alice Palmer was the state senator Obama replaced in Illinois, his first elected seat, and a woman of the far left. As reported by the *New York Times*, it was with Alice Palmer that Obama met with Bill Ayers and Bernardine Dohrn to seek their political support and blessing in 1995 during his first run for office, the same year that *Dreams from My Father* was released. Obama met with Ayers and Dohrn in their Chicago living room.[14] Ayers and Dohrn had been domestic terrorists once pursued by the FBI as fugitives, before somehow escaping jail time on a legal technicality. ("Guilty as hell, free as a bird!" says Ayers today.[15]) They were communist revolutionaries, founders of the Weather Underground. In 1995, the two were still extremists, and remain so. Ayers would tell the *New York Times*—in an interview published, chillingly, on September 11, 2001—that he harbored "no regrets" about bombing targets in New York City and Washington, D.C., three decades earlier.[16]

Drew told me about the moment he, a well-known campus communist, first met Obama at Occidental. Obama was introduced to him as "one of us." "Obama was already an ardent Marxist when I met him in the fall of 1980," said Drew.

Drew is certainly cognizant of the gravity of that statement. "I know it's incendiary to say this," he continued, but Obama "was basically a Marxist-Leninist." He noted how Obama, in *Dreams*, noted that when he got to college he attended "socialist conferences" and "hung out" with Marxist professors, but what Obama did not explain, or clarify, said Drew, is that he "was in 100 percent, total agreement with these Marxist professors."

I asked Drew where, precisely, he believes Obama stands today. Drew, who today is a conservative, was quick to concede that he no longer knows Obama, and that his main goal in reaching out to me was to clarify where Obama stood at Occidental, which is information that Drew understands cannot be ignored, least of all for an accurate historical understanding of the background of the current president of the United States of America.

That said, Drew stressed: "There are a lot of brands of Marxism. That was one of the key ingredients of my argument with the young Barack Obama. I see evidence of [a] continuing commitment to Marxist ideology every time President Obama traces the furor of the public to underlying economic conditions and inevitable changes taking place

in society. In the Marxist model, the economy is the driving force behind change in the other spheres of society."

Drew shared those particular thoughts with me in the spring of
2010, by email. He was willing to go public and add further details. We
had an even more illuminating conversation when I interviewed him
for the Glen Meakem program. Here are edited excerpts of what Drew
told me on the air on October 16, 2010:

> **DREW:** As far as I can tell, I'm the only person in Obama's extended
> circle of friends who is willing to speak out and verify that he was
> a Marxist-Leninist in his sophomore year of college from 1980 to
> 1981. I met him because I graduated from Occidental College in
> 1979, and I was back at Occidental visiting a girlfriend.
>
> **KENGOR:** Was Occidental known for radical-left politics? Would that
> have been an attraction to Obama?
>
> **DREW:** It was considered the Moscow of southern California when I
> was there. There were a lot of Marxist professors, many of whom
> I got to know pretty well. . . . What I know absolutely for sure—
> and this is where I really sought you out and I really wanted to be
> helpful in terms of the historic record—was to verify that Barack
> Obama was definitely a Marxist and that it was very unusual for
> a sophomore at Occidental to be as radical or as ideologically
> attuned as young Barack Obama was.
>
> **KENGOR:** You said that Obama was introduced to you at Occidental
> College *as a Marxist*? Because you were one, a Marxist, at that point?
>
> **DREW:** Yeah, that's embarrassing for me, but I studied Marxist
> economics when I was at the University of Sussex in England.
> I had a junior-year scholarship over there and I did my senior
> honor's thesis on Marxist economics when I was at Occidental
> College. And I also founded [the] Democratic Student Socialist
> Alliance, under a different name, in 1976. . . .
>
> At the time I met [Obama]—this was probably around
> Christmastime in 1980, because I had flown out during
> Christmas break from Cornell, where I was doing my graduate
> work—young Obama was looking forward to an imminent social
> revolution, literally a movement where the working classes would

overthrow the ruling class and institute a kind of socialist utopia
in the United States. I mean, that's how extreme his views were
his sophomore year of college.

KENGOR: And you would know this because you were a *comrade*, so
to speak.

DREW: Yeah, I was a comrade, but I was kind of more what Michael
Savage called the "Frankfurt School" of Marxism at the time. I
was, you know, I felt like I was doing Obama a favor by pointing
out that the Marxist revolution that he and [our friends] were
hoping for was really kind of a pipedream, and that there was
nothing in European history or the history of developed nations
that would make that sort of fantasy—you know, Frank Marshall
Davis fantasy of revolution—come true.

KENGOR: So you had a realistic sense that even though you liked
these ideas, it [Marxist revolution] really couldn't happen or
really wouldn't even work?

DREW: Right. I was . . . still a card-carrying Marxist, but I was kind of
a more advanced, East Coast, Cornell University Marxist, I think,
at the time.

KENGOR: But Obama thought it was practical—he thought you
could make this [a Marxist revolution] happen in America?

DREW: Oh yeah, and he kind of thought I was, you know, a little
reactionary—like I was kind of insensitive to the needs of the
coming revolution. So that's why I said, [Obama] was full-bore,
100 percent into that simpleminded Marxist, revolutionary
mental framework.

I then asked John Drew how this information related to Barack
Obama today, as president—aside from the obviously relevant fact that
Americans ought to know such significant biographical information on
their presidents. In answering, Drew again acknowledged the Hawaii
years of Frank Marshall Davis:

DREW: I can definitely kick down some doors here intellectually by
nailing down that he [Obama] had a very consistent ideology,
probably from the time that he was [in Hawaii] until he was

there with Alice Palmer and Bill Ayers in Chicago. I think his
current behavior demonstrates that he does still have these
ideological convictions. Whenever he talks about taxing the
richest two percent, I think even though he knows that will
harm the economy—to him, that redistribution of wealth is
still *extremely* important. And I think the problem here is that
he never studied political science or economics the way I did.
He just went straight to law school. . . . He never had any real
business experience, never had a payroll to meet, and I think
he still is locked in a very dangerous mindset where I think if he
didn't fight to redistribute the wealth, he would feel guilty—as if
he were violating a John Rawls *Theory of Justice* ideology.

KENGOR: And that's what people need to understand. That's why
all of this matters. That's why the background is so crucial—
Frank Marshall Davis, what happened at Occidental, goes straight
to Columbia from Occidental, the Bill Ayers affiliation, no real
world experience—this matters. You need to know this in your
presidents. . . .

So it's not that he's right now trying to abolish all private
property, but you're saying he has a certain—he still holds to
certain tenets of a Marxist worldview.

DREW: Yeah, I think whenever he talks about people clinging to
their guns and their religion due to economic stress, that's just
the standard Marxist argument. In fact, that's the argument of
alienation and class-consciousness that [Marxists believe that
people] hold to, the superficial religious and cultural ideals of
the capitalist culture. [Marxists believe that people hold to that]
instead of paying attention to the root economic changes, which
are supposedly controlling their thoughts and their behavior. So,
he's still using the Marxist mental architecture in the way he talks
about things, and I really think he's surrounded by people that
share that mental architecture.

Drew expressed great frustration over the refusal by the media or
Obama biographers to call him about Obama, even as they consistently
contacted other classmates and quoted them at great length.

PREPARING FOR THE IMMINENT REVOLUTION

My exchanges with Dr. John Drew prompted demands upon Drew—
from conservatives, not liberals—to share more specifics. Drew com-
plied, writing a detailed twenty-five-hundred-word account titled
"Meeting Young Obama," published by *American Thinker* on February
24, 2011. Again, Drew's recollection points back to Frank, with still
more details.

"I met Obama in December of 1980, a couple of days after Christmas," wrote Drew, "in Portola Valley—a small town near Stanford University in Palo Alto, CA." Drew was a twenty-three-year-old, second-year
grad student in Cornell's Department of Government. He had flown to
California to visit his twenty-one-year-old girlfriend, Caroline Boss, who
was a senior at Occidental. In the fall of 1980, Boss had taken a course
with Occidental political theorist Roger Boesche, and it was there that
she met and befriended a nineteen-year-old Obama.

Drew's temperament in those days was that of a typical "angry Marxist revolutionary." In his sophomore year at Occidental, in the fall of
1976, Drew celebrated America's bicentennial by founding the Marxist-
socialist group on campus, which, befitting the communist tactic of
using a benign front name, was called the Political Awareness Fellowship. The group's core of about a dozen Marxist activists successfully attracted liberal/progressive dupes to their events, generating "crowds of
eighty or more." Like their CPUSA ancestors, they pushed whatever left-
wing hot button was within their reach, from the plight of homosexuals,
to the vagaries of capitalism, to the machinations of the campus administration, to the injustice of white apartheid rule in South Africa. Apartheid was an especially fertile area for communists in the late 1970s and
1980s, offering superb recruiting grounds to lure liberals/progressives,
with any detractors easily denounced as slack-jawed racists.

Why might there be detractors? Because anticommunists were
deeply concerned that if the white apartheid regime fell in South Africa, it might be replaced with a Soviet-proxy regime allied with the African National Congress as part of a larger African communist bloc. Such
opponents were dispatched by campus communists as loathsome racists, with the liberal/progressive echo chamber loudly following suit.

It was a tactic Frank Marshall Davis had mastered.

John Drew took a hiatus from Occidental in the fall of 1977 to study Marxist economics at the University of Sussex in England. He returned in the fall of 1978. By then, the interim president of the Political Awareness Fellowship, a student named Gary Chapman, had changed the group's name to the Democratic Socialist Alliance (DSA).

It was through DSA that Drew began his romance with Caroline Boss in the spring of 1979. She had been attracted to DSA through its antiapartheid outreach. But Boss was no liberal. "Like me, she was a committed Marxist," wrote Drew, "preparing for the approaching revolution."

Their political wedding was consummated when Drew completed his senior honors thesis on Marxist economics; the two danced together after Drew accepted his Occidental degree in June 1979, wearing less a cap and gown and more a red armband that, in Drew's words, "signified my solidarity with my Marxist brethren around the world and my commitment to the antiapartheid movement." Their relationship continued through the academic year of 1979–80 and all the way to Ithaca, New York, where Boss stayed with Drew in the summer of 1980 while he was enrolled at Cornell. Upon her return to Occidental in the fall of 1980, as a senior, Boss met the sophomore Obama in Professor Boesche's course on European political thought.

It was thus that Obama came into Drew's orbit. Drew remembered well meeting Obama for the first time during a visit to Boss's parents' home:

> When I first saw Obama, I remember I was standing on the porch of Boss's parents' impressive home as a sleek, expensive luxury car pulled up the driveway. Two young men emerged from the vehicle. They were well-dressed and looked like they were born to wealth and privilege. I was a little surprised to learn they were Boss's friends from Occidental College until she articulated the underlying political connection. "They're on our side," she said.
>
> The taller of the two was Obama, then only nineteen, who towered over his five-foot-five companion, Mohammed Hasan Chandoo—a wealthy, twenty-one-year-old Pakistani student. Chan-

doo had a full dark black, neatly trimmed moustache, and was dressed in expensive clothes. Nevertheless, Obama was the more handsome of the two. At six foot two, Obama carried himself with the dignity and poise of a model.

Drew provided very specific details on Chandoo and Obama, from physical to ideological. He noted that even David Remnick was willing to mention the fact that Chandoo was a Marxist. In *The Bridge*, Remnick quoted Chandoo's girlfriend at the time, Margot Mifflin, who told Remnick: "In college, Hasan was a socialist, a Marxist."

Drew remembered Chandoo from his participation in their anti-apartheid rallies. Obama, on the other hand, was completely new to Drew. "This is Barack Obama," Boss said to Drew, making the friendly introduction. He recalled: "Since I was not much taller than Chandoo, I remember I looked up at Obama as we shook hands. I was completely mystified by the pronunciation of his name. He did not put up a fight over it, however." Obama graciously said to Drew, "You can call me Barry."

Boss and Chandoo informed Drew of Obama's elite prep-school credentials in Honolulu. "Obama seemed embarrassed by the fuss," Drew noticed. "Boss, I remember, wanted to make sure I understood that young Obama was not merely an attractive socialite dabbling in Marxist theory. 'You've worked with us,' she observed. 'You've been at our DSA meetings. You've been active in the antiapartheid movement.' "

The four retired to dinner with Boss's parents. Obama was polite to Boss's parents, calm, distinguished in his deference and manner. Drew did not come off quite as well, as Mr. Boss was not pleased with his daughter's radical politics and boyfriend, and could barely disguise his contempt.

After dinner, all four students lit up cigarettes in the Bosses' dining room, where they got to the more serious business of the revolution. Caroline Boss sat at the head of the table, to Drew's left. Obama sat directly across from Drew, and Chandoo sat on the other side, to Obama's left.

Most captivating was the talk not only of Karl Marx but of the long-anticipated Marxist revolution. Drew's studies at Sussex and Cornell had tempered his earlier enthusiasm. Oh, he was still a Marxist, but chastened, more realistic. He no longer thought revolution was imminent or "in the cards anymore." "There was no inevitability, in my mind, to the old idea that the proletariat would rise up and overthrow the ruling classes," recalled Drew. "The idea that we could entirely eliminate the profit motive from an advanced industrialized economy seemed like a childhood fantasy. The future, I now thought, would belong to nations with mixed economic systems—like those in Europe—where there was government planning of the economy combined with a greater effort to produce a more equitable distribution of wealth. It made more sense to me to focus on elections rather than on preparing for a coming revolution."

Here is where Drew's testimony is particularly significant, as Barack Obama disagreed with Drew's pessimism:

"Boss and Obama, however, had a starkly different view," said Drew. "They believed that the economic stresses of the Carter years meant revolution was still imminent. The election of Reagan was simply a minor setback in terms of the coming revolution. As I recall, Obama repeatedly used the phrase 'When the revolution comes. . . . ' "

"There's going to be a revolution," Obama affirmed. "We need to be organized and grow the movement." According to Drew, Obama argued that their role as Marxists was to educate others in order to more quickly usher in this inevitable revolution.

Drew also distinctly remembers being surprised by Obama's invoking Frantz Fanon's writings and colonialism generally—Frank's obsession. He was impressed by Obama's knowledge in this area. Here, on this ideological turf, Drew described Obama and Boss as aggressive, adamant: "Chandoo let Boss and Obama take the crux of the argument to me. Chandoo, in fact, seemed chagrined by the level of disagreement in the group."

It was a spirited debate, and Drew's pessimism could not be chalked up to inexperience. Drew had been to Europe. He studied there. He tried to convince Obama that revolution was not even imminent in Europe, where Ronald Reagan had not been recently elected. "Drawing on the history of Western Europe," stated Drew, "I responded it was unrealistic to think the working class would ever overthrow the capitalist system. As I recall, Obama reacted negatively to my critique, saying: 'That's crazy!' "

The sparring among the fellow Marxists went back and forth, from historical to theoretical, from practical to impractical. In Obama, Drew knew he was staring into the eyes of a true believer:

> Since I was a Marxist myself at the time, and had studied variations in Marxist theory, I can state that everything I heard Obama argue that evening was consistent with Marxist philosophy, including the ideas that class struggle was leading to an inevitable revolution and that an elite group of revolutionaries was needed to lead the effort. If he had not been a true Marxist-Leninist, I would have noticed and remembered. I can still, with some degree of ideological precision, identify which students at Occidental College were radicals and which ones were not.

Here was a very young but very informed Obama, reportedly professing Marxism with knowledge and nuance, with information and persuasiveness he clearly heard many times before—and that before could only have been in Hawaii.

John Drew concluded his account with an image of Obama as a peacemaker: "By the time the debate came to an end, Obama—although not Boss—was making peace, agreeing with the facts I had laid out, and demonstrating an apparent agreement with my more realistic perspective." Drew retains "a vivid memory of Obama surrendering to my argument, including signaling to the somewhat bewildered Chandoo—through his voice and body language—that the argument had concluded and had been decided in my favor."

Today, a lifetime away from those radical beliefs, Drew remembers that meeting with Obama as a "treasured" memory, a rare interaction with a future president. More than that, Drew believes he might have been one of the first to "directly challenge Obama's Marxist-Leninist mind-set and to introduce him to a more practical view that saw politics, rather than revolution, as the preferred route to socialism."

That is a compelling observation. Might this moment have signaled the start of a conversion or adjustment by Obama, from the fringe Marxist left to a softer leftism, perhaps a more benign socialism, a less extreme brand of collectivism and wealth redistribution? It is difficult to say. Liberal biographers and journalists will not dare entertain such an honest dialogue because of fears of exhuming their beloved leader's radical past—even if the ultimate answers might lead to a more full (and positive) portrait of Obama's belief system and how and where it developed.

For Drew and Obama, it was not their final encounter. Drew was "friendly" with Obama on at least four other occasions over the next months. In one instance, he and Boss visited Obama and Chandoo's apartment. "I certainly considered him a friend," said Drew, "a confidant and a political ally in the larger struggle against poverty and oppressive social systems."

And Drew definitively concludes this about the Barack Obama of 1980: "At that time, the future president was a doctrinaire Marxist revolutionary, although perhaps—for the first time—considering conventional politics as a more practical road to socialism. Knowing this, I think I have a responsibility to place on the public record my account of this incident from our president's past."

Drew recalls the moment not with bitterness or vindictiveness, but positively, as a treasured encounter with some significant history.

If this account by Dr. John Drew is accurate, and there is no reason to think it is not, what—or, better still, *who*—explains Obama's Marxist political thinking at the time, fresh out of Hawaii?

The obvious answer is Frank Marshall Davis.

WHERE'S THE CONVERSION NARRATIVE?

As I said from the outset of this book, my goal is not to declare President Barack Obama a communist or closet card-carrying member of CPUSA. Drew's account claims that Obama was a communist at Occidental College. To be sure, Drew is not convinced Obama has completely left behind all remnants of that philosophy. Nonetheless, all of this leads to a curious question, namely, where is the conversion narrative for Obama?

If Barack Obama had once been a communist, which is certainly not unusual for someone of his age, then when and where and why and how did he change, and why have we not read about it? Why was the change not broached in no fewer than two lengthy memoirs published before the man ever set foot in the Oval Office?

That question was insightfully raised by Selwyn Duke. Duke followed up the articles by myself and Drew with his own piece in *American Thinker*.[17] Duke thought: If Obama has changed, why? And where is the documented account? Duke wrote:

> Now, some may say that a person can change markedly over a thirty-year period. This is true. Yet not only do we have the recent evidence of Obama's radical communist appointments, but there's something else as well. It hit me just the other night. . . .
>
> [A] transition from flat-out "Marxist-Leninist" to someone who rejects the red menace is a pretty big change, don't you think? In fact, wouldn't such a personal evolution—some might say revolution— be a kind of *conversion*? I think so.
>
> Now, many people do experience conversions. I think here of erstwhile radical-leftist David Horowitz; ex-liberals Michael Savage and Robin of Berkeley; and President George W. Bush, who accepted Christ as an adult.
>
> And then there's me: I was never a liberal, but I did transition from being a scoffer at religion and an agnostic to a devout Catholic.
>
> There's an interesting thing, however, about conversions.
>
> *You hear about them.*
>
> You see, a conversion is a sea change, a rebirth, a turning point in your existence. . . . And those around you will know about it.
>
> As for this writer, everyone who knows me would say that my religious conversion was a seminal point in my life. Horowitz has spoken of his rejection of the "loony left," Bush's conversion is well known, Savage has talked about his on the radio, and Robin of Berkeley can't stop talking about hers. A conversion becomes part of your life narrative.
>
> Now consider something. Barack Obama is one of the most famous, most discussed individuals on the planet.

But we have not heard about any soul-changing conversion in his life.

Not a whisper.

Nothing.

Nothing that could reconcile the flat-out Marxist-Leninist Obama was in his college days with the man he supposedly is today. There's no one who says, "Yeah, he was a radical guy in his youth, and I just couldn't believe how he became disenchanted with his old ideas." There are no stories about a great epiphany, an overseas trip that opened his eyes, or a personal tragedy that inspired growth. There's nothing to explain how a radical Marxist became a reasonable politician. And if there is such an explanation, it's the most elusive of missing links.

I, myself, have a conversion narrative, similar to Duke's. John Drew has a conversion narrative. Glenn Beck has candidly said many times, to huge audiences, that he can recall the color of the paint on the walls when he finally began his awakening. In my last book, *Dupes*, I repeatedly touted ex-communists or onetime duped liberals/progressives who redeemed their earlier transgressions: Louis Budenz, Whittaker Chambers, Paul Douglas, William C. Bullitt, John Dewey, and even Ronald Reagan, to name a few among dozens. I dedicated that book to Herb Romerstein, arguably the greatest living expert on communism, who himself had been a communist—at the same age Obama would have been. Frank Marshall Davis comrades like Richard Wright and even Howard Fast changed, with Wright's reversal so profound that it was profiled in the bestseller *The God That Failed*. In the three spiritual biographies I have written, on Ronald Reagan, George W. Bush, and Hillary Clinton (who switched from conservative to liberal), I focus on when and why each of them changed. Reagan transformed from a young liberal actor repeatedly duped by communist front groups to a passionate, unwavering anticommunist who one day undermined the Evil Empire.[18]

Countless millions of Americans have had some kind of conversion, and most do not mind sharing it. Americans love to hear such stories because they remind them of themselves and their own ups and downs.

So, *where is Barack Obama's conversion,* assuming he was, perhaps, once on the communist left and left it behind?

Obama has never left the political left. In 2007, his final full year in the U.S. Senate, *National Journal,* the widely respected nonpartisan source that ranks the liberalism/conservatism of legislators, rated Barack Obama the most liberal member of the U.S. Senate—to the left of Ted Kennedy and Barbara Boxer.[19] Even among an extremely left-tilting Democratic Senate, no member was as far left as Senator Obama.

If Obama was on the Marxist-Leninist left, we have no accounting, from Obama or anyone, of a switch. Quite the contrary, in Obama's memoirs, we hear about him attending socialist conferences and "hanging out" with Marxist professors, but never any repudiation of those conferences, professors, or even a tiny, passing comment suggesting these were fanciful musings from a politically misguided youth.

FRANK'S ROLE

So, how much does this Occidental drama relate to Frank Marshall Davis? The answer is potentially quite a bit.

By Obama's own account in his memoirs, "Frank," who himself represented the furthest extreme of the left, was the last person Obama visited before heading to Occidental. The next time we hear about influences on Obama (in *Dreams*), we hear of him hanging out with Marxists at Occidental. And we now hear from John Drew that Obama was a Marxist himself, hanging out with Drew and their Marxist brethren.

Frank Marshall Davis would seem the obvious thread interweaving the sets of influences.

Obama hagiographers and defenders will not want to accept this; it does not reflect well on the politics of the current president—or at least his onetime politics. It would add fuel to claims by conservatives that Obama, at root, is a collectivist and redistributionist. On the other hand, the more alert Obama court composers might argue that there is no proof in Obama's memoirs that Frank influenced Obama's politics. There are, however, at least two core problems with that assertion:

For one, it would be naïve to think that Obama, who in *Dreams* fastidiously concealed Frank's full name and identity throughout 442 pages and dozens of direct references, would have included political sermons he gathered at the feet of Frank—a boldly pro-Soviet CPUSA agitator called to Washington by Democrats to be questioned about his loyalties. In other words, *of course* there is no mention of Frank's influencing Obama's politics in *Dreams from My Father*. To think there would be is silly, or would presuppose that Barack Obama is a political fool.

Second, while *Dreams* does not register Frank's extremist views on Harry Truman, the Marshall Plan, the USSR, and General Motors, it more than hints at Frank's worldview, especially his parting advice to Obama before college. There, we get a bitter Frank, the Frank of the *Chicago Star* and *Honolulu Record*, whose description of America does not ring of the Liberty Bell. Frank's farewell does not ring of Washington's or Reagan's Farewell Address.

It would be the height of gullibility to assume that Frank Marshall Davis, during those long evenings of talk and drink, never taught any politics to the wide-eyed Obama, or ruminated aloud with no effect whatsoever on the impressionable young man in the room—brought there (by a leftist grandfather) to be mentored in the first place. Frank lived his political philosophy, including direct work with communist fronts from the 1930s until the 1970s, when he knew Obama. Frank is the firmest political/ideological link between the adolescent Obama of Hawaii and the underclassman at Occidental.

Liberals should simply concede this logic and likelihood. A much better defense of their president would be to accept Frank's influence, accept that Obama was on the fringe left at Occidental—like many college students—and argue that Obama gradually or quickly moved from the fringe toward mainstream liberalism or even centrism. That would be a more saleable retreat.

I believe that liberals believe just that, even as they are afraid to say so publicly. The proof of that is that no liberal journalist, to my knowledge, has bothered to ask Obama about Frank's political/ideological influence and what Obama thought about communism when he was at Occidental. They are afraid of the answer. Of course, even if they did ask, I would expect Obama to be as forthcoming as he was about the identity of "Frank" in *Dreams*.

"POP"

Finally, a potentially tantalizing insight into the Obama-Frank relationship during the Occidental years is a poem written by Obama called "Pop."

As a student at Occidental, the young Obama followed Frank's footsteps by trying his hand at poetry. He published two poems that appeared in the 1981 edition of the college's literary magazine, *Feast*. One was titled "Underground," the other was titled "Pop." An Occidental student named Kevin Batton found the poems once Obama achieved celebrity and published them in the March 2007 edition of the *Occidental Weekly*.[20] No less an authority than *The New Yorker* followed up, publishing both poems in full and running an article by writer Rebecca Mead analyzing the poems.[21]

"Pop" is the poem of interest here. In it, Obama does not disclose the identity of "Pop," just as he did not reveal the identity of "Frank" in *Dreams*. Curiously, Rebecca Mead concluded that the subject of "Pop" "appears to be a loving if slightly jaded portrait of Obama's maternal grandfather." Her conclusion, however, does not stack up at all, as Barack Obama never referred to his grandfather as "Pop." In *Dreams* and elsewhere, he always referred to Stanley Dunham as "Gramps," as is evident from a cursory reading of his memoirs.

Moreover, a careful reading of *Dreams* reveals that Obama never once used the word "Pop" or "Pops" for anyone, including his Kenyan father, whom he called "Dad," "Father," "old man," but never "Pop."

Rather, the "Pop" that is the subject of Obama's Occidental poem is an intriguing poet from his adolescence—and neither Obama's father nor maternal grandfather was, for starters, a poet. Further, this poet drinks whiskey, smokes, and gives the young man advice, as the young man continues to "listen." Here is the opening to the poem:

> *Sitting in his seat, a seat broad and broken*
> *In, sprinkled with ashes,*
> *Pop switches channels, takes another*
> *Shot of Seagrams, neat, and asks*
> *What to do with me, a green young man*

Who fails to consider the
Flim and flam of the world, since
Things have been easy for me;
I stare hard at his face . . .
I listen, nod . . .

As a "green" Obama listens and nods, staring at the man's face and "dark, watery eyes," taking in the advice and hard-earned knowledge, it is evident that this old, whiskey-drinking man of the world is unhappy. The man seems angry but keeps talking, or, as Obama puts it, "he's still telling." The poem continues:

[S]o I ask why
He's so unhappy, to which he replies . . .
But I don't care anymore, cause
He took too damn long, and from
Under my seat, I pull out the
Mirror I've been saving; I'm laughing,
Laughing loud, the blood rushing from his face
To mine, as he grows small,
A spot in my brain, something
That may be squeezed out, like a
Watermelon seed between
Two fingers.

The man remains discontented, and Obama "pulls out a mirror" as if to endeavor to see something of himself or for himself in the old fig-ure. Indeed, he feels the blood rushing from the old man's face into his own. Obama continues:

Pop takes another shot, neat,
Points out the same amber
Stain on his shorts that I've got on mine, and
Makes me smell his smell, coming
From me; he switches channels, recites an old poem
He wrote before his mother died,

Stands, shouts, and asks
For a hug, as I shink, my
Arms barely reaching around
His thick, oily neck, and his broad back; 'cause
I see my face, framed within
Pop's black-framed glasses
And know he's laughing too.

Though much of the content of this poem is inexplicable, its subject is not. This mystery man does not seem all that mysterious. He bears an uncanny resemblance (including physically) to "Frank."

The poem begins with the broad-backed man "sitting in his seat," just as Obama starts his most vivid description of Frank in *Dreams*, where Frank is "sitting in his overstuffed chair, a book of poetry on his lap." Roughly three lines after that descriptive item in *Dreams*, Obama writes of Frank drinking whiskey. Here, in this poem, three lines later, Obama describes "Pop" drinking Seagram's whiskey.

In both cases, the book *Dreams* and poem "Pop," the subject is wondering what to do with this green young man, and seems frustrated, bitter, unhappy, shouting, peers through "black-framed glasses," but Obama listens and nods. In "Pop," the subject indignantly tells the young man that things "have been easy" for him, and he fails to understand "the flim and flam of the world"—just like "Frank" in *Dreams*.

The man "recites an old poem," as Frank always did, and this time a poem "he wrote before his mother died." That item right there fits Frank, who was composing poems in Kansas well before his mother died in the summer of 1926, and wrote eloquently of her death for years to come, including in his memoirs;[22] it rules out Stanley Dunham ("Gramps"), who was not a poet and whose mother died when he was very young (age eight).[23]

Far and away the one subject who uniquely matches "Pop" is Frank Marshall Davis, a further reflection of his significant, lasting impact on Barack Obama—and into the Occidental years specifically. Indeed, the core message of the poem is indicative of an even deeper impact: The young Obama speaks of pulling out a "mirror I've been saving." Why? He seems to say that he sees himself in "Pop," or is looking for himself there. The poet's influence is so direct and so lasting that he seems to have inspired Obama to pay him tribute through poetry.

And what of the word "Pop"? That, of course, is the enigma. The paternal word has even prompted speculation by some conservatives that Frank is actually Obama's biological father and, by others with a less riotous take, that Frank is Obama's "surrogate father."[24]

I cannot resolve all of the arcane recesses of the riddle of "Pop," and I am certainly not prepared to argue that it means Frank was Obama's biological father. Rather, I can imagine how "Pop" simply might be a term of endearment for Frank. Recall that Dawna Weatherly-Williams, Frank's neighbor who was there when Obama and Frank first met, referred to Frank as "Daddy."

"Pop" was not an uncommon term of endearment. In fact, when Obama published this poem, I was a fifteen-year-old from Pittsburgh who counted among my heroes the Pittsburgh Pirates' iconic slugger Willie Stargell, whom everyone, from fans to teammates, referred to as "Pops." Stargell headed the famous Pirates "Family," the "We-Are-Family" club that even President Jimmy Carter glowed about. That team won the World Series in the fall of 1979, when Obama enrolled at Occidental and probably wrote this poem.

Whatever the reason for cloaking his subject as "Pop," there is no question that no other man in young Obama's life fits the bill like Frank Marshall Davis. And, again, if this was Frank Marshall Davis, then Barack Obama continued to carry Frank with him, far away from Hawaii, to the mainland, and onward farther still.

20

Frank Re-Emerges—and the Media Ignore Him

FOR OBAMA, LIFE after Hawaii and Occidental and New York meant Chicago. Just as Frank had done, it was there, in the 1980s, that he spread his wings. Both men established themselves in the Windy City, making political contacts that somehow ultimately helped lead Obama to the White House.

While Obama's horizons expanded, however, Frank's horizons narrowed. By the 1980s, the enemy now was not colonialism, not anticommunists, not Harry Truman or Winston Churchill, not corporate profits and General Motors, but mortality. Frank no longer faced the FBI or Senate Judiciary Committee but Father Time.

On July 26, 1987, Frank Marshall Davis took his last gasp of breath. In that final moment, all the bitterness and anger and injustice dissipated. He died in Honolulu at the age of eighty-one. The cause of death was a heart attack.

Let's hope that Frank passed to a place of no anger, no bitterness, no racism, no colonialism, no imperialism—and certainly no communism. Perhaps to an existence that featured long-overdue retribution for the Tulsa riots of the 1920s, for that young black mom burned at the stake while a diabolical mob laughed at her cries, for the Scottsboro Boys. A time of reckoning for those vile policemen who harassed Frank in Arkansas City while he was home from college, or for those two junior rednecks who fitted a five-year-old Frank with a noose.

Frank perished shortly after Ronald Reagan's speech at the Brandenburg Gate in West Berlin, where Reagan commended forty years of Americans and West Germans banding together to resist the Soviet menace. Frank had once smeared those efforts, particularly in that especially bad column for the *Honolulu Record* way back in May 1950—the one mockingly titled "Our New 'Democratic' Partner." Frank had stood on the other side of that wall.

The world had since changed dramatically. Within just two years of Frank's death, that Berlin Wall would collapse, and the people of Germany rapidly reunited just a year later—with no new "Nazification." Frank was not around to agitate and insist that a fascist/racist axis was emerging between nascent German Nazis and American anticommunists. That kind of propaganda work by Frank was finished.

A year after Germany reunited, the USSR that Frank and his comrades had promoted disintegrated. The Soviet collapse occurred in 1991, with the final nail in its atheist coffin coming Christmas Day 1991, when Mikhail Gorbachev resigned his post as head of the USSR, and thereby turned out the lights on what Ronald Reagan—a Republican whom Frank surely did not support for president—had described as an "Evil Empire." With the communist system collapsed, former Soviet officials came out of the woodwork to agree with Reagan—and not with the likes of Frank and Paul Robeson and William Patterson and CPUSA— that the Soviet Union had been a truly evil place.

Andrei Kozyrev, Boris Yeltsin's foreign minister, finally free to speak in his own country, stepped forward to declare it was a mistake to call it "the Union of Soviet Socialist Republics. It was, rather, [an] Evil Empire, as it was put."[1] A slight dissent came from another influential Soviet official, Genrikh Trofimenko, director of the prestigious Institute for U.S. and Canada Studies of the Russian Academy of Sciences. Trofimenko complained that Ronald Reagan's description of the USSR as an Evil Empire "was probably too mild."[2]

Frank Marshall Davis had been wrong about that one.

ARCHIVES—AND "PAUL"

With Marxism-Leninism on the ash heap of history, Russia's new anti-communist president, Boris Yeltsin, threw open the Soviet archives. Free citizens could now see evidence of what Yeltsin called the "horror house" that was the USSR and its worldwide web of accomplices. In the United States, the Library of Congress purchased from Russia a damning collection of declassified Soviet Comintern Archives on CPUSA. They are stunning to behold, particularly the complicity not only of lying CPUSA hacks but of the oblivious liberal/progressive dupes they manipulated. Elsewhere, FBI files and other Cold War materials were released, from holdings all over Washington, D.C., to libraries in New York, Chicago, California, and the Soviet Bloc. As these materials were opened, crucial information on men who thought like Frank—and Frank himself—became available.

With the Soviet implosion, even CPUSA revealed occasional facts about suspected (but deceased) erstwhile comrades. Among them, in 1998, the one hundredth anniversary of Paul Robeson's birth, CPUSA celebrated with full disclosure, publishing an eleven-page pamphlet proudly titled *Paul Robeson: An American Communist*.[3] The document is the text of a May 31, 1998, tribute to Robeson, presented in New York by longtime CPUSA head Gus Hall, the man who for decades secretly accepted multimillion-dollar subsidies from the Soviet Central Committee to clandestinely fund the American Communist Party throughout the most ominous days of the Cold War.[4]

In its birthday tribute to "Comrade Paul," CPUSA came bearing gifts. "We have a birthday present for Paul that no one else can give," said Hall, "the full truth and nothing but the truth. Just as we have had to tell and retell the truth about the Communist Party, so we have had to undo the lies about our Communist heroes." Hall was criticizing not anticommunists as liars (or *racists*, in Frank-speak), but liberals/progressives for denying or omitting Robeson's communist past. "Paul was a proud member of the Communist Party USA," stated Hall un-equivocally. In fact, said the CPUSA national chairman, Robeson did not "declare his Party membership openly" because such was CPUSA "policy" for "well-known, public personalities" who were members.

Paul had been a man of communist "conviction." Hall said that com-munism "defined, guided and motivated his [Robeson's] whole life," his "every word and deed." This was "an indelible fact of Paul's life," in "every way, every day of his adult life." He "never forgot he was a Com-munist." "Marxism-Leninism and the Communist Party gave Paul's life meaning and direction," gushed Gus Hall. "Comrade Robeson's mag-nificent life was nourished and sustained by Marxism-Leninism and the ever-growing Communist Party." A teary-eyed Hall recalled that his "own most precious moments with Paul were when I met with him to accept his dues and renew his yearly membership in the CPUSA."

This public disclosure by Hall and CPUSA sealed the case on Robe-son, well before the public posting of his 2,680-page FBI file.[5]

Sadly, however, such smoking guns are never enough for de-niers who still frame Paul Robeson as yet another innocent hounded by Joe McCarthy.[6] Gus Hall was frustrated, even disgusted at liberals/progressives for repressing the obvious fact that Robeson was a commu-nist. "Unfortunately," lamented Hall, "most try to deny or simply omit 'Communist' from the list of his enormous achievements. Most deny that Paul was a proud member of the Communist Party USA." A vigilant Hall said that communists "cannot allow . . . liberal, progressive" forces "to turn Robeson into a liberal. The real Robeson was a revolutionary, a Communist. . . . Paul Robeson was one of ours—a Communist leader, a beloved comrade."[7]

POST–COLD WAR RECORDS ON FRANK

Gus Hall further hoped that others would "honor Paul Robeson and the history of our whole Party," by joining CPUSA. Well, that was pre-cisely what Frank Marshall Davis had done in the 1940s.

As for post–Cold War documentation on the truth about Frank, the first key bits came with his memoir, *Livin' the Blues*, published posthu-mously in 1992, just after the Soviet disintegration. Frank's closeness to the Party and Party members was a salient thread throughout the book, even as he warily concealed his Party membership.

Then, too, came the work of serious biographers, particularly specialists on African-American poets and the African-American radical left. These scholars were not right-wingers, and all were sympathetic to Frank, clearly desiring not to rock the boat. Exposing certain "progressives" as closet communists could get them blacklisted by their colleagues in the academy. And none of them could have imagined Frank's relevance in the century to come with someone named Barack Obama.

Paramount among these scholars is John Edgar Tidwell. As noted, in Tidwell's most important work on Frank, *Frank Marshall Davis: Black Moods, Collected Poems*, released in 2002, he wrote: "Sometime during the middle of the war [World War II], he [Frank] joined the Communist Party." Tidwell produced the smoking gun: the letter from Frank to Irma Wassall confiding he had "joined the Communist party." [8] Five years later, in a 2007 work, continuing his study as Frank's biographer, Tidwell could write with confidence and almost in passing that Frank "became a closet member of the Communist Party." [9]

Another seemingly fair-minded scholar is James Edward Smethurst, a University of Massachusetts professor and Harvard Ph.D. At Harvard, Smethurst wrote *The New Red Negro*, published in 1999 by Oxford University Press, which focused on a broader group of African-American writers. There, Smethurst quoted Frank's poetry and noted his involvement in various fronts, such as being a teacher at CPUSA-sponsored schools like the Abraham Lincoln School—which, noted Smethurst, was "sponsored by the CPUSA or organized by CPUSA members and sympathizers." Writing of the 1930s and 1940s, Smethurst conceded the obvious: "Davis worked closely with the Communist Left both as a journalist and as a poet through virtually the entire period—and was almost certainly a CPUSA member for at least part of those years." [10]

Both Smethurst's and Tidwell's works on Frank are scholarly, not partisan; they are sympathetic authors whose interest in Frank is outside the political realm. This is especially true for Tidwell, who is unaware of the severity of the Soviet aspect of his subject and the very real danger and duplicity of American communists in this period—which is not surprising, given his interest in Frank as a literary figure. Tidwell's

and Smethurst's treatments appeared well before the meteoric rise of
a young politician named Barack Obama. Again, neither scholar could
imagine the political sensitivity of their earlier research.

The grandest disclosure of Frank came with Obama's 1995 book,
Dreams from My Father. Much as with his association with Jeremiah
Wright, the hip-gyrating, pelvis-thrusting, blaspheming, Bill Clinton–
bashing, ranting, raving reverend at the Trinity United Church of Christ
in Chicago, Obama knew that he needed safe distance from Frank, all
the while understanding that Frank had been too important and formative in his life to be ignored. Nonetheless, the CPUSA cat was out of
the bag.

Once it was acknowledged during the 2008 presidential campaign
that Obama's "Frank" was Frank Marshall Davis, suspected communist,
three things happened: 1) Conservatives began digging and reporting;
2) pro-Obama liberal journalists and biographers did backflips to avoid
Frank's shady past, and mocked and ridiculed conservatives daring to
investigate; and 3) modern American communists were thrilled about
the connection between Obama and Frank, and did not hesitate to affirm, endorse, and even emulate them.

Consider each of these three dynamics:

Among conservatives, the most exhaustive initial effort to reveal
Frank and his past was done by Cliff Kincaid and Herb Romerstein.
Romerstein has spent his entire life researching the communist movement. As a young man, he had been a communist himself. Growing up
in New York, his views changed dramatically during the Korean War,
which sent him fleeing the Party. He became a highly sought investigator for Congress, testifying predominantly under Democrat-led committees. When the crucial Venona transcripts were released after the Cold
War, Romerstein was front and center in interpreting them for posterity.

Romerstein became a common face at the Library of Congress
throughout the 1990s and into the 2000s, where he studiously combed
Comintern archives on CPUSA and any number of additional archives
that only someone of his unique background and understanding
could comprehend. He remains in demand in the United States and
around the world for his fairness and meticulous research. He is completely credible and highly respected, and no one, Democrat or Re-

publican, had ever accused Herb Romerstein of being a McCarthyite witch-hunter. He was the epitome of responsible anticommunism, always pushing other researchers never to exaggerate, to treat individuals fairly, to not sloppily lump together liberals with communists, to distinguish small "c" communists from Party members, to amply credit those who left and rejected the Party.[11]

So, when Frank Marshall Davis's name arose during the 2007–8 presidential candidacy of Barack Obama—thanks to Obama's own memoir—it was Romerstein who knew about Frank, his past, his many colleagues in the movement, and his dealings and motivations. Romerstein endeavored to show not only that Frank was a communist, but that Frank and his comrades had subverted the dearest liberal causes, such as stopping Hitler after the Hitler-Stalin Pact; they did so because of their unflagging loyalty and lockstep subservience to the Comintern and the USSR. If that did not concern liberals, Romerstein charged that Frank, like other CPUSA members, had used the civil-rights movement for the purpose of advancing Moscow's goals.

Romerstein worked with Cliff Kincaid to produce several in-depth reports on Frank. Kincaid, at his website, USASurvival.org, posted thousands of pages of publicly available congressional testimony and reports on Frank and his associates dating back to the 1950s, as well as declassified government documents. The best available primary-source material on Frank is today easily available because of the efforts of Romerstein and Kincaid.

FRANK'S LIBERAL PROTECTORS

It was patently cruel, but not surprising, that when Romerstein and Kincaid held a press conference on Capitol Hill in May 2008 to announce what they had found on Frank, loaded with primary-source exhibits, they were mocked and ridiculed, but mostly ignored. The snubbing was a sign they had their facts right. One member of the media who did not ignore them was the *Washington Post*'s liberal columnist Dana Milbank, who ridiculed them.

Milbank described the press conference as a conspiracy theorist's dream, a gathering of right-wing wackos—"a UFO convention."[12]

Romerstein and Kincaid might as well have held their press conference at Area 51, or Roswell, New Mexico. A new Vast Right-Wing Conspiracy was being uncorked, this time against Barack Obama. Milbank
framed the press conference as a 2008 version of the 2004 Swift Boat
veterans who damaged the candidacy of John Kerry, the previous Democratic presidential nominee. In a particularly mean swipe, Milbank referred to Romerstein as "a living relic from the House Committee on
Un-American Activities."

The *Washington Post* reporter laughed off the very worthwhile point
by Romerstein and Kincaid that because of associations like Frank Marshall Davis, not to mention Bill Ayers and other communist radicals,
Barack Obama would have difficulty getting a security clearance for a
job as a clerk in a government agency, let alone a pass to sit in the Oval
Office. Recall that Frank had been on the federal government's Security
Index.

Milbank's article was a shot across the bow of the right: a warning
by an influential Obama supporter that conservatives not dare bring up
the communists in Obama's past. Anyone who committed such a transgression could face exposure in the *Washington Post*. *Are you now, or have
you ever been, an* anti*communist investigating Barack Obama's past?*

As some conservatives complained about Frank—though not as
loudly as they complained about Bill Ayers and Jeremiah Wright—other
liberals were forced to at least acknowledge him. As they did, however,
they quickly covered for him, serving the role that liberals/progressives
have long served for communists: as dupes denouncing not the communists who covertly fronted for Stalin but the anticommunists who raised
questions.

Consider the work of the Associated Press, which ran two articles on
Barack Obama's life in Hawaii, and one specifically on Frank Marshall
Davis,[13] at the height of the 2008 presidential campaign. In an extraordinary display of journalistic bias, the AP managed to share only one
line worthy of quotation from all of Frank's outrageous articles in the
Honolulu Record: "I refuse to settle for anything less than all the rights
which are due me under the constitution."

In the AP's portrait, Frank was an unflagging advocate of "civil rights
amid segregation," a crusader for the U.S. Constitution, suffering the

jackboot of segregation. There was no sign of the unyielding basher of Harry Truman, of the bomb-thrower accusing the Democratic president of pursuing a neocolonial state, a fascist-imperialist state, a racist state, a third world war. There was not a whiff of Sovietism. The word "communism" was never mentioned. Worse, the article dismissively claimed that charges of Frank's "allegedly anti-American views" had been soundly rejected by "those who knew Davis and his work," people who maintained that "his activism was aimed squarely at social injustice."

Frank Marshall Davis: champion of social justice.

Aside from the AP, other leading media sources put their top (liberal) talent on the subject. This included David Maraniss, Jon Meacham, and David Remnick, all respected voices who have done excellent work in other contexts, including (in some cases) on the Soviets and the Cold War.

The *Washington Post* placed star reporter David Maraniss on a story about Obama's Hawaii years. Maraniss had earned a Pulitzer Prize for his probing in the past. He did superb work on the early life of the previous Democratic president, Bill Clinton. Maraniss's research on Obama produced a ten-thousand-word piece for the *Post*. And yet, among all those words on Obama's upbringing in Hawaii, there was not a single mention of Frank Marshall Davis. This was a slight of Frank that Obama himself could not even carry out.[14]

Jon Meacham and David Remnick managed more than that, but, in so doing, did more harm to the truth. They mentioned Frank all right, but defended him as a staunch, stoic civil-rights crusader hounded by McCarthyites, even though Joe McCarthy never came anywhere near Frank. Quite the contrary, as noted, the senator who questioned Frank was the same senator who headed the special committee that pursued Joe McCarthy.

Meacham, the gifted writer for *Newsweek*, told readers that Frank wrote about "civil-rights and labor issues," and was a relentless advocate for racial and social justice. Frank's columns were a platform for his "strong voice" on such matters. This was Frank's form of "political activism"—note, not communism or pro-Soviet activism or vilifying every foreign-policy move of the Truman administration. And it was this, lamented Meacham, that ramped up the Red-under-every-bed brigade of McCarthy witch-hunters. "His political activism," claimed Meacham of Frank, "especially his writings on civil-rights and labor issues, prompted a McCarthyite denunciation by the House Un-American Activities Committee."[15]

This statement was wholly inaccurate. Frank's writings on civil rights and "labor issues" were not, by any stretch of the imagination, what got him noticed in Washington. Moreover, there was no denunciation of Frank by Joe McCarthy or the House Committee on Un-American Activities—of which McCarthy had never been a member. It had been the Senate Judiciary Committee that called Frank out. It was the Democratic-run Senate that in 1956 called him to testify and in 1957 accurately described him as "an identified member of the Communist Party." Joe McCarthy that year was out of the Senate and nearly in his grave.

Rather astonishingly, Meacham had unwittingly adopted one of Frank's favorite propaganda lines, namely that the congressmen on the House Committee on Un-American Activities were motivated not by anticommunism or concerns over Soviet infiltration, but by unadulterated racism. Frank would have been thrilled with Meacham's take. Frank had honed this argument as a gambit to dupe liberals/progressives in Hawaii in the 1940s and 1950s; he could scarcely have imagined its being picked up by liberals/progressives in Washington some fifty to sixty years later.

Meacham's angle on Frank has become the standard liberal narrative.[16] And why wouldn't it be? For liberals in the mainstream press, it is a narrative that not only protects but actually helps Barack Obama.

To be fair, Meacham is hardly alone. His severely mistaken interpretation is repeated by David Remnick, who magnified it to outrageous proportions.

Remnick is a *Washington Post* and *New Yorker* journalist who, ironically, did outstanding work on the Soviet collapse.[17] He won the Pulitzer for his marvelous 1994 work, *Lenin's Tomb*, in which he demonstrated piercing insight into the defunct Soviet empire. That perceptiveness, however, was jettisoned when Remnick dealt with Frank Marshall Davis.

In his lengthy, best-selling biography of Barack Obama, *The Bridge*, which stands as the definitive work on Obama's life thus far, Remnick introduced Frank as "one of the more interesting men in Honolulu," regularly visited by Obama's grandfather. He should have stopped there.[18]

Remnick did not ignore Frank; he simply ignored all the negatives. His treatment is scandalous in its omissions.

In one section, Remnick wrote sympathetically of this grandson of a slave with a "fantastically deep Barry White voice." Frank had escaped Kansas, "a land of lynchings and frontier racism." From there, he established a "distinguished career as a columnist and editor in the world of the black press."

Remnick noted Paul Robeson's impact on Frank's coming to Hawaii. Robeson had visited Hawaii because of a concert tour sponsored by the ILWU, which Remnick described as a "left-wing union." Remnick, who, again, is a liberal journalist with an unusually sophisticated knowledge of the communist world, made not a single mention of Harry Bridges or the communist infiltration at the ILWU, which was well known by everyone in Hawaii, to the point where it was an everyday news item. Remnick also failed to mention the elephant in the living room: communism in Robeson's checkered career. Nor did he mention communism as a factor in Robeson's flying to Hawaii to provide his services for Harry Bridges's ILWU. Remnick noted only Robeson's glowing comments about racial harmony in Hawaii—just like the alleged harmony Robeson had somehow discovered in Stalin's Russia.

Remnick's account of Frank's work for the *Record* became progressively more outrageous. He benignly wrote that Frank "worked with the ILWU and wrote for its weekly newspaper, the *Honolulu Record*. . . . Some of his 'fellow freedom fighters' back in Chicago accused him of 'deserting the battle,' he [Frank] wrote, but in Hawaii he was less angry than he had been on the mainland, more at ease, though he never gave up his political views."

At this point in Remnick's recording, a confused reader would wonder what were Frank's "less angry" "political views" expressed in the *Record*. Remnick gave his answer in the next sentence, and thereby also leaves us wondering if he actually read Frank's columns: "He wrote fierce columns about the suppression of unions, conditions on the plantation, the power of the oligarchic Hawaiian families, race relations."

Remnick made not a single mention of Frank's fierce columns tearing up Harry Truman and the Marshall Plan, or blasting America's alleged plot to re-enslave and recolonize the world, or the so-called attempt by Uncle Sam to re-Nazify Germany, or, generally, Frank's intrepid defense of the USSR and the communist line at every twist and turn. None of this was mentioned by Remnick, who, as a Cold War Democrat, should have been aghast at Frank's positions. Instead, Remnick's very next line made it sound as if Frank was crucified by racist McCarthyites for his championing of "human dignity" and for his role as a civil-rights freedom fighter. "He was," explained Remnick of Frank, "one of many leftists who, in the nineteen-fifties, were investigated, and tainted, by the House Un-American Activities Committee."

Remarkably, Remnick (or his editor) even went so far as to use a derivation of the CPUSA name for the House Committee (as had Jon Meacham): the dread "HUAC" label that Frank and other communists employed to suggest the congressmen were un-American. (Of course, the American left en masse does this.) But more serious was Remnick's charge of *tainting*: In truth, Frank sufficiently tainted himself. He did so via a decades-long record of unmistakably pro-Soviet writings, thereby earning the suspicion not so much of the Democrat-run House Committee on Un-American Activities, which first began flagging Frank's communist associations in a 1944 report—precisely the period when Frank joined the Party—but, again, of the Democrat-run Senate Judiciary Committee.

In Remnick's section on Frank, the words "communist," "Marxist," "CPUSA," "Soviet Union," "USSR," "Russia," or host of other words that established the dominant extreme-left themes in Frank's political writings across multiple decades, especially at the *Honolulu Record*, appear just once; Remnick concluded his discussion of Frank with a shot at the "right-wing blogosphere," which, when Obama was running for president, allegedly smeared Frank as (in Remnick's words) "a card-carrying Communist, a pornographer, a pernicious influence. The attacks were loud and unrelenting."

Any reader of Remnick's definitive biography would, at this point, conclude that such right-wingers were beyond the pale, perhaps certifiably insane, and unquestionably delusional. After all, where would this crazy "card-carrying Communist" charge come from? It was certainly nowhere to be seen in Remnick's recording of things. Frank Marshall Davis, a communist? What smear-monger could have ever conjured up such libelous political fantasy?

And yet, Remnick's conclusions somehow got even worse.

After devoting four pages to Frank and Obama; after noting how Obama as a teen drove to Frank's house for advice; after conceding that "Davis, by Obama's own accounting, made the young man feel something deep and disorienting"; after quoting his eyewitness to the Frank-Obama relationship, Dawna Weatherly-Williams, so intimately close that she was there the first time Frank and Obama met, and who described the relationship as influential and consequential, and "about social justice, about finding out more about life, about what's important, about how to use your heart and your mind"; Remnick then dismissed it all by claiming that the Frank-Obama "relationship was neither constant nor lasting, certainly of no great ideological importance."[19]

Not lasting? It lasted long enough for Obama to expend thousands of words on Frank in his memoirs—the reason we know of the relationship to begin with.

Not of great ideological importance? Of course, on that matter, a reader of Remnick's book would again immediately ponder: *What ideology?* Remnick's account made no mention of Frank Marshall Davis's ideology. Readers would be thoroughly confused by Remnick's remark here: *Did Frank Marshall Davis even have a political ideology?* Readers of this authoritative account of the life of Barack Obama might want to know. Actually, more likely, they would simply chalk up all charges of Frank's being a communist to Neanderthal McCarthyism.

To be fair to Remnick, the pressures in dealing with Frank must have been immense. He likely had to steer clear of Frank's Soviet loyalties for fear of infuriating his liberal colleagues and tarnishing his liberal credentials by being labeled a McCarthyite who hurt Barack Obama. For liberals, few sins are as egregious as anticommunism, especially anticommunism that damages one of their own—and, in this case, a uniquely historic one of their own. Given the liberal/progressive circles that Remnick frequents, he was right to be afraid. To this day, any accusation of communism, no matter how perfectly fitting, no matter how unerringly accurate, is grounds to get any journalist blacklisted by the left. Just ask Hollywood conservatives.

Remnick's fears are understandable—as are those of Jon Meacham, David Maraniss, or other journalists from the mainstream press who have been fair and credible in the past. It is best to leave this territory to conservatives, whom the left can ignore as anti-Obama "morons" possessed by the unholy ghost of Joe McCarthy.

Herein, then, is the ultimate irony: The McCarthyism that supposedly once hounded the likes of Frank Marshall Davis has become one of Frank's best covers.

CONTEMPORARY COMMUNISTS FOR FRANK

For honest reporting on Frank from the left, one had to look much further left—all the way to the modern communist left.

One source not downplaying Frank, his mentoring of Obama, or the "c" word, was Alan Maki, a CPUSA member who, shockingly—and quite tellingly—blogged on the official "Obama '08" website. During the 2008 presidential campaign, Maki ran a blog called "Communist Manifesto," in which he picked up the Frank-Obama mandate for "change." Maki excitedly announced a "Frank Marshall Davis roundtable for change" on the Obama website.

And it was there that Maki was open about Frank's communism and his enthusiasm for Frank's communism. "Reading Barack Obama's book I learned about his mentor, Frank Marshall Davis," wrote Maki. "Of course, as we all know, Frank Marshall Davis was a communist." Maki noted that Frank "understood through his thorough studies of the situation that socialism provided the only workable alternative to capitalism."

Maki was learning from Frank, and he publicly expressed gratitude to Obama for helping him advance his communist beliefs through new study in the writings of Frank Marshall Davis. "Now I can say that Frank Marshall Davis is in many ways my mentor, too," Maki wrote.[20]

Taking a more jaded but likewise truthful tone about Frank's past was Dr. Gerald Horne, a professor of history and African-American studies with a Ph.D. from Columbia University and a J.D. from Cal-Berkeley—and a Marxist. His books include, among others, *The Final Victim of the Blacklist,* a defense of John Howard Lawson, Hollywood's commissar, and *Race War! White Supremacy and the Japanese Attack on the British Empire.*

Horne spoke at the reception for the opening of the CPUSA archives at NYU's Tamiment Library. In a transcript of his remarks published in *Political Affairs* magazine, the longtime "theoretical" journal of CPUSA, Horne started his lecture pessimistically, upset at how "the right-wing" in America had long "profited so handsomely" from the "infestation of anti-Sovietism and anti-communism." Among conservatives' scurrilous charges was that the USSR had been a "supposed 'Evil Empire.' " Quite the contrary, averred Horne, "the fall of the USSR was the greatest geo-political catastrophe of the 20th century."[21]

But not all was lost. There was hope and change afoot, and reason for optimism. Writing in 2007, Horne discerned a new political star on the horizon, and its name was Barack Obama. And, lo and behold, the star's mentor was none other than Frank Marshall Davis, who, Horne noted, "was certainly in the orbit of the CP—if not a member." Horne stated: "In his best-selling memoir, '*Dreams from My Father,*' the author speaks warmly of an older black poet he identifies simply as 'Frank,' as being a decisive influence in helping him to find his present identity."

The hopeful professor envisioned a day when America's youth would study Obama's memoirs "alongside Frank Marshall Davis's equally affecting memoir, 'Living the Blues.' " "When that day comes," said Horne, buoyantly, "I'm sure a future student will not only examine critically the Frankenstein monsters that US imperialism created in order to subdue Communist parties but will also be moved to come to this historic and wonderful [CPUSA] archive in order to gain insight on what has befallen this complex and intriguing planet on which we reside."

That CPUSA archive, as Horne and his comrades realize, holds information on Frank Marshall Davis's communist dealings. It is information the communist faithful are willing to concede, even if liberal/

progressive friends in the mainstream press refuse to consider and expose it at Obama's peril.

DECLASSIFIED FILES ON FRANK AND THE "CHURCH"

It was precisely such archives—all opened after the Cold War ended—that formed the heart of my research on Frank Marshall Davis. The material ranged from boxes and shelves and bound volumes at NYU's Tamiment Library, to the Comintern Archives on CPUSA at the Library of Congress, to Frank's huge declassified FBI file, plus more.

One of the most illuminating was Frank's six-hundred-plus-page FBI file, which was only recently made available to researchers, and which officially closed the case on whether Frank had joined the Party.[22] That file started in 1944, when Frank was in Chicago. It must have been Frank's staunchly pro-Soviet and anti-Churchill writings for the Associated Negro Press that prompted the FBI to begin collecting materials. Contrary to Frank's claim that the feds hounded him because he was a champion of racial justice and "democracy," the only articles excerpted by the FBI in that huge file are those in which Frank displayed unequivocal admiration for Soviet communism and relentlessly opposed U.S. foreign policy. It was not merely that Frank always opposed U.S. foreign policy, as the FBI noted in a January 4, 1952, document in his file, but he always did so "while praising Russia on every opportunity."[23]

In the FBI file, the collection of which stopped in 1963, we see an interest in communism by Frank dating back to 1931 and the Scottsboro and Herndon cases. We also see constant references to Paul Robeson and William Patterson, with Patterson a kind of communist mentor to Frank—mentioned probably more than any other figure in the file. One document quotes Patterson (April 1944) referring to Frank as a member of the "Church," evidently a reference to CPUSA. Another document reported a May 16, 1949, meeting of the Hawaii Civil Liberties Committee, the front group that Frank immediately sought to affiliate with Patterson and Robeson's Civil Rights Congress. Frank, who had just started his *Honolulu Record* column, was the speaker that evening. Following his talk, Frank was presented with a framed picture of

Robeson, which he held up for the audience as he beamed: "This is the great one."

We can also view in the FBI file Frank's continued placement on the Security Index, dating back to at least 1951.[24] We can even observe a May 6, 1949, document officially authorizing the transfer of Frank's file from the Chicago office to the Honolulu office. The document is personally signed by J. Edgar Hoover.

One FBI informant who had been a member of the Hawaiian branch of the Party—having joined CPUSA in San Francisco in 1946 before transferring his membership to Hawaii in January 1947—recounted how he had personally transmitted dues from Frank to the Party.[25] In a sworn statement given to FBI agent Leo S. Brenneisen in Honolulu on November 10, 1953, the informant also explained that the Hawaiian Party had been reorganized to go underground, with the Party divided into various "groups." He said that Frank was chairman of Group 10, which also included his wife, Helen. The informant also confirmed that the *Honolulu Record* had been started and controlled by the executive board of the Communist Party of Hawaii.

We also finally see in Frank's FBI file the long-awaited smoking gun: his CPUSA card number. Frank Marshall Davis's CPUSA number was 47544.

The case on Frank's Party membership and involvement is closed, as is abundantly evident in massive post–Cold War files now available to the public, some stored in hard-to-reach libraries, others (including the FBI file) easily retrievable online in a Google search.[26] Those files are also open, of course, to the pro-Obama media and biographers who insist on sugarcoating Frank Marshall Davis and his relationship with Barack Obama. In so doing, they dutifully protect a man who once demonized their own Democratic presidents and public officials, and whom their Democratic predecessors did not dare ignore.

21

Conclusion

Echoes of Frank

THIS BOOK HAS taken us through a long political journey. As a crucial parting thought, we must consider the extent to which the politics and ideology of Frank relate to Obama. Can we point to, say, a direct policy impact by Frank Marshall Davis on President Barack Obama?

That is a tricky business that invites a whole host of unwelcome criticisms. The nature of this book has been to rely not on conjecture but on evidence—that is, a long trail of written, undeniable, unmistakable statements by Frank, backed up by carefully detailed archival material collected by Congress, the FBI, the Soviet Comintern, CPUSA, and others. This is not a wise moment to radically depart from that evidentiary method.

Muddying the waters even further is the fact that President Obama is not about to step forward and admit that Frank directly influenced him on specific policy. Obama would never do that, given Frank's demonstrated extremist past as a loyal pro-Soviet member of CPUSA who opposed American foreign policy at each juncture in the hottest days of the Cold War. There is no way that Obama would affirm from the Oval Office that this American Bolshevik might have helped form some of his policy initiatives.

Yet we can count on Obama supporters to demand precisely such unreasonable standards. They will maintain that there is no stated proof offered by Obama in *Dreams from My Father* that Frank influenced him on policy matters. Of course, there isn't—for reasons I noted earlier and also because *Dreams* avoids policy matters altogether.

This does not mean that we cannot reasonably speculate or make certain policy connections between Obama and Frank. And to the extent there are similarities—and there most certainly are—they no doubt derive from a simple fact: Obama and Frank share elements of the same broader leftist philosophy. By nature of being politically on the left, communists, socialists, progressives, and liberals cross many areas of mutual interest, even when not inhabiting the same precise location on the ideological spectrum.

Just as starters, they tend to share a desire for reducing income inequality, for spreading and redistributing wealth, for workers' rights, for central planning and management of the economy, for expanding the power and scope of the federal government (at the expense of local government), for favoring the public sector over the private sector, for championing progressive or graduated federal income-tax rates, for expressing cynicism about business and capitalism and the wealthy, for engaging in heated class-based rhetoric and even class envy—to name merely a few commonalities. The differences among fellow travelers on the left are matters of degree more than a matter of principle. The communist will take all of your property and income and inheritance; the liberal/progressive will take varying portions of it. Both plan to redistribute it in a more "equitable" way, with the communist going much further.

The commonalities between Frank and Obama are reflective of these patterns.

Yet, more fundamentally, aside from policy matters, both men from the outset of their defining missions fancied themselves as agents of "change." Obama's famous campaign mantra was "change." Frank, too, saw himself as an agent of change. While Obama kicked off his historic presidential campaign with talk of "change," Frank kicked off his "Frank-ly Speaking" column in the inaugural issue of the *Chicago Star* with similar language. In the piece titled "Those Radicals of '76," Frank and his comrades claimed to be the true "spiritual descendants of . . . 1776." There, they invoked a mantra of "change." "If history teaches us anything," wrote Frank, "it teaches that any fundamental change advancing society is spearheaded by strong radicals."[1] Obama famously pledged to "fundamentally transform" America.

Both Frank and Obama were radical change agents. Remember from the start of this book the words of Dr. Kathryn Takara, the University of Hawaii professor who knew and interviewed Frank. She stated that Frank "nurtured a sense of possibility" in Obama, including "a sense of believing that change can happen."

Furthermore, and less general than "change," there are some quite specific and rather stunning similarities between what Barack Obama has favored and said and done as president and what Frank argued as a communist. Some of these could be happenstance, others perhaps not. Nonetheless, here I will offer just a few examples worth pondering, beginning with the start of Barack Obama's presidency.

REJECTING CHURCHILL

An auspicious start to the Obama presidency came when the new president sent back to the British embassy a bust of Winston Churchill that had resided in the White House. The bust had sat there with, of course, no objection from anyone. President Bush had placed it in a special spot in the Oval Office after the attacks of September 11, 2001. Americans have long revered Churchill, with end-of-the-century surveys citing him as the Man of the Century. He remains America's beloved, heroic World War II and Cold War ally. Brits, who once voted Churchill the greatest Brit in history, correctly saw Obama's action as a snub.[2]

Was there any American who would have endorsed Obama's action? Ironically, yes. Frank Marshall Davis.

An auspicious start to Frank's political commentary came when the new columnist for the Associated Negro Press began attacking Winston Churchill. He excoriated Churchill as an imperialist, a warmonger seeking domination and "supremacy." "The only people Churchill gives a rap about," charged Frank, "are the white people of the British Empire." Churchill hoped to "bludgeon all other countries into submission."

This thinking on Churchill—which no doubt first got Frank noticed by anticommunists and probably by the FBI—was as alien to Americans then as it is today.

This similarity is so unusual that it is hard to imagine it as a coincidence. Did Obama first learn to dislike Churchill from Frank? Could that dislike have come from a rant against colonialism by Frank? We do not know, but the parallel is extraordinary.[3]

To be sure, there have been positive areas of distinct departure between Obama and Frank in foreign policy. Recall Frank's demonization of postwar West Germany, arguing that America (under Harry Truman) was willfully handing Germany back to the Nazis. To the contrary, in July 2008, Senator Barack Obama, then the Democrats' presidential nominee, made an eloquent speech in Berlin, in which he fondly noted how America and West Germany stood together during those awful, trying days after the war.

"The only reason we stand here tonight," Obama told citizens of a unified Berlin, "is because men and women from both of our nations came together." They had done so in defiance of the dark, ominous "Soviet shadow" that had "swept across Eastern Europe." And which American policy had been most helpful, most generous? It was, said Obama, "the generosity of the Marshall Plan," which had helped create "a German miracle." It was also NATO, "the greatest alliance ever formed to defend our common security," and that had "face[d] down the Soviet Union." It was such things that produced "victory over tyranny."[4]

Barack Obama's speech was spot-on, but at each and every point, it was utterly contrary to the Stalin/Molotov line unerringly toed by Frank Marshall Davis in his columns.

Here, we can thankfully say, Frank left no impact on Obama.

That said, Obama seems closer to Frank in favoring or accommodating Russia on policy questions, once even privately assuring Russia's leaders that he would have more "flexibility" to deal with their concerns "after my election."[5] He has been troublingly pro-Russia at the expense of key U.S. allies like Poland and the Czech Republic. He accepted the Russian position on American missile defense, a stance that is explicitly anti-Poland and anti-Czech. In a move of terrible historical/symbolic significance, it was on September 17, 2009, that President Obama canceled America's plans for joint missile defense with Poland and the Czech Republic. Few partnerships made Poles and Czechs so proud; they cherished this defense alliance. It was the crowning touch, a peaceful one, forged from the Cold War crucible. It was *defensive*, not offensive. It hurt no one. But worst of all was the date of Obama's move, which struck Poles in particular as an ugly pro-Russia gesture, whether intentional or not: September 17, 2009, was seventy years to the day since Stalin's Red Army, in compliance with the Hitler-Stalin Pact, invaded Poland.

Frank had excused that pact, and even joined CPUSA after it was signed.

ON ECONOMIC RECOVERY

The most striking similarities between Obama and Frank occur in economic and domestic policy.

In his August 25, 1949, article for the *Honolulu Record*, Frank addressed a struggling economy saddled by continuing layoffs and teetering on the brink of another depression. He suggested economic-recovery ideas hauntingly close to what President Barack Obama and the Democratic Congress pursued in 2009 and 2010. He demanded a "living wage," "higher minimum pay," and a stop to the flow of "huge funds" into "Wall Street," "corporations," "Big Business," and "the pockets of our gigantic trusts and monopolies." "Instead," insisted Frank, tax money should flow into shovel-ready "public works projects" and be redirected and redistributed into "increased social security benefits, health insurance, education and low-cost housing."

Like President Obama, Frank had in mind "stimulus" of a strictly public-sector variety. The business world's investors and entrepreneurs could stimulate the economy only through their "taxes"—that is, wealth—redistributed by the federal government. Economic "growth" would come by spreading the wealth.

Generally, Frank's writings evinced a confidence that government central planners could resolve the nation's economic crisis. One thinks of President Obama's declaration that "only government," and specifically the federal government, could save America from its economic crisis. "At this particular moment," said the man who had sought Frank's advice, "the federal government is the only entity left with the resources to jolt our economy back into life. It is only government that can break the vicious cycle where lost jobs lead to people spending less money which leads to even more layoffs."[7]

Obama said this on February 9, 2009, just days into his presidency. Mere hours earlier, Senate Democrats had paved the way for the unprecedented $800-billion "stimulus" package that Obama desired as a cure for the fledgling economy. Washington's central planners had seized the reins to rescue the nation from another depression.

This "only government" sentiment was expressed in Obama's very first presidential press conference. It was a lifetime removed from the previous Democratic president, Bill Clinton, a fiscal moderate who famously declared "the era of big government is over," or Republican president Ronald Reagan, who, likewise facing a terrible economy, said, "In this present crisis, government is not the solution . . . government is the problem."[8]

Reagan spoke those words not long after young Obama digested Frank's words on the American way. Obama was listening to Frank Marshall Davis, not Ronald Reagan.

More ironic still is that this Obama statement in his first press conference came roughly six decades to the day, February 9, 1950, after Frank wrote his *Honolulu Record* column mocking "the incomes of the poor millionaires"; blasting "Big Business," "big stockholders," "dividend diplomats," and "giant corporations getting fat contracts"; and asking "how could General Motors make $600,000,000 in one year in the face of rising unemployment?"[9]

Frank's words seem a chilling bellwether of Obama's rhetoric going forward.

CLASS-BASED RHETORIC AND TAX CUTS

We can hear echoes of Frank in President Obama's unceasing class rhetoric and warfare—his constant negative references to "the wealthy" and blaming of the nation's fiscal and economic woes on anonymous "millionaires and billionaires" and nefarious "corporate jet owners." This is such a common tendency by Obama that we need not waste time here documenting it. One example, however, is particularly illustrative and reminiscent of Frank.

In early December 2010, President Obama made a remarkable announcement. He had compromised with the incoming Republican House majority on a "framework" to extend the Bush tax cuts. Obama thereby violated one of his core campaign promises. In so doing, he pleased and surprised conservatives and many moderates, and gravely disappointed his left-wing base.[10]

It seemed immediately clear, however, that Obama was motivated entirely by politics and not at all by ideology; that he responded to the Republican electoral rout that had just taken place in November. This impression was reinforced on Tuesday morning, when Obama, almost chastising his disappointed left-wing base for not understanding political realities, analogized Republicans to "hostage takers." It was as if the GOP were holding Obama and America and its poor and proletariat ransom to tax cuts for the bloody rich. The president bemoaned his moral dilemma, forced to "negotiate" with Republicans who kneel before what Obama described as "their Holy Grail": "tax cuts for the wealthy." It was an arresting metaphor: That cup overfloweth, apparently, with the real presence of the blood of the workers, which Republicans and their factory bosses and greedy landlords slurp up from the fruits of the assembly line.

"These tax cuts for the wealthy," said a visibly bitter Obama. "This is, seems to be, their central economic doctrine."[11]

Well, it was not Republicans' "central economic doctrine." But here was the telling item in Obama's assessment: Watching these words leave his lips, it was obvious this was not simply the standard class-warfare rhetoric typical of Democrats. This was not a mere political/rhetorical bone to toss to unions. No, Barack Obama had uttered these words with such conviction and such contempt that one could tell they came from the heart. This came off not as Democratic demagoguery, but as the class-based worldview many suspect is the core Barack Obama.

Of course, Frank Marshall Davis was not beyond this sort of rhetoric. In one column for the *Record*, he wrote indignantly that a proposal by liberals to increase wages was a "holy horror" to Republicans.[12] In another column, he scoffed at the "holy war to contain 'Russian communism,' " by Republicans and Truman Democrats alike.[13]

Aside from religious metaphors, recall the January 11, 1947, issue of Frank's *Chicago Star*, in which the lead headline bemoaned how the "GOP would 'spare rich' with 20 percent tax cut plan." The *Star* accused Republicans of wanting to hurt the poor and pad the wallets of the wealthy with "phony" tax cuts that only "benefit millionaires" and the "corporation executive." Frank's *Star*, sounding just like Obama and the Nancy Pelosi/Harry Reid Democratic leadership, insisted that America needed a more "fair" and "equitable" tax code that did not benefit millionaires at the expense of the poor. The wealthy, in the view of Frank and the *Star*, were not paying their "fair" share.

Generally, the pages of the *Star* regularly featured anti-Republican language and class-based demagoguery very similar to President Obama's rhetoric.

GHOSTS OF MAY DAYS PAST

Another eerily unusual similarity rising from the past is May Day, a national holiday to the communist world. And here, too, the tentacles stretch not only from Obama to his mentor but to the Canter family that mentored David Axelrod, the man who in 2008 got Obama elected president under the banner of "hope" and "change."

Remember that David Canter was a mentor to David Axelrod. David and his father, Harry, were intimately acquainted with Chicago's left-wing political scene. Harry had been secretary of Boston's Communist Party, and both father and son spent the 1930s in Moscow, with Harry working for the Soviet government as a translator of Lenin's writings. As noted, Harry was among the small group that purchased the *Chicago Star* from Frank. His name was familiar to *Star* readers. Among other instances, his name appeared in the April 28, 1947, edition, wishing "May Day Greetings" to fellow comrades.

Frank would have joined Harry at that May Day parade in Chicago. He editorialized in support of the 1947 May Day.[14] His newspaper was gung-ho for every May Day, which was accorded more fanfare (and ink) in the *Star* than Christmas and Independence Day combined. Each May Day, it was all hands on deck at the *Star*, from Frank to Howard Fast, from the editorial department to news and advertising. May Day was like a test of loyalty.

Not many American presidents have marched in May Day rallies, but Barack Obama did so as a U.S. senator for May Day 2006.[15] And speaking of loyalty on May Day, it is uncanny that, as president, Obama issued a formal presidential proclamation declaring a national "Loyalty Day" for "May 1 of every year"—that is, every May Day. In an almost creepy Frank-like way, Obama presented his proclamation in the language of the Founding Fathers, their Declaration, and their Constitution. The very first words of the proclamation are: "When our Nation's Founders adopted the Declaration of Independence . . ."[16]

THE OLD FOLKS AT HOME: THE JARRETT AND AXELROD CONNECTIONS

These are just a few peculiar Obama-Frank connections, with many more that could be cited.[17] The connections go beyond policy and philosophy to people—to White House staff, *top* advisors, *very* top advisors.[18]

With Axelrod, there is the Canter family. With Valerie Jarrett, the links are likewise deep. Recall that Valerie Jarrett's father-in-law, Vernon Jarrett, and her maternal grandfather, Robert Taylor, both worked with Frank as joint members of communist fronts or in suspected front activities. In a surreal twist of fate, Barack Obama, once he landed in Frank's Chicago, would come face-to-face with Valerie Jarrett, child of these forebears, and initially through Michelle Obama.

Michelle Robinson, then Obama's fiancée, met Jarrett in July 1991, when Jarrett was deputy chief of staff to Mayor Daley, whom David Axelrod helped elect. Michelle was working for the law firm Sidley Austin. Michelle impressed Jarrett, who was a power broker in Chicago political circles. Michelle told Jarrett she should meet Barack Obama. They did, and hit it off in a way that would change the world.[19]

Valerie later said of the meeting, "Barack felt extraordinarily familiar." Indeed, there was much between them that was truly extraordinarily familiar. Beyond their common political/ideological ancestry, the two of them, said Jarrett, "shared a view of where the United States fit in the world." According to David Remnick, this shared view was a more "objective" view of America—a view in which America was not "the center of all wisdom and experience."[20] In other words, this was not an exceptional America. It was closer to a Frank Marshall Davis view of America. It was a different vision of the American way.

Valerie Jarrett and Barack Obama became extremely close politically, personally, and professionally. Obama checked with Valerie every step of the way to the White House. He and Michelle regularly vacation with Valerie at Martha's Vineyard. She is their top advisor and confidante. Michelle told the *New York Times* that Jarrett "automatically understands" the "values" and "vision" of the two Obamas, "never afraid" to tell them the truth. Michelle speaks of Jarrett like both a sibling and a mother: "Like a mom, a big sister, I trust her implicitly." So does Barack, who refers to Jarrett as "someone I trust completely." "She is family." The president trusts her so much that he permits Jarrett "to speak for me, particularly when we're dealing with delicate issues."[21]

From November 2008 to November 2010, it was Valerie Jarrett at Obama's side as the new "progressive" president pushed a radical-left agenda, from nationalizing GM to an $800-billion government "stimulus" for public-work projects, just as Frank and Valerie's father-in-law and grandfather had once stood side by side pushing a radical-left agenda.

And to think that Frank—Obama's Frank—had worked with Valerie Jarrett's father-in-law, Vernon Jarrett, and with Valerie Jarrett's maternal grandfather, Robert Taylor, is kind of mesmerizing. It is a political/historical irony that is profound.

GM AND HEALTH CARE

Most extraordinary is the GM parallel between Frank and Obama. Of all the automakers, both Frank and Obama happened to zero in on GM for government action—draconian government action. In Frank's *Honolulu Record* columns from January to February 1950 in particular, he seemed to favor a government takeover of enterprises like General Motors, a company he eviscerated because of its profits—profits Frank deemed excessive. Before those columns, Frank's *Chicago Star* had been relentless in bashing GM. He described the company as a "branch of U.S. imperialism" lowering its own "iron curtain" across the continent. He vilified GM's management as "General Motors' Hitlers."

Frank's antipathy for GM makes Obama's actions toward GM all the more startling, and hard to chalk up as a fluke. Only one president ever, of all presidents, was willing to nationalize General Motors. That president, Barack Obama, just happens to be the one mentored by Frank Marshall Davis.

That kind of radical government intervention is historically alien to the American way. It is reminiscent of the Attlee government in Britain after World War II, when Prime Minister Clement Attlee and his band of Keynesians nationalized numerous industries, from car companies to health care. Attlee won the prime ministership by defeating and unseating no less than Winston Churchill.

Speaking of health care, Frank championed an expanded federal role there as well. He favored redistributing wealth from "rich" "corporations" toward "health insurance," and explicitly advocated taxpayer funding of universal health care. In his July 1955 column for the *Honolulu Record*, Frank stated: "I would rather see my tax dollars go to insure health care for everybody."[22] Recall, too, that Frank's fellow columnist at the *Chicago Star*, Senator Claude Pepper, with the help of his chief of staff, Charles Kramer—who we now know was a literal Soviet agent—authored the first major legislation seeking to socialize American medicine.

Where Frank's *Chicago Star* companions failed, the young man he mentored in Hawaii one day picked up. President Obama's "health-care reform," that is, "Obamacare," is the closest America has come to Pepper's socialist pipedream.

FRANK'S MAN IN THE OVAL OFFICE

Likewise profound are some fascinating parting thoughts in Frank's memoirs that relate precisely to Obama's election to the Oval Office.

Frank cited various national and global "problems" that he believed posed the "prospect of annihilation." These included the earth's alleged "finite quantities of coal, oil," and other "disappearing natural resources." Frank also feared a "mushrooming world population" and a "population explosion" in America. He prophesied bleak times: "What will we do with the 300,000,000 to 400,000,000 or more that is expected in thirty years?"

The coming generation would deal with these perceived crises. In fact, Frank was worried about precisely the time when Barack Obama would become president, with a population of 300-plus million Americans.[23]

Speaking of those prophecies, and of President Obama—America's first black president—Frank finished his life's story with a particularly prescient thought: He noted that until the election of President Franklin Roosevelt, black Americans could never aspire to anything higher than the president's "Kitchen Cabinet." Yet Frank harbored a rare glimmer of hope in his otherwise pessimistic, bitter outlook. "We have been inching our way slowly toward the Oval Room," stated Frank.[24]

Amazingly, it was that young man whom Frank helped mentor in Hawaii who would become the first black American to occupy that Oval Room.

For a man for whom race was always the paramount issue, this was Frank's grandest prediction—one that would have had him weeping tears of joy. No matter what one's politics, it is hard not to appreciate the fulfillment of that dream. The little boy who was nearly lynched a century earlier in Arkansas City had mentored an African-American boy who made it to the Oval Room. Imagine that. It is hard not to be touched.

If only the politics weren't so bad.

Again, there are plenty of other Obama-Frank parallels that could be drawn out in this final chapter.

The primary goal of this book, however, has been to reveal the mystery and the man behind the "Frank" in *Dreams from My Father*. Never before, to my knowledge, has a president (gingerly) acknowledged such a radical early influence only to have the dominant press utterly ignore that influence, if not downplay or dismiss that influence altogether. It was my lot as a Cold War researcher to find all the material on Frank Marshall Davis. With this book, readers can now glimpse that material themselves.

Frank was a complex man. Most often I shook my head in disgust as I read his pro-Soviet propaganda work, then recoiled again as I read his writings on Mao's China, on Korea, on Vietnam, and more.

Still, all along, I could never escape that little boy in Kansas who was forever traumatized by what Frank and I finally would agree were white-hooded mini-Hitlers. That colossal sin coarsened Frank's soul.[25] It was so devilish that it separated him from God, pushing him away from the light and closer to the darkness, where communism lurked. For that transgression alone, Frank earned my sympathy. He suffered a great injustice, and it was merely the first.

On the other hand, Frank earned my disapproval for the mud and hate he slung where it absolutely did not belong. This included a vicious, sustained rhetorical lynching of the likes of President Harry Truman, among countless others who fought the good fight to stop the Soviets. Frank's mistreatment of these good men was itself a great injustice. Here, his bitterness was completely misplaced, even as it was most appropriate back in Arkansas City.

And why is this particular injustice so relevant right now? It is relevant on its own merits. There were hundreds of thousands of American communists like Frank who agitated throughout the twentieth century. They chose the wrong side of history, a horrendously bloody side that left a wake of over 100 million corpses from the streets of the Bolshevik Revolution to the base of the Berlin Wall—double the combined dead of the century's two world wars. And they never apologized. Quite the contrary, they cursed their accusers for daring to charge (correctly) that they were communists whose ideology threatened the American way and the greater world and all of humanity. They took their denials to the grave, and still today their liberal/progressive dupes continue to conceal their crimes and curse their accusers for them. We need hundreds and thousands more books on American communists like Frank, so we can finally start to get this history right—and, more so, learn its vital lessons. To fail to do so is a great historical injustice.

We especially need to flesh out these lessons, which are morality tales in the truest sense of the word, when we find the rarest case of a man like "Frank" managing to influence someone as influential as the current president of the United States of America—the leader of the free world and driver of the mightiest political/economic engine in history. Such figures cannot be ignored.

The people who influence our presidents matter.

Motivation and Acknowledgments

SOMEONE NEEDED TO take the time to deal with Frank Marshall Davis. Given that I came into possession of Frank's political writings, and that my area of research is the Cold War and the American communist movement, I took up the task, for better or worse. I could not ignore it.

A book on Frank's political past had to be done, particularly as liberal Obama biographers frame Frank as a stoic civil-rights crusader who battled slanderous McCarthyites who unfairly hounded him for *trumped-up* communist activities. That false narrative is pushed by liberals to protect Barack Obama.

On the matter of Frank's impact on Obama, I will say, definitively, that Frank's far-left extremism is reflective of, and may help explain, how and why our president is further to the left than any other president of our generation if not American history. More than that, Frank even more likely explains how and why our president, as a young man at Occidental College circa 1980, was possibly once on the Marxist left.

I understand I will be accused of a conservative bias for having the impudence to investigate this. The greater bias is the liberal bias that refuses to ponder this elephant in young Obama's living room—a serious influence on the current president of the United States of America, the mightiest political-economic behemoth in history, governing 300-plus million citizens and affecting many more worldwide. This nation won the Cold War, defeating Soviet communism in a battle in which this influence to the current president stood on the wrong side. To ignore the deep track record of public writings by this influence is scandalous.

Let's all be honest: Such a ludicrous demand could be advanced only because the president's protectors do not want exposed what plainly exists. They do not want this information out there because of what it might suggest about the president's thinking. There is no way that liberals would insist on such a hands-off approach if a conservative Republican president had a mentor this extreme to the right. The mentor would have been exposed in front-page profiles early in the 2008 presidential campaign.

At the same time, conservatives must also concede political biases: They want this disturbing information to see the light of day.

Nonetheless, whatever our biases, reality is reality, history is history, truth is truth. And you do not ignore the influences on our presidents, especially one like Frank Marshall Davis.

My task as an orthodox Roman Catholic who endeavors to be a Christian scholar has been to try to report fairly, accurately, and, above all, truthfully the vast volume of remarkable Frank Marshall Davis writings that I could have never imagined finding. In December 2010, one year before I finished this manuscript, I had no intention of writing this book. I do not need the grief. My next book was going to be a leisurely follow-up to my most recent book, *Dupes*. Nonetheless, I got ahold of this material on Frank. And as someone who for a long time has taught and written about this era, I understand it. I had to write it.

Here is how I arrived at this point: In the course of researching a follow-up to *Dupes*, I came across more and more on Frank. I came into possession of the rarest of his writings. His columns from the *Chicago Star* and the *Honolulu Record* seem to exist in only two libraries, where I had two students (one former, one current) photocopying from microfiche. The Library of Congress does not have this material. In the case of the *Star*, the Library of Congress claims to have the archives but, upon taking a closer look, discovered it does not. The reels of microfiche from the *Chicago Star* seem to have disappeared from the shelf.

Beginning in the spring of 2011, I became riveted by Frank. He fascinated me, alternately outraging me and inspiring empathy; the former because of Frank's communism, the latter because of the racism he painfully endured. Some people can't put a book down; I couldn't pull myself away from doing this one.

I have dedicated this book to Spyridon Mitsotakis, a brilliant young man with a promising career ahead of him as a top-notch Cold War scholar, if he chooses. This book would not exist if not for Spyridon's digging. I met Spyridon at a conference in February 2011 at a book signing for my book *Dupes*. Once Spyridon had my ear, I couldn't shut him up, and neither could the folks behind him in line. He spoke a mile a minute, a walking encyclopedia of Cold War knowledge. I promised Spyridon that if he emailed me with his innumerable follow-up questions on the American communist movement, I would respond. He did so right away, and I responded.

Almost immediately in our continued email correspondence, Spyridon reminded me that he is a student at New York University, which is home to the Tamiment Library, which happens to hold CPUSA's archives. "Is there any research I could do for you here?" Spyridon enthusiastically offered.

I told Spyridon that I was already researching a follow-up book to *Dupes*. I told him that among the characters I wanted to continue to examine was Frank Marshall Davis. I told Spyridon that I had librarians searching everywhere for the *Chicago Star*, but they came up empty, including at the Library of Congress. "Could you look in NYU's Tamiment to see if they have the *Star*?" I wrote to Spyridon.

In mere hours, Spyridon excitedly emailed me back with the good news that Tamiment not only had the *Star* but had every issue. Attached were samples that Spyridon had already started copying and emailing to me. When I looked at the columns, I was blown away.

Over the course of the next several weeks, I soon had a literal stack of pages from the *Star* traversing the entirety of its existence, including every article by Frank. My jaw hit the floor as I digested these pro-Soviet columns one by one. It was then, in the spring of 2011, that I knew I had no choice but to convert this material into a book. I knew I would take some arrows, but I had no choice.

I must add that Spyridon built on the superb efforts of Emily

Hughes, a former student of mine at Grove City College who happened to live in Hawaii and ventured into a University of Hawaii library that has every copy of the *Honolulu Record*. Emilyix, another very impressive young person, got me every Frank column for the *Record* from 1949 to 1957. She had already gotten a bunch of them for me for *Dupes* (the 1949–50 columns) and went back again for my renewed research into a *Dupes* follow-up (the 1951–57 columns). And before Emily, another wonderful student, Anthony Maneiro, had also located a cache of Frank columns.

Still, it was not until Spyridon's excavations that I realized I was peering into a gold mine of information that demanded a separate book just on Frank. Without Spyridon's tireless work, of which this was just the start, I would not have considered a full book strictly on Frank Marshall Davis. Once Spyridon had vetted the *Star*, he began finding more and more Frank gems, including those from the American Committee for Protection of Foreign Born and rare microfiche of the *Atlanta Journal World*.

So I quickly put together a book proposal that I began sending to publishers, a process that transpired rapidly between roughly mid-May and late June 2011.

That brings me to Mercury Ink, and a word of appreciation.

I had shared this book concept with a few other conservative imprints and publishing houses. All were respectful and gave my proposal immediate consideration. Unfortunately, I was very surprised and dismayed at the failure (by some) to appreciate the historical significance. "People aren't interested in the Cold War anymore," one editor told me. There was also a failure to see the contemporary political relevance, which surprised me even more.

Two houses/editors did appreciate it, but had other reasons why they were not interested in a manuscript. For one, the 2012 titles were already etched in stone, and my proposal was indeed last-minute.

To the contrary, Glenn Beck, and specifically his editor, Kevin Balfe, immediately grasped the full significance, and especially appreciated the history. They responded instantly. I emailed the proposal to Kevin on a Friday morning, June 17 (with the recommendation of my friend Peter Schweizer, who knew Kevin). Kevin responded that day, asking me a few questions concerning documentation and where I found the materials. I told him and forwarded some jpgs and PDFs of Frank's columns. Kevin sent the proposal to Glenn over the weekend, and Glenn read it on the spot. (I had never met Glenn other than doing his radio show in 2004 on my book, *God and Ronald Reagan*. I had learned then that Glenn is a talk-show host who actually reads books cover to cover.) Kevin and I were talking on Monday morning.

Enthusiasm is extremely important in a publisher. Here it was.

Most important, and a huge relief to me, was Glenn's insistence—in keeping with my own insistence in the proposal—that the book not overstate anything. Glenn relayed this through Kevin: There should be no exaggeration or hyperbole. I should simply start the book by noting the relationship between Frank and Obama—and what we know about it—and then focus on Frank and his vast volume of writings. Speaking for Glenn, Kevin told me, "Simply tell the reader who Davis was and what he believed. This man was a mentor of some type. He shouldn't be ignored. Give people the facts and they can make up their own minds."

This reaction by Glenn was completely contrary to the caricature by his critics.

Glenn and Kevin and Mercury Ink wanted a book on Frank Marshall Davis's ideas, thinking, ideology, and history. They agreed with my desire to avoid the seedy sexual allegations against Frank. "Let's stay focused on what Davis believed and why that matters," said Kevin, as I vigorously nodded.

Glenn also had some highly informed follow-up questions concerning my proposal. These were insightful, probing into historical context and previous presidential mentors. He noted the lack of a conversion narrative by Obama between his Occidental and White House years, and how odd and telling that is. Glenn has frequently observed the lack of a "pivot point" by Obama in his memoirs and interviews—unlike Ronald Reagan, George W. Bush, Hillary Clinton (all subjects of mine), or even Glenn himself in his own life.

All of these factors drew me to want to sign with Mercury Ink. The fact that it is partners with Simon & Schuster, the largest and most prestigious publishing house in the world, made it even more attractive.

In one more conversation, Kevin reiterated that they didn't want me to be partisan, lobbing bombs and ad hominem attacks. They wanted to go with me because they safely assumed I wouldn't do that. They wanted something "levelheaded," "nonhysterical," "reasonable," "respectable," and "scholarly while still readable and accessible to a general audience." No sensationalism or hyperbole, no partisanship. I couldn't have been more pleased. It was a perfect match. On June 28, I signed the contract. I thank everyone who has played a role at Mercury Ink and Simon & Schuster. Most notably, that includes the editing hands of David Harsanyi and Dan Smetanka. Dan did a great job helping shape and focus the manuscript. His work was superb. Likewise, Simon & Schuster editorial assistant Natasha Simons did excellent work, as did many other players at Simon & Schuster, including Mitchell Ivers.

I'm also grateful to Alex Welch and Soren Kreider, two current Grove City College students, for their assistance. Alex, in particular, was my steady on-campus researcher. He was always there to grab whatever request I emailed, answering cheerfully and promptly. I'm also grateful to Matt Costlow, an outstanding Grove City College student who graduated in 2010, and was a tremendous help and go-to guy for my book *Dupes*. Matt today is in graduate school, and often emailed me offering to help on this book as well—for fun, not pay. "Once a researcher, always a researcher," Matt would sometimes preface his emails, with a grin, before sending me some tidbit he happened upon and figured I could find useful. Matt had regular access to archives of the *Daily Worker*, and was always eager to dive into the archives to track down whatever I needed.

Finally, as always, I thank everyone at Grove City College and the Center for Vision & Values for their support, particularly Lee Wishing and Brenda Vinton for helping me find the time to write, and especially Cory Shreckengost, who was involved in every step of the process, including suggesting publishers (Mercury Ink among them). And I'm most grateful to my family—my wife, my children, my brother and sister, and my parents. Most of all, I'm grateful to the God who gave me life and through whose sanctifying grace alone I'm able to occasionally squeeze out a modicum of virtue. Any mistakes or personal vices evident in this final product are no doubt mine alone, and no surprise given my many daily faults and insufficiencies.

Appendix:
Frank Marshall Davis Documents

BIOGRAPHICAL DATA

FRANK DAVIS

FRANK M. DAVIS
MARSHALL DAVIS
F. M. DAVIS

Name: Frank Marshall Davis

Born: 12/31/05, Arkansas City, Kansas

Description: Race: Negro
                     Height: 6'1"
                     Weight: 230
                     Eyes: Brown
                     Hair: Black
                     Complexion: Light Brown

Communist Party No: 1946 CP #47544

Social Security No: 337-16-3458

Addresses: 1923-1934: 1014 North Summit, Arkansas
                     City, Kansas.

                     1944-   : 3559 South Vincennes Avenue,
                     Chicago, Illinois.

                     1944-   : 3507 South Parkway, Chicago.

                     -1948: 3852 South Lake Park Avenue,
                     Chicago.

                     1948-1950: 1830 Waiola, Apt. #1,
                     Honolulu, T.H.

                     1950-1953: Punaluu, Kapaka District,
                     Windward Oahu, T.H., c/o Post Office
                     at Hauula, Oahu, T.H.

Marital Status: Wife - Thelma B. Davis, born 5/8/03,
                     place not stated. Married on 7/12/31 at
                     Atlanta, Georgia.
                     Wife - [   ] a
         b6   member of the white race, born
         b7C   at [   ] Date of
                     marriage not stated.

-3-

Figure 1: Summary page from Frank's six-hundred-page FBI file, which includes his Communist Party number: 47544 (FBI file).

DETAILS: AT HONOLULU, HAWAII

I. BACKGROUND

On September 5, 1963, [____] reported that DAVIS still resides at 2994 Kalihi Street with his wife and four children. DAVIS is a Salesman for the Wright Company of Syracuse, New York, working out of his home. He handles mainly advertising specialties. He also works as a free-lance salesman for other Mainland business firms.

      b2
      b7D

II. EVIDENCE OF ANY COMMUNIST PARTY (CP) ACTIVITY

On August 2, 1963, DAVIS was contacted on Waikamilo Road and was asked if he was willing to be interviewed by FBI Agents. DAVIS claimed he had no time for an interview that date but believed he would be willing to furnish his observations to questions that might be put to him. He requested that he be contacted the following week to set up an appointment.

It was not until August 26, 1963, when DAVIS agreed to a definite appointment and met SA's ROBERT F. RYAN and LEO S. BRENNEISEN in Kapiolani Park, Honolulu. At the start of the interview DAVIS stated that since first being contacted by the FBI, he had come to the opinion that little could be gained from the interview and he did not see where it would be to his advantage to talk to Agents.

He was asked specifically if he was a member of the Communist Party. He stated that as far as he knew, there was no Communist Party in existence in Hawaii. He was next asked why and when he had broken with the Communist Party. DAVIS then went on at length to state that he had never gone on record as having been a member of the Communist Party, and he, therefore, did not see what could be gained by answering that question.

DAVIS related that he had been associated with a large number of radical organizations in the past, and he had been motivated solely by his fight for racial equality. He took the position that he would "consort with the devil to gain his ends," and his end was the fight against racial discrimination. DAVIS related that he had been born and

- 2 -

Figure 2: FBI report on Frank's August 1963 meeting with FBI agents in Honolulu (FBI file).

SAC, Honolulu (100-5082)   August 15, 1962
                    REC- 135
            Director, FBI (100-328955) — 58

                                                    1 - Mr. Pettit

        FRANK MARSHALL DAVIS
        SECURITY MATTER - C

            Reurlet 7-30-62.

                Subject is a Negro male, 56 years of age, who
        has been employed most of his life as a reporter. He was
        a Communist Party (CP) member in Chicago from 1945 until
        1948 when he moved to Hawaii. He was very active in the
        Party there until Party activity as such ceased in 1952.
        He was active in front groups in a leadership capacity
        until such front groups became inactive in 1956. When
        questioned before the Senate Internal Security Subcommittee
        in 1956, Davis took the Fifth Amendment.

                He wrote a column which constantly followed the
        CP line in the now defunct "Honolulu Record" until 1957.
        In 1958 he frequented the premises of this newspaper. He
        contributed to "The Worker" prior to 1956.

                He was listed as a sponsor for the 27th National
        Conference of the American Committee for Protection of
        Foreign Born in December, 1960.

                In 1957 he championed the policies of Soviet
        Russia.

                His name is being retained on the Security Index
        at this time.

                                        ALL INFORMATION CONTAINED
        NOTE ON YELLOW: HEREIN IS UNCLASSIFIED
                                        DATE 4-25-77 BY

                    Relet recommended deletion from SI.

        Tolson
        Belmont
        Mohr
        Callahan
        Conrad   BGLP:bmt
        DeLoach   (4)
        Evans
        Malone
        Rosen
        Sullivan
        Tavel
        Trotter
        Tele. Ro   56 AUG 22 1962
        Holmes
        Gandy   MAIL ROOM ☑   TELETYPE UNIT ☐

Figure 3: A biographical page from Frank's FBI file noting his Communist Party membership (FBI file).

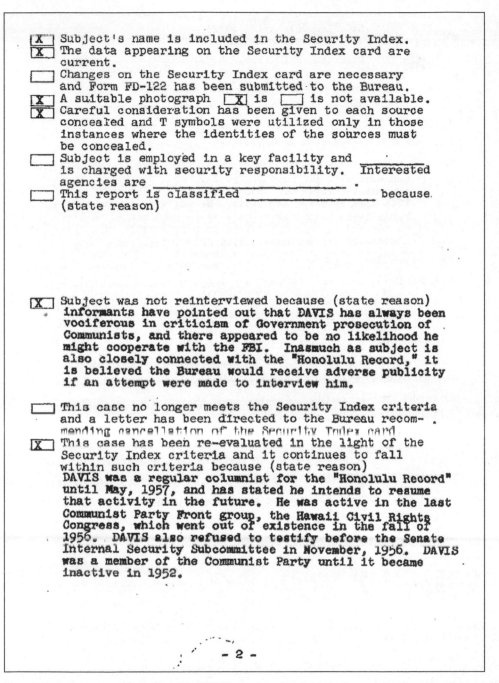

[X] Subject's name is included in the Security Index.
[X] The data appearing on the Security Index card are
    current.
[ ] Changes on the Security Index card are necessary
    and Form FD-122 has been submitted to the Bureau.
[X] A suitable photograph [X] is [ ] is not available.
[X] Careful consideration has been given to each source
    concealed and T symbols were utilized only in those
    instances where the identities of the sources must
    be concealed.
[ ] Subject is employed in a key facility and _____ .
    is charged with security responsibility. Interested
    agencies are _____ .
[ ] This report is classified _____ because.
    (state reason)

[X] Subject was not reinterviewed because (state reason)
    informants have pointed out that DAVIS has always been
    vociferous in criticism of Government prosecution of
    Communists, and there appeared to be no likelihood he
    might cooperate with the FBI. Inasmuch as subject is
    also closely connected with the "Honolulu Record," it
    is believed the Bureau would receive adverse publicity
    if an attempt were made to interview him.

[ ] This case no longer meets the Security Index criteria
    and a letter has been directed to the Bureau recom- .
    mending cancellation of the Security Index card.
[X] This case has been re-evaluated in the light of the
    Security Index criteria and it continues to fall
    within such criteria because (state reason)
    DAVIS was a regular columnist for the "Honolulu Record"
    until May, 1957, and has stated he intends to resume
    that activity in the future. He was active in the last
    Communist Party Front group, the Hawaii Civil Rights
    Congress, which went out of existence in the fall of
    1956. DAVIS also refused to testify before the Senate
    Internal Security Subcommittee in November, 1956. DAVIS
    was a member of the Communist Party until it became
    inactive in 1952.

- 2 -

Figure 4: A cover page from Frank's FBI file noting that he is being retained on the federal
government's Security Index (FBI file).

"8"
3546/3
vt-copy
2.iv.41

Confidential - USA

THE AMERICAN PEACE MOBILISATION.

The American Peace Mobilisation (APM) –– which was organised on the initiative of our Party in Chicago in September, 1940 at a national anti-war conference representing approximately 12 million working people from the progressive labor, youth, farm and Negro movements, the Townsend Old Age pension movement, and progressive Protestant church organisations –– has become the main coordinating and leading center of the people's anti-imperialist and anti-war movement. The national leadership of the organisation is of a broad, anti-war, people's front character, under militant labor influence, and includes progressive ministers, authors, etc. and left-wing and Communist leaders from the progressive unions, farm groups, youth and Negro movements.

In its formative period, the program of APM was built around the following main slogans of action: a) Keep America out of the war; Get out and stay out of the war; No aid to Either Belligerent group; Against Yankee Imperialism in Latin America; Aid the Chinese People; b) Defeat Militarisation and Regimentation; c) Restore the Bill of Rights; d) Stop war profiteering; e) Guarantee a decent standard of living to all.

But in the first days of its existence, the APM did not take a clear-cut anti-imperialist position on such questions as the character of the war, national defence and the issue of peace. And it evaded taking an official stand on, or raising the, burning question of friendship with the great Land of Socialism.

In the six months since its existence, APM has initiated and set in motion important mass activities and campaigns against the enactment of military conscription, and subsequently for the improvement of the wages, conditions and democratic rights of those conscripted for military service; for the defeat of the War Powers Bill; for the defence of the right to strike and the enforcement of labor legislation /6

Figure 5: A confidential document by the Soviet Comintern notes that the American Peace Mobilization was organized by the Comintern and CPUSA in Chicago in September 1940 (Soviet Comintern Archives on Communist Party USA).

THE CHICAGO

★ STAR

Vol. 1, No. 1   Chicago, July 6, 1946   5¢

What to do about Prices

1 Wire or write your Congressman and Senators Brooks and Lucas. Tell them to pass a resolution at once, extending OPA as is for another year. Tell them to act now, before prices and rents get out of hand.

2 Support the national buyers' strike against inflation. Buy only what are bare essentials—basic foods and medicines—until Congress renews price control. Refuse to pay any increase in rent.

Demand Congress act!

Nation fights to halt price disaster; Buyer strike on!

Death of the OPA may set off the biggest buyers' strike in history.

More than 2,000,000 Chicago consumers this week prepared for a bitter strike to stop zooming prices.

The blast at inflation came in answer of the wiping out of rent and price control by a Big Business-minded block of Congressmen despite overwhelming demands for the continuation of the OPA.

Mobilization for the buyers strike got under way here in cooperation with a nationwide wave of consum-

ers protests as civic, labor, women's and church organizations pledged to purchase only essential commodities.

Revolt against the lynching of OPA was touched off here for the Extension Committee for the Extension of Price and Rent Control, representatives of more than a million consumers, who called for a buyers' strike and stated:

"In this period, in which we are waiting the action of Congress, and in which the consumer is left unprotected from greedy business and real estate interests, we are calling upon every individual to protect himself and his neighbor by joining a nationwide movement of consumers to refuse to pay over ceiling prices for goods and services."

* * *

ISSUED by Mrs. Manuel Robin executive director of the Committee, the statement urged a barrage of telegrams to the White House "until even the present Congress will be forced to obey the peoples' will."

The American Veterans Committee with 3000 members in Chicago, a fighting stand against the OPA-killing as Sidney Ordower, executive secretary of the Chicago chapter, declared:

"We're playing for keeps, no holds barred, to get back OPA. We're going to institute buyers' strikes. We are going to investigate every eviction that takes place in the city—especially where a veteran is concerned—and we're urging our people to stay in their places and refuse to pay any additional rent hike.

We're selling apples on street corners called "The Taft Apples" he stated.

* * *

BETTY Dashew, head of the Chicago Action Council, representative of 3,000 business and professional groups, stated that her organization felt "the only thing left for consumers to do is to take action in a nationwide consumers' strike," and said the CAC was already working with other groups in mobilizing for the nationwide buyers' strike.

Others on early record supporting the nationwide buyers' strike included the National Negro Congress, The United Electrical Workers, the League of Women Voters, and the Chicago Federation of Consumers.

Mrs. Lillian Inke, chairman of the Independent Voters of Illinois, declared that her group had "tremendous sentiment" in favor (Continued on back page)

Chicago fights race covenants

by Richard Durham

See Page 8

★

Bribery behind the Iran crisis

by Johannes Steel

See Page 5

'Trampling out the vintage . . .'

Figure 6: A newsstand view of the front page of the kickoff edition of Frank's *Chicago Star*, July 6, 1946.

THE STAR IS BORN

An Editorial

HERE is your Star!

Here is the newspaper you own and control and which will speak for the plain people of Chicagoland. This is your answer to the prostitute press which peddles its favors to the big money boys and the high priests of rising American fascism.

* * *

THE STAR comes into being at a critical time.

We have seen congress turn against the people since V-J Day; we have watched the Truman administration shelve the policies of Franklin Delano Roosevelt. Progressive legislation has been sidetracked or emasculated. The FEPC is no more. The full employment bill is but a farce. The Murray-Wagner-Dingell bill gathers dust. The only measures certain of passage are those designed to cripple labor or wallop the common man in his pocketbook.

The plain people have but a handful of spokesmen in high places. The decisive leaders of both the Republican and Democratic parties are but mouthpieces for monopolists. Such a situation demands dynamic independent political action and support only of those candidates committed to a progressive program, no matter what their label.

* * *

WE are unalterably opposed to a foreign policy based on either the preservation of the pre-war status quo or its replacement by a new American big money imperialism. We believe unity between the United States, Great Britain and the Soviet Union is necessary to preserve world peace and are convinced that our foreign policy is being determined by those forces in America who work night and day to condition this nation for an atomic bomb attack on our great ally of less than a year ago.

* * *

IT IS the goal of the Star to arouse and unify the plain people into a dynamic, aggressive whole to make democracy a reality. To that end we invite the complete cooperation of all progressive forces from liberals to Communists; of all religions; of Negroes and whites; and of all minority groups.

The Star will expose and resist in every way possible the divide and rule strategy of our entrenched reactionaries and their spokesmen. The Star looks upon labor-baiting, anti-Semitism, Negro-hating and Red-baiting as weapons of fascism.

* * *

THIS, then, is what your Star believes and its program for the future.

We have faith in ourselves and our ability, with your help, to carry on. Realizing the need for this newspaper, many have contributed at a considerable sacrifice, many have spent hours obtaining subscriptions for a publication that, until now, did not exist.

And so the Star is born. How it grows, progresses and develops is up to all of us. Let's fight — but let's fight together to solve the problems of plain people everywhere.

Figure 7: In his inaugural editorial for the *Chicago Star,* Frank elicits "the complete cooperation of all progressive forces."

Frank-ly speaking

By FRANK MARSHALL DAVIS

I'm tired of being beaned with those double meaning words like "sacred institutions" and "the American way of life" which our flag-waving fascists and lukewarm liberals hurl at us day and night. I've been slapped slogan silly, and I'm ready to snap out of it.

Last week I read in an Arkansas newspaper that Sen. John L. McClellan told civic club members in Pine Bluff that he was opposed to the "infamous FEPC bill" because it would "deprive an employer of the fundamental right of selecting his own employes." He vowed he would continue to "adhere to the principles and fundamentals that made America" and would do all in his power "to defeat measures tending to deprive individuals of their liberties."

In the New York Times right before the election I also read where Sen. James M. Mead said he repudiated "the support of anyone advocating beliefs or philosophies of government alien to our own. These foreign ideologies are repugnant to the practices of my faith, the dictates of my conscience and the institutions of my country. I have dedicated my efforts to the advancement of the American system."

DAVIS

HERE were two Senators pounding their chests and renewing allegiance to the American way of life, which incidentally nobody ever doubted in the first place. They used similar words, yet obviously did not mean the same thing. On the ground of Americanism, McClellan is against FEPC, the anti-lynching bill, anti-poll tax bill and labor. The record shows that Mead, on the ground of Americanism, favors these measures. Obviously something is wrong. Could it be the slogan?

Just what are our "sacred institutions" anyway? Do they include discrimination based on religion, color or origin? That has been an American institution since slavery became a money making "free enterprise" 300 years ago. Anti-Semitism is a standard paying business. Traditionally Catholics cannot be placed in high offices. You know what happened to Al Smith in 1928. And that fascist agency called the Ku Klux Klan has been a going concern long enough to merit rating as an institution. Are those the "sacred" things?

What is the "American way of life" that both fascists and liberals shout that they want to preserve? Is it the crazy cycle of boom and bust, wild inflation and breadlines? Is it the privilege shared exclusively by the Big Money Boys of tightening the vise when they will on American economy, such as keeping meat off the market to wreck price controls? Is it cracking down on organized labor, sending our warships "where we damn please" and building a huge stockpile of atom bombs to impress... the rest of the world with our... diplomats?

IF THAT'S what they mean, then I'm for blasting our "sacred institutions" and "the American way of life" into ancient history. They've brought me nothing but worry and grief all my life. I've had enough of being hypnotized with flags and slogans.

I cannot reconcile the basic idea of our founding father that "all men are created equal" with hardboiled reality. When I see four GI families crowded into one six room flat while an industrialist who made millions out of war contracts locks his 14-room apartment on the Gold Coast and vacations in Florida, equality becomes hazy myth. I say that if this is the "American way of life," then it has got to go.

You see, I've got the screwy idea that America with all its riches and its plenty should belong to the people. I have the "foreign" belief that those other "foreigners," the forefathers of America, meant what they said back in 1776, and that you and I and the other little people should have some say so about food and clothing and housing and health instead of leaving our control in the hands of the economic dictators sitting in Wall Street offices.

That's the only kind of Americanism that I can welcome and respect.

Figure 8: In the *Chicago Star*, Frank rips "the American way"—right aside a promotional ad for CPUSA's William Z. Foster.

An Editor's Report to the Readers:-

There is no crisis.

That's the important fact about this, the 12th issue of your Chicago Star.

We are not going to sound the alarm that all kinds of horrible things are about to happen to the Star unless you mortgage the old homestead to save the paper from imminent disaster.

On the contrary, the progress of the paper has been good and the prospects are even better.

Our main problems today are:

1. Putting the paper on a solid, self-sustaining basis.

2. Improving and enlarging the paper and the staff and expanding its coverage and its effectiveness.

• • •

The answer to this problem lies in 12,000 additional readers.

Why 12,000?

That's the difference between the 18,-000 readers we have now and the 30,000 that it will take to put the paper on a solid, solvent footing.

And today the 1,400 members of the People's Publishing Association are launching a drive to secure 12,000 new subscribers, by January 1, 1947.

• • •

This job could be easy with your help.

We are asking you to do the following things:

1. Get another subscriber.

2. Speak up about this campaign at the next meeting of your union, lodge or other organization.

3. If you feel you can do it, join the ranks of the Star Boosters who are pledging at least five subs by January 1.

FRANK MARSHALL DAVIS,
Executive Editor.

Figure 9: In this appeal to the *Chicago Star*'s readership, Frank seeks some capitalist dollars.

By FRANK MARSHALL DAVIS

How Our Democracy Looks To Oppressed Peoples

For a nation that calls itself the champion of democracy, our stupendous stupidity is equalled only by our mountainous ego. Our actions at home and abroad are making American democracy synonymous with oppression instead of freedom.

Four years ago, we had the opportunity for world leadership. This was near the end of World War II, a global conflict for freedom and liberation. We shouted our antagonism toward the "superior race" theories of the Nazis.

MR. DAVIS

But before the guns grew cold, we interpreted freedom and liberation to be the exclusive possession of the imperialist governments of Europe. I h a v e watched with growing shame for my America as our leaders have used our golden riches to re-enslave the yellow and brown and black peoples of the world.

As the colonials see it, the Marshall plan is a device to maintain what they call "white imperialism," and no manner of slick phrases can convince them otherwise. They also see our congressional failure to pass the civil rights program as merely the domestic side of the same coin of the oppression of non-white peoples everywhere.

Billions To Bolster Empires

Under the Marshall plan, billions of U. S. dollars have been used to bolster the tottering empires of England, France, Belgium, Holland and the other western exploiters of teeming millions of humans. The Dutch have used their share to make war upon the Indonesians who are guilty of wanting self-government; France and England have gotten the financial means of crushing rebellions against white imperialism in Asia and Africa. With callous disregard for the natural rights of the subject peoples, we have told Western Europe to rebuild itself through taking out tremendous profits by robbing the 150,000,000 black Africans who get only ignorance and poverty and the print of the aggressors' heels stamped hard into the face.

With our usual genius for suppressing the common people, we backed the oppressors in China. We poured in a Niagara of cash to the corrupt Kuomintang, thus insuring the enmity of millions of Chinese who thereby faced a harder fight for freedom and the end of feudalism.

Figure 10: Frank assails the Marshall Plan as "white imperialism" in his *Honolulu Record* column.

Notes

INTRODUCTION: PAST IS PROLOGUE

1 This particular oath was issued in 1935, at the heart of Stalin's rampage. Printed in "The Communist Party of the United States of America: What It Is, How It Works," Committee on the Judiciary, U.S. Senate, 84th Congress, 2nd Session, April 23, 1956 (Washington, DC: U.S. GPO, 1956), p. 2.

2 See: Paul Kengor, *God and Ronald Reagan: A Spiritual Life* (New York: HarperCollins, 2004), pp. 32–40.

3 "The heart of darkness" was Reagan's description. Reagan would have learned anticommunism from the intensely anticommunist Cleaver.

4 See: Paul Kengor, *God and Hillary Clinton: A Spiritual Life* (New York: HarperCollins, 2007), pp. 13–23.

5 See: Ibid.; and Roger Morris, *Partners in Power: The Clintons and Their America* (Washington, DC: Regnery, 1996).

6 "Unsinkable Hyman Rickover," *Time*, May 23, 1977.

7 In his memoir, *My Life*, Bill Clinton twice lists Fulbright as "my mentor." See: Bill Clinton, *My Life* (New York: Random House, 2004), p. 518 and caption at picture insert.

8 For an interesting piece on Gore and Revelle in disagreement, see: "Gore's guru disagreed," *National Post*, May 19, 2007.

9 See: Jules Witcover, *Joe Biden: A Life of Trial and Redemption* (New York:

HarperCollins, 2010), p. 168; and Sam Youngman, "Biden remembers Byrd as mentor and 'dear friend,' " *The Hill,* June 28, 2010.

10   Ronald Reagan, *An American Life* (New York: Simon & Schuster, 1990).

11   Hillary Clinton, *Living History* (New York: Simon & Schuster, 2003), pp. 22–23, 77.

12   This CPUSA number is listed in Davis's FBI file, which I obtained via a FOIA request that was submitted by a colleague. The document with the number was first published on p. 607 of my book *Dupes: How America's Adversaries Have Manipulated Progressives for a Century* (Wilmington, DE: ISI Books, 2010).

13   Frank leveled these charges in his columns for the *Honolulu Record* on September 15, 1949, April 13, 1950, and April 20, 1950.

14   That particular senator was a Republican, not a Democrat. I will address this at length later.

15   Frank Marshall Davis was so elected in April 1950. This information comes from his FBI file. It will be quoted later in the narrative.

16   "Investigation of Un-American Propaganda Activities in the United States," Special Committee on Un-American Activities, House of Representatives, 78th Congress, Second Session, on H. Res. 282, App. Part IX, Vol. 1 (Washington, DC: U.S. GPO, 1944), pp. 340–55.

17   See: Kengor, *Dupes,* pp. 265–66, 313.

18   Obviously, in some of these, Frank was much more extreme than Obama, with Obama sharing a similarity but not approaching Frank's level of extremism. On the other hand, in other cases, Obama went further than Frank.

19   As a parallel to Barack Obama, here I'm thinking of Obama's HHS mandate compelling all Catholic institutions to forcibly provide insurance coverage for contraception, sterilization services, and abortion drugs—a huge violation of the constitutional freedom of religion/conscience of Roman Catholics (among other believers). Few (if any) policy actions by a president have so outraged and unified the American bishops. See: Paul Kengor, "Obama's Catholic Church Gambit," *American Thinker,* February 16, 2012. Among Frank Marshall Davis's articles objecting to the Catholic Church (specifically, the Church's anticommunism and anti-Soviet stances) are: "The church's weakness," *Chicago Star,* October 4, 1947, and "Challenge to the Church," *Honolulu Record,* September 29, 1949. Also see my articles, "The Catholic Bishops v. Obama?" and "The Obama Mandate to Catholics: 'To Hell with You?' " posted at the website of the Center for Vision & Values.

20   Recall President Obama's April 2012 assessment that it would be "unprecedented," "extraordinary," and an act of "judicial activism" for "unelected"

judges on the Supreme Court to rule the individual mandate in "Obama-care" unconstitutional.

21 As this book goes to press, the 2012 Obama campaign has just announced (on May Day eve) "Forward!" as its 2012 campaign slogan. "Forward!" happens to be a very common communist slogan, and can be found in Frank Marshall Davis's work, including a bold banner on the front page of the May Day 1948 issue of the *Chicago Star*. For an in-depth analysis, including an image of the May 1948 issue, see: Paul Kengor, "'Forward!' with Obama, Axelrod, Jarrett, and Frank Marshall Davis," *American Thinker*, May 8, 2012.

22 I will detail this in the chapter examining the contents of the *Chicago Star*.

23 Obama, *Dreams from My Father* (New York: Times Books, 1995), p. 97.

24 See Paul Kengor, "Obama's 'Missing Link': Dr. John Drew on Obama's Marxism," *American Thinker*, December 10, 2010, and John Drew, "Meeting Young Obama," *American Thinker*, February 24, 2011.

25 See: Scott Shane, "Obama and '60s Bomber: A Look Into Crossed Paths," *New York Times*, October 4, 2008, p. A1.

26 While writing this book, I typed into Google the words "Obama mentor." The first subjects to come up were all Frank-specific: "Obama mentor in Hawaii," "Obama mentor communist," and "Obama mentor Davis."

27 Stanley grew up in Wichita, Kansas. Frank grew up in Arkansas City, Kansas. They did not know each other, as far as we know. Stanley was considerably younger, by about fourteen years.

28 Many conservative authors likewise cite Frank as a "mentor" (or more) to Obama. Among others, these include: Dinesh D'Souza, *The Roots of Obama's Rage* (Washington, DC: Regnery, 2010), p. 89; Michael Savage, *Trickle Up Poverty* (New York: HarperCollins, 2010), pp. 33–35, 54, 75; David Freddoso, *The Case Against Barack Obama* (Washington, DC: Regnery, 2008), p. 136; David Limbaugh, *Crimes Against Liberty* (Washington, DC: Regnery, 2010), pp. 40, 50, 325; Jack Cashill, *Deconstructing Obama* (New York: Threshold Editions, 2011), pp. 274–83; Stanley Kurtz, *Radical-in-Chief* (New York: Threshold Editions, 2010), pp. 10, 16, 54, 87, 90, 387

29 *Merriam-Webster* defines a mentor as "a trusted counselor or guide." *Oxford* defines a mentor as "an experienced and trusted adviser."

30 Sudhin Thanawala, "Writer offered a young Barack Obama advice on life," Associated Press, August 2, 2008.

31 Toby Harnden, "Frank Marshall Davis, alleged Communist, was early influence on Barack Obama," *London Telegraph*, August 22, 2008; Toby Harnden, "Barack Obama's True Colours: The making of the man who would be US president," *London Telegraph*, August 21, 2008.

32 Jennifer Steinhauer, "Charisma and a Search for Self in Obama's Hawaii Childhood," *New York Times*, March 17, 2007.

33 Gerald Horne, "Rethinking the History and Future of the Communist Party," posted at PoliticalAffairs.net, March 28, 2007.

34 Sudhin Thanawala, "Writer offered a young Barack Obama advice on life," Associated Press, August 2, 2008.

35 David Remnick, *The Bridge: The Life and Rise of Barack Obama* (New York: Knopf, 2010), pp. 96–97.

36 Kathryn Waddell Takara, *Frank Marshall Davis: The Fire and the Phoenix* (Kaaawa, Hawaii: Pacific Raven Press, 2012), pp. x–xi, 106, 178, and 181.

37 Takara quoted in report by Herb Romerstein and Cliff Kincaid, "Communism in Hawaii and the Obama Connection," May 2008, posted at the website of usasurvival.org.

38 Quoted by Harnden, "Barack Obama's True Colours."

39 Takara told this to Cliff Kincaid. Romerstein and Kincaid, "Communism in Hawaii and the Obama Connection."

40 Barack Obama, *Change We Can Believe In* (New York: Crown, 2008).

41 Garen Thomas, *Yes We Can: A Biography of Barack Obama* (New York: MacMillan, 2008), pp. 57–61.

42 Ron Jacobs, *Obamaland: Who Is Barack Obama?* (Honolulu: Trade Publishing, 2009), pp. 28–29, 147.

43 Richard Wolffe, *Renegade: The Making of a President* (New York: Crown, 2009), pp. 147–49.

44 Patricia Cohen, "In Writings of Obama, a Philosophy Is Unearthed," *New York Times*, October 27, 2010.

45 James T. Kloppenberg, *Reading Obama: Dreams, Hope, and the American Political Tradition* (Princeton, NJ: Princeton University Press, 2011), pp. 15, 24–25, 190, 215, 253, 270.

46 Kloppenberg writes this on p. 190. Kloppenberg and I differ, however, in our interpretation of what that might mean. I view it in the sense of Obama being on the economic far left, or socialist left—like Frank. Kloppenberg states it in the sense of Obama being "trained" or selling out in the way that Frank warned Obama before Obama left Hawaii for Occidental College. I will quote those words from Frank at length later in this book.

47 As for Remnick's personal appraisal of the relationship and of Frank generally, it is highly problematic, as I will show at length later. Remnick, *The Bridge*, pp. 96–97.

48 One of the earliest statements from the 2008 Obama campaign conceding that "Frank" was Frank Marshall Davis was a document paid for and published by "Obama for America" in response to Jerome Corsi's book *The Obama Nation*. The document was titled *Unfit for Publication*. A petulant childish rant, unbefitting a presidential campaign, the document none-

theless affirms on pp. 9–10 that the "Frank" of Obama's memoirs is Frank Marshall Davis.

49 Bob Greene, *Sex Rebel: Black (Memoirs of a Gash Gourmet)*, (San Diego: Greenleaf Classics, 1968).

50 Frank Marshall Davis, *Livin' the Blues: Memoirs of a Black Journalist and Poet* (Madison, WI: University of Wisconsin Press, 1992), p. xxvi.

51 Davis, *Livin' the Blues*, p. 346. Also in *Livin' the Blues*, the introduction by Frank's biographer, John Edgar Tidwell, confirms the authorship. The authorship is so certain that even Wikipedia, which otherwise tiptoes around troubling claims like Frank's communist work, writes that "Davis also authored a hard core pornographic novel, which was published in 1968 under a pseudonym. The book, titled *Sex Rebel: Black (Memoirs of a Gash Gourmet)*, was written under the pseudonym, 'Bob Greene.' " Source: "Frank Marshall Davis," Wikipedia, retrieved March 17, 2011.

52 Here, too, see Tidwell's introduction in *Livin' the Blues*, p. xxvi. Tidwell likewise struggles with this.

53 Karl Marx and Friedrich Engels, *The Communist Manifesto* (New York: Penguin Signet Classics edition, 1998), pp. 71–74.

54 Davis, *Livin' the Blues*, p. 230.

55 Ibid., pp. xxvi, 21, 42, 72, 84, 229, 241, 333, 347.

56 In *Livin' the Blues*, Frank twice notes the restaurant of "the Spanish Jew" in Atlanta. On "slant eyed natives," see: Frank Marshall Davis, "Touring the World," *Atlanta Daily World*, February 10, 1932.

CHAPTER 1: GROWING UP FRANK

1   Davis, *Livin' the Blues*, p. 3.

2   Ibid., p. 3.

3   Ibid.

4   Ibid., p. 4.

5   Ibid.

6   Ibid., p. 13.

7   Ibid.

8   For a timeline, also see: John Edgar Tidwell, ed., *Frank Marshall Davis, Black Moods: Collected Poems* (Urbana and Chicago: University of Illinois Press, 2002), pp. xvii–xx.

9   Davis, *Livin' the Blues*, pp. 94–96.

10 Among others, see: Davis, *Livin' the Blues*, pp. 21, 42, 72, 84. The reference on p. 84 is especially crude.

11 Davis, *Livin' the Blues*, p. 7.

12 Ibid., pp. 7, 101.

13   Ibid., p. 64.

14   Ibid.

15   Ibid.

16   Gary Smith, "Race, Segregation, and Heaven," posted at the website of the Center for Vision & Values, August 31, 2011.

17   *Newsweek* described Obama's faith as a patchwork of divergent beliefs, philosophies, and influences, from a "Christian-turned-secular mother"—her own views a product of "two lapsed Christian" parents and a Bill Moyers book—to a "Muslim-turned-atheist African father" to a stepfather with a "unique brand of Islam." See: Lisa Miller and Richard Wolffe, "Finding His Faith," *Newsweek*, July 12, 2008. On this, including more on the *Newsweek* analysis, see my article: "God and Barack Obama," October 24, 2008, posted at the website of the Center for Vision & Values.

18   That church was located in Bellevue, Washington, one of the areas where the family lived. Tim Jones, "Obama's roots are steeped in tradition," *Chicago Tribune*, March 26, 2007. Also see Andrew Walden, "Obama's *Other* Controversial Church," *American Thinker*, June 14, 2009.

19   Davis, *Livin' the Blues*, p. 64.

20   Ibid.

21   Ibid.

22   President Harry Truman, "Remarks Before a Joint Session of Congress Announcing Aid to Greece and Turkey," March 12, 1947.

23   Davis, *Livin' the Blues*, p. 297.

24   He could not be certain that "the excellent relationship between Moscow and Washington would have continued had Roosevelt lived," said Frank, "but I firmly believe it would not have deteriorated so rapidly as occurred under Truman." Davis, *Livin' the Blues*, p. 297.

25   Ibid., p. 98.

26   Ibid., pp. 132–34.

27   Ibid., p. 107.

28   Frank's dating is not precise. See: Davis, *Livin' the Blues*, pp. 137–42; Tidwell, *Frank Marshall Davis, Black Moods*, p. xvii.

29   Davis, *Livin' the Blues*, pp. 159–79; Tidwell, *Frank Marshall Davis, Black Moods*, p. xvii.

CHAPTER 2: ATLANTA, 1931–32:
THE COMMUNISTS SWARM TO SCOTTSBORO

1   Davis, *Livin' the Blues*, p. 180.

2   Ibid., pp. 180–81.

3   Ibid.

4   Davis, *Livin' the Blues*, pp. 180–85; Tidwell, *Frank Marshall Davis, Black Moods*, p. xviii.

5   Davis, *Livin' the Blues*, pp. 180–81.

6   Frank's wondrous changes and Scott's overall operations could never have happened in the USSR, from the mere concept of ownership and management, to the incentive and innovation and independence, to the pay and the production, to the freedom of thought and expression and association. And if by some miracle of secrecy such a paper ever made it out the door in the Soviet system, it would be shut down at the barrel of a gun the moment an editor like Frank dared to issue a dissenting editorial.

7   Frank Marshall Davis, "Touring the World," *Atlanta Daily World*, December 18, 1931.

8   On "slant eyed natives," see: Frank Marshall Davis, "Touring the World," *Atlanta Daily World*, February 10, 1932.

9   Davis, *Livin' the Blues*, pp. 188–90.

10 Ibid., pp. 187–88.

11 Malia in Stephane Courtois et al., *The Black Book of Communism* (Harvard University Press, 1999), p. x.

12 *The Black Book of Communism* tabulated a toll of 100 million. Courtois, *Black Book*, p. 4. That ghastly figure is actually among the more conservative, mainly because it estimates *only* 20 million dead in the USSR. Alexander Yakovlev, the esteemed Soviet reformer who was one of Gorbachev's most instrumental aides, was given the task in the 1990s of scouring archives to try to determine a more accurate figure. Yakovlev reported that Stalin alone "annihilated . . . sixty to seventy million people." See: Alexander Yakovlev, *A Century of Violence in Soviet Russia* (New Haven, CT: Yale University Press, 2002), p. 32. Those numbers are consistent with those provided in the 1970s by the likes of dissident and Nobel winner Alexander Solzhenitsyn, among others. See: Alexander Solzhenitsyn, *Alexander Solzhenitsyn Speaks to the West* (London: The Bodley Head, 1978), p. 17; Lee Edwards, ed., *The Collapse of Communism* (Stanford, CA: Hoover Institution Press, 1999), p. xiii. Citing figures by political scientist R. J. Rummel, who specializes in this area, and who draws on the research of Robert Conquest, Solzhenitsyn, and others, Lee Edwards projects that the USSR took the lives of 61.9 million people from 1917 to 1987. When one adds in at least 60-70 million dead under China's Tse-tung, plus the killing fields of Cambodia, Cuba, North Korea, Ethiopia, Eastern Europe, Africa, and more, we see a figure closer to 140 million. For Mao, the *Black Book of Communism* lists 65 million dead (p. 4). The latest figures on Mao, rising to 70 million-plus, are recorded in the seminal work by Jung Chang and Jon Halliday, *Mao: The Unknown Story* (New York: Knopf, 2005).

13   The highest early estimates on the sixty-four-year Spanish Inquisition (1481–1545) reported 31,912 killed. See, for instance, the early authoritative work on the subject: J. A. Llorente, *A Critical History of the Inquisition of Spain* (1823), pp. 575–83. More recent figures claim a much smaller number.

14   Marx and Engels, *The Communist Manifesto*, p. 91.

15   The 1920 Comintern congress further added as a condition for admission and membership to the Comintern: "Every party which wishes to join the Communist International is obligated to give unconditional support to any Soviet republic in its struggle against counter-revolutionary forces." See: Richard Pipes, *Communism: A History* (New York: Modern Library, 2001), p. 93; Courtois et al., *The Black Book of Communism*, pp. 271–75; V. I. Lenin, *Collected Works*, Vol. 28 (Moscow: Progress Publishers, 1965), pp. 477–80; Brian Crozier, *The Rise and Fall of the Soviet Empire* (Rocklin, CA: Forum, 1999), pp. 38–40; Jane Degras, ed., *The Communist International, 1919–1943: Documents*, vol. I (London, 1956), pp. 166–72.

16   William Z. Foster authored a book by that title: *Toward Soviet America*. William Z. Foster, *Toward Soviet America* (New York: Coward-McCann, 1932).

17   This exchange appears in "Investigation of Un-American Activities and Propaganda," Special Committee on Un-American Activities, 75th Congress, House of Representatives, January 3, 1939, pp. 18–21. On Hamilton Fish and his Fish Committee, which ran from June 1930 through early 1931, see: Richard Gid Powers, *Not Without Honor: The History of American Anticommunism* (New Haven, CT: Yale University Press, 1998), p. 89.

18   Communist Party USA in the Comintern Archives, Library of Congress, Fond 515, Opis 1, Delo 9.

19   One well-known ex-party member, Theodore Draper, who famously went public when he left the communist movement, shared the language inscribed on his party registration card when he joined in New York in the 1920s: "The undersigned, after having read the constitution and program of the Communist Party, declares his adherence to the principles and tactics of the party and the Communist International, agrees to submit to the discipline of the party as stated in its constitution, and pledges to engage actively in its work." Theodore Draper, *American Communism and Soviet Russia: The Formative Period* (New York: Viking, 1960), p. 162.

20   See: Degras, *The Communist International, 1919–1943: Documents*, pp. 166–72; O. Piatnitsky, *The Twenty One Conditions of Admission Into the Communist International* (New York: Workers Library Publishers, February 1934), pp. 29–31.

21   This fealty would continue throughout the existence of the American Party and the Soviet Party. As noted by Herb Romerstein, a former com-

munist who to this day remains America's leading authority on domestic communism, "from 1919, when it [CPUSA] was formed, to 1989, when the Soviet Union collapsed, it was under total Soviet control." (Source: e-mail correspondence with Herb Romerstein, April 16, 2007.) The most telling evidence of that Soviet control, which emerged only after the Cold War ended, was the fact that CPUSA had received funding all along from the Soviet communist government, beginning in 1919 and continuing until the collapse of the Soviet empire in 1989. We now know this was not some piddling sum; it was a lifeline that kept CPUSA afloat, to the tune of annual stipends of millions of dollars. The funding continued for so long and at such a high level that it reached nearly $2.8 million for 1980 alone. The most intriguing source documenting the funding from 1958 to 1980, told through a remarkable story, is in John Barron, *Operation Solo: The FBI's Man in the Kremlin* (Washington, DC: Regnery, 1996), pp. xv, 339–40.

22 The one hundred thousand peak membership was conceded by Earl Browder himself. See: Earl Browder, "Socialism in America," in David Footman, ed., *International Communism* (Carbondale, IL: Southern Illinois University Press, 1960), p. 101.

23 See examples throughout my book, *Dupes.*

24 Source: repeated conversations with Romerstein.

25 See report titled "Communist Propaganda in the United States, Part VIII, Campaigns," June 1959, Federal Bureau of Investigation. Declassified copy on file at Harvard University (where I found the report) under the formal citation "The Communist Party and Radical Organizations, 1953–1960, FBI Reports from the Eisenhower Library."

26 See: Harvey Klehr, John Earl Haynes, and Kirill Anderson, *The Soviet World of American Communism* (New Haven, CT: Yale University Press, 1998), p. 219. This source specifically points to this 1928–30 period. Beyond this source, one can see this reality abundantly evident in the materials from the late 1920s and early 1930s in the Comintern Archives on CPUSA. Also on the "Black Belt," see: "The American Negro in the Communist Party," Committee on Un-American Activities, U.S. House of Representatives, 79th Congress, Second Session, Washington, DC, December 22, 1954, pp. 5–7.

27 I have read hundreds of reels of microfiche from these archives, and the effort by CPUSA to recruit black Americans is one of the things that most consistently strikes the reader.

28 This information became well known once published in the huge 1958 bestseller *Masters of Deceit*, by FBI director J. Edgar Hoover, which, of course, was assembled by his staff. See: J. Edgar Hoover, *Masters of Deceit* (New York: Henry Holt, 1958), pp. 250–51.

29 "Black and Red," *Time*, November 9, 1925.

30 All of this information (which, to my knowledge, is accurate) was recently reported by Tony Pecinovsky, "Remembering James W. Ford," *People's World*, February 16, 2010.

31 Pecinovsky, "Remembering James W. Ford."

32 See: "The American Negro in the Communist Party," Committee on Un-American Activities, U.S. House of Representatives, 79th Congress, Second Session, Washington, DC, December 22, 1954.

33 Ibid.

34 V. I. Lenin's "Letter to American Workers" was written August 20, 1918, and published in *Pravda*, August 22, 1918. It is easily available at (among other sources) www.marxists.org.

35 "The American Negro in the Communist Party," pp. 2–3.

36 See: Glenda Elizabeth Gilmore, *Defying Dixie* (New York: W.W. Norton, 2008), pp. 118–19.

37 CPUSA in the Comintern Archives, Reel 259, Opis 1, Delo 3364.

38 James Edward Smethurst, *The New Red Negro: The Literary Left and African American Poetry, 1930–46* (Oxford University Press, 1999), p. 141.

39 "Guide to Subversive Organizations and Publications (and Appendices)," revised and published December 1, 1961, to supersede Guide published on January 2, 1957 (including Index), prepared and released by the Committee on Un-American Activities, U.S. House of Representatives, Washington, DC, 87th Congress, 2nd Session, House Document No, 398, pp. 88–89.

40 "Guide to Subversive Organizations and Publications," pp. 88–89.

41 "Civil Rights Congress as a Communist Front Organization," Committee on Un-American Activities, House of Representatives, 80th Congress, First Session, Public Law 601, September 2, 1947 (Washington, DC: U.S. GPO, 1947), pp. 1–2.

42 "Civil Rights Congress as a Communist Front Organization," pp. 1–2.

43 "Guide to Subversive Organizations and Publications," pp. 88–89.

44 "Civil Rights Congress as a Communist Front Organization," pp. 1–2. Given his vast activities and enormous amount of personal support of blatantly pro-Soviet communist activities, it is hard to imagine that Marcantonio was not a Party member, or at the very least a communist in his philosophy. John Abt, the prominent CPUSA attorney and activist, who willingly listed two other congressmen as Party members, stated that Marcantonio was friendly to the Party but was not a formal member. John J. Abt, *Advocate and Activist: Memoirs of an American Communist Lawyer* (Urbana and Chicago: University of Illinois Press, 1993), p. 117.

45 CPUSA in the Comintern Archives, Reel 195, Delos 2585–86.

46 CPUSA in the Comintern Archives, Reel 302, Delo 3973.

47 It was also known as the Methodist Federation for Social Action.

48 The January 14–16, 1945, editions of the *Daily Worker* included three articles glowing about Harry Ward's contributions. Of the three, the most gushing was a January 14, 1945, feature by Art Shields, titled "One Man's Quest."

49 For a picture of the *New Masses* page that includes this offer, see: Kengor, *Dupes*, p. 189.

50 "Investigation of Communist Activities in the New York Area," Parts 6 to 8, Committee on Un-American Activities, House of Representatives, 83rd Congress, July 7–8 and 13–14, 1953, pp. 2082, 2201–2, 2229, 2266.

51 On this, see: Paul Kengor, "Christmas with Clarence (Darrow)," *American Spectator*, December 20, 2010, and Kengor, *Dupes*, pp. 83, 121–22.

52 The "Fourth Report of the Senate Fact-Finding Committee on Un-American Activities: Communist Front Organizations," published by the California legislature in 1948, affirmed the 1943 report. On p. 107, it stated, "The American Civil Liberties Union may be definitely classed as a Communist front or 'transmission belt' organization. At least 90 percent of its efforts are expended on behalf of Communists who come in conflict with the law." For a summary of these and more, see "The Truth About the American Civil Liberties Union," remarks entered into the *Congressional Record* by Congressman John Rousselot, September 20, 1961.

53 To cite just one example of Frank's advocacy in his writings, the words "civil liberties" appear eight times in his *Honolulu Record* columns from 1949 to 1950, roughly half of which are part of the formal name of organizations. In his March 23, 1950, column, "Congress Considers 'Communist Control,' " he defends the ACLU specifically.

54 "Guide to Subversive Organizations and Publications," pp. 107, 151.

55 Davis, *Livin' the Blues*, p. 184.

56 CPUSA in the Comintern Archives, Fond 515, Opis 1, Reel 195, Delo 2591.

57 Wilkins wrote this in a November 22, 1949, letter to communist William L. Patterson, who headed the front-group Civil Rights Congress. Wilkins and the NAACP made it available to the media in a November 23, 1949, press release, which I have in my possession.

58 Hill published this in the June–July 1951 edition of *Crisis* magazine, pp. 365–71, 421–22. Herb Romerstein cited this article as well as the two previous letters in the three previous paragraphs in his May 2008 report, "The Communist Assault on Hawaii." We are indebted to Herb Romerstein for his report and for sharing this information.

59 In the utmost irony, given the true contrast with Stalin's reign of terror, not one of the Scottsboro Boys was executed. One of the trials was not

resolved for over twenty years after the original incident. Several of the boys did some hard jail time—particularly Charlie Weems—before being ultimately paroled.

60 Davis, *Livin' the Blues*, p. 194.

61 Ibid.

CHAPTER 3: FRANK'S WORK FOR THE *ATLANTA DAILY WORLD* (1931–34)

1 This again is due entirely to the extraordinary research skills of Spyridon Mitsotakis.

2 "Spelman Schedules Langston Hughes for Lecture," *Atlanta Daily World*, December 11, 1931.

3 On "major outlet," see: Arnold Rampersad, *The Life of Langston Hughes: 1902–1941* (New York: Oxford University Press, 2002), p. 215.

4 "Langston Hughes Will Speak Thursday Night," *Atlanta Daily World*, December 16, 1931.

5 See: Jean Wagner, *Black Poets of the United Sates: From Paul Laurence Dunbar to Langston Hughes* (Chicago and Urbana: University of Illinois Press, 1973), p. 435; Faith Berry, *Langston Hughes: Before and Beyond Harlem* (New York: Citadel Press, 1992), pp. 296–97.

6 Langston Hughes, *Essays on Art, Race, Politics, and World Affairs* (Columbia, MO: University of Missouri Press, 2002), p. 207.

7 Ibid. This famous Hughes poem is titled "Goodbye Christ."

8 Frank Marshall Davis, "Touring the World," *Atlanta Daily World*, December 25, 1931.

9 "Scottsboro Defense," *Atlanta Daily World*, December 27, 1931.

10 "Darrow, Hayes and Reds Leave Birmingham at Odds," *Atlanta Daily World*, January 1, 1932.

11 On this, see: Powers, *Not Without Honor*, pp. 109–12.

12 Ibid.

13 Quoted in Hoover, *Masters of Deceit*, p. 252.

14 Editorial, "The N.A.A.C.P. Withdraws," *Atlanta Daily World*, January 6, 1932.

15 Frank Marshall Davis, "Touring the World," *Atlanta Daily World*, January 15, 1932.

16 See: John Dewey, "Why I Am Not a Communist," *Modern Monthly*, Vol. VIII, April 1934, pp. 135–37. The article was also reprinted in Sidney Hook, ed., *The Meaning of Marx: A Symposium by Bertrand Russell, John Dewey, Morris Cohen, Sidney Hook, and Sherwood Eddy* (New York: Farrar & Rinehart, 1934).

17 For instance, there were two deadlines on the front page of the February 3, 1932, edition.

18 "Reds Say They've Spent $10,000 in Defense of Condemned 8 Boys," *Atlanta Daily World*, February 26, 1932.

19 "Red Scottsboro," *Atlanta Daily World*, March 27, 1932.

20 My copy of the editorial does not include a date. It was likely the spring of 1932.

21 "Communism Argued By 7 Editors," *Atlanta Daily World*, March 24, 1933.

22 Particularly loathsome was Aptheker's *The Truth About Hungary*, a horrible defense of the Soviet slaughter of tens of thousands of freedom-loving Hungarians in the Budapest uprising of October–November 1956. Herbert Aptheker, *The Truth About Hungary* (New York: Mainstream Publishers, 1957).

23 See: Christopher Lehmann-Haupt, "Herbert Aptheker, 87, Dies; Prolific Marxist Historian," *New York Times*, March 20, 2003.

24 Published in Herbert Aptheker, ed., *A Documentary History of the Negro People in the United States: From the NAACP to the New Deal, 1910–32* (New York: Citadel Press, 1993), pp. 705–6.

CHAPTER 4: PAUL ROBESON AND PROGRESSIVE DUPES

1 Alden Whitman, "Paul Robeson Dead at 77," *New York Times*, January 24, 1976.

2 I detailed this concept in my book *Dupes*. I had not heard this term used before. To my knowledge, this is my term alone. Other scholars, such as Paul Hollander, have used the term "Political Pilgrims."

3 See my discussion in *Dupes*, pp. 100–109.

4 The word is traced to Russian official Grigori Aleksandrovich Potemkin, who purportedly ordered the construction of fake settlements in the Crimea to fool Catherine II during a visit in the eighteenth century.

5 See: S. J. Taylor, *Stalin's Apologist: Walter Duranty, the New York Times's Man in Moscow* (New York: Oxford University Press, 1990).

6 Malcolm Muggeridge, *Chronicles of Wasted Time, Chronicle 1: The Green Stick* (New York: Quill, 1982), p. 244.

7 Malcolm Muggeridge, *The Sun Never Sets: The Story of England in the 1930s* (New York: Random House, 1940), p. 79.

8 Muggeridge, *Chronicles of Wasted Time*, pp. 211–13.

9 H. G. Wells, *An Experiment in Autobiography: Discoveries and Conclusions of a Very Ordinary Brain (Since 1866)* (New York: Little, Brown & Co., 1984), pp. 215, 667, 687–89. Wells made several trips to the USSR in the 1920s and 1930s. See: H. G. Wells, *Russia in the Shadows* (New York: George H. Doran Company, 1921), pp. 160–62.

10 Shaw wrote this in a letter to the editor of the *Manchester Guardian*, pub-

lished March 2, 1933. He was the author and lead signatory of the letter, followed by twenty other signers. As the letter itself stated, Shaw and all of the twenty others had been "recent visitors to the USSR."

11 Ralph de Toledano, *Spies, Dupes, and Diplomats* (New York: Duell, Sloan and Pearce, 1952), p. 190.

12 Corliss and Margaret Lamont, *Russia Day By Day: A Travel Diary* (New York: Covici-Friede Publishers, 1933).

13 William W. Brickman, ed., *John Dewey's Impressions of Soviet Russia and the Revolutionary World, Mexico-China-Turkey 1929* (New York: Bureau of Publications, Teachers College, Columbia University, 1964), pp. 19–20, 58n.

14 The collection of essays was published in 1929 by The New Republic, Inc., as well as in subsequent Dewey writings and a later (1964) volume edited by William W. Brickman, produced and published by the Teachers College at Columbia University. See earlier note for full citation of Brickman volume.

15 Dewey wrote this in his third article for the *New Republic* series.

16 Margaret Sanger, "Birth Control in Russia," *Birth Control Review*, June 1935.

17 See Martin Duberman, *Paul Robeson: A Biography* (New York: Knopf, 1989); the review of Duberman's biography by Harvey Klehr, "People's Artist," *Commentary*, May 1989, pp. 70–71; and Whitman, "Paul Robeson Dead at 77."

18 Ibid., Duberman.

19 Robeson relayed these details in an interview with the *Daily Worker* on January 15, 1935. Full citation follows below.

20 In his memoirs, Gorbachev repeatedly expressed his frustration at not being able to find out how much his nation was spending on the military, nor being able to discern the nation's true figures for GDP.

21 On the number of blacks in the USSR, I consulted a number of colleagues who are sociologists/demographers. As I expected, I was told that they were unaware of any reliable statistics on race in Russia from the Cold War period.

22 At the time of the writing of this book (fall 2011), the latest figures on Russia provided by the online *World Factbook* (based on Russia's most recent census data) list this demographic breakdown: Russian 79.8%, Tatar 3.8%, Ukrainian 2%, Bashkir 1.2%, Chuvash 1.1%, other or unspecified 12.1%. The *Factbook* uses designations of "black" or "African descent" when describing what Americans commonly refers to as "black Americans" or "African-Americans."

23 Young said this in May 1977. See: "Young Statements—and Reactions to Them," *Washington Post*, August 16, 1979. Bear in mind, Young, like his

boss, President Carter, was known for his naïveté in foreign policy; coming from Young, this was a stinging statement. The most infamous example of this was Young's February 1979 remark that the Ayatollah Khomeini "will be some kind of saint when we finally get over the panic of what is happening [in Iran]."

24 Some sources describe this as a "Comintern school" and others as the Lenin School. See: "Black and Red," *Time*, November 9, 1925; Raymond Arsenault, "Forgotten Revolutionaries," *Washington Post*, January 13, 2008; Klehr, Haynes, and Anderson, *The Soviet World of American Communism*, pp. 218–23; CPUSA files on Fort-Whiteman, Box 9, Folder 57, Tamiment Library, New York University; and "Investigation of Un-American Propaganda Activities in the United States," pp. 1001, 1282, 1452.

25 Klehr, Haynes, and Anderson, *The Soviet World of American Communism*, pp. xi, 218–23.

26 Among others, see: Klehr, "People's Artist," p. 70; and Paul Robeson and Philip Sheldon Foner, *Paul Robeson Speaks: Writings, Speeches, Interviews, 1918–1974* (New York: Citadel Press, 1978), p. 109.

27 Vern Smith, " 'I Am at Home,' says Robeson At Reception in Soviet Union," *Daily Worker*, January 15, 1935.

28 I quote these in detail in *Dupes*, pp. 93–98.

29 To cite just one of thousands of examples that could be cited, and a fairly mild one, see: Judy Kaplan and Linn Shapiro, eds., *Red Diapers: Growing Up in the Communist Left* (Urbana and Chicago: University of Illinois Press, 1998), p. 319. They write: "Although he was not a member of the CP, Robeson's political positions often coincided with the Party's." To say "often coincided" is a tremendous understatement. The authors write that Robeson thus suffered "punishment for his views" by the federal government.

30 And when not using the "c" word, Robeson would long express what he coyly called "my belief in the principles of scientific socialism"—a term the Soviets themselves used—and a "deep conviction that for all mankind a socialist society represents an advance to a higher stage of life." See Robeson's *New York Times* obituary: Whitman, "Paul Robeson Dead at 77." Tellingly, in his May 31, 1998, birthday tribute to Paul Robeson at Winston Unity Auditorium in New York City, CPUSA national chairman Gus Hall referred to Robeson's "belief in the revolutionary science of Marxism-Leninism" (Text published in *Paul Robeson: An American Communist*. The 11-page booklet was initially published in 1998 by CPUSA. I was able to get a copy via interlibrary loan. It has also been published in the Marxist journal *Political Affairs*. See: Gus Hall, "Paul Robeson: Artist, Freedom Fighter, Hero, American Communist," *Political Affairs*, July 1998).

31 Robeson's "To You Beloved Comrade" was published in the April 1953 edi-

tion of the *New World Review*. It is republished in Robeson and Foner, *Paul Robeson Speaks*, pp. 347–49.

32 This was admitted by longtime CPUSA head Gus Hall, in a May 1998 speech that CPUSA quickly published in several sources, from the Marxist journal, *Political Affairs*, to a booklet. See: Gus Hall, "Paul Robeson: Artist, Freedom Fighter, Hero, American Communist," *Political Affairs*, July 1998. I will discuss this at length later in the book.

33 The index flags only two references to Robeson. Davis, *Livin' the Blues*, p. 372.

34 Ibid., p. 344.

35 Ibid., p. 311.

CHAPTER 5: BACK TO CHICAGO: "PEACE" MOBILIZATION AND DUPING THE "SOCIAL JUSTICE" RELIGIOUS LEFT

1 Davis, *Livin' the Blues*, p. 226; Tidwell, *Frank Marshall Davis, Black Moods*, p. xviii.

2 Davis, *Livin' the Blues*, pp. 238–39.

3 Wright, *Black Boy*, pp. 294–97.

4 Ibid., pp. 294–97, 315, 333–35.

5 Davis, *Livin' the Blues*, pp. 238–44.

6 Ibid., p. 243.

7 Ibid.

8 Ibid., p. 244.

9 See: "Soviet Continues Selling to Italy," *New York Times*, January 17, 1936.

10 Davis, *Livin' the Blues*, p. 245.

11 Ibid., pp. 245–46.

12 Ibid., pp. 245 and 250–51.

13 To view these actual flyers, including this incendiary language, see: Kengor, *Dupes*, pp. 113–19.

14 For a list of these, see: Kengor, *Dupes*, pp. 160–81.

15 Davis, *Livin' the Blues*, pp. 296–97.

16 Ibid., pp. 262–63.

17 Ibid., pp. 263, 268–70.

18 Ibid., p. 275.

19 See Kennan's classic "X" article, "The Sources of Soviet Conduct," *Foreign Affairs*, July 1947.

20 Henry Winston, "Our Tasks Today," report to the national committee of the Young Communist League, July 19, 1941. The text was published in *Clarity*, the self-described "Theoretical Organ of the Young Communist League, U.S.A.," Summer 1941, Vol. II, No. 2, pp. 30–40.

21 The emergency meeting would be held July 19–20, 1941.

22 Sources: "Investigation of Un-American Propaganda Activities in the United States," p. 431; "Guide to Subversive Organizations and Publications," pp. 26–28.

23 "Clergymen Group Charges War Aim," *New York Times*, January 10, 1941.

24 This is seen in two documents in the Comintern Archives: the Ryan/Dennis memo (which I will discuss and cite momentarily) and also a handwritten March 29, 1941, document personally written by Comintern head Georgi Dimitroff. To see the documents (and further discussion), see: Kengor, *Dupes*, pp. 150–51.

25 The actual flyers and resolutions from this event are published in full in Kengor, *Dupes*, pp. 147–57.

26 "Call, American People's Meeting," New York City, April 5–6, 1941.

27 Kengor, *Dupes*, pp. 145–46.

28 In total, eighteen were listed as "Rev.," including the Reverend F. Hastings Smyth, the lone Catholic. The remainder of the eighteen were Protestants.

29 Herbert Romerstein and Eric Breindel, *The Venona Secrets: Exposing Soviet Espionage and America's Traitors* (Washington, DC: Regnery, 2000), p. 114.

30 Kengor, *Dupes*, pp. 149–50.

31 Some of these individuals were more open about their Party membership, even if only later in life. Pete Seeger, interviewed for a 2008 episode of the PBS series *American Masters*, and by then an old man, conceded that he had been a communist. He first joined the Young Communist League as a student at Harvard (in the mid-1930s) and then later (in the early 1940s) joined CPUSA as a card-carrying member. Ron and Allis Radosh refer to "The Almanacs" as "the Communist folk-singing group." See Ron and Allis Radosh, *Red Star Over Hollywood: The Film Colony's Long Romance with the Left* (Jackson, Tenn.: Encounter Books, 2005), p. 78. Also see: Paul C. Mishler, *Raising Reds* (New York: Columbia University Press, 1999), pp. 7, 101, 105–6. On Guthrie, see: John Pietaro, "Book Review: Woody Guthrie: An American Radical," *Political Affairs*, July 5, 2011.

32 For a published copy of the original program, including Robeson's performance, see: Kengor, *Dupes*, pp. 152–53.

33 Kengor, *Dupes*, pp. 152–53.

34 Comintern Archives on CPUSA, Library of Congress, Fond 515, Opis 1, Delo 4091.

35 See: David H. Anthony, "Max Yergan," *Encyclopedia of the American Left*, 2nd ed., eds. Mary Jo Buhle, Paul Buhle, and Dan Georgakas (New York: Oxford University Press, 1998), p. 912.

36 On Dorothy Taylor's support of Planned Parenthood, see: "Journal of the Proceedings of the City Council of the City of Chicago, Illinois," Regular

Meeting, Wednesday, January 12, 1994, 10:00 a.m., Council Chambers, City Hall, Chicago Illinois, pp. 44318–20.

37   "Investigation of Un-American Propaganda Activities in the United States," pp. 609, 2100.

38   See: Robert Draper, "The Ultimate Obama Insider," *New York Times*, July 26, 2009; Jodi Kantor, "An Old Hometown Mentor, Still at Obama's Side," *New York Times*, November 24, 2008.

39   Dana Milbank, "Valerie Jarrett: The real center of Obama's inner circle," *Washington Post*, September 29, 2010.

40   See: Christi Parsons, "The president's right-hand woman," *Chicago Tribune*, February 19, 2011; Draper, "The Ultimate Obama Insider"; Kantor, "An Old Hometown Mentor, Still at Obama's Side"; Milbank, "Valerie Jarrett."

41   Information published in "Investigation of Un-American Propaganda Activities in the United States," pp. 1284–85.

42   Among others, see: "Civil Rights Congress as a Communist Organization," p. 10.

43   This is the description of Earl Ofari Hutchinson. It is not clear to me when (precisely) Frank advocated this, whether before or after he joined CPUSA. See: Earl Ofari Hutchinson, *Blacks and Reds: Race and Class in Conflict, 1919–1990* (East Lansing: Michigan State University Press, 1995), p. 166.

44   I cited this same document earlier. It is from Wilkins in a November 22, 1949, letter to communist William L. Patterson, who headed the frontgroup Civil Rights Congress. Wilkins and the NAACP made it available to the media in a November 23, 1949, press release.

CHAPTER 6: WAR TIME AND PARTY TIME (1943–45): FRANK WITH CPUSA AND ASSOCIATED NEGRO PRESS

1   That said, congressional investigators did catch other items missed by Frank watchers and biographers since, including an April 1944 roundtable on the war held at Chicago's Hamilton Hotel by a group called "Friends of the New Masses in Chicago," moderated by *New Masses'* Washington editor, Bruce Minton. The small group of a dozen sponsors included William Patterson and executive editor of the Associated Negro Press Frank Marshall Davis. "Investigation of Un-American Propaganda Activities in the United States," pp. 566, 974, 978, 1353.

2   This poem appears in Tidwell, ed., *Frank Marshall Davis: Black Moods, Collected Poems*, pp. 169–70. Tidwell lists it first among unpublished and uncollected poems by Frank in the 1948–84 timeframe. It is clear, however, that

the poem would have been written not long after Hitler invaded the Soviet Union in June 1941. More precisely, the poem refers to the USSR planting itself "twenty-five years ago." The year of that planting was 1917; thus, this poem almost certainly was written in 1942.

3   Davis, *Livin' the Blues*, pp. 276–78.

4   See Tidwell's endnote (p. 21) on p. 365 of his edited edition of Frank's memoirs, *Livin' the Blues.*

5   Tidwell, *Frank Marshall Davis: Black Moods, Collected Poems*, p. xxviii.

6   Davis, *Livin' the Blues*, pp. 265–67.

7   Tidwell, ed., *Frank Marshall Davis: Black Moods, Collected Poems*, p. xxxv.

8   Ibid.

9   As Tidwell notes, the letter is not dated, which, as any historian knows, is quite common in biographical research. Tidwell has a "Note on the Text" that discusses Davis's undated letters.

10 John Edgar Tidwell, ed., *Writings of Frank Marshall Davis: A Voice of the Black Press* (Jackson, MS: University Press of Mississippi, 2007), p. xxv.

11 Tidwell says this in note 29 of p. xxxv of his book. Tidwell has the letter in his possession.

12 Cliff Kincaid and Herb Romerstein, "Who was Frank Marshall Davis?" report posted at usasurvival.org, p. 1.

13 Davis, *Livin' the Blues*, p. 277.

14 Ibid.

15 Ibid.

16 Ibid., pp. 277, 281.

17 Ibid., p. 277.

18 Ibid., p. 227.

19 See also: Davis, "Check Your Dagger, Mister?" February 9, 1944.

20 The three parts were published, respectively, on September 15 and 22, 1943, and October 7, 1943.

21 Tidwell's reproduction of this column does not include commas in that final sentence. I have inserted commas where I believe Frank would have intended them.

22 Equally remarkable, this was Frank's first of his ANP commentaries. He had started with a bang.

23 Davis, "Ben and the Reds."

24 Frank wrote this in another column, "Willkie Helps Roosevelt," April 12, 1944.

25 Ellsworth Barnard, *Wendell Willkie: Fight for Freedom* (Northern Michigan University Press, 1966), p. 359.

26 "The Press: Politicians and Love," *Time,* July 26, 1943.

27 Davis, *Livin' the Blues*, p. 282.

28   This point merits a lengthy side discussion, given that certain defenders of
     Frank today, including a person online claiming to be his son, Mark, argue
     that Frank was not pro-Stalin, even if he was pro-Soviet. This reveals a fun-
     damental misunderstanding of the nature of CPUSA and what it meant to
     be a Party member. For these defenders of Frank, their only form of evi-
     dence seems to be a statement from James Edward Smethurst's book stat-
     ing that Frank "wrote poetry attacking Stalin by name, which appeared in
     his collections *I Am the American Negro* (1937) and *47th Street Poems* (1948)."
     (Smethurst, *The New Red Negro*, p. 48.) In March 2011, a person claiming
     to be Mark Davis engaged in several exchanges with Dr. John Drew online
     at Drew's blog, "Anonymous Political Scientist." Mark Davis maintained
     that his father was not pro-Stalin. As evidence, he cited the Smethurst quo-
     tation. (On Mark Davis and this issue, see: Cashill, *Deconstructing Obama,*
     p. 281.)

     As I dug into these poems, I did not see much in the line of staunch
     criticism of Stalin. I found that Frank mentions Stalin twice in *I Am the
     American Negro.* There, I interpreted him as somewhat critical of Stalin, but
     not exactly scathingly, and based on the Trotsky trials, which was a very
     common criticism of Stalin by American communists and leftists gener-
     ally, embodied in John Dewey's famous Trotsky Commission. (See: Kengor,
     Dupes, pp. 105–9.) Specifically, in his poem, "They All Had Grand Ideas,"
     Frank wrote: "Lenin and Trotsky fought for a Russia without czars and ar-
     istocracy . . . today both are in the city dump as Stalin and his crew strong-
     arm the liberated peasants into accepting state control and ownership."
     That is Frank's strongest criticism, which is mild in light of Stalin's murder-
     ous rampage against tens of millions, which was taking place at the time.
     In the other poem, Frank gently jabbed: "Will Stalin sniffle in his vodka?"
     See: Frank Marshall Davis, *I Am the American Negro* (Chicago, IL: Black Cat
     Press, 1937), pp. 26, 34. (It is also in this book that Frank penned a much-
     quoted poem titled "Christ Is a Dixie Nigger.")

     Of course, even with these slight criticisms, this was before Frank joined
     the Party.

     Spyridon Mitsotakis also reviewed the poems and wrote to me in an
     e-mail: "It appears that the 1937 issue with Stalin, which is only in two
     poems, revolves around the party's treatment of FMD's friend Richard
     Wright. It's all circumstantial. . . . I don't see outright criticism of Stalin in
     the 1948 one, only one or two possible." Referring to one of the poems,
     Mitsotakis continued: "Stalin is mentioned where Frank writes 'Will Sta-
     lin sniffle in his vodka?' But the scene that is mentioned directly before
     this, black men trying to imitate Russian Bolsheviks and their sloganeering
     in Washington Park in Chicago, is taken directly from Richard Wright's

experience. This is a significant clue. I'm sure you are familiar with the incident where Richard Wright was picked up and thrown head first onto the sidewalk by a white Communist when he tried to take part in a May Day march, this happened in 1937. Wright's friend Frank would have been completely enraged by this at the time he was finishing his book. . . . It could well be a combination of both the Trotsky trials and the attack on Wright that inspired FMD's ire against Stalin—and this combination theory is what I recommend."

29 That cult was so devout that Stalin's successor, Nikita Khrushchev, was forced to publicly repudiate it in scathing terms in his February 1956 "Crimes of Stalin" speech. When Khrushchev did, he devastated countless CPUSA members, whose world was shattered. See, among others: Billingsley, *Hollywood Party*, p. 255; David Horowitz, *Radical Son* (New York: The Free Press, 1997), pp. 83–84.

30 Davis, *Livin' the Blues*, p. 297.

31 Ibid., p. 273. In this passage, Frank hoped that integrated armed forces would be an "antidote" to that image.

CHAPTER 7: THE LATTER 1940S: FRANK AND THE CHICAGO CREW

1 Davis, *Livin' the Blues*, pp. 283–84.

2 "Investigation of Un-American Propaganda Activities in the United States," p. 268.

3 Frank himself noted this. See: Davis, *Livin' the Blues*, p. 289.

4 "Investigation of Un-American Propaganda Activities in the United States," p. 566.

5 Frank Marshall Davis FBI file. This information is found on p. 4 of Honolulu File 100–5082.

6 Davis, *Livin' the Blues*, pp. 285, 299–302. Helen was actually Frank's second wife. His first wife was named Thelma, on whom there is surprisingly little information. The FBI file says that Frank married Thelma in 1931.

7 Ibid., pp. 289–90.

8 Ibid., pp. 283, 292–93.

9 In his memoirs, Frank calls it by both "union" and "committee." The editor, Tidwell, and index use "committee." See: Davis, *Livin' the Blues*, pp. xxiii, 278, 295, and 370.

10 "Investigation of Un-American Propaganda Activities in the United States," p. 1972.

11 Ibid., p. 2043; "Civil Rights Congress as a Communist Front Organization," p. 16.

12 Davis, *Livin' the Blues*, p. 296.

13 "Investigation of Un-American Propaganda Activities in the United States,"
    p. 610.

14 "Civil Rights Congress as a Communist Front Organization," p. 9.

15 Davis, *Livin' the Blues*, p. 296.

16 "Guide to Subversive Organizations and Publications," pp. 44–45; "Civil
    Rights Congress as a Communist Front Organization," pp. 9–10.

17 Ibid.

18 Ibid., pp. 1–6.

19 Ibid., p. 6.

20 Ibid., pp. 1, 11, 14–18, 24–25, 40–45.

21 For an extended analysis of Arthur Miller's communist sympathies and
    likely Party membership, including a photo of his apparent application for
    membership, see: Kengor, *Dupes*, pp. 184–93.

22 "Civil Rights Congress as a Communist Front Organization," p. 19.

23 Davis, *Livin' the Blues*, p. xxiii.

24 "Civil Rights Congress as a Communist Front Organization," pp. 24–25,
    28–29.

25 Among others, see: Margaret Sanger, "The Pope's Position on Birth Con-
    trol," *The Nation*, January 27, 1932, p. 103.

26 According to data currently posted by the Radiance Foundation, each year
    289,000 black Americans die from accidents, HIV, homicide, cancer, kid-
    ney, respiratory, and heart disease. This, however, is nothing compared to
    what Planned Parenthood has done to the black community. Each year,
    363,000 black Americans die from abortion.

27 "Five Hundred and Fifty Union Officials Assail 'Red-Hunt,'" *Daily Worker*,
    May 25, 1947, p. 9; "Civil Rights Congress as a Communist Front Organiza-
    tion," pp. 30–36.

28 Trevor Loudon, *Barack Obama and the Enemies Within* (Las Vegas, NV:
    Pacific Freedom Foundation, 2011), pp. 370–72.

29 This information was provided by testimony of Walter S. Steele to the Com-
    mittee on Un-American Activities on July 21, 1947. "Communist Activities
    in the United States," hearings before the Committee on Un-American Ac-
    tivities, U.S. House of Representatives, Washington, DC, 80th Congress, 1st
    Session, H.R. 1884, H.R. 2122, July 1947, pp. 75–6.

30 I credit Trevor Loudon for finding and sharing this information.

31 See my profile of Axelrod: Paul Kengor, "David Axelrod, Lefty Lumber-
    jack," *American Spectator*, March 2012, pp. 16–29.

32 Maria L. La Ganga, "The man behind Obama's message," *Los Angeles
    Times*, February 15, 2008. Also see: Amanda Paulson, "David Axelrod: ar-
    chitect of Obama's unlikely campaign," *Christian Science Monitor*, July 15,

2008; Patrick T. Reardon, "The Agony and the Agony," *Chicago Tribune*, June 24, 2007.

33 Ben Wallace-Wells, "Obama's Narrator," *New York Times*, April 1, 2007.

34 Jeff Zeleny, "President's Political Protector, Ever Close at Hand," *New York Times*, March 9, 2009.

35 Jeff Zeleny, "Long by Obama's Side, an Adviser Fills a Role That Exceeds His Title," *New York Times*, October 27, 2008.

36 See the I. F. Stone tribute website: http://www.ifstone.org/biography-refuted.php. The *Los Angeles Times* dubbed Stone the "conscience of investigative journalism," and CNN's Larry King called him a "hero." An Oliphant cartoon showed Stone outside the Pearly Gates, with Saint Peter telephoning God, "Yes, <u>THAT</u> I. F. Stone, Sir. He says he doesn't want to come in—he'd rather hang around out here, and keep things honest."

37 In their latest work, published by Yale University Press, historians John Earl Haynes, Harvey Klehr, and Alexander Vassiliev conclude that Stone was a "Soviet spy." In an article excerpted from the book and published in the April 2009 online version of *Commentary* magazine, titled, "Special Preview: I. F. Stone, Soviet Agent—Case Closed," they write: "To put it plainly, from 1936 to 1939 I. F. Stone was a Soviet spy." Haynes and Klehr have written about Stone for years. See, for example: John Earl Haynes and Harvey Klehr, *Venona: Decoding Soviet Espionage in America* (New Haven, CT: Yale University Press, 2002), pp. 247–49. Also closely studying Stone's case was Herb Romerstein, the authority on the Venona Papers. See: Romerstein and Breindel, *The Venona Secrets*, pp. 432–39. On p. 436, Romerstein and Breindel write: "it is clear from the evidence that Stone was indeed a Soviet agent." One of the stronger confirmations from the Soviet side is provided by retired KGB general Oleg Kalugin, who states flatly: "He [Stone] was a KGB agent since 1938. His code name was 'Blin.' When I resumed relations with him in 1966, it was on Moscow's instructions. Stone was a devoted Communist." Kalugin added that Stone "changed in the course of time like many of us"; in other words, he did not remain a communist—but for a time he was a Soviet agent. Oleg Kalugin, *Spymaster: My Thirty-Two Years in Intelligence and Espionage Against the West* (New York: Basic Books, 2009), p. 80.

38 Marc Canter is an especially good source on the Canter and Rose mentorship of Axelrod. At his blog, testmarcblog.wordpress.com, Marc, a Chicago-based IT consultant, posts an e-mail from Don Rose, who remains a close family friend. Rose was eager to set straight the "historical record" on when and where he and David Canter met Axelrod. According to Rose, Axelrod "was familiar with our paper [*Hyde Park-Kenwood Voices*] as a stu-

dent before he got the [Hyde Park] Herald job." In the next line, Rose confirmed to Marc: "Your dad and I 'mentored' and helped educate him [Axelrod] politically in that capacity, which is perhaps why you may recall seeing him hanging around the house. I later wrote a reference letter for him that helped him win an internship at the Tribune, which was the next step in his journalism career." Marc Canter posted this on November 3, 2008, under the headline, "My family has been outed—we're dam [*sic*] Commies—but we ain't paid to be." I retrieved the post on October 13, 2011. Significantly, Don Rose's influence on David Axelrod was so strong that even the mainstream media sometimes pause to interview him in profiles of Axelrod. Articles in *Chicago Magazine,* the *Chicago Tribune,* the *Christian Science Monitor,* and the *Los Angeles Times* pause to acknowledge Don Rose's influence on Axelrod—albeit avoiding David Canter like the plague. (See earlier Axelrod citations, especially Reardon, "The Agony and the Agony.") Some of them correctly refer to Rose as a "mentor"— the *Chicago Tribune* does so explicitly—and most note that Rose "recommended" Axelrod for the critical summer internship position that he won at the *Chicago Tribune* when he graduated from college, directly interviewing and quoting Rose. That internship launched Axelrod. For more on Don Rose, see: Kengor, "David Axelrod, Lefty Lumberjack."

39   See: "Investigation of Un-American Propaganda Activities in the United States," p. 292.

40   "David and Miriam Canter: Doing Right from the Left," *Chicago Jewish History,* Vol. 34, No. 2, Spring 2010. This article is an interview with Evan Canter, second child of David and Miriam Canter, conducted by Walter Roth, president of the Jewish Historical Society.

41   See: "Investigation of Un-American Propaganda Activities in the United States," p. 292.

42   Harry's grandson, Evan, recalls the year being "around 1930." Congress reported it as 1932, adding that he stayed "in Europe" until 1937. See: "Investigation of Un-American Propaganda Activities in the United States," pp. 292, 297–98, 301.

43   "David and Miriam Canter: Doing Right from the Left"; "Davis S. Canter, 81," *Chicago Tribune,* August 29, 2004.

44   House Resolution on David Canter by Illinois House of Representatives. He and his father both did work for the Packinghouse Workers Union. David's surviving son, Marc, recalls "all sorts of wild memories of being the son of one of the organizers of the meatpackers union. Don't get me started!" Canter, "My family has been outed."

45   David Canter was subpoenaed on July 12, 1962. "Communist Outlets for the Distribution of Soviet Propaganda in the United States," Part 1, Hear-

ings Before the Committee on Un-American Activities, House of Representatives, 87th Congress, Second Session, May 9, 10, and 17 and July 12, 1962, pp. 1687–99.

46 Congress was also curious about Canter, an attorney, being listed in the 1960 and 1962 editions of the *Lawyers Referral Directory*, published by the National Lawyers Guild, an infamous communist front classified by Congress as the "legal bulwark of the Communist Party." "Subversive Involvement in Disruption of 1968 Democratic Party National Convention," p. 2260. On the National Lawyers Guild, see: "Report on the National Lawyers Guild: Legal Bulwark of the Communist Party," House Committee on Un-American Activities, House of Representatives, September 17, 1950.

47 "Communist Outlets for the Distribution of Soviet Propaganda in the United States," p. 1697.

48 For the exchange on this point with Canter, see: "Communist Outlets for the Distribution of Soviet Propaganda in the United States," p. 1681.

49 These words appear in: "Subversive Involvement in Disruption of 1968 Democratic Party National Convention," Part 1, Hearings Before the Committee on Un-American Activities, House of Representatives, 90th Congress, Second Session, October 1, 3, and 4, 1968, p. 2260. Also see: "Communist Outlets for the Distribution of Soviet Propaganda in the United States," pp. 1673–99.

50 In his book, *Barack Obama and the Enemies Within*, Trevor Loudon, one of the few people in the world bothering to track this trail, has referred to David Canter as a "paid Soviet agent." Loudon has written this many times in articles and blog entries. For a single succinct statement, see: Loudon, *Barack Obama and the Enemies Within*, pp. 192–209 (especially p. 199), 365. Both of David's sons vigorously deny that David was a paid Soviet agent or spy. See: Canter, "My family has been outed"; "David and Miriam Canter: Doing Right from the Left."

51 "Investigation of Un-American Propaganda Activities in the United States," p. 298.

52 Ibid., p. 1353.

53 Wikipedia entry retrieved September 20, 2011.

54 William L. Patterson, *The Man Who Cried Genocide: An Autobiography* (New York: International Publishers, 1991), p. 97.

55 Ibid., pp. 156–60.

56 Once back in Chicago, Frank enlisted the reliable support of Marshall Field. Field was enthusiastic, as was singer Lena Horne, whom Patterson and his wife, Louise, tapped for a fundraiser for the school. Ibid., pp. 150–55.

57 Ibid., pp. 148–49.

58 Ibid., p. 156.

59 Davis, *Livin' the Blues*, p. 276.

60 To cite just one example, they together did a symposium put together for the group "Friends of the New Masses in Chicago." "Investigation of Un-American Propaganda Activities in the United States," p. 1343.

61 As I will note later, probably no other figure is mentioned as often in Frank's FBI file as Patterson. For the Romerstein quotation, see: Kincaid and Romerstein, "Who was Frank Marshall Davis?" p. 2.

62 Mary Louise Patterson shares her and her father's story in Kaplan and Shapiro, eds., *Red Diapers*, pp. 110–15.

63 Through an intermediary source, I asked Lieutenant General Ion Mihai Pacepa, the highest-level intelligence official to defect from the Soviet Bloc, about Patrice Lumumba and his connections to the KGB. In a June 16, 2011, e-mail, Pacepa wrote: "To the best of my knowledge, Lumumba was a Communist used by the KGB as an agent of influence. No wonder that in 1966 the Soviet Union's third largest university was given his name."

64 On Khamenei at the university, see: Ilan Berman, *Tehran Rising* (Lanham, MD: Rowman-Littlefield, 2005), p. 12.

65 Stephen Kinzer, "Soviet Help to Sandinistas: No Blank Check," *New York Times*, March 28, 1984.

66 Among others, see: Claire Sterling, *The Terror Network* (New York: Holt, Rinehart, and Winston, 1981), pp. 118–20, 137; Simon Reeve, *One Day in September: The Full Story of the 1972 Munich Olympics* (New York: Arcade Publishing, 2011), p. 148; Patrick Goodenough, "Abbas, Fatah Call Mastermind of Munich Olympics Attack a Hero," CNSNews.com, July 8, 2010.

CHAPTER 8: THE *CHICAGO STAR*: COMRADES, "PROGRESSIVES," AND SOVIET AGENTS

1 On the *Chicago Star* and Davis, see: "Fifth Report of the Senate Fact-Finding Committee on Un-American Activities, 1949," California Legislature, published by the California Senate, pp. 546, 562; Bill V. Mullen, *Popular Fronts: Chicago and African-American Cultural Politics, 1935–46* (Champagne, IL: University of Illinois Press, 1999).

2 Davis, *Livin' the Blues*, pp. 298–99.

3 Tidwell, *Frank Marshall Davis, Black Moods*, pp. xviii–xix.

4 John Edgar Tidwell reports that the newspaper launched on July 4, 1946. Perhaps it was released that day. The date on the newspaper (which I have) is July 6, 1946. Tidwell, *Writings of Frank Marshall Davis, A Voice of the Black Press*, p. xxiv.

5   I have more on this later in the book, including a full chapter.

6   Frank Marshall Davis, "Those Radicals of '76," *Chicago Star*, July 6, 1946.

7   "Reveal Pepper Columnist For Red-Tinged Newspaper," *Logansport* (Indiana) *Pharos-Tribune*, April 21, 1947. This was a syndicated UP piece.

8   "Investigation of Un-American Propaganda Activities in the United States," pp. 274–91.

9   Tidwell, *Writings of Frank Marshall Davis, A Voice of the Black Press*, p. xxiv.

10 Davis, *Livin' the Blues*, p. 308.

11 See index of "Investigation of Un-American Propaganda Activities in the United States," p. 1866.

12 Ibid., p. 2022.

13 "Fifth Report of the Senate Fact-Finding Committee on Un-American Activities, 1949," California Legislature, published by the California Senate, p. 546.

14 "Scope of Soviet Activity in the United States," Hearings Before the Subcommittee to Investigate the Administration of the Internal Security Act and Other Internal Security Laws of the Committee on the Judiciary, United States Senate, 84th Congress, Second Session, on Scope of Soviet Activity in the United States, December 5 and 6, 1956, Part 41 (Washington, DC: U.S. GPO, 1957), p. 2098.

15 Pepper did not appear nearly as frequently as Frank and Fast. That said, the only other op-ed contributor who rivaled Pepper in terms of appearances (but not prestige) was Herman Schendel. Pepper thus would have been probably the third or fourth most frequent contributor to the *Star*'s op-ed page.

16 Among other sources, see: Claude Pepper, *Pepper: Eyewitness to a Century* (New York: Harcourt Brace, 1987), p. 250.

17 Among the better historical accounts of this period and the AMA versus Pepper, see: Peter Conrad, *The Sociology of Health and Illness*, 8th ed. (New York: Macmillan, 2009), pp. 305–6. The source on a "terrific fight" is cited there.

18 See: Haynes, Klehr, and Vasilliev, *Spies: The Rise and Fall of the KGB in America* (New Haven, CT: Yale University Press, 2009), pp. 279–83.

19 Ibid.

20 See p. 16 of Romerstein's 2008 paper, "From Henry Wallace to William Ayers—the Communist and Progressive Movements," which can be found at the websites of www.aim.org and www.usasurvival.org. That paper features original documents, including pages from FBI files and a 1944 NKVD memo to the Comintern listing Kramer by name. Romerstein writes that Kramer, working as Pepper's staff director, "wrote a bill to establish a Na-

tional Health Program, which in 1946 was adopted by President Truman as the Truman Health Care Bill. It failed to pass. Its opponents called it social-ized medicine."

21 Reginald Thomas, "Claude Pepper, Fiery Fighter for Elderly Rights, Dies at 88," *New York Times*, May 31, 1989.

22 Among others, see: Romerstein and Breindel, *The Venona Secrets*, pp. 215–16; Harvey Klehr, John Earl Haynes, and Fridrikh Igorevich Firsov, *The Secret World of American Communism* (New Haven, CT: Yale University Press, 1995), pp. 96–97; Haynes, Klehr, and Vasilliev, *Spies*, pp. 427–28; and "The Shameful Years: Thirty Years of Soviet Espionage in the United States," prepared and released by the Committee on Un-American Activities, U.S. House of Representatives, 82nd Congress, 2nd Session, December 30, 1957 (Washington, DC: U.S. GPO, 1957), pp. 55–58.

23 I provide a lengthy discussion of this in *Dupes*, pp. 124–26, 160–66, among others. Also see: Romerstein and Breindel, *The Venona Secrets*, p. 214.

24 Romerstein, "From Henry Wallace to William Ayers—the Communist and Progressive Movements," p. 8.

25 See: Ernest DeMaio, "DeMaio gives analysis of CIO nat'l convention," *Chicago Star*, October 25, 1947; Lee Pressman, "An Analysis: Charter for Fascism," *Chicago Star*, May 15, 1948.

26 See: Tanenhaus, *Whittaker Chambers*, pp. 93–97, 223.

27 I. F. Stone, "What can a felon teach us . . . ," *Chicago Star*, July 31, 1948. A quotation from Stone also appeared in the August 21, 1948, edition, in a roundup by reporter Peter Williams, titled "Our Town."

28 My estimate of 1,500 pages is based on roughly 100–110 issues ranging from twelve to sixteen pages per issue.

CHAPTER 9: FRANK'S WRITINGS IN THE *CHICAGO STAR* (1946–48)

1 Editorial, "The Star is Born," *Chicago Star*, July 6, 1946.

2 "Liberals, Where Are You?" *Chicago Star*, May 8, 1948.

3 This is evident, for instance, on the front page of the newspaper of August 28, 1948.

4 Herb Romerstein writes that Wallace "became the point man for the com-munist assault on the Truman administration," and, "In reality, many Communist Party operatives were in control of the Progressive Party." Romerstein, "From Henry Wallace to William Ayers—the Communist and Progressive Movements," pp. 10–11.

5 While I cannot confirm the authenticity of the statement, the *Star* ran this text on p. 7 of its May 22, 1948, issue, under the headline "TEXT: A State-

ment from Stalin." The subhead claimed that the text came from a May 17, 1948, "Moscow Radio broadcast" by "Premier Stalin."

6 See: Kengor, *Dupes*, pp. 194–95.

7 "John Howard Lawson to speak at civil rights rally here Friday," *Chicago Star*, November 22, 1947.

8 In another piece, for instance, Frank noted that, of all the nations in the world, it was "only the Soviet Union which has abolished racism and color prejudice." Quoted in "Reveal Pepper Columnist For Red-Tinged Newspaper," April 21, 1947.

9 See my lengthy discussion of this in *Dupes*, pp. 172–73.

10 In his September 21, 1946, column, Frank attacked FDR's former Soviet ambassador William C. Bullitt, who once had been terribly pro-Bolshevik before making a wonderful conversion.

11 Editorial, "A yardstick for Soviet-baiters," *Chicago Star*, September 7, 1946.

12 This ad appeared on p. 15 of the November 2, 1946, edition.

13 Another blatant example was Frank's column in the February 1, 1947, issue, right alongside a huge (top-to-bottom of the page) ad for a February 4 "Lenin-Lincoln-Douglass Anniversary Meeting" at Chicago's Civic Opera House, featuring Eugene Dennis, CPUSA general secretary, and Gil Green, CPUSA candidate for mayor of Chicago.

14 "New cancer research told by Soviet scientist," *Chicago Star*, January 11, 1946.

15 There was good reason for that perception. Among others, see Daniel Doron, "The Pathology of Israel's Left," *Jerusalem Post*, December 19, 2003.

16 Senator Claude Pepper, "What's up in Greece?" *Chicago Star*, March 22, 1947.

17 Senator Claude Pepper, "Is the present Greek gov't worthy of support?" *Chicago Star*, March 22, 1947.

18 This was on page 11 of the next issue of the *Star*, March 29, 1947.

19 Frank Marshall Davis, "The people will not lose," *Chicago Star*, April 5, 1947.

20 On the rapes in East Germany, see: Antony Beevor, *The Fall of Berlin, 1945* (New York: Viking-Penguin, 2002), pp. 32–34, 410–14.

21 "U.S. ministers denounce Greece-Turkey plan," *Chicago Star*, April 12, 1947.

22 " 'Truman endangers peace'—Wallace," *Chicago Star*, April 12, 1947.

23 "Johannes Steel's exclusive interview with Molotov," *Chicago Star*, April 12, 1947.

24 See: Frank Marshall Davis, "The Bible 'subversive'?" *Chicago Star*, July 26, 1947; "The suppressed Bible," August 2, 1947.

25 That tradition dated back to Pope Pius IX's extremely early condemnation in 1846 (*Qui pluribus*), which affirmed that communism is "absolutely contrary to the natural law itself" and prophetically averred that if communism were adopted it would "utterly destroy the rights, property, and possessions of all men, and even society itself." Bear in mind that this was two years before the publication of Marx's *Communist Manifesto.* In 1878 (*Quod Apostolici muneris*), Pope Leo XIII followed by defining communism as "the fatal plague which insinuates itself into the very marrow of human society only to bring about its ruin." More statements from the Church followed, in 1924, 1928, 1930, 1931, two in 1932, 1933, all before the publication of *Divini Redemptoris* (on atheistic communism) in 1937. *Divini Redemptoris* accurately stated that the Church had called public attention to the perils of communism "more frequently and more effectively"—and earlier, it might have added—than "any other public authority on earth."

26 Frank Marshall Davis, "Barometer of progress," *Chicago Star*, October 25, 1947.

27 The "opiate of the masses" remark is well-known. The source for the quotation, "communism begins where atheism begins," is Fulton J. Sheen, *Communism and the Conscience of the West* (Indianapolis and New York: Bobbs-Merrill, 1948). Sheen, who spoke and read several languages, translated the quotation into English from an untranslated Marx work.

28 Lenin wrote this in a November 13 or 14, 1913, letter to Maxim Gorky. See: James Thrower, *God's Commissar: Marxism-Leninism as the Civil Religion of Soviet Society* (Lewiston, NY: Edwin Mellen Press, 1992), p. 39.

29 Quoted in Thrower, *God's Commissar*, p. 39. Another translation of this quotation comes from Robert Conquest, in his "The Historical Failings of CNN," in Arnold Beichman, ed., *CNN's Cold War Documentary* (Stanford, CA: Hoover Institution Press, 2000), p. 57.

30 See: J. M. Bochenski, "Marxism-Leninism and Religion," in B. R. Bociurkiw et al., eds., *Religion and Atheism in the USSR and Eastern Europe* (London: MacMillan, 1975), p. 11.

31 See: Daniel Peris, *Storming the Heavens: The Soviet League of the Militant Godless* (Ithaca, NY: Cornell University Press, 1998).

32 On this and more, see: Alexander Solzhenitsyn, *The Gulag Archipelago, 1918–1956* (New York: Harper and Row, 1974), pp. 29, 37–38, 325–27, 345–51.

33 Mikhail Gorbachev, *Memoirs* (New York: Doubleday, 1996), p. 328. For an analysis of this Soviet war on religion, see Kengor, *God and Ronald Reagan*, pp. 57–74.

34 Frank Marshall Davis, "Cold War in Church," *Honolulu Record*, September

22, 1949. As I write, the best current research on Stalin's campaign against Stepinac is being done by Ion Mihai Pacepa and Ron Rychlak, who are compiling a major work on Soviet disinformation against the religious.

35 The April 18, 1947, and October 25, 1947, issues of the *Star* are just two examples.

36 Frank Marshall Davis, "Another 'Peoria Affair,' " *Chicago Star*, August 23, 1947.

37 See: Frank Marshall Davis, "The Horatio Alger myth," *Chicago Star*, July 19, 1947, and "Today's independence," July 5, 1947.

38 Ronald Reagan, "Farewell Address," January 11, 1989.

39 "Packinghouse workers cut cows, but can't put meat on table," *Chicago Star*, September 20, 1947.

40 Frank Marshall Davis, "I got radical thoughts," *Chicago Star*, September 20, 1947.

41 Perhaps the best example is: Frank Marshall Davis, "Democracy—by Wall St.," *Chicago Star*, December 20, 1947.

42 Among others, see: "No sign of the 'Iron Curtain' in Czechoslovakia," *Chicago Star*, November 22, 1947.

43 "To General Motors," *Chicago Star*, October 16, 1947, and "Can't sing behind GM's iron curtain," *Chicago Star*, November 15, 1947.

44 "How the GM branch of U.S. imperialism works," *Chicago Star*, August 23, 1947.

45 Another notable anti-GM article was titled " 'Sure I duped GM workers'—Vincent," *Chicago Star*, November 22, 1947.

46 This headline ran in the January 4, 1947, issue. Also see: "GOP would spare rich' with 20% tax cut plan," *Chicago Star*, January 11, 1947.

47 This discussion was in the May 17, 1947, issue.

48 This was one of several features on May Day in the life of the *Star*. This particular feature ran in the April 26, 1947, issue; it included a lengthy analysis by Howard Fast.

49 This headline ran in the July 19, 1947, issue.

50 This headline ran in the May 15, 1948, issue.

51 This headline likewise ran in the May 15, 1948, issue. It ran on p. 1.

52 Frank Marshall Davis, "Ginger Rogers' hatred," *Chicago Star*, May 24, 1947. Ginger Rogers was a member of the prominent anti-communist group Motion Picture Alliance for the Preservation of American Ideals, which included the likes of John Wayne, Gary Cooper, Clark Gable, and Barbara Stanwyck. The group's statement of principles began with a very un-Frank-like thought: "We believe in, and like, the American way of life."

53 Frank Marshall Davis, "I've had enough," *Chicago Star*, August 9, 1947.

54 The full-page feature was in the June 14, 1947, issue, in addition to nu-

merous other articles supporting the Hungarian coup in other editions, including particularly awful pieces in the June 21 and 28, 1947, and July 26, 1947, editions. The article in the June 28 edition was titled "No 'coup' in Hungary."

55 Frank's worst piece on Czechoslovakia was titled "Czechs and the press," *Chicago Star*, March 6, 1948. In that same issue, the *Star* ran a horrible piece of Soviet propaganda with an article titled "Russian coup? City's Czechs laugh at wild press stories."

56 That crusade commenced with a *Star* editorial in the July 12, 1947, issue, titled "Who lost at Paris?" I will discuss the opposition to the Marshall Plan when I detail Frank's later columns for the *Honolulu Record*. He personally wrote more on the Marshall Plan in Hawaii than in Chicago.

57 "Behind Berlin ruckus," *Chicago Star*, July 17, 1948.

58 Frank Marshall Davis, "White House Harry," *Chicago Star*, June 22, 1947.

CHAPTER 10: FRANK HEADS TO HAWAII

1 "Progressive Party hails new paper," *Chicago Star*, September 4, 1948.

2 Canter was secretary and member of the four-man board of directors.

3 Tidwell, *Frank Marshall Davis, Black Moods*, p. xviii.

4 Ibid., p. 311.

5 Ibid.

6 See: Kengor, *Dupes*, pp. 198–99.

7 See: "Scope of Soviet Activity in the United States," Hearings Before the Subcommittee to Investigate the Administration of the Internal Security Act and Other Internal Security Laws of the Committee on the Judiciary, United States Senate, 84th Congress, 2nd Session, on Scope of Soviet Activity in the United States, Part 41-A, Appendix II, 1953 and 1954 Reports of The Commission on Subversive Activities of the Territory of Hawaii (Washington, DC: U.S. GPO, 1957), p. 2697.

8 Karl G. Yoneda, *Ganbatte* (*Steadfast*) (Los Angeles: Asian American Studies Center, University of California Press, 1983), pp. 145, 154.

9 Even Frank's biographer, John Edgar Tidwell, seems almost willing to call the *Record* a communist publication. Tidwell notes that the *Record* "grew out of the history of radical newspaper publishing that had been established by such predecessors as *People's World* on the West Coast." Of course, *People's World* was (and remains) CPUSA's West Coast organ. "Through its prolabor position," adds Tidwell, with tremendous understatement, "the *Record* was immediately associated with the Communist Party." No, through its obviously communist contents, the *Record* was immediately as-

sociated with the Communist Party. It was impossible to read the *Record* (especially Frank's writings) and not associate it with the Communist Party. See: Tidwell, *Writings of Frank Marshall Davis: A Voice of the Black Press,* pp. xxiv–xxvi.

10 See: "Scope of Soviet Activity in the United States," Hearings Before the Subcommittee to Investigate the Administration of the Internal Security Act and Other Internal Security Laws of the Committee on the Judiciary, p. 2696.

11 Ibid.

12 Pelosi said this in a July 27, 2001, tribute given on the one hundredth anniversary of Harry Bridges's birth. Bridges died in March 1990. Hon. Nancy Pelosi, "In Honor of Harry Bridges," *Congressional Record—Extension of Remarks,* July 27, 2001, p. E1460.

13 Ibid.

14 Among others, see: "Communist Legal Subversion: The Role of the Communist Lawyer," House Committee on Un-American Activities, U.S. House of Representatives, 86th Congress, 1st Session, February 16, 1959 (Washington, DC: U.S. GPO, 1959), p. 21.

15 Document filed in the Comintern Archives, Fond 495, Opus 74, Delo 467. This document is housed in the Moscow archives, and is now in a closed section of the archives. We can thank the diligence of Herb Romerstein for finding this document. Romerstein shared the document with me.

16 Frank's biographer states that the *Honolulu Record* was "affiliated" with the ILWU. Tidwell, *Frank Marshall Davis, Black Moods,* p. xix. Also, Frank acknowledge in his memoirs that the *Record* was "a newspaper supported mainly by the ILWU membership, and was openly friendly with its leadership." Davis, *Livin' the Blues,* p. 323.

17 "Scope of Soviet Activity in the United States," Hearings Before the Subcommittee to Investigate the Administration of the Internal Security Act and Other Internal Security Laws of the Committee on the Judiciary, p. 2696.

18 Ibid., p. 2697.

19 Frank Marshall Davis, "How to Become a Communist," *Honolulu Record,* June 2, 1949.

20 Jack Hall's bio at the ILWU website: http://www.ilwulocal142.org/new159/index.php?option=com_content&view=article&id=74:jack-hall&catid=52:leaders&Itemid=122, retrieved November 5, 2011.

21 Soviet Comintern Archives, Fond 495, Opus 72, Delo 277. See fuller citation below.

22 Among other sources, see Jack Hall's bio at the ILWU website. http://

www.ilwulocal142.org/new159/index.php?option=com;sfcontent&view=
article&id=74:jack-hall&catid=52:leaders&Itemid=122. The website says of
Hall's conviction and appeal: "The convictions were appealed, and in 1957
the Supreme Court threw out nearly all of the convictions as unconstitutional. Following the Supreme Court decision, the Ninth Circuit Court of
Appeals dismissed the convictions against Jack Hall on January 20, 1958."

23   Davis, *Livin' the Blues*, pp. 313–14, 324–25.

24   Ibid., p. 323.

25   Cashill, *Deconstructing Obama*, pp. 272–73.

26   This is written in the November 15, 1947, preface of Ichiro Izuka's self-
published memoir/pamphlet, "The Truth About Communism in Hawaii,"
provided to me by Herb Romerstein.

27   Material in the next several paragraphs first appeared in my book *Dupes*.

28   The document that forms the decision brief on this meeting was pulled
from the Comintern Archives in Moscow (it is not available in the United
States) by Herb Romerstein before the specific archives were reclosed.
This document is filed in Fond 495, Opus 72, Delo 277, with Opus 72 reclosed. Romerstein gave me a copy of the document.

29   See: Romerstein and Briendel, *The Venona Secrets*, pp. 73–77, 258–68.

30   This document, too, was obtained on-site in Moscow by Herb Romerstein.
He has given me a copy of the document.

31   This information is taken from a second document in the Comintern Archives in Moscow (not in the United States), this one filed under Fond
495, Opus 20, Delo 541. Herb Romerstein has written or spoken on it on
several occasions, as well as discussing it with me.

32   Ibid.

33   Ibid.

34   Quotation from Edward Berman in a 1949 letter to Roy Wilkins, acting
secretary of the national branch of the NAACP. The Berman letter—a
copy of which was given to me by Herb Romerstein—was included as part
of his testimony before HUAC in April 1950. "Hearings Regarding Communist Activities in the Territory of Hawaii—Part 3," Hearings before the
Committee on Un-American Activities, House of Representatives, 81st
Congress, 2nd Session, April 17, 18, and 19, 1950, Appendix, Index (Washington, DC: U.S. GPO, 1950), pp. 2065–68.

35   Quotation from Edward Berman in a 1949 letter to Roy Wilkins, cited in
House Committee on Un-American Activities testimony, April 1950.

36   Ibid.

37   Ibid.

38   A document in Frank's FBI file shows him speaking at a May 16, 1949,

HCLC event, revealing him to be immediately active in Hawaii. His *Honolulu Record* column started that same month.

39   "Communist Legal Subversion: The Role of the Communist Lawyer," p. 30.

CHAPTER 11: FRANK IN THE *HONOLULU RECORD* (1949–50): TARGET, HARRY TRUMAN

1   Among others, see: "The Billion-Dollar Empire Scheme for Europe," *Daily Worker*, June 14, 1947, p. 6; "Russian Comment on the Marshall Plan," *Daily Worker*, June 17, 1947, p. 2; "The Goal of the Marshall Plan," *Daily Worker*, June 18, 1947, p. 6; "The Marshall Plan: Truman's Doctrine in Different Words," *Daily Worker*, June 22, 1947, p. 12; "The Press and the Marshall Plan," *Daily Worker*, July 1, 1947, p. 2.

2   "Molotov Bars Pressure in Europe Aid," *Daily Worker*, July 1, 1947, p. 2.

3   Frank's June 16, 1949, article, "Murder in Guam."

4   Ion Mihai Pacepa, "Propaganda Redux," *Wall Street Journal*, August 7, 2007.

5   See: Kengor, *Dupes*, p. 195.

6   I am in possession of original documents, from programs to pamphlets, used at these festivals.

7   He used the "new democracies" phrase in his August 11, 1949, column, to cite just one example.

8   Frank's August 18, 1949, column.

9   Frank Marshall Davis, "End of an Era," *Honolulu Record*, November 10, 1949, and "Mobilizing for Civil Rights," *Honolulu Record*, January 5, 1950.

10   See: Frank Marshall Davis, "More 'civil rights' talk," *Chicago Star*, November 8, 1947.

CHAPTER 12: FRANK IN THE *HONOLULU RECORD* (1949–50): OTHER TARGETS, FROM "HUAC" TO "PROFITS" TO GM

1   See Frank's columns from August 4, 1949, and April 13, April 20, April 27, May 18, and June 8, 1950. Frank and his colleagues had also done so at the *Chicago Star*. See, for instance, "Threaten film folk with jail terms in 'red' hunt," *Chicago Star*, November 1, 1947.

2   The political left generally has applied this term for decades, and gotten away with it, to the point that the House Committee is today widely known as simply "HUAC." This is extremely ironic, given that liberals/progressives go into hysterics when "un-American" is used by others. Even more ironic, the left was, in effect, arguing that the *true* Americans were the card-carrying, closet American communists—literally pledged to Sta-

lin's USSR and the Comintern—whereas the un-Americans were the anti-communists, especially those elected to Congress and fulfilling their duty of investigating possible secret Soviet agents.

3   The National Emergency Civil Liberties Committee was founded in the early 1950s. Some online sources claim 1951; others claim 1954.

4   As cited earlier: I. F. Stone, "What can a felon teach us . . . ," *Chicago Star*, July 31, 1948. A quotation from Stone also appeared in the August 21, 1948, edition, in a roundup by reporter Peter Williams, titled "Our Town."

5   As testified by the feature source in the hearings before the Senate Judiciary Committee, the *Times* was one of the primary "organs of anti-anti-communism," doing so *ad nauseum* with "heavyweight, comatose gibberish." See: "The New Drive Against the Anti-Communist Program," Hearing Before the Subcommittee to Investigate the Administration of the Internal Security Act and Other Internal Security Laws of the Committee on the Judiciary, United States Senate, 87th Congress, 1st Session, July 11, 1961 (Washington, DC: U.S. GPO, 1961), p. 11.

6   This example is a post–Cold War one, showing the lasting power of these vicious words among communists and the American left, taken from the precise words of Gus Hall, CPUSA national chairman, in his May 31, 1998, tribute to Paul Robeson at Winston Unity Auditorium in New York City, text published in *Paul Robeson: An American Communist.*

7   The column was titled "Dailies and the Racists," June 29, 1950.

8   Frank used the word "domestic fascists" in his September 29, 1949, column "Challenge to the Church."

9   Frank Marshall Davis, "Paul Robeson's Last Stand," *Honolulu Record*, August 13, 1949.

10 "Russia continues to point to the fact that discrimination and segregation based on race does not exist there," Frank reported in his first column, "How Our Democracy Looks To Oppressed Peoples," *Honolulu Record*, May 1949.

11 As CPUSA national chairman Gus Hall later put it, "Unlike Comrade W. E. B. DuBois, Paul Robeson was not able to declare his Party membership openly." See: Hall, *Paul Robeson: An American Communist*, p. 3.

12 Davis, "Democracy is Indivisible," *Honolulu Record*, September 1, 1949.

13 Ibid.

14 Ibid.

15 Also see Frank Marshall Davis, "Test of Democracy," *Honolulu Record*, November 17, 1949; Frank Marshall Davis, "Africa is Next Door," *Honolulu Record*, January 12, 1950.

16 See: Kaplan and Shapiro, eds., *Red Diapers*, p. 319.

17 Horowitz, *Radical Son*, p. 72.

18 "For Freedom and Peace," transcript of Paul Robeson's remarks at the "Welcome Home Rally," New York, June 19, 1949.

19 Harten was cited in the *Daily Worker* at least fifteen times from 1942 to 1950. The source for this, which indexes and details each occasion by name and date and title, is the well-known "658/NCC" compilation: "A Compilation of Public Records of 658 Clergymen and Laymen connected with the National Council of Churches," published in April 1962 by Circuit Riders, Inc. (Cincinnati, OH), pp. 65–66. The chief investigator was J. B. Matthews. They also appear prominently in "A Compilation of Public Records, 20.5%, 1411 Protestant Episcopal Rectors (as of 1955)," published in March 1958 by Circuit Riders.

20 Ibid.

21 Melish took up two pages, whereas his son, William Howard Melish (more on him in a moment), took up nine pages. Together, they filled pp. 102–12 of the "20.5%/Episcopal" compilation.

22 "Guide to Subversive Organizations and Publications," pp. 117–18.

23 "20.5%/Episcopal" compilation, pp. 104–12.

24 See: Paul Kengor, "Buchenwald and the Totalitarian Century," *The Center for Vision & Values*, March 2010.

25 Frank Marshall Davis, "How to Block Both," *Honolulu Record*, August 25, 1949.

26 I am here pausing to make this distinction in order to pre-empt arguments. In 2010, I wrote a piece on this particular article by Frank for National Review Online. In a "readers' comments" response, a pro-Obama reader accused me of distortion, noting that Frank did not explicitly state (in the article) which option he preferred, and thus suggesting he may have favored free enterprise. This was quite a stretch, evident of the depths of desperation of Frank's (and Obama's) defenders. Not long after, in March 2011, a source claiming to be Mark Davis, Frank's son, used the same argument at the blog of Dr. John Drew. I was accused of misrepresentation.

27 This is point seven in Marx's ten-point plan. See: Mark and Engels, *The Communist Manifesto*, p. 75.

28 Robeson said this in May 1948 Senate hearings on the "Act to Protect the U.S. Against Un-American and Subversive Activities," in response to questions from Senator William Langer (R-ND). It is telling that this exchange, and call for nationalizations, was highlighted in a glowing tribute to Paul Robeson by CPUSA on the hundredth anniversary of his birth. See: *Paul Robeson: An American Communist*, p. 9.

CHAPTER 13: FRANK AND THE FOUNDERS

1   Among them, Matthew Spalding and Joseph Postell have done yeoman's work on this subject in their work at the Heritage Foundation's B. Kenneth Center for Principles and Politics.

2   Frank wrote this in his June 23, 1949, column, "Hawaii's Loyalty Oath."

3   Quoted in Gerald Duchovnay, *Humphrey Bogart: A Bio-Bibliography* (Westport, CT: Greenwood Press, 1999), p. 29.

4   Communist Party USA in the Comintern Archives, Library of Congress, Fond 515, Opis 1, Delo 9.

5   Fraina laid this out at great length in the August 23, 1919, edition of *Revolutionary Age*, reprinted in its entirety in: "Organized Communism in the United States," Committee on Un-American Activities, U.S. House of Representatives, 85th Congress, 2nd Session, August 19, 1953 (Washington, DC: U.S. GPO, 1958), pp. 25–29. In this same report, see pp. 4, 10, 29, and 141 for more on Fraina.

6   Darrow was posed in contrast to Woodrow Wilson's attorney general, Alexander Mitchell Palmer, an anticommunist progressive whom American Reds despised. Among other issues of the *Chicago Star*, these items were carried in the April 19 and 26, 1947, editions.

7   For an insightful analysis of Paine's faith, see: Michael Novak, *On Two Wings: Humble Faith and Common Sense at the American Founding* (San Francisco: Encounter Books, 2002), pp. 162–65.

8   Howard Fast, *Citizen Tom Paine* (New York: Grove Press, 1943).

9   "Civil Rights Congress as a Communist Front Organization," pp. 10–11.

10 Ibid.

11 See my two chapters on this period in Kengor, *Dupes*, pp. 182–230.

12 Gerald Cook, "Stars Arrive at LaGuardia on Bill-of-Rights Tour," *Daily Worker*, October 30, 1947.

13 I say there were "roughly two dozen" people who flew to Hollywood. For whatever reason, historians have differed on this point, saying anywhere from 19 to 29 people. Billingsley says 19. The Radoshes say 29. *The Daily Worker*, at the time, reported 26.

14 Ron and Allis Radosh, *Red Star Over Hollywood*, p. 152.

15 Ibid., p. 161.

16 Davis, "Those Radicals of '76."

17 Davis, "Today's independence."

18 Marx and Engels, *Communist Manifesto*, p. 67.

CHAPTER 14: 1951–57: FRANK ON RED CHINA, KOREA, VIETNAM, AND MORE

1 Wallace's statement was published in the August 26, 1950, issue of the leftist *New Leader* magazine.

2 Ronald Reagan, *An American Life*, p. 303.

3 Frank Marshall Davis, "What is 'Honorable Settlement'?" *Honolulu Record*, January 11, 1951.

4 For an excellent analysis of this, see the article by Dr. Nguyen Bich at the Global Museum on Communism website, www.victimsofcommunism.org.

5 Frank Marshall Davis, "We Must Give a War," *Honolulu Record*, January 25, 1951.

6 Frank Marshall Davis, "Why All the Shouting?" *Honolulu Record*, April 26, 1951.

7 Frank Marshall Davis, "Where the Blame Lies," *Honolulu Record*, page not dated.

8 Ibid.

9 See, especially: Frank Marshall Davis, "Our China Policy," *Honolulu Record*, March 14, 1957.

10 Frank Marshall Davis, "The Coming Year," *Honolulu Record*, January 1, 1953.

11 Many sources cite figures in the 60-plus-million range. Among the most credible and authoritative is Alexander Yakovlev, who was officially tasked with trying to verify Soviet atrocities during the Stalin era and throughout the Cold War. Yakovlev states that Stalin alone killed 60–70 million people. See: Yakovlev, *A Century of Violence in Soviet Russia*, p. 32.

12 Frank Marshall Davis, "There Is Hope At Geneva," *Honolulu Record*, July 21, 1955.

13 In this instance, Frank was writing post-Stalin, revealing that he perceived all Soviets leaders as desiring peace—as opposed to U.S. leaders. Frank Marshall Davis, "Friendship with Russia," *Honolulu Record*, February 2, 1956.

14 Frank Marshall Davis, "Let's Give Thanks," *Honolulu Record*, page not dated. While the photocopy in my possession is not dated, it would have been published in late November 1954, as it was a Thanksgiving column.

15 Frank Marshall Davis, "Just What Is Aggression?" *Honolulu Record*, April 8, 1954.

16 Ibid.

17 Frank Marshall Davis, "Christmas Story," *Honolulu Record*, December 17, 1953.

18 This item was published in the 2002 book by Alexander Yakovlev. See: Yakovlev, *A Century of Violence in Soviet Russia*, p. 157.

19 Davis, "There Is Hope At Geneva."

20 Among others, see: Antony Barnett, "Revealed: the gas chamber horror of North Korea's gulag," *London Observer,* January 31, 2004.

21 Barbara Crossette, "Korean Famine Toll: More Than 2 million," *New York Times,* August 20, 1999.

CHAPTER 15: MR. DAVIS GOES TO WASHINGTON

1 "The American Negro in the Communist Party," Committee on Un-American Activities, U.S. House of Representatives, 79th Congress, 2nd Session, Washington, DC, December 22, 1954.

2 Ibid., p. 1.

3 See: Mark Rudd, *Underground: My Life With SDS and the Weathermen* (New York: William Morrow, 2009).

4 "The American Negro in the Communist Party," pp. 1–2.

5 Ibid., pp. 4–5.

6 Ibid.

7 Ibid.

8 Ibid., pp. 8–9.

9 Ibid.

10 See: "Scope of Soviet Activity in the United States," Hearings Before the Subcommittee to Investigate the Administration of the Internal Security Act and Other Internal Security Laws of the Committee on the Judiciary, December 5 and 6, 1956, pp. 2518–19.

11 "Communist Legal Subversion: The Role of the Communist Lawyer," pp. 21, 30–32.

12 See: "Scope of Soviet Activity in the United States," pp. 2518–19.

13 "Communist Legal Subversion: The Role of the Communist Lawyer," pp. 21, 30–32.

14 See: "Scope of Soviet Activity in the United States," pp. 2518–19.

15 Ibid.

16 See: "Scope of Soviet Activity in the United States," Hearings Before the Subcommittee to Investigate the Administration of the Internal Security Act and Other Internal Security Laws of the Committee on the Judiciary, 1953 and 1954 Reports of The Commission on Subversive Activities of the Territory of Hawaii, pp. 2696–98.

17 "Guide to Subversive Organizations and Publications," pp. 237–45.

18 See: "Scope of Soviet Activity in the United States," pp. 2696–98.

19 See: M. Stanton Evans, *Blacklisted by History: The Untold Story of Senator Joe McCarthy* (New York: CrownForum, 2007), pp. 589–98.

CHAPTER 16: FRANK VERSUS "THE GESTAPO"

1 After describing the FBI's interest in his activities in Honolulu, Frank wrote, "It is only during the past twenty years that the FBI seems to have given up on me." This would seem to date the period as the late 1950s and possibly into the early 1960s. Davis, *Livin' the Blues*, pp. 325–26.

2 Ibid., p. 325.

3 Ibid.

4 Trevor Loudon has stated this in a number of writings. See: Loudon, *Barack Obama and the Enemies Within*, pp. 148–50.

5 Kincaid and Romerstein, "Who was Frank Marshall Davis?" p. 1.

6 Loudon, *Barack Obama and the Enemies Within*, p. 150; Loudon, "Vernon Jarrett's Father-in-Law Was a Communist"; Kincaid and Romerstein, "Who was Frank Marshall Davis?" p. 1.

7 Davis, *Livin' the Blues*, pp. 326–27.

8 Ibid.

9 Ibid.

10 Frank's FBI file contains many of these summary pages. This one is dated July 30, 1962.

CHAPTER 17: AMERICAN COMMITTEE FOR PROTECTION OF FOREIGN BORN

1 This is found on p. 2 of Frank's file record #100–5082. The FBI file provides some very personal information on their marital struggles.

2 "Investigation of Un-American Propaganda Activities in the United States," pp. 340–55.

3 See: Kengor, *Dupes*, p. 195; Billingsley, *Hollywood Party*, p. 230.

4 "Investigation of Un-American Propaganda Activities in the United States," pp. 340–41.

5 Ibid.

6 American Committee for Protection of Foreign Born Collection, Tamiment Library, New York University, Boxes 1 and 2.

7 Ibid.

8 Kincaid and Romerstein, "Who was Frank Marshall Davis?" p. 1.

9 See: "Investigation of Un-American Propaganda Activities in the United States," pp. 298, 301.

10 Romerstein and Breindel, *The Venona Secrets*, p. 216.

11 Abt said that Congressman Vito Marcantonio "was a friend of the Party but never a member." See: Abt, *Advocate and Activist, Memoirs of an American Communist Lawyer*, p. 117. Also see: Romerstein and Breindel, *The Venona Secrets*, p. 214.

12   "Investigation of Un-American Propaganda Activities in the United States,"
     p. 432.

13   Ibid., pp. 600, 622, 1127, 1203.

14   "Hugh DeLacy, Ex-Legislator Active in the Progressive Party," *New York
     Times*, August 21, 1986.

15   Frank Marshall Davis, "Davis Medina to Harris," *Honolulu Record*, December 1, 1949.

16   Robert Thomas, "George W. Crockett Dies at 88; Was a Civil Rights Crusader," *New York Times*, September 15, 1997.

17   Foner wrote this as part of a *London Review of Books* symposium/panel of
     reactions (by historians) to September 11. Source: "11 September," *London
     Review of Books*, October 4, 2001, Vol. 23, No. 19, pp. 20–25.

18   Matthew Rothschild, "The New McCarthyism," *The Progressive*, January
     2002.

19   "Columbia University Faculty Action Committee Statement of Concern,"
     New York Sun, November 12, 2007; Tamar Lewin and Amanda Millner-
     Fairbanks, "President of Columbia is Criticized," *New York Times*, November 14, 2007.

20   Jack Foner was Eric's father and Henry's brother. See: William H. Honan,
     "Jack D. Foner, 88, Historian and Pioneer in Black Studies," *New York
     Times*, December 16, 1999. This *New York Times* obituary characterized Jack
     Foner as a victim of a McCarthyite Red Scare in the 1930s, long before Joe
     McCarthy ever set foot in the Senate building.

21   For example, both Henry and Moe appeared together in a May 9, 1973,
     ACPFB letter. American Committee for Protection of Foreign Born Collection, Tamiment Library, New York University, Boxes 1 and 2.

22   As I write (October 12, 2011), this tag is attached to Francis Walter at his
     Wikipedia entry—sadly one of the few remarks on his character in a very
     brief and insufficient biography. See: Roger Daniels, *Guarding the Golden
     Door: American Immigration Policy and Immigrants since 1882* (Boston & New
     York: Hill and Wang, 2004), p. 129.

23   American Committee for Protection of Foreign Born Collection, Tamiment Library, New York University, Boxes 1 and 2.

24   Ibid.

25   "Investigation of Un-American Propaganda Activities in the United States,"
     pp. 614–16.

26   Ibid., pp. 612–17, 626.

27   Quoted in "Investigation of Un-American Propaganda Activities in the
     United States," p. 612.

28   Ibid., pp. 833–34.

29   Max Friedman's below-referenced piece for the Winter Soldier website

calls Feinglass a "probable KGB agent of influence." Also see Loudon, *Barack Obama and the Enemies Within,* pp. 194, 200, 424.

30 I have written about this at great length, with notes and images of documents, in Chapters 14–17 and 23 in *Dupes.* Chapter 23 is focused exclusively on Progressives for Obama.

31 An exhaustive analysis of this, including a huge amount of minute detail on Abe Feinglass, was posted at the website of WinterSoldier.com in an article by Max Friedman titled "John Kerry: Ambition and Opportunism," last updated on April 19, 2007.

32 On this, too, see my chapter (17) in *Dupes* titled "John Kerry—and Genghis Khan."

33 For example, see mentions of Feinglass in: "Chicago labor speaks out!" *Chicago Star,* April 26, 1947; "10,000 here march on May Day," *Chicago Star,* May 8, 1948 (Feinglass is pictured); and "Labor's best friend," *Chicago Star,* July 31, 1948.

34 "Progressive Party hails new paper," *Chicago Star,* September 4, 1948.

35 Ibid.

CHAPTER 18: WHEN FRANK MET OBAMA

1 This is the conclusion of Cliff Kincaid, who on September 19, 2009, submitted a FOIA request to the FBI requesting FBI files on Stanley Dunham. That request led to several letter exchanges between Kincaid and David M. Hardy, section chief of the Records Management Division of the FBI. Hardy requested additional information from Kincaid, including proof of Dunham's death. In a final letter from Hardy to Kincaid, dated March 26, 2010, Hardy wrote, "Records which may be responsive to your Freedom of Information-Privacy Acts (FOIPA) request [on Dunham] were destroyed on May 01, 1997." Kincaid includes this entire correspondence, in PDF format, on his website, www.usasurvival.org, under the post titled, "FBI Admits Destroying File on Barack Obama's Grandfather, Stanley Armour Dunham."

2 See, for instance, the journal article written by Obama's father: Barak [*sic*] H. Obama, "Problems Facing Our Socialism," *East Africa Journal,* July 1965, pp. 26–33. On this, see: Ben Smith and Jeffrey Ressner, "Long-lost scholarly article by Obama's dad surfaces," *USA Today,* April 16, 2008. Smith and Ressner were reporters for Politico.com, which tracked down the article. Also, of course, see Dinesh D'Souza's extended treatment in *The Roots of Obama's Rage.*

3 Davis Maraniss, "Though Obama Had to Leave to Find Himself, It Is Hawaii That Made His Rise Possible," *Washington Post,* August 24, 2008; D'Souza, *The Roots of Obama's Rage,* p. 70.

4   Sally H. Jacobs, *The Other Barack* (New York: Perseus, 2011), p. 113;
    Maraniss, "Though Obama Had to Leave to Find Himself." As noted ear-
    lier, Paul Robeson studied the Russian language for two years before trav-
    eling there. See: Vern Smith, " 'I Am at Home,' says Robeson At Reception
    in Soviet Union," *Daily Worker*, January 15, 1935.

5   Jacobs, *The Other Barack*, p. 113.

6   Ibid., pp. 114–15.

7   Ibid., pp. 115–16.

8   See: "March 12, 2009—Barack Obama Senior in 1962," posted at the
    website of the ILWU local 142 in Hawaii, http://www.ilwulocal142.org/
    new157/index.php?option=com_content&view=article&id=174:barack
    -obama-senior-&catid=1:latest-news&Itemid=50, retrieved November 6, 2011.
    Among other sources on Obama senior at this rally, see: Jacobs, *The Other
    Barack*, p. 108.

9   Davis, *Livin' the Blues*, p. 318. Another observer who made this connection
    is Jack Cashill in his *Deconstructing Obama*, p. 254.

10 Jack Cashill considers this. See: Cashill, *Deconstructing Obama*, p. 254.

11 Janny Scott, *A Singular Woman: The Untold Story of Barack Obama's Mother*
    (New York: Riverhead, 2011), pp. 82–83.

12 It is not clear (to me) when the two first met; accounts seem to differ.
    Broadly, it would have been in the 1930s.

13 Varying accounts report that Kenyatta in Moscow studied at "the Lenin
    School," at "a Comintern school," or at "Moscow University." Kenyatta
    himself, when asked which university he attended, once said only "Moscow
    University," which is how the *New York Times* subsequently referred to his
    university. It seems that the correct answer is that Kenyatta was enrolled
    in something called the Stalin Communist University of the Toilers of the
    East, known as "KUTV," located in Moscow, and which was Comintern-
    sponsored. For a superb article on this, see: Woodford McClellan, "Af-
    ricans and Black Americans in the Comintern Schools, 1925–1934,"
    The International Journal of African Historical Studies, Vol. 26, No. 2, 1993,
    pp. 371–90, especially pp. 378–82.

14 See: "Soviet-trained Mau Mau Terrorist Is Sentenced to 7 Years' Hard
    Labor," *New York Times*, April 9, 1953; "Kenya's Burning Spear: Jomo
    Kenyatta," *New York Times*, August 22, 1961.

15 See: "Kenyatta Works Closely With Reds But Ball Calls Him Independent,"
    Human Events, April 17, 1965. The socialist/communist divisions among
    Kenyans in this era are very complicated. It gets more complex still when
    considering Kenyatta's personal political evolution and his leanings for
    and against the USSR, the United States, and the West. Importantly, many
    years later, as Kenya's ruler, Kenyatta would reject communism and em-

brace Western capitalism as the key to advancing economic prosperity in Kenya. On this, the senior Obama would disagree and break ranks with Kenyatta, turning instead to Odinga Odinga. Kenyatta became a U.S. ally. In the 1930s and 1940s, however, Kenyatta was almost certainly a communist in ideology, if not a Party member; he was undoubtedly highly sympathetic. On the senior Obama's view on Kenyatta, Dinesh D'Souza writes: "Barack Obama Sr. was actually a political opponent of Kenyatta." D'Souza, *The Roots of Obama's Rage*, pp. 69–70.

16 I counted ten literal references to "Kenyatta," with one of the ten a reference to Kenyatta Airport. Of course, there were many more references to Kenyatta via pronouns.

17 *Dreams from My Father* was published by Times Book, an imprint of Crown Publishing Group, which is a division of Random House.

18 Barack Obama, *Dreams from My Father*, pp. 76–77.

19 Ibid.

20 Ibid., pp. 89–91.

21 Ibid., pp. 96–97.

22 Ibid.

23 Additional examples of Frank's using the phrase in the *Honolulu Record* include August 4, 1949, September 29, 1949, and December 22, 1949, columns.

24 Writing his memoirs in the 1990s, Obama figured that these words were probably (politically) safe to share, and probably could not imagine some Cold War researcher one day plucking the exact same Frank phrases from old library and CPUSA archives.

25 Obama, *Dreams from My Father*, p. 133.

26 Ibid., pp. 145–46.

27 Ibid., pp. 99, 103–4.

28 Though Obama's dating in *Dreams* is not clear (another similarity he shares with Frank's memoirs), he says that he decided to become a community organizer in 1983. In 1983, he would have been twenty-two years old—just like Frank. See: Obama, *Dreams from My Father*, pp. 133, 140, 143. Biographers tend to date his arrival in Chicago as 1985. David Remnick says that Obama arrived in Chicago in June 1985. See: Remnick, *The Bridge*, p. 142.

29 Ibid., p. 165.

30 As chief executive at The Habitat Co.—as well as in prior positions—Jarrett oversaw the management and development of huge housing projects in and around Chicago, including in Obama's district when he was Illinois state senator. Those projects received huge infusions of government dollars. They were also a wreck, suffering from pests, rats, mice, backed-up

sewage, and drug dealers—to cite a short list. The facilities were seized by federal authorities and shut down because of their deplorable conditions and litany of code violations. In a striking irony, Jarrett would preside over the demolition of some of the very housing projects that bore the name of her grandfathers. A symbol of the disaster is the housing complex in Obama's state district, Grove Parc Plaza, which had become uninhabitable because of unfixed problems ranging from fire damage to collapsed roofs. In one of the few national stories on this scandal, a shocking *Boston Globe* piece from June 2008 reported that in 2006 federal inspectors gave the complex of 504 apartments—which for eight years were part of Obama's district—a grade of "11" on a one-hundred-point scale. They were set for demolition. For more detail on this, see my piece on Valerie Jarrett: Paul Kengor, "Letting Obama be Obama," *American Spectator*, July/August 2011, pp. 12–19.

31   Obama, *Dreams from My Father*, p. 171.
32   Ibid., p. 220.
33   Ibid., p. 277.
34   Ibid., p. 330.
35   Ibid., pp. 96–97.
36   Remnick, *The Bridge*, pp. 96–97.
37   Ibid.
38   Ibid.
39   Ibid.
40   Ibid.
41   Ibid., p. 97.
42   Ibid., p. 94.
43   Toby Harnden, "Frank Marshall Davis, alleged Communist, was early influence on Barack Obama," *London Telegraph*, August 22, 2008.
44   Ibid.
45   Ibid.
46   Harnden, "Barack Obama's True Colours: The making of the man who would be US president."
47   Ibid.
48   Ibid.

CHAPTER 19: WHEN OBAMA LEAVES FRANK: OCCIDENTAL COLLEGE

1   Remnick, *The Bridge*, pp. 98–99.
2   Also see: Ibid.
3   Obama, *Dreams from My Father*, pp. 96–98.
4   Ibid.

5   Ibid., pp. 100–101.

6   Of course, Frank used the words constantly in other time periods and venues, but I am able to count (via electronic files) the number of times he used the words in his 1949–50 *Honolulu Record* columns.

7   On Fanon and Obama, see D'Souza, *The Roots of Obama's Rage*, pp. 13–14, 29–31, 91, 131.

8   Obama, *Dreams from My Father*, p. 122.

9   Ibid., pp. 98, 133.

10 Among journalists, *Time*'s dean of presidential correspondents, Hugh Sidey, said flatly: "No one can deny that Ronald Reagan restored morale to a country that needed it." This was a view seconded by veteran CBS reporter Mike Wallace, among numerous others. I document these assessments, including actual surveys of the question among academics, in Kengor, *The Crusader: Ronald Reagan and the Fall of Communism* (New York: HarperCollins, 2006), pp. 61–64.

11 The change was so quick, said Morris, "that it can only be ascribed to him." See: Morris in Robert Wilson, ed., *Power and the Presidency* (New York: Public Affairs, 1999), pp. 125–26; Edmund Morris, interviewed by Leslie Stahl of *60 Minutes*, September 26, 1999.

12 The Glen Meakem program is a radio talk show at 104.7 FM, WPGB, Pittsburgh, Pennsylvania, and is carried by several major stations throughout Pennsylvania and into parts of New York, New Jersey, Delaware, Maryland, West Virginia, and Ohio. I occasionally guest host for Glen Meakem, and did so on this occasion on which I interviewed John Drew.

13 Paul Kengor, "Obama's 'Missing Link,'" *American Thinker*, December 10, 2010.

14 Scott Shane, "Obama and '60s Bomber: A Look Into Crossed Paths," *New York Times*, October 4, 2008, p. A1.

15 This is a very well-known quote, probably first sourced by David Horowitz when he interviewed Ayers for the classic September 1982 *Rolling Stone* piece that Horowitz and Peter Collier wrote together. For a more recent account by Horowitz, see: Horowitz, *Radical Son*, pp. 333–34.

16 Dinitia Smith, "No Regrets for a Love of Explosives," *New York Times*, September 11, 2001, p. E1.

17 Selwyn Duke, "The Missing Link in the Evolution of Barack Obama," *American Thinker*, December 28, 2010.

18 See: Kengor, *Dupes*, pp. 203–16, 227, 229, 231.

19 Reagan's first memoirs, *Where's the Rest of Me?*, were published in 1965. He was elected in 1980. Obama's *Dreams from My Father* was first published in 1995. He was elected president in 2008.

20 Kevin Batton, "Ode to Obama," *Occidental Weekly*, March 2007.

21   See: Rebecca Mead, "Obama, Poet," *The New Yorker*, July 2, 2007; Primary
     Sources, "Two Poems, by Barack Obama," *The New Yorker*, July 2, 2007.

22   Davis, *Livin' the Blues*, p. 98.

23   Stanley's mother, Ruth Armour Dunham, committed suicide at the age
     of twenty-six, when Stanley was eight years old. Young Stanley found her
     body. See: Scott Fornek, "Stanley Armour Dunham: 'Gramps had entered
     the space age,'" *Chicago Sun-Times*, September 9, 2007.

24   See: Cashill, *Deconstructing Obama*, pp. 246–47, 269–85. See the 2012 docu-
     mentary video by Joel Gilbert, titled *Dreams from My Real Father*.

CHAPTER 20: FRANK RE-EMERGES—AND THE MEDIA IGNORE HIM

1   Kozyrev on ABC News, *This Week With David Brinkley*, August 25, 1991.
    From ABC News, Brinkley transcript #513, p. 7.

2   Genrikh Aleksandrovich Trofimenko, presentation at 1993 Hofstra Univer-
    sity conference on the Reagan presidency, published in Eric J. Schmertz et
    al., eds., *President Reagan and the World* (Westport, CT: Greenwood Press,
    1997), p. 136.

3   The book is posted at Amazon.com. I was able to get a copy via interlibrary
    loan. It has also been published in the Marxist journal *Political Affairs*. See:
    Gus Hall, "Paul Robeson: Artist, Freedom Fighter, Hero, American Com-
    munist," *Political Affairs*, July 1998.

4   In their spring 1992 article for *Labor History*, "Moscow Gold, Confirmed at
    Last?" Haynes and Klehr provide documentation on Moscow's funding, as
    does John Barron, *Operation Solo* (Washington, DC: Regnery, 1996), which
    details not only how and when Gus Hall received the Soviet money but
    the precise annual dollar amount, which Barron published in the appen-
    dix on pp. 339–40. Moreover, Herb Romerstein published images of the
    actual cash receipts between Gus Hall and the Kremlin, declassified from
    Soviet archives. Those images/receipts can be viewed on the web on p. 2
    (Exhibit 1) of Romerstein, "From Henry Wallace to William Ayers—the
    Communist and Progressive Movements."

5   Robeson's declassified FBI file is now posted and available for viewing at
    http://foia.fbi.gov/alpha.htm. It is one of the largest files at the site, cov-
    ering 2,680 pages.

6   For a very recent example, see: "Glenn Beck Targets Pro-Marxist at FCC,"
    Accuracy in Media, August 31, 2009.

7   Of course, Hall and his comrades have themselves to blame, as well as lib-
    erals/progressives never-ending blind eye and stunning naïveté when it
    comes to communism. The likes of Robeson and CPUSA lied to liberals/

progressives for so long that the lie became their truth. Indeed, Hall, in this same tribute to Robeson, admitted as much when he noted that Robeson would defend accused CPUSA members not as (himself) an open, fellow Party member, but "as a representative of progressive America." In reality, Robeson was not a progressive or a liberal, but a communist duping and using progressives and liberals. And with his and other communists' lies now exposed, liberals/progressives today have so much egg on their faces that they cannot bring themselves to reality. Ironically, those now speaking the truth on Robeson are communists and conservative anti-communists.

8   Tidwell, *Frank Marshall Davis: Black Moods, Collected Poems*, pp. xxviii and xxxv.

9   Tidwell, *Writings of Frank Marshall Davis: A Voice of the Black Press*, p. xxv.

10 Smethurst, *The New Red Negro*, pp. 35, 47–48.

11 I know this from personal experience, as Romerstein has constantly so cautioned me in writing books like this.

12 Dana Milbank, "Obama as You've Never Known Him!" *Washington Post*, May 23, 2008.

13 Sudhin Thanawala, "Writer offered a young Barack Obama advice on life," Associated Press, August 2, 2008. The other AP piece, by the same reporter, was titled "In multiracial Hawaii, Obama faced discrimination," May 19, 2008.

14 Maraniss, "Though Obama Had to Leave to Find Himself, It Is Hawaii That Made His Rise Possible." When asked about this slight of Frank, specifically by Cliff Kincaid, Maraniss had the courtesy to respond. He told Kincaid that he believed Frank's role had been "hyped," overstated, including "by Obama himself." It is striking here to see that even Obama's words on Frank's influence can be dismissed by reporters who do not want to touch this subject. I believe that Maraniss, like Remnick and others, is afraid to deal with Frank's communism because of the criticism it would bring from fellow journalists.

15 Jon Meacham, "On His Own," *Newsweek*, August 23, 2008.

16 For another example of attacking the accusers while defending Davis, see the press release by the Honolulu Community Media Council titled "The Honolulu Community-Media Council Condemns Shoddy Journalism and Smear Tactics by the Pittsburgh Tribune-Review and the Accuracy in Media Website," issued July 22, 2008.

17 I have long respected Remnick, using his books in my courses at Grove City College. I have used his *Lenin's Tomb* in my comparative politics course every semester since I began teaching the course. Thus, my criticisms of

his treatment of Frank come from no bias against his work—quite the contrary. My grave disappointment in his sugarcoating of Frank is magnified by my tremendous respect for his previous work.

18 See: Remnick, *The Bridge*, pp. 94–96.

19 Ibid., p. 97.

20 Maki was interviewed and is quoted by Cliff Kincaid, "Communist Party Backs Obama," Accuracy in Media, July 3, 2008. Kincaid's piece is posted at the AIM.org website.

21 Gerald Horne, "Rethinking the History and Future of the Communist Party," posted at PoliticalAffairs.net, March 28, 2007.

22 In 2008, Cliff Kincaid filed a FOIA request for Frank's FBI file and quickly received a copy. Kincaid told me (via a June 12, 2010, e-mail) that he believes that another researcher must have earlier filed a FOIA request, explaining the quick release. He believes that the other researcher was most likely Frank's biographer, John Edgar Tidwell.

23 To cite just one example, one page in the file excerpts three consecutive *Honolulu Record* columns by Frank from February 22, March 1, and March 8, 1951. All relate to communism and foreign policy.

24 This is evident in a January 4, 1952, document in the FBI file.

25 The informant has been widely cited as Robert M. Kempa. In fact, Kempa is so widely cited that Frank's Wikipedia entry (retrieved March 21, 2011) lists Kempa as the source. Herb Romerstein also lists the source as Kempa. See: Kincaid and Romerstein, "Who was Frank Marshall Davis?" pp. 3–4.

26 Cliff Kincaid posted Frank's entire FBI file online at www.usasurvival .org, where it has been posted since 2008. Researchers such as Remnick, Meacham, Maraniss, the Associated Press journalists, and countless others have no excuse for not reading the files.

CHAPTER 21: CONCLUSION: ECHOES OF FRANK

1 Frank Marshall Davis, "Those Radicals of '76," *Chicago Star*, July 6, 1946.

2 This has been widely reported by numerous sources. Among the most interesting are these from the British press and liberal American press: "Barack Obama sends bust of Winston Churchill on its way back to Britain," *London Telegraph*, February 14, 2009; "The White House Replaces Churchill Bust," *Daily Beast*, February 20, 2009; and "Obama Returns Churchill Bust to England: British Press Sees Snub," *Huffington Post*, February 22, 2009.

3 Dinesh D'Souza comments on this: "Perhaps we have a source here for why Obama removed that Churchill bust from the White House." D'Souza, *The Roots of Obama's Rage*, p. 91.

4   Transcript, "A World That Stands as One," Barack Obama, Berlin, Germany, July 24, 2008.

5   This was the infamous March 2012 "open mic" incident between Obama and Russian president Dmitri Medvedev.

6   Frank Marshall Davis, "How to Block Both," *Honolulu Record*, August 25, 1949.

7   President Barack Obama, Press Conference, February 9, 2009.

8   Clinton said this in his January 1996 State of the Union Address. Reagan made his statement in his January 20, 1981, Inaugural Address.

9   Frank Marshall Davis, "Onward with the Hydrogen Bomb," *Honolulu Record*, February 9, 1950.

10 "Obama Announces 'Framework' for Deal with Congress to Extend Bush-Era Tax Cuts," FoxNews.com, December 7, 2010.

11 See video clip posted at CBSNews.com, "Obama: Tax Cuts for Wealthy GOP's 'Holy Grail,' " December 7, 2010.

12 Frank Marshall Davis, "How to Become a Communist," *Honolulu Record*, June 2, 1949.

13 Frank Marshall Davis, "Africa is Next Door," *Honolulu Record*, January 12, 1950.

14 Editorial, "Labor fights back," *Chicago Star*, April 26, 1947.

15 In Brownsville, Texas, in February 2008, Obama recalled: "And I remember May Day 2006, when I marched should-to-shoulder with the Hispanic community." See: Maria Gavrilovic, "Obama Speaks to Hispanic Evangelicals," CBSNews.com, February 29, 2008.

16 See: "Presidential Proclamation—Loyalty Day," The White House, Office of the Press Secretary, April 29, 2011.

17 Among other areas, I see possible shades of Frank in President Obama's sometimes selective invoking of the American Founders. As noted at length, Frank had done this, often for purposes that distorted or were not a full reflection of what the Founders meant or intended. For Obama, consider his invocation of the Founders' inalienable rights, and, more so, their ultimate source. For example, President Obama has on several conspicuous occasions left out the word "Creator" in calling upon Americans' inalienable rights, including in a June 17, 2011, presidential statement responding to a U.N. resolution on sexual orientation. This was the third time in the first half of 2011 alone that Obama had used the language of "inalienable rights" but omitted the "Creator." Such a tendency began literally at the very start of his presidency. In quoting what seemed to be an amalgam of the American Declaration of Independence and the French Declaration of the Rights of Man, the new president excluded "life" among the inalienables, as well as the "Creator" that endows that right to

life. See: Jerad McHenry, "Obama Omits 'Creator' When Citing 'Inalienable Rights' of LGBTs," CNSNews.com, June 20, 2011; Paul Kengor, "Viva La Revolucion," posted at the website of the Center for Vision & Values, January 27, 2009.

18   As I write, Axelrod has left the White House. He was, however, Obama's most important political advisor, arguably the man who got Obama elected president. And he is now the president's point man for reelection in 2012.

19   See: Parsons, "The president's right-hand woman"; Draper, "The Ultimate Obama Insider"; Kantor, "An Old Hometown Mentor, Still at Obama's Side"; Milbank, "Valerie Jarrett: The real center of Obama's inner circle"; Kengor, "Letting Obama be Obama."

20   Ibid., Kengor.

21   Ibid.

22   Davis, "There Is Hope At Geneva."

23   Davis, *Livin' the Blues*, pp. 328–29.

24   Ibid., p. 332.

25   Incidents like these helped form in Frank what he called a "lifelong inferiority complex" that permanently resided "deep in my psyche." Davis, *Livin' the Blues*, p. 333.

Index

Abbas, Mahmoud, 117
Abolition, Operation, 166
Abraham Lincoln School, 105, 114, 116, 120, 144, 222, 272
 Davis's senatorial testimony and, 209–10
Abt, John, 222–23, 326n
Africa, 56, 94, 162, 194, 248, 323n
 Obama and, 15, 241
 Obama's father and, 230–31, 322n
 slavery and, 22, 25
African National Congress, 254
Ahmadinejad, Mahmoud, 224
Alger, Horatio, 139
Almanacs, The, 83
American Civil Liberties Union (ACLU), 65, 110, 114, 135, 166, 185
 communists and, 46–47, 327n
 Scottsboro Boys case and, 45–47
American Committee for Protection of Foreign Born (ACPFB), 220–25
 communists and, 8, 18, 220–22, 225
 Davis's affiliation with, 8, 220–22, 225, 228, 308

 on Internal Security Act, 224–25
 racial issues and, 8, 18, 221–22
American Council of Trustees, 224
American exceptionalism, 2, 9, 246–47, 294
American Life, An (Reagan), 3
"American Negro in the Communist Party, The," 40, 204–5
American Negro Labor Congress, 39, 68
American Peace Mobilization (APM), 120, 184
 antiwar resolution of, 82–83
 Chicago and, 84, 110, 223, 310
 CRC and, 109–10
 name change and mission of, 80–81
 New York City and, 81–84
 World War II and, 79–84, 86–87, 109–10, 162, 225–26, 310
American Revolution, 183–87
American Thinker, 249, 254, 260
American Youth for Democracy, 105–6, 112, 210
antiapartheid movement, 254–56

anticommunists, anticommunism, 5–6, 127,
   207, 230, 268–69, 274–75, 351*n*, 364*n*
   Christians and, 76, 137–38, 165, 171–72,
     174–75, 201–2, 345*n*–46*n*
   in Hollywood, 140, 347*n*
   as racism, 163, 166–69, 171
   and Remnick's profile of Davis, 277,
     280
   see also House Committee on
     Un-American Activities
Aptheker, Herbert, 61, 106, 329*n*
Ariyoshi, Koji, 144–45, 147–48, 194
Associated Negro Press (ANP), 28, 59
   Davis at, 74–75, 78, 90, 95–103, 283,
     287–88
   Davis's "Passing Parade" column for,
     95–97
   and Davis's politics and ideology, 76,
     97–98, 101–3
   World War II and, 90, 95–100
Associated Press (AP), 12, 170, 275–76
Atlanta, Ga., 51, 60–61, 96–97
   Davis's departure from, 61, 73
   Davis's life in, 29–31, 44, 53, 61, 93
Atlanta Daily World:
   Davis at, 31–32, 51, 53–62, 140, 172
   Davis's departure from, 61–62, 73
   and Davis's politics and ideology, 53,
     57, 61
   Davis's "Touring the World" column in,
     31, 55, 58–59
   Hughes and, 54–55, 206, 223
   and political home for blacks, 60–61
   Scottsboro Boys case and, 56–60
Atlanta Independent, 47
Atlanta World, 30–31, 44
atomic bomb:
   Chicago Star and, 125, 127, 312
   Honolulu Record and, 159–61, 197,
     200–201
   U.S. use of, 157–59, 161
Attlee, Clement, 157, 295
Auerbach, Sol (James S. Allen), 41
Axelrod, David, 112–15, 123, 339*n*–40*n*
   Canter and, 113–14, 228, 292–93, 339*n*
   Obama's relationship with, 112–13, 115,
     142, 228

Axelrod, Myril, 113, 123
Ayers, Bill:
   comparisons between Davis and, 4, 11
   Obama and, 11, 19, 227, 249–50, 253,
     275

Baldwin, Roger, 46, 65
Bates, Ruby, 36–37
Beck, Glenn, 261
Ben-Gurion, David, 131
Berlin, 117, 125, 134, 141, 269, 288
Berlin Wall, 269, 297
Berman, Edward, 152
Bernard, Johnny, 222
Bessie, Alvah, 188–89, 191
Biddle, Francis, 42, 108
Biden, Joe, 3
big business, 9, 111, 128
   ANP and, 100, 102
   Honolulu Record and, 146–48, 161–62,
     176–78, 289–90
Bill of Rights, 153, 169, 181–82, 310
biological weapons, 197
Black Book of Communism, The (Courtois
   et al.), 323*n*
Black Boy (Wright), 75
Black Man's Verse (Davis), 74
blacks, 59, 111, 152, 172, 278, 296, 338*n*
   APM and, 83–84, 310
   Chicago and, 28, 84–86, 143
   Chicago Star and, 126–27, 129, 139,
     312
   communists and, 38–41, 50, 61, 204–7
   and Davis's politics and ideology, 6, 17,
     94, 98, 102, 272
   discrimination against, 7, 17–18, 21–25,
     48, 79, 83, 85–87, 101–2, 164, 169
   education of, 21–22
   Herndon case and, 51–52
   Honolulu Record and, 156, 162, 168–69,
     173–74, 315
   Hughes and, 54–55
   in journalism, 28–31
   Livin' the Blues on, 25–26
   Obama and, 14, 233, 235–36, 240–42,
     244–45, 247
   Patterson and, 91, 115–17

politics of, 28, 39–40, 50, 60–61, 173–74, 204–7

Robeson and, 168–70, 173–74, 205

Schuyler and, 56–57

Scottsboro Boys case and, 32, 36–37, 44, 48–49, 52, 86–87, 205

USSR and, 39–41, 67–69, 86, 103, 115, 204–7, 330n

World War II and, 78–79, 83–87, 89, 206–7, 310

see also civil rights; race, racism; slaves, slavery

Boesche, Roger, 254–55

Bogart, Humphrey, 159, 189

Bollinger, Lee, 224

Borodin, Mikhail, 196

Boss, Caroline, 254–59

Boudia, Mohamed, 117

Bouslog, Harriet, 208–10, 222

Boxer, Barbara, 10, 262

Brenneisen, Leo S., 217–18, 284, 307

Bridge, The (Remnick), 12, 243, 256, 277–80

Bridges, Harry, 223, 278

Honolulu Record and, 144–47, 173–74, 221

ILWU and, 144–47, 208, 216, 221

Browder, Earl, 66, 110, 223, 228

Scottsboro Boys case and, 44–46

Bryan, William Jennings, 46–47, 184

Buchenwald, 176

Bush, George W., 1, 224, 287, 291

conversion of, 260–61

California Senate Fact-Finding Committee on Un-American Activities, 47, 120

Canter, David, 339n–41n

Axelrod and, 113–14, 228, 292–93, 339n

Canter, Harry Jacob, 113–14, 228, 292–93

Chicago Star and, 142–43, 292

Canter, Marc, 339n–41n

capitalists, capitalism, 58–59, 142, 161, 184, 201, 230, 254, 281, 286, 314, 360n

ANP and, 100–101

APM and, 81–82

Drew and, 257–58

Gitlow and, 185–86

Honolulu Record and, 160, 162, 176

Carter, Jimmy, 3, 68, 257, 267, 331n

Chambers, Whittaker, 66, 261

Chandoo, Mohammed Hasan, 255–59

Change We Can Believe In, 13

Chiang Kai-shek, 4, 128

Chinese civil war and, 156, 162

Honolulu Record and, 162–63

Chicago, Ill., 199, 205, 209, 225–28, 270, 273

APM and, 84, 110, 223, 310

Axelrod and, 112–13

CPUSA and, 33–34, 74, 84–86, 134, 183–84

Davis's departure from, 143, 148, 151–52, 278

Davis's life in, 5, 11, 28–30, 51, 72–74, 76–78, 83, 93–94, 105–7, 111–12, 143, 151, 153, 225, 233–34, 239–41, 268, 278, 283–84, 293–94, 308

and Davis's politics and ideology, 78, 93–94, 104–5, 111–12, 120, 188

D. Canter and, 114, 228, 292

Feinglass and, 225–26

Fraina and, 183–84

H. Canter and, 228, 292

Obama and, 28, 239–41, 245, 249–50, 253, 268, 293, 361n

public housing in, 240, 361n

Robeson and, 72–73, 139

United Packinghouse Workers and, 111–12, 115

World War II and, 84–86, 109–10, 226, 310

Wright and, 74, 336n

Chicago Civil Liberties Committee, 106–7, 153, 226

Chicago Conference on Race Relations, 85

Chicago Defender, 112, 116

Chicago *Evening Bulletin,* 28–29

Chicago Peace Congress, 226

Chicago Public Housing Authority (CHA), 240

Chicago Star, 118–45, 152, 227–28, 319*n*
  Davis at, 5–6, 9–10, 32, 124–41, 145,
    147, 163, 166, 182, 185–91, 193, 204,
    211, 221, 227, 232, 238–39, 263, 287,
    292–93, 295, 311–14, 343*n*
  Davis's "Frank-ly Speaking" column in,
    118–19, 126–27, 145, 189–90, 287, 313
  and Davis's politics and ideology, 104,
    118, 124, 126–30, 132, 134, 137, 140–
    41, 189–90
  founding of, 114, 118–20
  major contributors to, 10, 121–23, 343*n*
  sale of, 142, 227
Chicago Sun-Times, 112
Chicago Tribune, 105, 112, 340*n*
China, 4, 102, 116, 170, 174, 193, 196, 297,
    310
  ANP and, 100–101
  Chicago Star and, 127–28
  civil war in, 156–57, 162, 315
  comparisons between USSR and, 198–99
  Honolulu Record and, 157, 162–63, 198–
    201, 315
  Korea and, 194–95, 197
  legacy of communism in, 202–3
  U.S. trade with, 162–63, 199
Christians, Christianity, 25–27, 36, 55, 63,
    135, 322*n*
  anticommunism and, 76, 137–38, 165,
    171–72, 174–75, 201–2, 345*n*–46*n*
  Chicago Star and, 137–39
  Honolulu Record and, 171–75
  slavery and, 22, 26
  World War II and, 81–82, 175
  see also Roman Catholics, Roman
    Catholic Church
Christmas, 55, 202
Churchill, Winston, 122, 125, 268
  ANP and, 96–101, 103
  comparisons between Wallace and,
    99–101
  Davis's criticisms of, 5, 9, 91, 98–100,
    103, 109, 128, 283, 287–88
  Obama and, 9, 287–88
  World War II and, 82, 96, 99–100, 287
Citizens' Committee to Aid Packing-House
  Workers, 111–12, 115, 228

Citizen Tom Paine (Fast), 186–88, 190
civil rights, 25, 58, 61, 68, 78, 83, 108, 171,
    223, 299
  Chicago Star and, 130, 163
  CPUSA and, 50, 205
  and Davis's move to Hawaii, 151–52
  and Davis's politics and ideology, 6, 91,
    274–77, 279
  Honolulu Record and, 157, 168–69, 315
  Scottsboro Boys case and, 38–39
  see also blacks; race, racism
Civil Rights Congress (CRC), 107–11, 126,
    171, 186–88, 210
  Davis's affiliation with, 107–10
  and Fast's book on Paine, 187–88
  HCLC and, 153, 283
  inflammatory rhetoric of, 109–10
  members of, 110–11
  Patterson and, 49–50, 107, 116, 153, 170,
    187, 283
  Robeson and, 110, 170, 283
Clark, Tom, 6, 42, 81, 108, 222
  Honolulu Record and, 167, 171, 173
Cleaver, Ben, 1–3, 242
Clinton, Bill, 3, 273, 276, 290
Clinton, Hillary, 1–4, 10, 261
  Jones's relationship with, 2–3, 242
  presidential campaign of, 2, 4, 11
colonialism, *see* imperialists, imperialism
Columbia University, 12, 66, 166, 187, 224,
    227, 248–49, 282
  Obama's enrollment at, 239, 248, 253
  Potemkin Progressives and, 62, 65
Commission on Subversive Activities of the
  Territory of Hawaii, 211
Committee for the First Amendment,
  188–89
Common Sense (Paine), 186
Communist International (Comintern),
    47–48, 77, 83–85, 92, 119, 146, 173,
    183, 188, 196, 221, 231, 285, 324*n*,
    351*n*, 360*n*
  APM and, 79, 81, 83, 310
  blacks and, 39–40, 204, 206
  and Davis's politics and ideology, 137,
    274
  Fort-Whiteman and, 39, 68

Gitlow and, 42, 185–86
Hawaii Question and, 149–51
opening of archives of, 270, 273, 283
Scottsboro Boys case and, 43–44
World War II and, 79, 81, 85
Communist Manifesto, The (Marx and
    Engels), 17, 33, 186, 191
Communist Party, Californian, 150
Communist Party, Hawaiian, 7, 144–50, 220
    and Davis's politics and ideology, 149,
      217, 284
    and FBI investigation of Davis, 217–19
    Honolulu Record and, 144–46, 148–49, 284
Communist Party, Soviet, 173, 324n
    Hawaii Question and, 150–51
    Potemkin Progressives and, 65–66
Communist Party USA (CPUSA), 1, 46,
    103–8, 112–17, 125, 132, 158–59, 170,
    183–87, 189, 191, 221–22, 223–26, 254,
    259, 269, 324n–26n, 333n, 341n
    Abraham Lincoln School and, 105, 116,
      210, 272
    ANP and, 95, 97, 99, 103
    and anticommunism as racism, 166–69
    APM and, 79–84, 86, 310
    blacks and, 39–40, 50, 61, 204–7
    Bridges and, 145–46
    campaigns of, 37–41, 44, 158
    Chicago and, 33–34, 74, 84–86, 134,
      183–84
    Chicago Star and, 5, 118–21, 123, 126,
      128, 130, 134, 140–41, 144, 313
    concealment and advancement of,
      35–36, 38
    CRC and, 108, 110
    Darrow and, 47, 56
    and Davis's politics and ideology, 4–5,
      10, 15, 17–19, 51, 53, 57, 61–62, 75–79,
      89, 91–95, 97–98, 103–5, 137, 140–41,
      143–44, 149, 151, 167, 179, 205–6,
      211–12, 215–19, 235, 238, 245, 263,
      271–73, 277, 279, 282–86, 289, 306–9,
      335n–36n
    Davis's senatorial testimony and, 208–9
    and FBI investigation of Davis, 215–19
    Feinglass and, 8, 225
    finances of, 35, 39, 56, 270, 325n

founding of, 33–35, 181, 183–84
Gitlow and, 42, 185–86
goals of, 33–35
Hawaii Question and, 149–50
Honolulu Record and, 144–45, 348n
HUAC targeted by, 165–66
ILD and, 42, 44
Korea and, 194–95
Marshall Plan and, 154–56
NAACP and, 48, 50
opening of Soviet archives on, 270, 273,
    283
Patterson and, 91, 105, 115–17
Pressman and, 122–23
racial issues and, 8, 68
Robeson and, 69–72, 144, 270–71, 331n,
    364n
on Roosevelt, 77–78
Schuyler and, 56–57
Scottsboro Boys case and, 17, 32, 37–39,
    41, 43–45, 48, 51–52, 55–58, 86, 205
Soviet Negro republic and, 40, 103
World War II and, 79–86, 96, 206–7, 226
Wright and, 74–75, 336n
communists, communism, 29, 31, 99, 107,
    113, 136, 153, 172, 215–31, 250, 254,
    261, 268–87, 292–93, 297–300, 339n,
    351n
ACLU and, 46–47, 327n
ACPFB and, 8, 18, 220–22, 225
American Revolution and, 183–86
Atlanta Daily World and, 58–59
blacks and, 38–41, 50, 61, 204–7
campaign against Truman of, 157–59
Chicago Star and, 5, 118–21, 123–30, 132,
    134, 137–41, 144, 211, 238, 312–13,
    319n
Chinese civil war and, 156, 162
and Committee for the First
    Amendment, 188–89
concealment and deception tactics of,
    35–36, 38, 129
CRC and, 108–10, 187
Darrow and, 47, 56, 185
Davis's disappointment with, 58–59
Davis's liberal protectors and, 276–77,
    279–81

communists, communism (*cont.*)
  and Davis's politics and ideology, 4–8, 10,
    15, 17–19, 51, 53, 57–59, 61–62, 75–79,
    88–95, 97–98, 103–5, 118–19, 134,
    137, 140–43, 149, 151, 154, 157, 160,
    163–64, 167–68, 171, 173–75, 179, 194,
    197, 205–7, 209–12, 215–19, 222, 235,
    237–38, 245, 247, 249, 263, 271–74,
    276–77, 279, 281–87, 289, 293, 297–99,
    306–9, 335*n*–36*n*, 365*n*
  Davis's senatorial testimony and, 204,
    207–10
  and Davis's sins of omission, 54–56, 60
  DeLacy and, 222–23
  and Fast's book on Paine, 186–88, 190
  and FBI investigation of Davis, 215–20,
    222, 283
  Feinglass and, 8, 225–26
  Founders and, 181–88, 191–92
  Gitlow and, 42, 185–86
  Herndon case and, 51–52
  Hollywood and, 38, 140, 159, 182,
    188–89
  Honolulu Record and, 144–49, 154, 160,
    163, 168–69, 194, 197, 199, 201–2, 211,
    238, 284, 292, 348*n*
  HUAC targeted by, 165–66
  Hughes and, 54–55, 234
  ILD and, 42, 44, 47–49, 56–58, 108
  Jarrett and, 112, 293
  Kenyatta and, 231, 360*n*
  Korea and, 193–95, 201–3
  Matthews lecture and, 59–60
  NAACP and, 44, 47–50, 55–56, 58, 60
  Obama and, 8, 15, 18–19, 249, 259–60,
    262–63, 275, 281, 319*n*
  Obama's father and, 229–30
  Pickens and, 48–49, 78
  political carnage generated by, 32–33,
    64–65, 67, 199, 202–3, 323*n*
  Potemkin Progressives and, 63,
    65–66
  racial issues and, 8, 17–18, 68, 206
  religion and, 27, 36, 137–39, 174,
    345*n*–46*n*
  Robeson and, 69–72, 144, 170, 179,
    270–71, 278, 331*n*, 364*n*

  Scottsboro Boys case and, 17, 32, 36–39,
    41–45, 48–52, 55–60, 86–87, 205
  on sexual matters, 16–17
  social justice religious left and, 36, 81,
    134–35
  Truman Doctrine and, 131–33, 135
  United Packinghouse Workers and, 111,
    228
  and use of atomic bomb, 157–59
  Vietnam and, 4, 194, 196, 201, 227
  Wilkins and, 49–50
  on world revolution, 33–35
  World War II and, 79–86, 89, 96–97,
    206–7, 226, 310
  Wright and, 74–75, 91, 234, 336*n*
  see also anticommunists, anticommunism
Congress, U.S., 42, 47, 86, 105, 107,
    130–31, 153, 182, 218, 225, 273, 285,
    326*n*, 351*n*
  ACPFB and, 8, 221–22, 224
  on blacks in CPUSA, 204–6
  on Canter, 340*n*–41*n*
  CRC and, 108–10, 186–87
  and Davis's politics and ideology, 88, 274
  DeLacy and, 222–23
  and Fast's book on Paine, 186–87
  Gitlow and, 185–86
  Honolulu Record and, 162, 173, 195, 315
  recovery and, 289–90
  Robeson and, 71, 173–74
  Rosser's testimony for, 205–6
  Soviet Negro republic and, 40–41
  see also House of Representatives, U.S.;
    Senate, U.S.
Congressional Record, 205
conservatives, 2, 4, 56, 92, 181, 186, 215,
    267, 281–82, 299–300, 364*n*
  and Davis's politics and ideology, 77, 273
  Drew and, 249–50, 254
  Obama and, 12, 262, 275
  Reagan and, 246, 248
Constitution, U.S., 78, 107, 153, 168, 181,
    189–90, 293
  and AP's portrait of Davis, 275–76
  Davis's senatorial testimony and, 209–10
Cooke, Alistair, 182
"Credo of an American" (Robeson), 139

Crockett, George W., Jr., 222–23
Czechoslovakia, 131–32, 198
  Chicago Star and, 128–29, 132, 141
Czech Republic, 288–89

Daily Worker, 46, 74, 76, 97, 111, 120,
  144–45, 166, 173, 186–87, 189, 226
  Marshall Plan and, 155–56
  NAACP and, 48, 50
  Pickens and, 48–49, 78
  Robeson and, 69–71
  Scottsboro Boys case and, 49, 78
Darrow, Clarence, 56, 189
  ACLU and, 46–47
  Scopes Trials and, 47, 184–85
Davis, Benjamin J., Jr., 73, 91, 223
  Herndon case and, 52, 97
  Honolulu Record and, 168–69
  political campaigns of, 47, 97–98, 172
Davis, Benjamin J., Sr., 47
Davis, Frank Marshall:
  on American way, 238–39, 246, 290, 294,
    313
  attempted lynching of, 22, 269, 296
  awards and honors of, 74, 106
  birth of, 21, 28, 208
  change and, 9–10, 286–87
  childhood and upbringing of, 22, 24–26,
    269, 296–97
  death of, 92, 268–69
  death of mother of, 27–28
  divorces of, 220
  documents of, 306–15
  education and, 21–24, 27, 29, 93, 177,
    208, 237–38, 240, 269
  entrepreneurship of, 29
  ethnic insensitivity of, 17, 24, 31–32
  finances of, 23, 27–28, 30, 73–74, 78,
    142, 148
  individualism of, 29
  inflammatory rhetoric of, 6–7, 109, 140
  jazz enjoyed by, 31, 73, 105, 143
  journalism career of, 4–10, 27–32, 44,
    47, 51, 53–62, 72–75, 78, 90, 95–103,
    109, 114, 116, 118–19, 121–43, 145–48,
    152–57, 159–82, 185–91, 193–202, 204,
    206, 208, 211–13, 221, 223, 227, 232,

    238–39, 248, 263, 269, 271, 275–76,
    278–79, 283, 287–90, 292–93, 295,
    308–9, 311–15, 319n, 323n, 343n,
    348n, 353n
  marriages of, 106, 143, 220
  memoirs of, *see* Livin' the Blues
  notoriety of, 233–34
  persecution of, 17–18, 21–25, 269, 297
  personality traits of, 29
  photos taken by, 17, 215–16
  physical appearance of, 21, 52, 140–41,
    234, 239, 266
  poetry of, 23, 28, 31, 74, 89, 103, 233–34,
    264, 272, 334n, 336n
  politics and ideology of, 4–10, 15–19, 22,
    27–29, 32, 51–53, 55, 57–62, 67, 72–73,
    75–79, 84, 86–95, 97–98, 101–12, 116,
    118–20, 124–30, 132, 134, 137, 140–44,
    149, 151–57, 159–69, 171, 173–80, 182,
    188–92, 194–99, 201, 205–7, 209–13,
    215–22, 229, 232, 234–35, 237–38,
    244–45, 247, 249, 252, 262–63, 268–87,
    289, 293–94, 297–99, 306–9, 319n–21n,
    335n–36n, 365n
  on religion, 25–27, 137–39
  sexuality of, 16–17, 24, 31–32, 231, 321n
  sins of omission of, 54–56, 60
  teaching of, 105, 114
  writing talent of, 23–25, 27–28
Davis, Helen Canfield (second wife), 220
  move to Hawaii of, 143, 145, 148
  politics and ideology of, 105–6
Davis, Mark (son), 249, 336n, 353n
Declaration of Independence, 78, 119,
  181–82, 186, 190, 192, 293, 367n
DeLacy, Hugh, 222–23
DeMaio, Ernest, 114, 119–20
Democratic Socialist Alliance (DSA), 251,
  255–56
Democrats, Democratic Party, 42, 71, 92,
  127, 145, 157, 161, 165, 184–85, 187,
  203, 221, 224–26, 227, 248, 276–77,
  284, 341n
  Chicago Star and, 120, 312
  Darrow and, 46–47
  and Davis's politics and ideology, 5–8, 77,
    88, 98, 102, 245

Democrats, Democratic Party (*cont.*)
  Davis's senatorial testimony and, 204,
    207, 210–11, 263
  Hawaiian communist infiltration of,
    218–19
  Honolulu Record and, 167, 170–71,
    175–77
  HUAC and, 108, 114, 226, 279
  mentors of, 2–3
  Obama and, 11, 262
  and political home for blacks, 60–61
  racial issues and, 18, 167
  recovery and, 289–90
  Romerstein and, 273–74
  taxes and, 130, 292
Dennis, Eugene (Tim Ryan), 83–84, 134,
  223
Dewey, John, 59, 70, 261
  as Potemkin Progressive, 62, 65–66
Dewey, Tom, 102
Dies, Martin, 7, 92, 98, 226
Dimitroff, Georgi, 83–84
Dodd, Thomas, 207
Dohrn, Bernardine, 227, 250
Draper, Theodore, 324n
Dreams from My Father (Obama):
  comparisons between *Livin' the Blues*
    and, 25
  comparisons between "Pop" and, 264,
    266
  Davis in, 3, 10, 14–15, 232–45, 247,
    262–64, 266, 273–74, 282, 286, 297,
    320n–21n
  on Obama's Occidental years, 247–48,
    250, 262
  on Obama's search for role model,
    232–33
Dreiser, Theodore, 82
Drew, John, 353n
  Chandoo and, 255–56
  on Davis, 252–53
  Kengor's on-the-air interview with,
    251–52
  Obama and, 10, 249–60, 262
  politics of, 249–58, 261–62
DuBois, W. E. B., 14, 76, 110, 168
Duke, Selwyn, 260–61

Dulles, John Foster, 127, 132
  China policy and, 200–201
Dunham, Madelyn "Toot," 229, 235–36,
  239–40, 245
Dunham, Stanley, 26, 239, 359n
  and Davis's influence on grandson,
    11–12, 15
  Davis's poetry and, 233–34
  Davis's relationship with, 233–36,
    243–44, 278
  and grandson's introduction to Davis,
    11, 243–45
  grandson's relationship with,
    236–37
  and grandson's relationship with Davis,
    235–36, 244
  politics of, 229, 263
  "Pop" and, 264, 266
Dupes (Kengor), 261, 300

Earle, George, 127
Eastland, James, 207
economics, economy, 41, 58–59, 61, 63,
  70, 127, 134–35, 201, 230–31, 286,
  298–300
  Honolulu Record and, 155, 177–79, 199,
    289
  Marxism and, 251, 253, 255, 257
  Obama and, 14, 177, 250–51, 253, 257,
    289–91, 294, 320n
Egypt, 212
Eisenhower, Dwight, 132, 195, 200
Eisler, Gerhart, 151, 221, 231–32
employment, 206
  Honolulu Record and, 162, 169, 177, 179,
    289
  layoffs and, 177, 289–90
  similarities between Davis and Obama
    on, 289–90
  unemployment and, 179, 290
Ethiopia, 76, 323n

Fanon, Frantz, 247–48, 257
Fast, Howard, 110, 189, 191, 261
  Chicago Star and, 10, 121, 128, 131,
    186–87, 190, 293, 343n
  Paine and, 186–88, 190

Federal Bureau of Investigation (FBI), 38, 78, 106, 116, 205, 229, 250, 268, 270–71, 285, 288, 359n
  on ACPFB, 220, 222
  and Communist Party of Hawaii, 217–19
  Davis investigated by, 214–20, 222, 283–84, 306–9
  and Davis's move to Hawaii, 148–49
  and Davis's politics and ideology, 5, 51, 53, 90, 93–94, 306–9
  Kramer and, 121–22
  Robeson and, 271, 283
Federalist Papers, 184, 191
Feinglass, Abe, 8, 225–28
feminists, feminism, 17, 61, 247
Field, Marshall, 113
Fish, Hamilton, 33–34
Flynn, Elizabeth Gurley, 46, 110
Foner, Eric, 224
Foner, Henry, 222, 224, 226
Foner, Moe, 224
Ford, James W., 39–41
Fort-Whiteman, Lovett, 39, 68–69, 205
Foster, William Z., 33–34, 46, 120, 130, 313
Founders, Founding, 181–92
  American Revolution and, 183–86
  Chicago Star and, 182, 189–91, 287
  and Committee for the First Amendment, 188–89
  Davis's invocation of, 189–92, 198
  Davis's senatorial testimony and, 208, 210
  and Fast's book on Paine, 186–88, 190
  on job of government, 191–92
  Obama's invocation of, 293, 367n
Fraina, Louis C., 183–84, 186, 189
France, 193–94, 248, 367n
  Honolulu Record and, 162, 175, 212–13
  Marshall Plan and, 157, 162, 193, 315
  Suez Canal crisis and, 212–13
  Vietnam and, 194, 196, 201
Frank Marshall Davis (Tidwell), 92, 272
"Free Angelo Herndon," 51
Friends University, 22–23, 208
Fulbright, J. William, 3
Fur, Leather, and Machine (FLM) Workers Union, 224, 226

Gary American, 29, 73–74
General Motors (GM):
  Chicago Star and, 5, 140, 295
  Honolulu Record and, 178–80, 290
  Obama and, 9, 263, 294–95
  profits of, 178–80, 268, 290, 295
Germany, 15, 241–42
  reunification of, 269, 288
Germany, East, 4, 132, 134
Germany, Nazi, 134, 225
  APM and, 79–82, 86
  CRC and, 109–10
  World War II and, 79–82, 86, 88–89, 96–97, 207
Germany, West, 132, 136, 155, 158, 193, 269
  Honolulu Record and, 165, 175–77
  nazification of, 4, 176–77, 279, 288
Gitlow, Ben, 42, 185–86
God That Failed, The (Wright et al.), 74, 261
Goldwater, Barry, 2
Gorbachev, Mikhail, 68, 138, 269, 323n, 330n
Gore, Al, 3
Great Britain, 63, 102, 134, 182, 187, 194, 198, 287–88, 295, 312
  ANP and, 99–101
  APM and, 79–80, 82, 86
  Honolulu Record and, 162, 175, 212–13
  Kenyatta in, 231–32
  Marshall Plan and, 157, 162, 315
  Suez Canal crisis and, 212–13
  World War II and, 79–80, 82, 86, 89, 96, 99
Great Depression, 30, 95, 177–78
Great Leap Forward, 199
Great Purge, 64–65, 67
Greece:
  Chicago Star and, 128–29
  Honolulu Record and, 161–62, 198
  Truman Doctrine and, 131–36, 161–62, 193
Green, Gil, 134, 140
Guthrie, Woody, 83, 130

Hall, Gus, 72, 223, 270–71, 331n, 364n
Hall, Jack, 147–48, 231
Hammett, Dashiell, 110

Harnden, Toby, 244–45

Harten, Thomas S., 172

Havel, Vaclav, 68

Hawaii, 10–15
  and Davis's influence on Obama, 12,
    14–15, 267, 320n
  Davis's life in, 11, 51, 148, 214–15, 233,
    235–37, 241–45, 252, 277–78, 284,
    295–96, 307
  Davis's move to, 72, 143–45, 148–49,
    151–53, 190, 194, 208, 214–15, 278
  Davis's photos of shorelines of, 215–16
  and Davis's politics and ideology, 7–8,
    151
  and Davis's relationship with Obama,
    235, 240, 243–44
  and FBI investigation of Davis, 214–17
  ILWU and, 147–49, 222, 231, 278
  Obama's departure from, 10, 242, 245,
    268
  Obama's father and, 229–31
  Obama's life in, 233, 237, 247, 252–53,
    256, 258, 263, 275–76, 295–96
  Obama's politics and, 258–59, 263
  USSR and, 147, 149–51, 211

Hawaii, University of, 13, 229–31, 287

Hawaii Civil Liberties Committee (HCLC),
    152–53, 208, 283–84

Hayden, Tom, 227

health care, 140
  Honolulu Record and, 177–78, 202, 289,
    295
  Obama and, 9, 202, 295, 318n
  Pepper and, 10, 121–22, 295

Hearst, William Randolph, 127–28, 140

Hearst papers, 119–20

Henderson, Donald, 82–83

Herndon, Angelo, 51–52, 73, 80, 91, 93, 97,
    105–6, 205, 283

Hill, Herbert, 50

Hiroshima, 157–59

Hitler, Adolf, 33, 158, 187–88
  APM and, 79–82, 87, 110
  Chicago Star and, 134, 140
  CRC and, 109–11
  Honolulu Record and, 167, 175–77
  West Germany and, 176–77

World War II and, 69, 79–82, 87–88,
    95–96, 101, 155, 161, 165, 175, 206–7,
    225–26, 274, 289, 334n

Hitler-Stalin Pact, 69, 79, 95, 101, 161, 206,
    225–26, 274, 289

Ho Chi Minh, 196, 202

Hollywood, Calif., 70, 110, 120–21, 222,
    281–82
  anticommunists in, 140, 347n
  and Committee for the First
    Amendment, 188–89
  communists and, 38, 140, 159, 182,
    188–89
  Wallace and, 125–26

Honolulu, Hawaii, 5, 208, 256, 268
  Davis's life in, 5, 11, 208, 277–78
  and FBI investigation of Davis, 214,
    216–18, 284, 307

Honolulu Record, 144–49, 284
  Davis at, 32, 145–48, 154–57, 159–80,
    182, 190–91, 193–202, 204, 208,
    211–13, 223, 238, 248, 263, 269, 275,
    278, 283, 289–90, 292, 295, 308–9, 315,
    348n
  Davis's "Frank-ly Speaking" column in,
    145, 315
  Davis's liberal protectors and, 275,
    278–79
  and Davis's politics and ideology, 154–57,
    159–69, 171, 173–80, 190–91, 194–97,
    212–13, 278–79
  finances of, 148–49
  Founders and, 182, 190–91
  ILWU and, 146, 148–49, 221
  Senate and, 144–46, 211

Honolulu Star-Bulletin, 198–99

Hoover, Herbert, 102, 132

Hoover, J. Edgar, 121, 128, 140, 190
  and FBI investigation of Davis, 214, 284

Hopkins, Harry, 122

Horne, Gerald, 12, 282

House Committee on Un-American
    Activities (HUAC), 42, 81, 106, 111,
    114, 122, 151, 224–26, 275, 351n
  Chicago Star and, 123, 128, 139
  and Committee for the First
    Amendment, 188–89

CRC and, 108–10
and Davis's politics and ideology, 7,
  90–92, 98, 210–11
Honolulu Record and, 165–67, 176–77,
  191
Matthews and, 60, 172
and Remnick's profile of Davis, 277,
  279
Robeson and, 71, 139
West Germany and, 176–77
House of Representatives, U.S., 119–20,
  209, 291
see also Congress, U.S.
Hughes, Langston, 14, 110, 221
  Atlanta Daily World and, 54–55, 206, 223
  and blacks in CPUSA, 205–6
  Davis's relationship with, 54, 74, 233–34
  politics and ideology of, 54–55, 106, 234
  USSR trip of, 54–55, 205–6
Hungary, 141, 212, 329*n*
Hyde Park Herald, 113, 339*n*
hydrogen bomb, 159–61, 200–201

I Am the American Negro (Davis), 103
Illinois Standard, 142, 227–28
imperialists, imperialism, 40, 59, 77, 109,
  268–69, 282, 288, 310
  ANP and, 99–101
  Chicago Star and, 124, 140
  and Davis's politics and ideology, 4, 9,
    94, 276
  Hawaii Question and, 150–51
  Honolulu Record and, 155–57, 160, 162,
    176, 196, 248, 315
  Marshall Plan and, 155–57, 173–74
  Obama and, 247–48, 257
  Vietnam and, 194, 196, 201
Indonesia, 239, 245, 315
Internal Security Act, 108, 224–25
International Labor Defense (ILD), 47–50,
  52, 223
  CRC and, 49–50, 108
  NAACP and, 48–49, 58
  Patterson and, 115–16, 225–26
  Pickens and, 48–49, 78
  Scottsboro Boys case and, 42–45, 48–50,
    56–60, 78, 221

International Longshoremen's and
  Warehousemen's Union (ILWU):
  ACPFB and, 221–22
  Bridges and, 144–47, 208, 216, 221
  Hall and, 147–48, 231
  Hawaii and, 147–49, 222, 231, 278
  Honolulu Record and, 146, 148–49, 221
International Red Aid, 42
"Investigation of Un-American Propaganda
  Activities in the United States," 71,
  84–85, 88, 107, 119–20, 221–22
Israel, 131, 212
Izuka, Ichiro, 149

Jacobs, Ron, 13–14
Jacobs, Sally, 230
Japan, 151
  Chicago Star and, 128–29, 132
  use of atomic bomb on, 157–59, 161, 201
Jarrett, Valerie Bowman:
  Chicago public housing and, 240, 361*n*
  Obama's relationship with, 85, 107, 112,
    115, 228, 294
  Obama's wife and, 293–94
Jarrett, Vernon, 115, 240
  Davis's relationship with, 293–94
  journalism career of, 112, 116
  United Packinghouse Workers and,
    111–12, 139, 228
Jarrett, William Robert, 112
Jay, John, 190–91
Jefferson, Thomas, 78, 181–82, 184, 190–92
Jews, 43, 129
  APM and, 80, 82
  World War II and, 117, 225–26
Jones, Don, 2–3, 242
Justice Department, U.S., 6, 108

Kalugin, Oleg, 339*n*
Kansas, 76, 92, 229, 278
  Davis's life in, 11, 21–26, 28, 208, 266,
    269, 296–97
Kansas State University, 23, 29, 208
Katyn Woods massacre, 127
Kawano, Jack, 146
Kelly, Gene, 126, 159, 189
Kennan, George, 80, 161

Kenya, 231–32, 242, 264, 360n
    Obama's father and, 229, 231
Kenyatta, Jomo, 231–32, 360–61n
Kerry, John, 227, 275
Keynesians, 157, 295
KGB, 43, 117, 121, 123, 137, 227, 339n
Khrushchev, Nikita, 218, 337n
Kim Il-Sung, 202–3
Kim Jong-Il, 202–3
Kincaid, Cliff, 215, 273–75, 359n, 365n
Kloppenberg, James, 14, 320n
Korea, 4, 132
    communists and, 193–95, 201–3
    division of, 193–94
    Honolulu Record and, 195, 197
    North, 193–95, 202–3, 323n
Korean War, 154, 194, 197, 200, 273, 297
Kozyrev, Andrei, 269
Kramer, Charles, 10, 121–22, 134, 222,
    295
Ku Klux Klan (KKK), 6, 77, 111, 140
    Chicago Star and, 127–28
    Honolulu Record and, 168, 170
    Peekskill riots and, 170–71

Labor Institute, 59–60
labor issues, 286, 310, 348n
    Chicago Star and, 118, 129, 142–43
    Davis's liberal protectors and, 276–78
Lamont, Corliss, 65–66, 166
Landon, Alf, 5, 76
Latimer, Ira, 107, 110, 226
Lawson, John Howard, 159, 188–89, 191,
    282
    CRC and, 110–11, 126
League of American Writers, 76, 88, 210,
    214
left, 4, 6, 32, 35, 41, 47, 66, 70, 87, 113,
    132–33, 166, 170, 211, 223–24, 229,
    250, 260, 278–79, 291–92, 310, 336n,
    351n
    in Chicago, 73, 76
    and Davis's politics and ideology, 7, 62,
        76, 78, 88, 124, 179, 244, 272, 279, 281,
        286, 294, 299
    Founders and, 182, 190
    Honolulu Record and, 162, 190

Obama and, 8–10, 12, 14, 18–19, 259,
    262, 286, 294, 299, 320n
    Occidental and, 249, 251, 263
    Potemkin Progressives and, 63–64
    and use of atomic bomb, 158–59
    see also social justice religious left
Lenin, Vladimir, 17, 33, 40–41, 46, 55, 63,
    91, 101, 113, 138, 175, 179, 184–86,
    190, 199, 202, 336n
Leninism, see Marxism-Leninism
Lenin's Tomb (Remnick), 277
"Letter to American Workers" (Lenin),
    40
"Letter to the CPUSA on Hawaii," 150
liberals/progressives, liberalism/
    progressivism, 2–3, 17, 47, 86, 107–8,
    111, 116, 122, 129, 134–36, 145, 157,
    159, 172, 177, 181, 183, 211, 224,
    227–28, 230, 246, 248–49, 254, 259–63,
    272, 286, 292, 297–300, 351n
    ACPFB and, 221–22, 225
    APM and, 79, 81–84, 223
    Canter and, 113, 143
    Chicago Star and, 118, 124–26, 130, 239,
        312
    and Committee for the First
        Amendment, 188–89
    communist manipulation and, 35–36,
        38
    Darrow and, 184–85
    Davis defended by, 274–81, 284, 353n
    and Davis's politics and ideology, 67, 77,
        88, 90, 98, 124–26, 152, 163, 273–79
    and Hawaiian communist infiltration of
        Democratic Party, 218–19
    McCarthyism and, 7, 276–77, 279–81
    Obama and, 3, 12–15, 227, 259, 262–63,
        275, 277, 294, 299–300, 353n
    Potemkin, 62–66, 72, 166
    Robeson and, 66–67, 70, 72, 170, 270–71,
        364n
    Stone and, 113, 123, 166
Library of Congress, 270, 273
Liebowitz, Samuel, 43
Lifson, Thomas, 249
Lightfoot, Claude, 126
Lincoln, Abraham, 1, 28, 41, 191

Livin' the Blues (Davis), 16, 24–28, 54, 56, 75, 116, 118, 120, 148, 231, 237, 248, 266, 282, 296, 321*n*

  Chicago and, 28, 73–74, 76, 143

  comparisons between *Dreams from My Father* and, 25

  on Davis's high school graduation, 21–22

  and Davis's politics and ideology, 89, 91–92, 94–95, 103, 106–8, 262, 271–72

  and FBI investigation of Davis, 214, 216–17

  on Herndon case, 51–52

  Robeson and, 72, 107

London Telegraph, 12, 244

Los Angeles Times, 112

Loudon, Trevor, 111, 215–16

Luce, Henry, 101, 127, 140

MacArthur, Douglas, 128, 197

McCarran, Pat, 207, 224–25

McCarthy, Joe, 7, 115, 224, 271, 281

  Davis's liberal protectors and, 276–77

  demagogic statements of, 6–7

  Watkins Committee and, 211–12

McCarthyites, McCarthyism, 126, 145, 148, 169, 202, 274, 299

  and anticommunism as racism, 166–67

  Davis's senatorial testimony and, 211–12

  liberals and, 7, 276–77, 279–81

Maki, Alan, 281

Malia, Martin, 32–33

Maltz, Albert, 188–89, 191, 222

Mao Tse-tung, 91, 128, 144, 179, 193, 195–96, 202, 297, 323*n*

  Chinese civil war and, 156, 162

  and Davis's politics and ideology, 4, 163, 198

  Honolulu Record and, 157, 162–63, 199

Maraniss, David, 276, 281, 365*n*

Marcantonio, Vito, 42, 82, 115, 326*n*

March, Herbert, 111, 114, 226

Marshall, George C., 200

  Davis's criticisms of, 132, 140, 155–57

  and Davis's politics and ideology, 4, 6–7, 163

Marshall, Thurgood, 6

Marshall Plan, 4, 27, 91, 131, 169, 193, 263, 288

  Chicago Star and, 141, 190

  Honolulu Record and, 154–57, 161–62, 173–74, 177–79, 197, 279, 315

Marx, Karl, 17, 33, 58–59, 91, 138, 186, 191–92, 256

Marxism, Marxists, 60–61, 105, 147, 183, 190, 248, 282

  Chicago Star and, 128, 140

  and Davis's politics and ideology, 92, 124

  Drew and, 249–58, 262

  Hughes and, 54–55

  Obama and, 10, 247, 250–53, 256–59, 261–62, 299

  Occidental and, 250–51, 254

Marxism-Leninism, 1, 18, 132, 150, 181, 194, 209, 270–71, 331*n*

  and Davis's politics and ideology, 27, 124

  Obama and, 250–51, 258, 260–62

Matthews, J. B., 59–60, 172

May Day, 9, 44, 77, 140, 142, 227, 292–93

Mboya, Tom, 229

Meacham, Jon, 276–77, 279, 281

Mead, Rebecca, 264

Meakem, Glen, 249, 251

"Meeting Young Obama" (Drew), 254

Melish, John Howard, 172–74

Melish, William Howard, 8, 110, 135, 172–74, 222

Milbank, Dana, 274–75

Mingulin, I., 150–51

Minor, Robert, 42, 45

Mitsotakis, Spyridon, 336*n*

Molotov, Vyacheslav, 70–71, 129, 132

  Chicago Star interview with, 136–37

  Marshall Plan and, 155–56

Morehouse College, 54, 223

Morris, Robert, 207–10

Moyers, Bill, 322*n*

Moynihan, Daniel Patrick, 3

Muggeridge, Malcolm, 63–64

Mussolini, Benito, 76

Nagasaki, 157
National Association for the Advancement
    of Colored People (NAACP), 61, 91,
    168
    communists and, 44, 47–50, 55–56, 58,
        60
    and Davis's move to Hawaii, 151–52
    ILD and, 48–49, 58
    Scottsboro Boys case and, 44, 48–50,
        55–58, 60
    Wilkins and, 49–50, 86, 115, 152
    World War II and, 86, 206
National Council of American-Soviet
    Friendship (NCASF), 135, 173, 223
National Council of Churches, 172, 225
National Emergency Civil Liberties
    Committee (NECLC), 166
National Journal, 10, 262
National Lawyers Guild, 208, 223,
    340*n*–41*n*
National Negro Congress, 84, 86, 88, 108,
    110, 116, 210
New Deal, 7, 77, 167
"New Drive Against the Anti-Communist
    Program, The," 166
New Masses, 46, 54, 71, 74, 120, 173, 189
New Red Negro, The (Smethurst), 272
Newsweek, 14, 26, 276, 322*n*
New York, 3, 42–43, 45–47, 65, 74, 97, 106,
    109, 113, 115–16, 135–36, 187, 199,
    218, 239, 268, 270, 273
    ACPFB and, 8, 222
    APM and, 81–84
    9/11 and, 224, 250
    Scottsboro Boys case and, 43, 45
New Yorker, The, 12, 264, 277
New York Times, 12, 14, 61–62, 64, 81, 122,
    166, 171, 197, 200, 223, 250, 360*n*
    Axelrod and, 112–13
    and Obama's relationship with Jarrett,
        85, 294
New York University, 282–83
9/11, 224, 250, 287
North Atlantic Treaty Organization
    (NATO), 4, 158, 200, 288
    Honolulu Record and, 162, 177, 197
Nowell, William Odell, 40–41, 86

Oakes, Grant, 120
Obama, Auma, 241
Obama, Barack, Jr., 2–5, 52, 72, 168, 211,
    218–19, 276
    absence of conversion of, 260–62
    Axelrod's relationship with, 112–13, 115,
        142, 228
    change and, 13, 248, 286–87
    Chicago and, 28, 239–41, 245, 249–50,
        253, 268, 293, 361*n*
    Churchill and, 9, 287–88
    class-based rhetoric of, 291–92
    community organizing of, 15, 239
    Davis's influence on, 8–16, 18–19, 22,
        180, 219, 237–47, 249, 259, 262–64,
        266–67, 280–83, 285–86, 290, 292,
        295–96, 298–300, 320*n*
    Davis's introduction to, 11, 228, 243–45,
        267, 280
    Davis's poetry and, 233–34
    Davis's relationship with, 3–4, 12, 16,
        18–19, 115, 232, 234–38, 240, 243–45,
        264, 272–75, 277, 280, 284
    Drew and, 10, 249–60, 262
    economy and, 9, 14, 177, 250–51, 253,
        257, 289–91, 294, 320*n*
    education of, 8, 10, 15, 237–40, 245–56,
        258–59, 261–64, 266–67, 299, 320*n*
    Founders invoked by, 293, 367*n*
    health care and, 9, 202, 295, 318*n*
    Jarrett's relationship with, 85, 107, 112,
        115, 228, 294
    liberal defenders of, 299–300, 353*n*
    memoirs of, *see* Dreams from My Father
    physical appearance of, 243, 255–56
    poetry of, 264–67
    politics and ideology of, 8, 10, 15,
        18–19, 227, 240, 247–53, 256–63,
        268, 275, 281, 286, 291, 294, 299,
        319*n*–20*n*
    presidential campaigns of, 2, 11, 13–14,
        115, 142, 227, 273–75, 279, 281, 287,
        292, 319*n*–21*n*
    religion and, 26, 322*n*
    and Remnick's profile of Davis, 277–78,
        280
    role model sought by, 232–33

senatorial career of, 10, 240, 262, 293,
    361*n*
similarities and differences between
    Davis and, 8–9, 286–95
state political career of, 126, 242, 249–50,
    361*n*
taxes and, 130, 253, 286, 291–92
Obama, Barack, Sr., 15, 233, 322*n*
    Davis's possible encounter with, 230–31
    death of, 239, 241
    education of, 229–30
    Kenyatta and, 232, 360*n*
    politics of, 229–31
    "Pop" and, 264
Obama, Michelle Robinson, 293–94
Obamaland (Jacobs), 13–14
"Obama's Missing Link" (Kengor), 249
Occidental College, 268
    Dreams from My Father on, 247–48, 250,
        262
    Drew and, 249–55, 258–60
    Obama's enrollment at, 8, 10, 237–39,
        246–55, 258–59, 262–64, 266–67, 299,
        320*n*
    politics at, 249–51, 254–55, 258,
        262–63
Other Side, The (Abbas), 117

Pacepa, Ion Mihai, 158
Paine, Thomas, 181, 186–88, 190
Palmer, Alice, 249–50, 253
Patterson, Louise T., 115–16, 120
Patterson, Mary Louise, 117
Patterson, William L., 269
    Abraham Lincoln School and, 105, 116
    Chicago Star and, 120, 126, 187
    CRC and, 49–50, 107, 116, 153, 170, 187,
        283
    and Davis's politics and ideology, 91,
        116, 283
    Davis's relationship with, 85, 115–17,
        127, 137, 283
    ILD and, 115–16, 225–26
    Scottsboro Boys case and, 49–50, 115
    Soviet trip of, 115–17
Paul Robeson, 270–71
Peabody, Endicott, 3

Peekskill, N.Y.:
    rioting in, 170–71, 175
    Robeson's appearance at, 169–71, 175
Pelosi, Nancy, 6, 8, 145, 218, 292
People's Friendship University, 117
People's World, 145–46, 348*n*
Pepper, Claude "Red":
    Chicago Star and, 10, 121–22, 128, 131,
        133–34, 295, 343*n*
    on Greek crisis, 133–34
    health care and, 10, 121–22, 295
Pickens, William, 48–49, 78
Pittsburgh Courier, 31, 56
Pittsburgh Pirates, 267
Pius IX, Pope, 346*n*
Pius XII, Pope, 201–2
Planned Parenthood, 65–66, 84, 111,
    338*n*
PM, 113, 123
Poland, 127–29, 131–32, 198
    Chicago Star and, 127–28, 132
    Obama's pro-Russian policies and,
        288–89
Political Affairs, 106, 282, 331*n*
Political Awareness Fellowship, 254–55
"Pop" (Obama), 264–67
Popular Front for the Liberation of
    Palestine (PFLP), 117
Potemkin Progressives, 62–66, 72, 166
poverty:
    Honolulu Record and, 162, 315
    Obama and, 240–41, 259, 291
Pressman, Lee, 122–23, 222
Price, Victoria, 36–37
private property, 191–92, 263
Progressive Citizens of America, 159
progressives, *see* liberals/progressives,
        liberalism/progressivism
Progressives for Obama, 227

Quill, Michael, 107, 110

race, racism, 30, 59, 75, 108–9, 116, 225,
        254, 268–69, 283, 296
    ACPFB and, 8, 18, 221–22
    anticommunism as, 163, 166–69, 171
    Chicago and, 84, 143

race, racism (*cont.*)
  Chicago Star and, 126–28, 130, 133–34, 140
  communists and, 8, 17–18, 68, 206
  Davis's journalism career and, 7, 31–32
  Davis's liberal protectors and, 276–79
  and Davis's politics and ideology, 4, 6–7, 17–18, 76, 90–91, 95, 97–98, 101–2, 152, 167
  Honolulu Record and, 156–57, 166–67, 169, 173–74, 176–77, 198
  HUAC and, 167, 176–77
  in Kansas, 21–25
  Marshall Plan and, 156–57
  Obama and, 9, 15, 25, 240–42, 244, 247
  Robeson and, 18, 67, 69–70, 94, 168–70, 173–74, 278
  Sanger and, 84, 111
  Scottsboro Boys case and, 17, 32, 37, 41, 167
  Truman and, 18, 163–64, 169–71
  USSR and, 8, 18, 39–43, 67–70, 94, 103, 115, 126–28, 133, 139, 168–69, 173–74, 204–7, 330n
  Willkie and, 101–2
  World War II and, 84, 104
  see also blacks; civil rights
Rankin, John, 7, 167, 176–77
Reading Obama (Kloppenberg), 14
Reagan, Ronald, 139, 194, 218, 246, 257, 290
  Brandenburg Gate Speech of, 269
  Cleaver's relationship with, 1–3, 242
  Farewell Address of, 2, 263
  morale restored by, 248, 362n–63n
  on USSR as Evil Empire, 261, 269–70
Remnick, David, 256, 294
  Davis profiled by, 276–81
  and Davis's influence on Obama, 12–14
  and Davis's introduction to Obama, 243–44
  and Davis's relationship with Obama, 237, 243–44, 280
Renegade (Wolffe), 14
Republicans, Republican Party, 41, 66, 132, 187, 195, 200, 269, 290–92, 300
  Chicago Star and, 130, 140, 292

Chinese civil war and, 156–57
  and Davis's politics and ideology, 5–7, 9, 76–78, 102
  Davis's senatorial testimony and, 207–12
  Honolulu Record and, 173, 176, 292
  HUAC and, 108, 226
  and politics of blacks, 28, 60–61, 173–74
  Romerstein and, 273–74
Revelle, Roger, 3
Revolutionary Age, 184
Rickover, Hyman, 3
right, 4, 272, 274–75, 279, 282
Robeson, Pauli, 70–71
Robeson, Paul L., 66–74, 110, 112, 116, 120–22, 125, 139, 168–71, 205, 221, 231, 269
  APM and, 83, 223
  birthday tribute to, 270–71, 331n, 364–65n
  and Davis's move to Hawaii, 144, 278
  Davis's relationship with, 62, 72, 74, 107, 127, 137, 278, 283–84
  entertainment career of, 66–67, 71, 144, 169–70, 278
  Honolulu Record and, 168–69, 171, 173–74
  in Peekskill, 169–71, 175
  politics and ideology of, 62, 66–67, 69–72, 106–7, 144, 170, 179, 270–71, 278, 331n, 364n
  as Potemkin Progressive, 62, 66, 72
  racial issues and, 18, 67, 69–70, 94, 168–70, 173–74, 278
  Stalin and, 62, 67, 69–72, 83, 278
  USSR and, 18, 62, 67–72, 83, 94, 168–70, 173–74, 278
Robinson, Edward G., 159, 221
Rogers, Ginger, 140, 347n
Roman Catholics, Roman Catholic Church, 129, 202, 224, 260
  anticommunism of, 76, 137–38, 201, 345n–46n
  Honolulu Record and, 174–75
  Obama and, 9, 318n
Romania, 158

Romerstein, Herb, 36, 94, 116, 121–23, 151, 261, 324n–25n, 344n
and Davis's politics and ideology, 273–75
on Kramer, 121–22
Milbank on, 274–75
Roosevelt, Franklin D., 3, 42, 49, 60, 99, 108–9, 121–23, 127, 144, 155, 296, 312, 322n
ANP and, 96–97
APM and, 79, 82
and Davis's politics and ideology, 5, 28, 77–78, 102
Pressman and, 122–23
World War II and, 79, 82–83, 85, 96, 226
Rose, Don, 113, 339n–40n
Rosenberg, Julius and Ethel, 58, 201–2
Rosser, Louis, 40, 205–7
Rush, Benjamin, 186
Russian Federation, 288–89
Ruthenberg, Charles (Anna Damon), 34, 45, 221
Ryan, Robert F., 217–18, 307
Ryan, Tim (Eugene Dennis), 83–84, 134, 223

Sanger, Margaret:
as Potemkin Progressive, 65–66
on racial eugenics, 84, 111
Santa Claus, Davis's parody on, 202
Savage, Michael, 252, 260
Schneiderman, William, 150–51
Schuyler, George, 56–57
scientific socialism, 70, 331n
"Scope of Soviet Activity in the United States," 7
Scopes Monkey Trials, 47, 184–85
Scott, W. A., 30–32, 55, 323n
Scottsboro Boys case, 48–53, 62, 91, 93, 113, 163, 167, 269, 283
ACLU and, 45–47
Atlanta Daily World and, 56–60
Browder and, 44–46
communists and, 17, 32, 36–39, 41–45, 48–52, 55–60, 86–87, 205
ILD and, 42–45, 48–50, 56–60, 78, 221
NAACP and, 44, 48–50, 55–58, 60

Patterson and, 49–50, 115
resolution of, 50, 57–58, 327n–28n
Scottsboro Defense Committee, 44–45
Security Index, 5, 216, 275, 284, 309
Seeger, Pete, 83, 333n
Senate, U.S., 120, 166, 179, 203, 268, 279
and Davis's politics and ideology, 7, 93, 210
Davis's testimony for, 7, 204, 207–12, 222, 263, 276–77, 308–9
Honolulu Record and, 144–46, 211
McCarthy investigated by, 211–12
Obama's career in, 10, 240, 262, 293, 361n
Pepper and, 121–22
see also Congress, U.S.
Sennett, William, 119–20, 142
Sex Rebel (Davis), 16, 24, 321n
sexuality, communists on, 16–17
Shaw, George Bernard, 62, 64–67
Sheen, Fulton, 138
Sidey, Hugh, 363n
slaves, slavery, 25, 40, 48, 60, 69, 164, 169
Marshall Plan and, 156–57, 161–62, 169, 177
religion and, 22, 26
Truman Doctrine and, 161–62
Sloan, Alfred, 178
Smethurst, James Edward, 41, 336n
on Davis's politics and ideology, 272–73
Smith, Gary, 26
Smith Act, 145, 147–48, 223
socialists, socialism, 1, 10, 44, 46, 64, 92, 137, 179, 229, 254, 256, 286, 295, 360n
and Davis's politics and ideology, 59, 90, 281
Obama and, 248, 250, 252, 258–59, 262, 320n
Robeson and, 67, 70, 331n
scientific, 70, 331n
social justice religious left, 8, 36, 45, 225
and anticommunists as un-Christian, 171–72, 174
APM and, 81–82, 84, 134
Chicago Star and, 135–36
and Davis's influence on Obama, 9, 12
Truman Doctrine and, 134–35

Soetoro, Lolo, 15, 239, 245
Soetoro, Stanley Ann, 11, 15, 229–31, 233, 238–39
  education of, 229–30
  religion and, 26, 322*n*
Soetoro-Ng, Maya, 12, 245
Soviet Negro republic, 40–41, 86, 103, 115, 204–6
Soviet Spirit, The (Ward), 46
Spanish Civil War, 76, 119
Spellman, Cardinal Francis, 127, 138
Spelman College, 54
Stalin, Joseph, 33, 46, 77–80, 91–92, 99, 113, 122, 170, 179, 185–88, 190, 198–203, 210, 275, 351*n*
  ANP and, 96, 100–101
  anticommunism and, 166–67, 172
  APM and, 79–80, 110
  Bolshoi Theatre speech of, 161
  Chicago Star and, 5, 10, 124–29, 132–33, 137, 140
  Davis's criticisms of, 103, 336*n*–37*n*
  and Davis's politics and ideology, 4–6, 95, 101–4, 124, 129, 137, 152, 154, 159–60, 163, 166–67, 169, 196, 198, 335*n*–36*n*
  death of, 71–72, 103, 200
  Hawaii Question and, 149–50
  Honolulu Record and, 154, 159–60, 163, 176, 196, 200–201
  Hughes and, 54–55
  Khrushchev's criticism of, 218, 337*n*
  Korea and, 194–95, 200
  Marshall Plan and, 155–56
  Potemkin Progressives and, 62–65
  purges of, 64–65, 67, 69–70, 72, 75, 96, 166, 200, 323*n*, 327*n*, 336*n*
  racial issues and, 8, 18, 41, 206
  Robeson and, 62, 67, 69–72, 83, 278
  Truman and, 27, 158, 195
  Truman Doctrine and, 131–33, 135
  World War II and, 69, 79–80, 89, 95–97, 101, 104, 158, 161, 165, 206–7, 225–26, 274, 289
Standard Oil, 100, 128, 162, 177
Stargell, Willie, 267
State Department, U.S., 116, 200
Steel, Johannes, 121, 128, 136–37

Stepinac, Archbishop Aloysius, 138–39
stimulus, 9, 177, 289–90, 294
Stone, I. F., 113, 123, 166, 339*n*
Students for a Democratic Society (SDS), 227
Suez Canal crisis, 212–13
Supreme Court, U.S., 6, 97, 108, 148

Taft-Hartley Act, 123, 143, 173–74
Takara, Kathryn, 13, 287
taxes:
  Chicago Star and, 130, 139, 292
  health care and, 9, 202, 295
  Honolulu Record and, 177, 202, 289
  Obama and, 130, 253, 286, 291–92
Taylor, Dorothy, 84
Taylor, Robert Rochon, 107, 115, 228
  Chicago antiwar rally and, 84–85
  Davis's relationship with, 293–94
Tehran Conference, 96
terrorists, terrorism, 117, 232
  on 9/11, 224, 250, 287
Thomas, Garen, 13
Tidwell, John Edgar, 321*n*
  Chicago Star and, 118–19, 348*n*
  and Davis's politics and ideology, 92–93, 272–73
Time, 39, 101, 127, 362*n*
Tith, Naranhkiri, 230
Tito (Josip Broz), 132, 152
"To the Red Army" (Davis), 89
"To You Beloved Comrade" (Robeson), 71–72
trade, 162–63, 199
Translation World Publishers, 114
Treasury Department, U.S., 49, 78
Trofimenko, Genrikh, 269–70
Trotsky, Leon, 17, 80, 103, 138, 185, 336*n*–37*n*
Truman, Harry S., 4–8, 81, 104, 108, 121, 151, 197–200, 203, 218, 263, 268, 344*n*
  Chicago Star and, 6, 124–25, 128, 140–41, 163, 312
  Chinese civil war and, 157, 162
  CRC and, 109–10, 171
  Davis's criticisms of, 4, 91, 128, 140–41, 154–57, 160–63, 165, 167, 169, 171,

173, 175–76, 178, 195, 197–98, 222, 276, 279, 288, 297
Davis's liberal protectors and, 276, 279
and Davis's politics and ideology, 4–7, 102, 163
Honolulu Record and, 154–57, 160–63, 165, 167, 169–71, 173, 175–76, 178, 195, 197–98, 200, 279, 292
Marshall Plan and, 155, 161
racial issues and, 18, 163–64, 169–71
Robeson and, 169, 171, 173–74
State of the Union Address of, 195
and use of atomic bomb, 157–59, 161
USSR and, 27, 158–59, 163, 194–95, 322n
Truman Doctrine, 4, 27, 130–36, 193
Chicago Star and, 130–36, 190
Honolulu Record and, 161–62, 197
social justice religious left and, 134–35
Trumbo, Dalton, 126, 159, 188–89, 191
Tulsa riots, 25, 269
Turkey, 128, 193
Truman Doctrine and, 131–36, 161–62
"Twenty One Conditions of Admission into the Communist International, The," 35

"Underground" (Obama), 264
Unfit for Publication, 320n–21n
Union of Soviet Socialist Republics (USSR), 1–5, 27, 31, 38, 46–48, 51, 57–58, 61–72, 74, 76, 107–10, 113–17, 119, 136, 144, 146, 172–76, 179, 181, 188, 190, 193, 208, 210, 254, 288, 300, 331n, 351n
ACPFB and, 18, 221–22, 225
ANP and, 95–97, 99–101, 103
anticommunism and, 167, 172
APM and, 79–82, 87, 110, 310
Aptheker and, 61, 329n
Canters and, 113–14, 143, 228, 292, 341n
Chicago Star and, 5, 10, 32, 118, 121–30, 132–34, 137, 141, 312
collapse of, 269–71, 277, 282, 325n
comparisons between China and, 198–99
CPUSA funding and, 35, 39, 325n
Davis's liberal protectors and, 276–77, 279–80

and Davis's politics and ideology, 4–5, 7, 10, 19, 94–95, 97, 101–3, 129–30, 137, 141, 152–54, 159–61, 163–64, 166–67, 175, 196–97, 201, 215–16, 263, 272, 274, 280, 283, 285–86, 297, 308, 335n
as Evil Empire, 261, 269–70, 282
expansionism of, 94, 155, 194
Feinglass and, 226–27
Fort-Whiteman and, 39, 68–69, 205
Fraina and, 183–84
Gitlow and, 185–86
Hawaii and, 147, 149–51, 211
Honolulu Record and, 32, 154, 159–63, 165, 169, 175, 178, 197–98, 200, 212–13, 292
Hughes and, 54–55, 205–6
Hungary invaded by, 212, 329n
hydrogen bomb and, 160–61, 200
Kenyatta and, 231–32, 360n
Korea and, 194–95, 200
Marshall Plan and, 154–56
NAACP and, 48, 50
Obama's father and, 230–31
opening of archives of, 270, 273, 283
Patterson and, 115–17
and political carnage of communism, 33, 323n
Potemkin Progressives and, 62–66
racial issues and, 8, 18, 39–43, 67–70, 86, 94, 103, 115, 126–28, 133, 139, 168–69, 173–74, 204–7, 330n
religion and, 138–39, 174
Robeson and, 18, 62, 67–72, 83, 94, 168–70, 173–74, 278
Rosenbergs and, 201–2
Stone and, 113, 123, 166, 339n
Truman and, 27, 158–59, 163, 194–95, 322n
Truman Doctrine and, 131–33, 135
U.S. trade with, 162–63
war on Christmas of, 202
West Germany and, 175–76
Willkie and, 101–2
on world revolution, 33–35, 63
World War II and, 79–82, 86–89, 96–97, 99, 104, 158–60, 175, 206–7, 289, 334n
see also Stalin, Joseph

United Nations, 68, 194, 199, 367n
United Packinghouse Workers of America,
    111–12, 114–16, 139, 228, 340n
USASurvival.org, 274

Venona Papers, 122, 273
Vietnam, 4, 201–3, 227, 297
    French in, 194, 196, 201
    Honolulu Record and, 195–97, 201
Vietnam War, 196, 227, 246

Wallace, Henry, 7, 122–23, 194, 218, 344n
    ANP and, 99–103
    Chicago Star and, 125–26, 128–29,
        135–36
    and Davis's politics and ideology,
        101–3
    presidential campaign of, 101–2, 123,
        125–26
    Truman Doctrine and, 135–36
Walter, Francis, 7, 224–25
Ward, Harry, 46, 65, 110–11, 135
Ware, Harold, 83, 122
Warsaw Pact, 200
Washington Post, 12, 85, 112, 277
    and Davis's politics and ideology,
        274–75
Wassall, Irma, 92–93, 272
Watkins, Arthur V., 207–12
Watkins Committee, 211–12
wealth redistribution, 9, 253, 259, 262, 286,
    289, 295
Weatherly-Williams, Dawna:
    on Davis's introduction to Obama, 12,
        243–44, 267, 280
    on Davis's relationship with Obama,
        12–13, 280
Wells, H. G., 64, 66
White, Harry Dexter, 78
Wilkins, Roy, 115, 152
    Scottsboro Boys case and, 49–50, 86–87
Willkie, Wendell:
    and Davis's politics and ideology, 101–3
    presidential campaign of, 5, 76–77, 101
    USSR and, 101–2

Winston, Henry, 83, 106, 116, 205
    Honolulu Record and, 168–69
    World War II and, 80–81
Wolffe, Richard, 14
Wood, John, 176–77
World Factbook, 68, 330n
World Peace Conference, 170
World War I, 33, 79
World War II, 27, 33, 105, 121, 144, 173,
    287
    ANP and, 90, 95–100
    APM and, 79–84, 86–87, 109–10, 162,
        225–26, 310
    blacks and, 78–79, 83–87, 89, 206–7,
        310
    Davis's opposition to, 78–79, 86, 88–89
    and Davis's politics and ideology, 88–89,
        165, 272, 274
    and FBI investigation of Davis, 214–15
    Honolulu Record and, 156, 159–60, 167,
        175–76, 315
    Jews and, 117, 225–26
    Marshall Plan and, 155–56
    Stalin and, 69, 79–80, 89, 95–97, 101,
        104, 158, 161, 165, 206–7, 225–26,
        274, 289
    USSR and, 79–82, 86–89, 96–97, 99, 104,
        158–60, 175, 206–7, 289, 334n
World Youth Festivals, 159
Wright, Jeremiah, 4, 11, 19, 273, 275
Wright, Richard, 223, 261
    Davis's relationship with, 74–75, 205,
        233–34, 336n–37n
    politics and ideology of, 74–75, 91, 234,
        336n

Yakovlev, Alexander, 323n
Yeltsin, Boris, 269–70
Yergan, Max, 84, 110
Yes We Can (Thomas), 13
Young, Andrew, 68, 330n–31n
Young Communist League, 51, 80–81, 83,
    205, 333n
Young Worker, 51
Yugoslavia, 127–28, 132, 152, 198